80,000
HOURS

80,000 Hours
Trajan House
Mill Street
Oxford
OX2 0DJ
United Kingdom

www.80000hours.org

First published 2016, second edition 2023.

ISBN 978-1-3999-5709-0

Second edition edited by Benjamin Hilton.
Images by Maria Gutierrez and Nik Mastroddi (unless otherwise credited).

80,000 HOURS

FIND A FULFILLING CAREER THAT DOES GOOD

BENJAMIN TODD
AND THE 80,000 HOURS TEAM

About the authors

80,000 Hours provides research and support to help students and recent graduates switch into careers that effectively tackle the world's most pressing problems.

It's a Y Combinator-backed nonprofit entirely funded by philanthropic donations.

Benjamin Todd is the co-founder and president of 80,000 Hours.

Ben managed 80,000 Hours while it grew from a lecture, to a student society, to the organisation it is today. Before 80,000 Hours, he was the first undergraduate to intern as an analyst at a top investment fund. He has a 1st from Oxford in Physics and Philosophy, has published in Climate Physics, once kick-boxed for Oxford, and speaks Chinese, badly.

Ben is advised by the rest of the 80,000 Hours team.

Contents

Introduction

You'll spend about 80,000 hours working in your career: 40 hours a week, 50 weeks a year, for 40 years. So how to spend that time is one of the most important decisions you'll ever make.

Choose wisely, and you will not only have a more rewarding and interesting life — you'll also be able to help solve some of the world's most pressing problems. But how should you choose?

Back in 2011, we were students at Oxford in the UK. We wanted to figure out how we could do work we loved while having a positive impact.

We wondered: should we work at a nonprofit? Go to grad school? Try to earn high salaries and give back through philanthropy? Give up and go meditate in a cave? Or something else entirely?

Most career guides we read were about how to land different jobs, but few gave advice on what jobs to aim for in the first place. Most people we knew didn't even use formal career advice, relying instead on conversations with friends.

As for doing good with your career, people suggested things like medicine, social work, teaching, or (most thrillingly) working in corporate social responsibility. But, valuable as these careers are, we felt like there might be even higher-impact options out there.

For instance, we recognised that some of the highest-impact people in history came from different fields. Martin Luther King, Jr. was a pastor who shaped the US civil rights movement. Marie Curie was a scientist who pioneered life-saving medical technologies through her research into radioactivity.

Since founding 80,000 Hours, our team has spoken to hundreds of experts, spent hundreds of hours reading the relevant literature, and conducted our own analyses of the many job options available. We still have a lot to learn: these questions are difficult to settle, and we've made some mistakes, but we don't think anyone else has spent as long researching these topics as we have.

Among the things we've learned:

- If you want a satisfying career, "follow your passion" can be misleading advice.
- You might be able to do more good as a bureaucrat than a charity worker.
- Many conventional approaches to making the world a better place don't actually work.

We've also come up with more research-backed and hopefully better ways to approach age-old questions like how to figure out what you're good at, and how to be more successful.

One of the most important things we've learned is that if lots of people already work on an issue, the best opportunities to help are more likely to have already been taken. But that means the most common and popular issues to work on, like health and education in rich countries, are precisely not the ones where you can have the biggest impact — instead, you need to find something more unconventional.

At the same time, we found real ways to help with important neglected problems. For instance, by focusing on the world's poorest people, it's really possible to save hundreds of lives, while doing work you enjoy too.

We've even found that our generation faces issues that could affect the entire future of civilisation, and that relatively few people focus on them. This includes issues such as pandemics even worse than COVID-19 and the creation of smarter-than-human AI (which we've been recommending people work on since 2014!).

As of today, thousands of people have significantly changed their career plans based on our advice. Some of them are researching ways to prevent the next pandemic, some are working on neglected areas of government policy, some are developing groundbreaking technology, and others have used our research to figure out their own paths.

How to use this guide

Here's what we'll cover:
1. What makes for a dream job?
2. Can one person make a difference?
3. How to have a real positive impact in any job
4. How to choose which problems to focus on
5. What are the world's biggest and most urgent problems?
6. What types of jobs help the most?
7. Which jobs put you in a better position?
8. How to find the right career for you
9. How to write a career plan
10. How to get a job
11. How our community can help

The first four chapters are about what options to aim for long term. The rest is about how to get there and take action.

We designed the guide especially for English-speaking students and recent graduates in their 20s, who are lucky enough to have the security and ability to make helping the world an important goal. However, we also have advice about all kinds of career decisions, and many of the core ideas apply to readers of any age or circumstance.

At the end, there are also a few more resources:

- Some additional articles that further explore our key ideas
- Summaries of our career reviews
- Summaries of our top problem area profiles

To get the most out of this guide, we recommend reading each chapter, then doing the exercises that go with each one. If you complete them, you'll have applied the ideas to your own career, and it'll be easy to use our online career template to make your new career plan:

https://80k.link/NCP

When we've delivered this content over an afternoon, often over half the people who attended changed what they had planned to do with their lives.

So let's get started. What's the best way you can use your 80,000 Hours?

Benjamin Todd
Co-founder and President, 80,000 Hours

CHAPTER 1

What makes for a dream job?

BY THE FIFTH YEAR, JIM REALLY REGRETTED FOLLOWING HIS CHILDHOOD PASSION FOR ICE CREAM...

We all want to find a dream job that's enjoyable and meaningful, but what does that actually mean?

Some people imagine that the answer involves discovering their passion through a flash of insight, while others think that the key elements of their dream job are that it be easy and highly paid.

We've reviewed three decades of research into the causes of a satisfying life and career, drawing on over 60 studies, and we didn't find much evidence for these views. Instead, we found six key ingredients of a dream job. They don't include income, and they aren't as simple as "following your passion."

In fact, following your passion can lead you astray. Steve Jobs was passionate about Zen Buddhism before entering technology. Maya

Angelou worked as a calypso dancer before she became a celebrated poet and civil rights activist.

Rather, you can develop passion by doing work that you find enjoyable and meaningful. The key is to get good at something that helps other people.

(For a full survey of the evidence on job satisfaction, follow the link in the footnote.[1])

Where we go wrong

The usual way people try to work out their dream job is to *imagine* different jobs and think about how satisfying they seem. Or they think about times they've felt fulfilled in the past and self-reflect about what matters most to them.

If this were a normal career guide, we'd start by getting you to write out a list of what you most want from a job, like "working outdoors" and "working with ambitious people." The bestselling career advice book of all time, *What Color is Your Parachute*, recommends exactly this.[2] The hope is that, deep down, people know what they really want.

However, research shows that although self-reflection is useful, it only goes so far.

You can probably think of times in your own life when you were excited about a holiday or party — but when it actually happened, it was just OK. In the last few decades, research has shown that this is common: we're not always great at predicting what will make us most happy, and we don't realise how bad we are. You can find an overview of some of this research in the footnotes.[3]

It turns out we're even bad at remembering how satisfying different experiences were. One well-established mistake is that we often judge experiences mainly by their endings:[4] if you missed your flight on the last day of an enjoyable holiday, you'll probably remember the holiday as bad.

"The fact that we often judge the pleasure of an experience by its ending can cause us to make some curious choices."
– Prof Dan Gilbert, *Stumbling on Happiness*[5]

This means we can't just trust our intuitions; we need a more systematic way of working out which job is best for us.

The same research that proves how bad we are at self-reflection can help us make more informed choices. We now have three decades of research into positive psychology — the science of happiness — as well as decades of research into motivation and job satisfaction. We'll summarise the main lessons of this research and explain what it means for finding a fulfilling job.

Two overrated goals for a fulfilling career

People often imagine that a dream job is well paid and easy.

In 2015, one of the leading job rankings in the US, provided by *CareerCast*, rated jobs on the following criteria:[6]

1. Is it highly paid?
2. Is it going to be highly paid in the future?
3. Is it stressful?
4. Is the working environment unpleasant?

Based on this, the best job was: actuary.[7] That is, someone who uses statistics to measure and manage risks, often in the insurance industry.

It's true that actuaries are more satisfied with their jobs than average, but they're not among the most satisfied.[8] Only 36% say their work is meaningful,[9] so being an actuary isn't a particularly fulfilling career.

So the *CareerCast* list isn't capturing everything. In fact, the evidence suggests that money and avoiding stress aren't that important.

Money makes you happier, but only a little

It's a cliche that "you can't buy happiness," but at the same time, better pay is people's top priority when looking for new jobs.[10] Moreover, when people are asked what would most improve the quality of their lives, the most common answer is more money.[11]

What's going on here? Which side is right?

A lot of the research on this question is remarkably low quality. But several major studies in economics offer more clarity. We reviewed the best studies available,[12] and the truth turns out to lie in the middle: money does make you happy, but only a little.

For instance, here are the findings from a huge survey in the United States in 2010:[13]

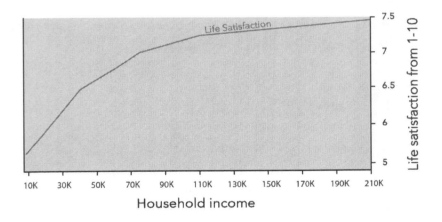

People were asked to rate how satisfied they were with their lives on a scale from 1 to 10. The result is shown on the right, while the bottom shows their household income.

You can see that going from a (pre-tax) income of $40,000 to $80,000 was only associated with an increase in life satisfaction from about 6.5 to 7 out of 10. That's a lot of extra income for a small increase.

This is hardly surprising — we all know people who've gone into high-earning jobs and ended up miserable.

But this result may be too optimistic. If we look at day-to-day happiness, income seems even less important. "Positive affect" is whether people reported feeling happy *yesterday*. The left axis of the chart below shows the fraction of people who reported "yes." This line goes flat around $50,000, showing that beyond this point, income had no relationship with day-to-day happiness in this survey.

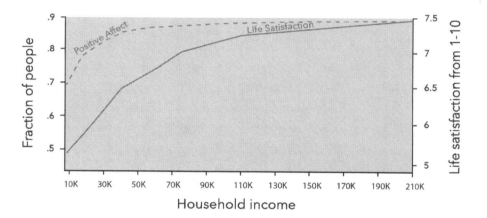

The picture is similar if we look at the fraction who reported being "not blue" or "stress free" yesterday.

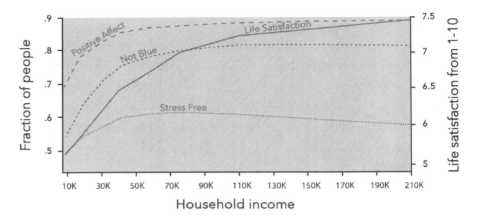

These lines are completely flat by $75,000, so beyond this point, income had no relationship with how happy, sad, or stressed people felt.

We think there's a good chance this result is an error, and day-to-day happiness does continue to increase with income, at least a little bit. A more recent study found exactly this, though it found that day-to-day happiness increases more slowly than life satisfaction.[14]

Everything we've covered above is only about the correlation between income and happiness. But the relationship might be caused by a third factor. For example, being healthy could both make you happier and allow you to earn more. If this is true, then the effect of earning extra money will be even weaker than the correlations above suggest.

Finally, $75,000 of household income is equivalent to an individual income of only $40,000 if you don't have kids.[15]

To customise these levels for yourself, make the following adjustments (all pre-tax):

- The $40,000 figure was for 2009. Due to inflation, it's more like

$55,000 in 2023.

- Add $25,000 per dependent who does not work that you fully support.
- Add 50% if you live in an expensive city (e.g. New York or San Francisco), or subtract 30% if you live somewhere cheap (e.g. rural Tennessee).
- Add more if you're especially motivated by money (or subtract some if you have frugal tastes).
- Add 15% in order to be able to save for retirement (or however much you personally need to save in order to maintain the standard of living you want).

As of 2023, the average college graduate in the United States can expect to make about $77,000 per year over their working life, while the average Ivy League graduate earns over $120,000.[16] The upshot is that if you're a college graduate in the US (or a similar country), then you'll likely end up well into the range where more income has little effect on your happiness.

Don't aim for low stress

Many people tell us they want to find a job that's not too stressful. And it's true that in the past, doctors and psychologists believed that stress was always bad. However, we did a survey of the modern literature on stress[17], and today, the picture is a bit more complicated.

One puzzle is that studies of high-ranking government and military leaders found they had lower levels of stress hormones and less anxiety, despite sleeping fewer hours, managing more people, and having higher occupational demands. One widely supported explanation is that having a greater sense of control (by setting their own schedules and determining how to tackle the challenges they face) protects them against the demands of the position.

There are other ways that a demanding job can be good or bad depending on context:

Variable		Good (or neutral)	Bad
Type of stress	Intensity of demands	Challenging but achievable	Mismatched with ability (either too high or too low)
	Duration	Short-term	On-going
Context	Control	High control and autonomy	Low control and autonomy
	Power	High power	Low power
	Social Support	Good social support	Social isolation
How to cope	Mindset	Reframe demands as opportunities, stress as useful	View demands as threats, stress as harmful to health
	Altruism	Performing altruistic acts	Focusing on yourself

This means the picture looks more like the following graph. Having a very undemanding job is bad — that's boring. Having demands that exceed your abilities is bad too: they cause harmful stress. The sweet spot is where the demands placed on you match your abilities — that's a fulfilling challenge.

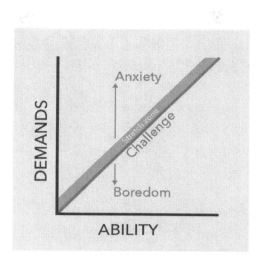

Instead of seeking to avoid stress, seek out a supportive context and meaningful work, and then challenge yourself.

What should you aim for in a dream job?

We've applied the research on positive psychology about what makes for a fulfilling life and combined it with research on job satisfaction to come up with six key ingredients of a dream job.

These are the six ingredients.

1. Work that's engaging

What really matters is not your salary, status, type of company, and so on, but rather what you do day by day and hour by hour.

Engaging work is work that draws you in, holds your attention, and gives you a sense of flow. It's the reason an hour spent editing a spreadsheet can feel like pure drudgery, while an hour spent playing a computer game can feel like no time at all: computer games are designed to be as engaging as possible.

What makes the difference? Why are computer games engaging while office admin isn't? Researchers have identified four factors:

1.   The **freedom** to decide how to perform your work.
2.   **Clear tasks**, with a clearly defined start and end.
3.   **Variety** in the types of tasks.
4.   **Feedback**, so you know how well you're doing.

Each of these factors has been shown to correlate with job satisfaction in a major meta-analysis ($r=0.4$), and they are widely thought by experts to be the most empirically verified predictors of job satisfaction (Judge et al., 2010).

That said, playing computer games is not the key to a fulfilling life (and not just because you won't get paid). That's because you also need...

2. Work that helps others

The following jobs have the four ingredients of engaging work that we discussed. But when asked, over three quarters of people doing them say they don't find them meaningful:[18]

- Revenue analyst
- Fashion designer
- TV newscast director

These jobs, however, are seen as meaningful by almost everyone who does them:

- Fire service officer
- Nurse / midwife
- Neurosurgeon

The key difference is that the second set of jobs seem to help other people. That's why they're meaningful, and that's why helping others is our second factor.

There's a growing body of evidence that helping others is a key ingredient for life satisfaction. People who volunteer are less depressed and healthier. A meta-analysis of 23 randomised studies showed that performing acts of kindness makes the *giver* happier.[19] And a global survey found that people who donate to charity are as satisfied with their lives as those who earn twice as much.[20]

Helping others isn't the only route to a meaningful career, but it's widely accepted by researchers that it's one of the most powerful.

(We explore jobs that really help people in the next chapter, including jobs that help indirectly as well as directly.)

3. Work you're good at

Being good at your work gives you a sense of achievement, a key ingredient of life satisfaction discovered by positive psychology.

It also gives you the power to negotiate for the other components of a fulfilling job — such as the ability to work on meaningful projects, undertake engaging tasks, and earn fair pay. If people value your contribution, you can ask for these conditions in return.

For both reasons, skill ultimately trumps interest. Even if you love art, if you pursue it as a career but aren't good at it, you'll end up doing boring graphic design for companies you don't care about.

That's not to say you should only do work you're already good at — but you do want the potential to get good at it.

(In chapter 8 we'll look in more detail at how to work out what you're good at.)

4. Work with supportive colleagues

Obviously, if you hate your colleagues and work for a boss from hell, you're not going to be satisfied.

Since good relationships are such an important part of having a fulfilling life, it's important to be able to become friends with at least a couple of people at work. And this probably means working with at least a few people who are similar to you.

However, you don't need to become friends with everyone, or even like all of your colleagues. Research shows that perhaps the most important factor is whether you can get help from your colleagues when you run into problems. A major meta-analysis found "social support" was among the top predictors of job satisfaction (r=0.56).[21]

People who are disagreeable and different from you can be the people who'll give you the most useful feedback, provided they care about your interests. This is because they'll tell it like it is, and have a different perspective. Professor Adam Grant calls these people "disagreeable givers."[22]

When we think of dream jobs, we usually focus on the role. But who you work with is almost as important. A bad boss can ruin a dream position, while even boring work can be fun if done with a friend. So when selecting a job, will you be able to make friends with some people in the workplace? And more importantly, does the culture of the workplace make it easy to get help, get feedback, and work together?

5. Work that doesn't have major negatives

To be satisfied, everything above is important. But you also need the absence of things that make work unpleasant. All of the following tend to be linked to job *dis*satisfaction.

- A long commute, especially if it's over an hour by bus
- Very long hours
- Pay you feel is unfair

- Job insecurity

Although these sound obvious, people often overlook them. The negative consequences of a long commute can be enough to outweigh many other positive factors.

6. Work that fits with the rest of your life

You don't *have* to get all the ingredients of a fulfilling life from your job. It's possible to find a job that pays the bills and excel in a side project; or to find a sense of meaning through philanthropy or volunteering; or to build great relationships outside of work.

We've advised plenty of people who have done this. There are famous examples too — Einstein had his most productive year in 1905, while working as a clerk at a patent office.

So this last factor is a reminder to consider how your career fits with the rest of your life.

Recap

Before we move on, here's a quick recap of the six ingredients. This is what to look for in a dream job:

1. Engaging work that lets you enter a state of flow (freedom, variety, clear tasks, feedback).
2. Work that helps others.
3. Work you're good at.
4. Supportive colleagues.
5. No major negatives, like long hours or unfair pay.
6. A job that fits your personal life.

How can we sum this all up?

Should you just follow your passion?

"Follow your passion" has become a defining piece of career advice.

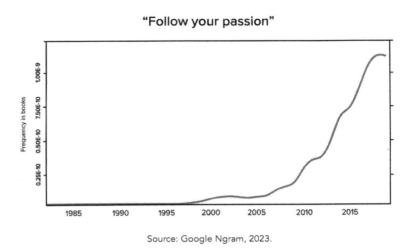

"Follow your passion"

Source: Google Ngram, 2023.

The idea is that the key to finding a great career is to identify your greatest interest — "your passion" — and pursue a career involving that interest. It's an attractive message: just commit to your passion, and you'll have a great career. And when we look at successful people, they *are* often passionate about what they do.

Now, we're fans of being passionate about your work. The research above shows that intrinsically motivating work makes people a lot happier than a big paycheque.

However, there are three ways "follow your passion" can be misleading advice.

One problem is that it suggests that passion is all you need. But even if you're deeply interested in the work, if you lack the six ingredients from above, you'll still be unsatisfied. If a basketball fan gets a job involving basketball, but works with people they hate, receives unfair pay, or finds the work meaningless, they are still going to dislike their job.

In fact, "following your passion" can make it harder to satisfy the six ingredients, because the areas you're passionate about are likely to be the most competitive, which makes it harder to find a good job.

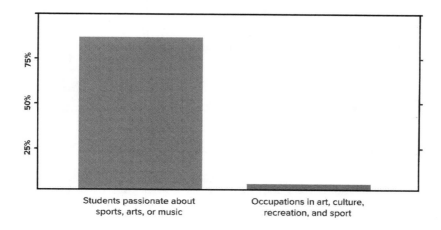

Source: Vallerand et al., 2003.

A second problem is that many people don't feel like they have a career-relevant passion. Telling them to "follow their passion" makes them feel inadequate. If you don't have a "passion," don't worry — you can still find work you'll become passionate about.

And the third problem is that it can make people needlessly limit their options. If you're interested in literature, it's easy to think you must become a writer to have a satisfying career, and ignore other options. It's also easy to have the idea that your "one true passion" will be immediately obvious, and eliminate options that aren't immediately satisfying.

But in fact, you can become passionate about new areas. If your work helps others, you practice to get good at it, you work on engaging tasks, and you work with people you like, then you'll become passionate about it.

The six ingredients are all about the context of the work, not the content. Twenty years ago, we would never have imagined being passionate about giving career advice, but here we are, writing this book.

Many successful people are passionate, but often their passion developed alongside their success, and took a long time to discover, rather than coming first. Steve Jobs started out passionate about Zen Buddhism. He got into technology as a way to make some quick cash. But as he became successful, his passion grew, until he became the most famous advocate of "doing what you love."[23]

In reality, rather than having a single passion, our interests change often, and more than we expect. Think back to what you were most interested in five years ago, and you'll probably find that it's pretty different from what you're interested in today. And as we saw above, we're bad at knowing what really makes us happy.

This all means you have more options for a fulfilling career than you think.

Do what contributes

Rather than "follow your passion," our slogan for a fulfilling career is: get good at something that helps others. Or simply: *do what contributes.*

We highlight "get good" because if you find something you're good at that others value, you'll have plenty of career opportunities, which gives you the best chance of finding a dream job with all the other ingredients — engaging work, supportive colleagues, lack of major negatives, and fit with the rest of your life.

You can have all the other five ingredients, however, and still find your work meaningless. So you need to find a way to help others too.

If you prioritise making a valuable contribution to the world first, you'll develop passion for what you do — you'll become more content, ambitious, and motivated.

This is what we've found in our career advising. For instance, Jess was interested in philosophy as an undergraduate, and considered pursuing a PhD. The problem was that although she finds philosophy interesting, it would have been hard to make a positive impact within it. Ultimately, she thought this would have made it unfulfilling. Instead, she switched into psychology and public policy, and became one of the most motivated people we know.

To date, thousands of people have made major changes to their career path by following our career advice. Many switched into a field that didn't initially interest them, but that they believed was important for the world. After developing their skills, finding good people to work with, and finding the right role, they've become deeply satisfied.

Here are two more reasons to focus on getting good at something that helps others.

You could be more successful

If you make it your mission to help others, then people will want to help you succeed.

This sounds obvious, and there's now empirical evidence to back it up. In the excellent book *Give and Take*, Professor Adam Grant argues that people with a "giving mindset" end up among the most successful. This is both because they get more help, and because they're more motivated by a sense of purpose.[24]

One caveat is that givers also end up unsuccessful if they focus too much on others, and burn out. So you also need the other ingredients of job satisfaction we mentioned earlier, and to set limits on how much you give.

It's the right thing to do

The idea that helping others is the key to being fulfilled is hardly a new one. It's a theme from most major moral and spiritual traditions:

> *"Set your heart on doing good. Do it over and over again and you will be filled with joy."*
> – Buddha

> *"A man's true wealth is the good he does in this world."*
> – Muhammad

> *"Love your neighbour as you love yourself."*
> – Jesus Christ

> *"Every man must decide whether he will walk in the light of creative altruism or in the darkness of destructive selfishness."*
> – Martin Luther King, Jr.

What's more, as we'll explain in the next chapter, as a college graduate in a developed country today, you have an enormous opportunity to help others through your career. Ultimately, this is the real reason to focus on helping others — the fact that it'll make you more personally fulfilled is just a bonus.

Conclusion

To have a dream job, don't worry too much about money and stress, and don't endlessly self-reflect to find your one true passion.

Rather, get good at something that helps others. It's best for you, and it's best for the world. This is the reason we set up 80,000 Hours — our mission is to help you find a career that contributes.

But which jobs help people? Can one person really make much difference? That's what we'll answer in the next chapter.

APPLY THIS TO YOUR OWN CAREER

These six ingredients, especially helping others and getting good at your job, can act as guiding lights — they're what to aim to find in a dream job long term.

Here are some exercises to help you start applying them.

1. Practice using the six ingredients to make some comparisons. Pick two options you're interested in, then score them from 1 to 5 on each factor.
2. The six ingredients we list are only a starting point. There may be other factors that are especially important to you, so we also recommend doing the following exercises. They're not perfect — as we saw earlier, our memories of what we've found fulfilling can be unreliable — but completely ignoring your past experience isn't wise either.[25] These questions should give you hints about what you find most fulfilling:
    *   When have you been most fulfilled in the past? What did these times have in common?
    *   Imagine you just found out you're going to die in 10 years. What would you spend your time doing?
    *   Can you make any of our six factors more specific? For example, what kinds of people do you most like to work with?
3. Now, combine our list with your own thoughts to determine the four to eight factors that are most important to you in a dream job.

4. When you're comparing your options in the future, you can use this list of factors to work out which is best. Don't expect to find an option that's best on every dimension; rather, focus on finding the option that's best on balance.

THE BOTTOM LINE:
WHAT MAKES FOR A DREAM JOB?

To find a dream job, look for:
1. Work you're good at.
2. Work that helps others.
3. Supportive conditions: engaging work that lets you enter a state of flow, supportive colleagues, lack of major negatives like unfair pay, and work that fits your personal life.

CHAPTER 2

Can one person make a difference?
What the evidence says.

It's easy to feel like one person can't make a difference. The world has so many big problems, and they often seem impossible to solve.

So when we started 80,000 Hours — with the aim of helping people do good with their careers — one of the first questions we asked was, "How much difference can one person really make?"

We learned that while many common ways to do good (such as becoming a doctor) have less impact than you might first think, others have allowed certain people to achieve an extraordinary impact.

In other words, one person can make a difference — but you might have to do something a little unconventional.

In this chapter, we start by estimating how much good you could do by becoming a doctor. Then, we share some stories of the highest-impact people in history, and consider what they mean for your career.

How much impact do doctors have?

Many people who want to help others become doctors. One of our early readers, Dr Greg Lewis, did exactly that. "I want to study medicine because of a desire I have to help others," he wrote on his university application, "and so the chance of spending a career doing something worthwhile I can't resist."

So, we wondered: how much difference does becoming a doctor really make? We teamed up with Greg to find out.[26]

Since a doctor's primary purpose is to improve health, we tried to figure out how much extra "health" one doctor actually adds to humanity. We found that, over the course of their career, an average doctor in the UK will enable their patients to live about an extra combined 100 years of healthy life, either by extending their lifespans or by improving their overall health. There is, of course, a huge amount of uncertainty in this figure, but the real figure is unlikely to be more than 10 times higher.

Using a standard conversion rate (used by the World Bank, among other institutions) of 30 extra years of healthy life to one "life saved," 100 years of healthy life is equivalent to about three lives saved.[27] This is clearly a significant impact; however, it's less of an impact than many people expect doctors to have over their entire career.

There are three main reasons this impact is lower than you might expect:

1. Researchers largely agree that medicine has only increased average life expectancy by a few years. Most gains in life expectancy over the last 100 years have instead occurred due to better nutrition, improved sanitation, increased wealth, and other factors.
2. Doctors are only one part of the medical system, which also relies on nurses and hospital staff, as well as overhead and equipment. The impact of medical interventions is shared between all of these elements.
3. Most importantly, there are already a lot of doctors in the developed world, so if you don't become a doctor, someone else will be available to perform the most critical procedures. Additional doctors therefore only enable us to carry out procedures that deliver less significant and less certain results.

This last point is illustrated by the chart below, which compares the impact of doctors in different countries. The y-axis shows the amount of ill health in the population, measured in disability-adjusted life years (DALYs) per 100,000 people, where one DALY equals one year of life lost due to ill health. The x-axis shows the number of doctors per 100,000 people.

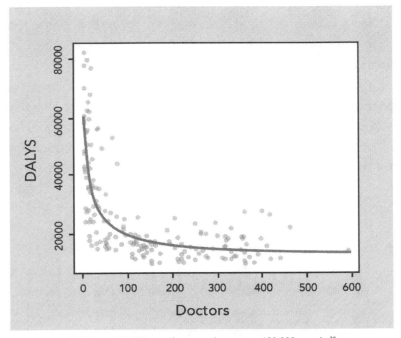

DALYs per 100,000 people versus doctors per 100,000 people.[28]

You can see that the curve goes nearly flat once you have more than 150 doctors per 100,000 people. After this point (which almost all developed countries meet), additional doctors only achieve a small impact on average.

So if you become a doctor in a rich country like the US or UK, you may well do more good than you would in many other jobs, and if you are an exceptional doctor, then you'll have a bigger impact than these averages. But it probably won't be a huge impact.

In fact, in the next chapter, we'll show how almost *any* college graduate can do more to save lives than a typical doctor. And in the rest of the career guide, we'll cover many other examples of common but ineffective attempts to do good.

These findings motivated Greg to switch from clinical medicine into biosecurity, for reasons we'll explain over the rest of the guide.

Who were the highest-impact people in history?

Despite this uninspiring statistic about how many lives a doctor saves, some doctors have had much more impact than this. Let's look at some examples of the highest-impact careers in history, and see what we might learn from them. First, let's turn to medical research.

By 1968, it had been shown that a solution of glucose and salt, administered via feeding tube or intravenous drip, could prevent death due to cholera. But millions of people were still dying every year from the disease. While working in a refugee camp on the border of Bangladesh and Burma, Dr David Nalin sought to turn this insight into a therapy that could be used in poor rural areas. He showed in a study that simply drinking a solution made at the right concentration and consumed at the right rate could be almost as effective as delivery via feeding tube or IV.[29]

This meant the treatment could be delivered with no equipment, and using extremely cheap and widely available ingredients.

Since then, this astonishingly simple treatment has been used all over the world, and the annual rate of child deaths from diarrhoea has plummeted from around 5 million to 1.5 million.[30] Researchers estimate that the therapy has saved over 50 million lives to date, mostly children's.[31]

If Dr Nalin had not been around, someone else would, no doubt, have discovered this treatment eventually. However, even if we imagine that he sped up the roll-out of the treatment by only five months, his work alone would have saved about 500,000 lives. This is a very approximate estimate, but it makes his impact more than 100,000 times greater than that of an ordinary doctor:

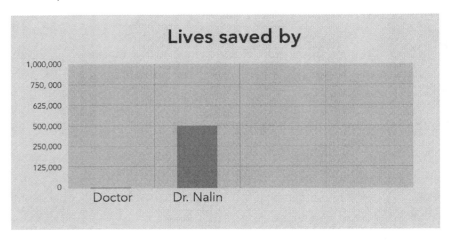

But even just within medical research, Dr Nalin is far from the most extreme example of a high-impact career. For example, one estimate puts Karl Landsteiner's discovery of blood groups as saving tens of millions of lives by enabling transfusions.[32]

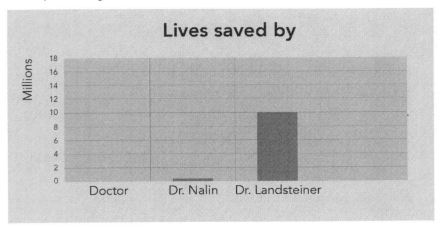

Beyond the medical field, later in the guide we'll cover the stories of a hugely impactful mathematician, Alan Turing, and bureaucrat, Viktor Zhdanov.

Or, let's think even more broadly. Roger Bacon and Galileo pioneered the scientific method — without which none of the discoveries we covered above would have been possible, along with other major technological breakthroughs like the Industrial Revolution. These individuals were able to do vastly more good than even outstanding medical practitioners.

The unknown Soviet Lieutenant Colonel who saved your life

Or consider the story of Stanislav Petrov, a Lieutenant Colonel in the Soviet Army during the Cold War. In 1983, Petrov was on duty in a Soviet missile base when early warning systems apparently detected an incoming missile strike from the United States. Protocol dictated that the Soviets order a return strike.[33]

But Petrov didn't push the button. He reasoned that the number of missiles was too small to warrant a counterattack, thereby disobeying protocol.

If he had ordered a strike, there's at least a reasonable chance hundreds of millions would have died. The two countries may have even ended up engaged in an all-out nuclear war, leading to billions of deaths and, potentially, the end of civilisation. If we're being conservative, we might quantify his impact by saying he saved a billion lives. But that's almost certainly an underestimate, because a nuclear war would also have devastated scientific, artistic, economic, and all other forms of progress, leading to a huge loss of life and wellbeing over the long run.

Later in the guide we'll discuss why we think these long-run effects could be vastly more important than "just" saving a billion lives from nuclear catastrophe.

Yet even with the lower estimate, Petrov's impact likely dwarfs that of Nalin and Landsteiner.

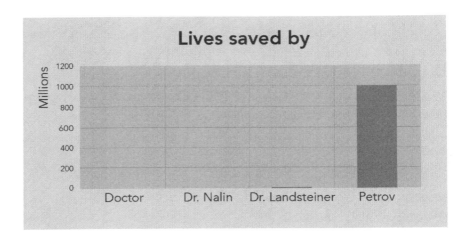

What do these differences in impact mean for your career?

We've seen that some careers have had huge positive effects, and some have vastly more than others.

Some component of this is due to luck — the people mentioned above were in the right place at the right time, giving them the opportunity to have an impact that they might not have otherwise received. You can't guarantee you'll make an important medical discovery.

But it wasn't *all* luck: Landsteiner and Nalin chose to use their medical knowledge to solve some of the most harmful health problems of their day, and it was foreseeable that someone high up in the Soviet military might have the opportunity to have a large impact by preventing conflict during the Cold War.

So, what does this mean for you?

People often wonder how they can "make a difference," but if some careers can result in thousands of times more impact than others, this isn't the right question. Two different career options can both "make a difference," but one could be dramatically better than the other.

Instead, the key question is: *What are some of the best ways to make a difference?* In other words, what can you do to give yourself a chance of having one of the highest-impact careers? Because the highest-impact careers achieve so much, a small increase in your chances means a great deal.

The examples above also show that the highest-impact paths might not be the most obvious ones. Being an officer in the Soviet military doesn't sound like the best career for a would-be altruist, but Petrov probably did more good than our most celebrated leaders, not to mention our most talented doctors. Having a big impact might require doing something a little unconventional.

So how much impact can *you* have if you try, while still doing something personally rewarding? It's not easy to have a big impact, but there's a lot you can do to increase your chances. That's what we'll cover in the next couple of chapters.

But first, let's clarify what we mean by "making a difference." We've been talking about lives saved so far, but that's not the only way to do good in the world.

What does it mean to "make a difference"?

Everyone talks about "making a difference" or "changing the world" or "doing good," but few ever define what they mean.

So here's a definition. Your social impact is given by:

> *The number of people*[34] *whose lives you improve, and how much you improve them, over the long term.*[35]

This means you can increase your social impact in three ways:
1. By helping more people.
2. By helping the same number of people to a greater extent (pictured below).
3. By doing something which has benefits that last for a longer time.

We think the last option is especially important, because many of our actions affect future generations. For example, if you improve the quality of government decision-making, you might not see many quantifiable short-term results, but you will have solved lots of other problems over the long term.

Two ways to have more social impact

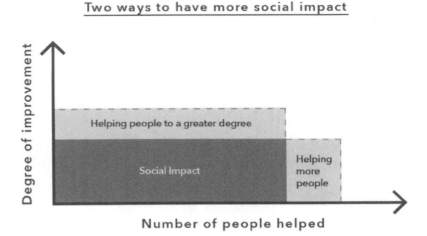

(There's more information about what it means to make a difference in appendix 1.)

So how can you improve lives with your career?

In the next chapter, we'll cover how any college graduate can make a big impact in any job. After that we'll cover how to choose a job in which you can fulfil your potential for impact.

CHAPTER 3

Three ways anyone can make a difference, no matter their job

No matter which career you choose, anyone can make a difference by donating to charity, engaging in advocacy, or volunteering.

Unfortunately, many attempts to do good in this way are ineffective, and some actually cause harm.

Take sponsored skydiving. Every year, thousands of people collect donations for good causes and throw themselves out of planes to draw attention to whatever charity they've chosen to support. This sounds like a win-win: the fundraiser gets an exhilarating once-in-a-lifetime experience while raising money for a worthy cause. What could be the harm in that?

Quite a bit, actually. According to a study of two popular parachuting centres, over a five-year period (1991 to 1995) approximately 1,500 people went skydiving for charity and collectively raised more than £120,000. That sounds pretty impressive — until you consider a few caveats.

First, the cost of the diving expeditions came out of the donations. So of the £120,000 raised, only £45,000 went to charity.

Second, because most of the skydivers were first-time jumpers, they suffered a combined total of 163 injuries, resulting in an average hospital stay of nine days.

In order to treat these injuries, the UK's National Health Service spent around £610,000. That means that for every £1 raised for the charities, the health service spent roughly £13, so the net effect was to *reduce* resources for health services. Ironically, many of the charities supported focused on health-related matters.[36]

What about volunteering? One problem is that volunteers need to be managed. If untrained volunteers use the time of trained managers, it's easy for them to cost the organisation more than the value they add.

In fact, the main reason many volunteering schemes persist is that if someone is a volunteer for an organisation, they are more likely to donate. When the organisation FORGE cut its volunteering scheme to be more effective, it inadvertently triggered a big drop in donations.[37]

So while volunteering can be effective in the right circumstances, it's often not.

In our research, we've found that *any college graduate in a rich country can do a huge amount to improve the lives of others* — and they can do this without changing jobs, or making big sacrifices.

We'll cover three examples:
- Donating 10% of your income to effective charities.
- Advocating for important causes.
- Helping others be more effective.

Donating effectively

How can you take whichever job you find the most personally rewarding, *and* do a huge amount of good?

Give 10% of your income to the world's poorest people. It's as simple as that.

How much good can donations do? A lower bound

Since 2008, GiveDirectly has made it possible to give cash directly to the poorest people in East Africa via mobile phone.

We don't think this the most effective way to donate to charity by any means — later we'll discuss higher-impact approaches — but it's simple and quantifiable, so it makes a good starting point.

As we saw in chapter 1, the more money you have, the less additional money will improve your life. For instance, in the US, doubling your income is only associated with about a half-point gain in life satisfaction on a scale of 1 to 10.

These surveys have been extended across the world. There are examples in the chart below.[38]

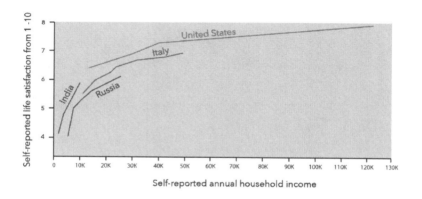

Self-reported annual household income

Poor people served by GiveDirectly in Kenya have an average individual consumption of about $800 per year.[39] This figure is based on how much $800 could buy in the US, meaning it already takes account of the fact that money goes further in poor countries.

The average US college graduate has an annual individual working income of about $77,000 (in 2023), or $54,500 post-tax.[40] This means that, assuming the above relationship holds, a dollar will do about 68 times more good if you give it to someone in Kenya rather than spending it on yourself.[41]

If someone earning that average level of income were to donate 10%, they could *double the annual income of seven people* living in extreme poverty each year. Over the course of their career, they could have a major positive impact on hundreds of people.

Grace is a typical recipient of donations from GiveDirectly.[42] She's a 48-year-old widow who lives with four children:

> "I would like to use part of the money to build a new house, since my house is in a very bad condition. Secondly, I would wish to pay fees for my son to go to a technical institute...
>
> My proudest achievement is that I have managed to educate my son in secondary school.
>
> My biggest hardship in life is [that I] lack a proper source of income.
>
> My current goals are to build and own a pit latrine and dig a borehole since getting water is a very big problem."

GiveDirectly conducted a randomised controlled trial of their programme, and found that recipients experienced significant reductions in hunger, stress, and other bad outcomes for years after receiving the transfers. These results add to substantial existing literature showing that cash transfers have significant benefits.[43]

How much sacrifice will this involve?

Normally when we think of doing good with our careers, we think of paths like becoming a teacher or charity worker, which often pay under half what you could earn in the private sector, and may not align with your skills or interests. Compared to switching to those careers, giving 10% of your income could easily be less of a sacrifice.

Moreover, as we saw in chapter 1, once you start earning more than about $55,000 per year,[44] extra income won't affect your happiness that much — while acts that help others, like giving to charity, probably make you happier.

To take just one example, one study found that in 122 of 136 countries, if respondents answered "Yes" to the question "Did you donate to charity last month?," their life satisfaction was higher by an amount also associated with a doubling of income.[45] In part, this is probably because happier people give more, but we expect some of the effect runs the other way too.

How to have a bigger impact than being a doctor

The reason donations can be so effective is that it's possible that you can send your money to the best organisations in the world, working on the biggest and most neglected issues. Although many charities aren't effective, the best are.

And while GiveDirectly is certainly an effective charity, there are others that some experts argue are even better. GiveWell, a leading independent charity evaluator,[46] estimates that its top charities (such as Helen Keller International and the Against Malaria Foundation) can prevent a death for about every $5,000 in donations it receives.[47] In addition, this provides other benefits that come with the treatment of malaria — such as improved overall quality of life and increased income — which causes further positive ripple effects over time.

With a typical US graduate salary, donating 10% of your income to the Against Malaria Foundation could therefore save more than one life every year.

These kinds of proven, cost-effective health programmes offer such a good opportunity to do good that even the most prominent aid sceptics have offered few arguments against them.

One life saved per year would amount to 40 lives saved over a 40-year career. In the previous chapter, we estimated that a typical doctor in clinical medicine saves three lives over their career. So by donating 10% of your income, you could achieve around 10 times as much impact.

We've just used the Against Malaria Foundation and GiveDirectly to provide a concrete lower bound on what you can achieve. We actually think there are many charities that are even more effective.

Some charities work on issues that seem even higher stakes and more neglected, such as preventing a catastrophic pandemic. We'll discuss why we think pandemics are more pressing than global health later in the guide.

If everyone in the richest 10% of the world's population donated 10% of their income, that would be $5 trillion per year.[48] That would be enough to double scientific research funding, raise everyone in the world above the $2.15 per day poverty line, provide universal basic education, and still have plenty left to fund a renaissance in the arts, go to Mars, and then invest $1 trillion in mitigating climate change. None of this would be straightforward to achieve, but it at least illustrates the enormous potential of greater giving.[49]

How is this possible?

It's astonishing that we can do so much good while sacrificing so little. How is this possible?

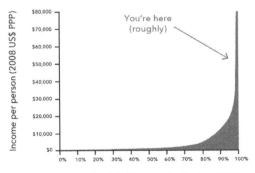

Percentile global income distribution, 2008

http://80k.link/income

Consider one of the most important graphs in economics, the graph of world income:[50]

The x-axis shows the percentage of people in the world who earn each level of income (as indicated by the y-axis). Income has been adjusted to indicate how much that specific dollar amount will buy in a person's home country (i.e. "purchasing power parity"). If the world were completely equal, the line would be horizontal.

As citizens of countries like the US and the UK, we know we're rich by global standards, but we don't usually think of ourselves as the richest people in the world — we're not the bankers, CEOs, or celebrities, after all. But actually, if you earn $60,000 per year after taxes and don't have kids, then globally speaking, *you are the 1%*.

These numbers are approximate, but it's still the case that if you're reading this, you are very likely in that big spike on the right of the graph (and perhaps even way off the chart), while almost everyone else in the world is in the flat bit at the bottom that you can hardly even see.

There's no reason to be embarrassed by this fact, but it does emphasise how important it is to consider how you can use your good fortune to help others. In a more equal world, we could just focus on helping those around us, and making our own lives go well. But it turns out we have an enormous opportunity to help other people with little cost to ourselves — and it would be a terrible shame to squander it.

Take action right now

Many of the staff at 80,000 Hours have been so persuaded by these arguments that we've pledged to give at least 10% of our lifetime income to the world's most effective charities.

We did it through an organisation called Giving What We Can, with whom we are partnered.[51]

Giving What We Can enables you to take a public pledge to give 10%

of your income to the charities you believe are most effective.

You can take the pledge in just a few minutes. It's likely to be the most significant thing you can do right now to do more good with your life.

It's not legally binding, you can choose where the money goes, and if you're a student, it only commits you to give 1% until after you graduate. You'll be joining over 9,000 people who've collectively pledged over $3 billion.

The pledge is not for everyone. We'd recommend being cautious if you're planning to have an impact mainly through your work (especially if that might involve lower-wage work, like at a charity), if you have significant debt or financial problems, or if you're not sure you can stick to it.

And if you're not quite ready yet, Giving What We Can allows you to take a "trial pledge" to give as little as 1% of your income for any period you choose, to see how it goes before making any long-term commitment.

Take the pledge here:
https://80k.link/GWC

What if you don't want to give money? How to help through effective political advocacy

Just as we happen to be rich by virtue of where we were born, we also happen to have political influence for the same reason.

Rich countries have a disproportionate impact on issues like global trade, migration, climate change, and technology policy, and are generally at least partly democratic. So if you'd prefer to do something besides giving money, consider advocating for important issues.

We were initially sceptical that one person could have real influence through political advocacy — but when we dug into the numbers, we changed our minds.

Let's take perhaps the simplest example: voting in elections. Several studies have used statistical models to estimate the chances of a single vote determining the US presidential election. Because the US electoral system is determined at the state level, if you live in a state that strongly favours one candidate, your chance of deciding the outcome is effectively zero. But if you live in a state that's contested, your chances rise to between 1 in 10 million and 1 in a million. That's quite a bit higher than your chances of winning the lottery.

Remember, the US federal government is very, very big. Let's imagine one candidate wanted to spend 0.2% more of GDP on foreign aid. That would be about $187 billion in extra foreign aid over their four-year term.[52] One millionth of that is $187,000. So if voting takes you an hour, it could be the most important hour — the highest in expected value — you'll spend that year. (The figures are similar in other rich countries; smaller countries have less at stake, but each vote counts for more.[53])

We've used the example of voting since it's quantifiable, but we expect the basic idea — the very small chance of changing a very big thing — applies to other forms of (well-chosen) advocacy, such as petitioning your congressperson, getting out the vote for the right candidate, or going to a town hall meeting. We think this is likely to be even more true if you're careful to focus on the right issues (more on this in the next chapter).

Being a "multiplier" to help others be more effective

Suppose you don't have any money or power, and you don't feel like you can contribute by working on an important problem. What then?

One option is to try to change that. We cover how to invest in yourself — no matter what job you have — in appendix 2.

That aside, you might know someone who does have some money, power, or skills. So you can make a difference by helping them achieve more.

For instance, if you could enable two other people to give 10% of their income to charity, that would have even more impact than doing it yourself.

These are both examples of being a *multiplier*. By mobilising others, it's often possible to do more than you could through just your own efforts.

Suppose you've come across a high-impact job, but you're not sure it's a good fit for your skills. If you can tell someone else about the job, and *they* take it, that does as much good as taking it yourself — and in fact more if they're a better fit for it than you.[54]

It's often possible to raise more for charity through fundraising than you might be able to donate yourself. Or, if you work at a company with a donation-matching scheme, you might be able to encourage other employees to use it.

What matters is that more good gets done — not that you do it with your own hands.

We're reminded of an old (most likely fictional) story about a time when President John F. Kennedy visited NASA. Upon meeting a janitor, Kennedy asked him what he was doing. The janitor replied, "Well, Mr. President, I'm helping put a man on the moon."

Conclusion: anyone can make a difference

So, good news: you don't need to throw yourself out of a plane to do good. In fact, there are far easier (and safer) ways to have an impact that are much more effective.

Due to our fortunate positions in the world, there's a lot we can do to make a difference without making significant sacrifices, whatever jobs we end up in.

Here are some key ways to make a big positive impact without changing jobs:

1. Give 10% of your income to effective charities.
2. Use your political influence, such as by voting.
3. Help others have an impact.

You might like to consider taking the 10% pledge right now.

Or take a moment to consider how else you might be able to make a big impact with little sacrifice.

What if you want to make a difference *directly* through your career? If you can achieve so much with just 10% of your income, then what you could achieve with your entire job over decades could be huge. That's what we'll cover in the next three chapters.

CHAPTER 4

Want to do good? Here's how to choose an area to focus on.

If you want to make a difference with your career, one place to start is to ask which global problems most need attention. Should you work on education, climate change, poverty, or something else?

The standard advice is to do whatever most interests you, and most people seem to end up working on whichever social problem first grabs their attention.

That's exactly what I (Benjamin) did. At age 19, I was most interested in climate change.

However, my focus on climate change wasn't the result of a careful comparison of the pros and cons of working on different problems. Rather, I'd happened to read about it, and found it engaging because it was sciency (and I was geeky).

The problem with this approach is that you might happen to stumble across an area that's just not that big, important, or easy to make progress on. You're also much more likely to stumble across the problems that already receive the most attention, which makes them lower impact.

So how can you avoid these mistakes, and do more good?

We've developed three questions to ask yourself to work out which social problems are most urgent — where an extra year of work will have the greatest impact.

It's based on work by Open Philanthropy,[55] a foundation with billions of dollars of committed funds, and the (modestly named) Global Priorities Institute, a research group at Oxford.

You can use these steps to compare areas you could enter (e.g. pandemic prevention, risks from AI, or global health), or if you're already committed to an area, you can compare projects *within* that area (e.g. research into malaria or HIV).

1. Is this problem large in scale?

We tend to assess the importance of different social problems using our intuition, i.e. what seems important on a gut level.

For instance, in 2005 the BBC wrote:

> *"The nuclear power stations will all be switched off in a few years. How can we keep Britain's lights on? ...unplug your mobile-phone charger when it's not in use."*

This so annoyed David MacKay, a Physics professor at Cambridge, that he decided to find out exactly how bad leaving your mobile phone plugged in really is.[56]

The bottom line is that even if *no mobile phone charger were ever left plugged in again*, Britain would save at most *0.01%* of its personal power usage (and that's leaving aside industrial usage and the like). So even if entirely successful, a quick estimate shows that this BBC campaign could have no noticeable effect. MacKay said it was like "trying to bail out the Titanic with a tea strainer."

Instead, that effort could have been used to change behaviour in a way that could easily have 1,000 times as much impact on climate change, such as installing home insulation.[57]

Decades of research has shown that we're bad at intuitively assessing differences in scale. For instance, one study found that people were willing to pay about the same amount to save 2,000 birds from oil spills as they were to save 200,000 birds, even though the latter is objectively 100 times better. This is an example of a common error called scope neglect.

To avoid scope neglect, we need to use numbers to make comparisons, even if they're very rough.

In chapter 2, we said that social impact depends on the extent to which you help others live better lives. So based on this definition, a problem has greater scale:

- The larger the number of people affected.
- The larger the size of the effects per person.
- The larger the long-run benefits of solving the problem.

Scale is important because the effect of activities on a problem is often proportional to the size of the problem. Launch a campaign that ends 10% of the phone charger problem, and you achieve very little. Launch a campaign that persuades 10% of people to install home insulation, and it's a much bigger deal.

If we cared so little about the relative importance of different problems in our personal lives.

2. Is this problem neglected?

In a previous chapter, we saw that medicine in the US and UK is a relatively crowded problem: there are already over 850,000 doctors in the US and health spending is high, which makes it harder for an extra person working on health to make a big contribution.[58]

Health in poor countries, however, receives much less attention, and that's one reason why it's possible to save a life for only about $5,000.

The more effort that's already going into a problem, the harder it is for *you* to be successful and make a meaningful contribution. This is due to *diminishing returns*.

When you pick fruit from a tree, you start with those that are easiest to reach: the low-hanging fruit. When they're gone, it becomes harder and harder to get a meal.

It's the same with social impact. When few people have worked on a problem, there are generally lots of great opportunities to make progress. As more and more work is done, it becomes harder and harder to be original and have a big impact. It looks a bit like this:

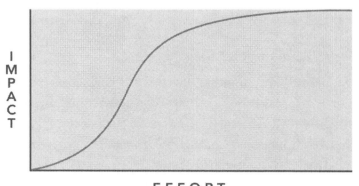

EFFORT

The problems your friends are talking about and interested in working on are exactly those where everyone else is already focused. So they're not the neglected problems, and probably not the most urgent.

Rather, the most urgent problems — those where you have the greatest impact — are probably areas you've never thought about working on.

We all know about the fight against cancer, but what about parasitic worms? It doesn't make for such a good charity music video, but these tiny creatures have infected one billion people worldwide with neglected tropical diseases.[59] These conditions are far easier to treat than cancer, but we never even hear about them because they very rarely affect rich people.

So instead of following the trend, seek out problems that other people are systematically missing. For instance:

1. Does the problem affect neglected groups, like those far away from us, nonhuman animals, or future generations rather than us?
2. Is the problem a low-probability event, which might be getting overlooked?
3. Do few people know about the problem?

Following this advice is harder than it looks, because it means standing out from the crowd, and that might mean looking a little weird.[60]

3. Is this problem solvable?

Scared Straight is a programme that takes kids who have committed misdemeanours to visit prisons and meet convicted criminals, confronting them with their likely future if they don't change their ways. The concept proved popular not just as a social programme but as entertainment; it was adapted for both an acclaimed documentary and a TV show on A&E, which broke ratings records for the network upon its premiere.[61]

There's just one problem with Scared Straight: it probably causes young people to commit *more* crimes.

Or more precisely, the young people who went through the programme *did* commit fewer crimes than they did before, so superficially it looked like it worked. But the decrease was smaller compared to similar young people who never went through the programme.

The effect is so significant that the Washington State Institute for Public Policy estimated that each $1 spent on Scared Straight programmes causes more than $200 worth of social harm.[62] This estimate seems a little too pessimistic to us, but even so, it looks like it was a huge mistake.

No one is sure why this is, but it might be because the young people realised that life in jail wasn't as bad as they thought, or they came to admire the criminals.

Some attempts to do good, like Scared Straight, make things worse. Many more fail to have an impact. David Anderson of the Coalition for Evidence Based Policy estimates:[63]

> *"Of [social programmes] that have been rigorously evaluated, most (perhaps 75% or more), including those backed by expert opinion and less-rigorous studies, turn out to produce small or no effects, and, in some cases negative effects."*

This suggests that if you choose a charity to get involved in without looking at the evidence, you'll most likely *have no impact at all.*

Worse, it's very hard to tell which programmes are going to be effective ahead of time. Don't believe us? Try our 10-question quiz at 80000hours. org/articles/can-you-guess/, and see if you can guess what's effective. The quiz asks you to guess which social interventions work and which don't. We've tested it on hundreds of people, and they hardly do better than chance.

So, before you choose a social problem to work on, ask yourself:

1. Is there a way to make progress on this problem with rigorous evidence behind it? For instance, lots of studies have shown that malaria nets prevent malaria.

2. Alternatively, is there a way to test promising but unproven programmes that could help solve this problem, and find out whether they work?
3. Is this a problem where there's a small but realistic chance of making a massive impact? For instance, stopping catastrophic pandemics via better policy.

If the answer to all of these is no, then it's probably best to find something else.

Look for the best balance of the factors

You probably won't find something that does brilliantly on all three dimensions. Rather, look for what does best on balance. A problem could be worth tackling if it's extremely big and neglected, even if it seems hard to solve.

Your personal fit and expertise

There's no point working on a problem if you can't find any roles that are a good fit for you: you won't be satisfied or have much impact.

So while it's a great idea to find a problem that has a good combination of being big, neglected, and solvable, you'll *also* want to find a specific role that's a good fit for you.

As we'll cover in chapter 8, personal fit is so important that it can easily be better to focus on an area you think is less pressing in general, if it's a sufficiently good fit for you.

Early in your career, you only need to have a vague idea of what problems you might want to work on in the future. Your main focus should be exploring to figure out what you're good at, and building skills that will plausibly be useful — which we cover in the next two chapters. Later you can use those skills to tackle the most pressing problems at the time.

If you're already an expert in a certain skill, then your focus should be on finding a way to use that expertise to tackle a pressing problem. It wouldn't make sense for, say, a great economist who's crushing it to go and become a biologist. Rather, there is probably a way to apply economics to the issues you think are most pressing. You can also use the framework above to narrow down subfields (e.g. development economics vs employment policy).

So what *are* the world's most urgent problems?

What are the biggest problems in the world that no one is talking about and are possible to solve? That's what we'll cover next.

THE BOTTOM LINE:
HOW CAN YOU FIND THE WORLD'S MOST
PRESSING PROBLEMS?

The most pressing problems are likely to have a good combination of the following qualities:

1. **Big in scale**: What's the magnitude of this problem? How much does it affect people's lives today? More crucially, how much of an effect will solving it have in the long run (including the very, very long run, if there are any such effects?)
2. **Neglected:** How many people and resources are already dedicated to tackling this problem? How well allocated are the resources that are currently being dedicated to the problem? Are there good reasons why markets or governments aren't already making progress on this problem?
3. **Solvable:** How easy would it be to make progress on this problem? Do interventions already exist to solve this problem effectively, and how strong is the evidence behind them?

To find the problem *you* should work on, also consider **personal fit**. Could you become motivated to work on this problem? If you're later in your career, do you have relevant expertise?

See how we apply this framework in the next chapter.

CHAPTER 5
The world's biggest problems and why they're not what first comes to mind

We've spent much of the last 10+ years trying to answer a simple question: what are the world's biggest and most neglected problems?

We wanted to have a positive impact with our careers, and so we set out to discover where our efforts would be most effective.

Our analysis suggests that choosing the right problem could increase your impact by over 100 times, which would make it the most important driver of your impact.

Here, we give a summary of what we've learned. Read on to hear why ending diarrhoea might save as many lives as world peace, why artificial intelligence might be an even bigger deal, and what to do in your own career to make the most urgent changes happen.

In short, the most pressing problems are those where people can have the greatest impact by working on them. As we explained in the previous chapter, this means problems that are not only big, but also *neglected and solvable*. The more neglected and solvable, the further extra effort will go. And this means they're not the problems that first come to mind.

If you just want to see what we think the answer is, go to appendix 9, where you can also see summaries of our problem profiles.

Why issues facing rich countries aren't always the most important — and why charity shouldn't always begin at home

Most people who want to do good focus on issues in their home country. In rich countries, this often means issues like homelessness, inner-city education, and unemployment. But are these the most urgent issues?

In the US, only 5% of charitable donations are spent on international causes.[64] The most popular careers for talented graduates who want to do good are teaching and health, which together receive around 40% of graduates, and mainly involve helping people in the US.[65]

There are some good reasons to focus on helping your own country — you know more about the issues, and you might feel you have special obligations to it. However, back in 2009, we encountered the following series of facts. They led us to think that the most urgent problems are not local, but rather poverty in the world's poorest countries — especially efforts within health, such as fighting malaria and parasitic worms. (And as we'll come onto later, we now think there are *even more pressing issues* than global poverty — in particular, catastrophic risks that could affect the whole world and future.)

Why do we say the most urgent problems aren't local? Well, remember the distribution of world income that we came across in chapter 2.

Even someone living on the US poverty line of $14,580 per year (as of 2023)[66] is richer than about 85% of the world's population,[67] and about 20 times wealthier than the world's poorest 700 million, who mostly live in Central America, Africa, and South Asia on under $800 per year.[68] These figures are already adjusted for the fact that money goes further in poor countries (purchasing power parity).[69]

As we also saw earlier, the poorer you are, the bigger difference extra money makes to your welfare. Based on this research, because poorer people in Africa are 20 times poorer, we'd expect resources to go about 20 times further in helping them.

There are also only about 40 million people living in relative poverty in the US, about 6% as many as the 650 million in extreme global poverty.[70]

There are also far more resources dedicated to helping this smaller number of people. Overseas development aid from the world's developed countries is, in total, only about $200 billion per year, compared to $1.7 trillion spent on welfare in the US alone (OECD 1-15).[71]

Finally, as we saw earlier, a significant fraction of US social interventions probably don't work. This is because problems facing the poor in rich countries are complex and hard to solve. Moreover, even the most evidence-backed interventions are expensive and have modest effects.[72]

The same comparison holds for other rich countries, such as the UK, Australia, Canada, and the EU. (Though if you live in a low-income country, then it may well be best to focus on issues there.)

All this isn't to deny that the poor in rich countries have very tough lives, perhaps even worse in some respects than those in the developing world. Rather, the issue is that there are far fewer of them, and they're harder to help.

So if you're not focusing on issues in your home country, what should you focus on?

Global health: a problem where you could really make progress

Earlier we told the story of Dr Nalin, who helped to develop oral rehydration therapy as a treatment for diarrhoea.

What if we were to tell you that, over the second half of the 20th century, efforts by Dr Nalin and others did as much to save lives as achieving world peace over the same period would have done?

The number of deaths each year due to diarrhoea have fallen by 3 million over the last five decades due to advances like oral rehydration therapy.

Meanwhile, all wars and political famines killed about 2 million people per year over the second half of the 20th century.[73]

And we've had similar victories over other infectious diseases.

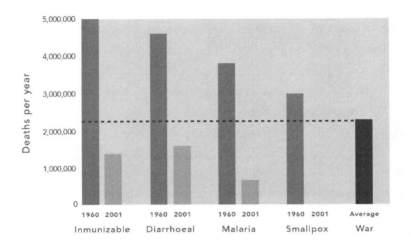

The global fight against disease is one of humanity's greatest achievements, but it's also an ongoing battle that you can contribute to with your career.

A large fraction of these gains were driven by humanitarian aid, such as the campaign to eradicate smallpox.[74] In fact, although many experts in economics think much international aid hasn't been effective, even the most sceptical agree there's an exception: global health.

For instance, William Easterly, author of *The White Man's Burden: Why the West's Efforts to Aid the Rest Have Done So Much Ill and So Little Good* wrote:

> *"Put the focus back where it belongs: get the poorest people in the world such obvious goods as the vaccines, the antibiotics, the food supplements, the improved seeds, the fertilizer, the roads.... This is not making the poor dependent on handouts; it is giving the poorest*

people the health, nutrition, education, and other inputs that raise
the payoff to their own efforts to better their lives."

Within health, where to focus? An economist at the World Bank sent
us this data, which also amazed us.

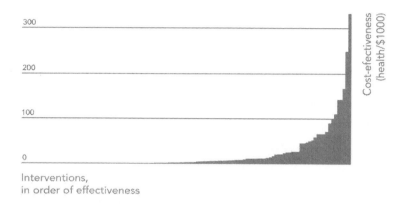

Cost-effectiveness of health interventions as found in the Disease Controls Priorities Project 2.[75]

This is a list of health treatments, such as providing tuberculosis
medicine or surgeries, ranked by how much health they produce per dollar,
as measured in rigorous randomised controlled trials. Health is measured
in a standard unit used by health economists, called the "quality-adjusted
life year."

The first point is that all these treatments are effective. Essentially all
of them would be funded in countries like the US and UK. People in poor
countries, however, routinely die from diseases that would certainly have
been treated if they'd happened to have been born somewhere else.

Even more surprising, however, is that the top interventions are far
better than the average, as shown by the spike on the right. The top
interventions, like vaccines, have been shown to have significant benefits,
but are also extremely cheap. The top intervention is over 10 times more

cost-effective than the average, and 15,000 times more than the worst.[76] This means if you were working at a health charity focused on one of the top interventions, you'd expect to have 10 times as much impact compared to a randomly selected one.

This study isn't perfect — there were mistakes in the analysis affecting the top results[77] (and that's what you'd expect due to regression to the mean) — but the main point is solid: the best health interventions are many times more effective than the average.

So how much more impact might you make with your career by switching your focus to global health?

Because, as we saw in the first chart, the world's poorest people are over 20 times poorer than the poor in rich countries, resources go about 20 times as far in helping them.[78]

Then, if we focus on health, there are cheap, effective interventions that everyone agrees are worth doing. We can use the research in the second chart to pick the very best interventions, letting us have perhaps five times as much impact again.[79] In total, this makes for a 100-fold difference in impact.[80]

Does this check out? The UK's National Health Service and many US government agencies are willing to spend over $30,000 to give someone an extra year of healthy life.[81] This is a fantastic use of resources by ordinary standards.

However, research by GiveWell has found that it's possible to give an infant a year of healthy life by donating around $100 to one of the most cost-effective global health charities, such as Against Malaria Foundation. This is about 0.33% as much.[82] This suggests that, at least in terms of improving health, one career working somewhere like AMF might achieve as much as 300 careers focused on one typical way of doing good in a rich country. (Though our best guess is that a more rigorous and comprehensive comparison would find a somewhat smaller difference.[83])

It's hard for us to grasp such big differences in scale, but that would mean that one year of (equally skilled) effort towards the best treatments within global health could have as much impact as what would have taken others 100 years working on typical rich country issues.

These discoveries caused many of us at 80,000 Hours to start giving at least 10% of our incomes to effective global health charities. No matter which job we ended up in, these donations would enable us to make a significant difference. In fact, if the 100-fold figure is correct, a 10% donation would be equivalent to donating 1,000% of our income to charities focused on poverty in rich countries.

However, everything we learned about global health raised many more questions. If it's possible to have 10 or 100 times more impact with just a little research, maybe there are even better areas to discover?

We considered lots of avenues to help the global poor, like trade reform, promoting migration, crop yield research, and biomedical research.

To go in a very different direction, we also seriously considered working to end factory farming. The idea — in brief — is that the interests of animals get very little protection by our current economic and political systems, but there are huge numbers of them: around 100 billion animals die every year in factory farms. For example, we helped to found Animal Charity Evaluators, which does research into how to most effectively improve animal welfare. We still think factory farming is an urgent problem (see appendix 9). But in the end, we decided to focus on something else.

Why focusing on future generations might be even more effective than tackling global health

Which would you choose from these two options?

1. Prevent one person from suffering next year.
2. Prevent 100 people from suffering (the same amount) 100 years from now.

Most people choose the second option. It's a crude example, but it suggests that they value future generations.

If people didn't want to leave a legacy to future generations, it would be hard to understand why we invest so much in science, create art, and preserve the wilderness.

We would certainly choose the second option. And if you value future generations, then there are powerful arguments that helping them should be your focus. We were first exposed to these by researchers at the University of Oxford's (modestly named) Future of Humanity Institute.

So, what's the reasoning?

First, future generations matter, but they can't vote, they can't buy things, and they can't stand up for their interests. This means our system neglects them. You can see this in the global failure to come to an international agreement to tackle climate change that actually works.

Second, their plight is *abstract*. We're reminded of issues like global poverty and factory farming far more often. But we can't so easily visualise suffering that will happen in the future. Future generations rely more on our goodwill, and even that is hard to muster.

Third, there will probably be many more people alive in the future than there are today. The Earth will remain habitable for at least hundreds of millions of years.[84] We may die out long before that point, but if there's a chance of making it, then many more people will live in the future than are alive today.

To use some hypothetical figures: if each generation lasts for 100 years, then over 100 million years there could be one million future generations.[85]

This is such a big number that any problem that affects future generations potentially has a far greater scale than one that only affects the present — it could affect one million times more people, and all the art, science, culture, and wellbeing that will entail. So problems that affect future generations are potentially the largest in scale and the most neglected.

What's more, because the future could be long and the universe is so vast, almost *no matter* what you value, there could be far more of what matters in the future.

This suggests that we have much greater reason than people usually realise to help the future — and not just the near future but also the very long-run future — go well.[86]

But can we actually help future generations, or improve the long term? Perhaps the problems that affect the future are big and neglected, but not solvable?

One way to help future generations: avert neglected existential risks

In the summer of 2013, Barack Obama referred to climate change as "the global threat of our time."[87] He's not alone in this opinion. When many people think of the biggest problems facing future generations, climate change is often the first to come to mind.

One reason for that is that many fear that climate change could lead to a catastrophic civilisational collapse — and could even lead to the end of the human species.[88]

We think this thought is, to some extent, on the right track. The most powerful way we can help future generations is, we think, to prevent a catastrophe that could end advanced civilisation, or even prevent any future generations from existing. If civilisation survives, we'll have a chance to later solve problems like poverty and disease; while anything that poses a truly *existential* threat will prevent any such progress.[89]

However, climate change is also widely acknowledged as a major problem (conspiracy theorists aside), and receives tens or even hundreds of billions of dollars of investment. Our guess is also that there are issues that pose much greater risks of ending civilisation.

So while we think tackling climate change is an important way to help future generations, we think it's likely even higher impact for many to focus on more neglected and more existentially dangerous issues.[90]

Biorisk: the threat from future disease

In 2006, *The Guardian* ordered segments of smallpox DNA via mail. If assembled into a complete strand and transmitted to 10 people, a study estimated it could infect up to 2.2 million people in 180 days — potentially killing 660,000 — if authorities did not respond quickly with vaccinations and quarantines.[91]

We first wrote about the risks posed by catastrophic pandemics back in 2016. Seven years later, and three years after the emergence of COVID-19, we're still concerned.

COVID-19 disrupted the world and has, so far, killed over 10 million people.[92] But it's easy to imagine scenarios far worse.

In the future, we might face diseases even deadlier than COVID-19 or smallpox — whether through natural evolution, or created through bioengineering (the technology for which is becoming cheaper and more accessible every year).

In our eyes, the chance of a pandemic that kills over 100 million people over the next century seems similar to and likely greater than the risk of nuclear war or runaway climate change. So it poses a threat that's at least similar in magnitude to both the present generation and future generations.

But risks from pandemics are even now far more neglected than either of these. We estimate that over $600 billion is spent annually on efforts to fight climate change, compared to $1–$10 billion towards biosecurity aimed at addressing the worst-case pandemics.

Moreover, there are some ways the risks from pandemics could be even greater. It's very difficult to see how nuclear war or climate change could kill *literally everyone*, and permanently end civilisation — but bioweapons with this power seem very much within the realm of possibility, if given enough time.

At the same time, there's plenty of relatively straightforward things that could be done to improve biosecurity, such as improving regulation of labs, building bigger stockpiles of personal protective equipment (PPE), and developing cheap diagnostics to detect new diseases quickly. Overall, we think biosecurity is likely more pressing than climate change. We currently think that biosecurity is one of the world's *most* pressing problems.[93]

But there are issues that *might* be even *more* important, and seem to be even more neglected.

Preventing an AI-related catastrophe

Around 1800, civilisation underwent one of the most profound shifts in human history: the Industrial Revolution.[94]

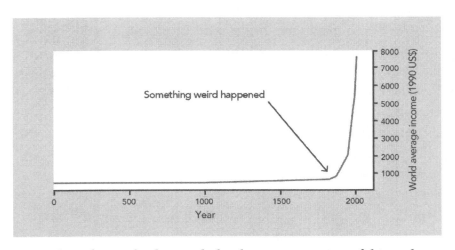

Looking forward, what might be the *next* transition of this scale — the next pivotal event in history that shapes what happens to all future generations? If we could identify such a transition, that may well be the most important area in which to work.

One candidate is bioengineering — the ability to fundamentally redesign human beings — as discussed, for example, by Yuval Noah Harari in *Sapiens.*

But we think there's an issue that's even more neglected, and is developing far more rapidly: artificial intelligence.

Billions of dollars are spent trying to make artificial intelligence more powerful, but hardly any effort is devoted to making sure that those added capabilities are implemented safely and for the benefit of humanity.

This matters for two main reasons.

First, powerful AI systems have the potential to be misused. For instance, they might be used to develop dangerous new technology, such as new and more powerful weapons.

Second, there is a risk of accidents when powerful new AI systems are deployed. This is especially pressing due to the "alignment problem." This is a complex topic, so if you want to explore it properly, we recommend reading our full problem profile on artificial intelligence:

https://80k.info/AI

But here's a quick introduction.

In the 1980s, chess was held up as an example of something a machine could never do. But in 1997, world chess champion Garry Kasparov was defeated by the computer program Deep Blue. Since then, computers have become far better at chess than humans.

In 2004, two experts in artificial intelligence used truck driving as an example of a job that would be really hard to automate. But today, self-driving cars are already on the road.[95]

In August 2021, a team of expert forecasters predicted that it would take five years for a computer to be able solve high school competition–level maths problems.[96] Less than a year later, Google built an AI that could do just that.[97]

At the end of 2022, ChatGPT became the fastest growing web platform ever.[98]

The most recent of these advances are possible due to progress in *machine learning*. In the past, we mostly had to give computers detailed instructions for every task. Today, we have programs that *teach themselves*. The same algorithm that can play Space Invaders has also learned to play about 50 other arcade games, caption images, chat with humans, and manipulate a real robot arm.[99]

Machine learning has been around for decades, but improved algorithms (especially around *deep learning* techniques), faster processors, bigger datasets, and huge investments by companies like Google and Microsoft have led to amazing advances far faster than expected.

Due to this, many experts think human-level artificial intelligence could easily happen in our lifetimes. Here are the results of a 2022 survey of hundreds of top AI researchers (AI Impacts):[100]

	Median response	Mean response	Standard deviation
10% chance of human-level machine intelligence	2032	2042	40 years
50% chance of human-level machine intelligence	2052	2127	530 years
90% chance of human-level machine intelligence	2086	5406	40,000 years

You can see half the experts give a 50% (or higher) chance of human-level AI happening by 2050, just 30 years in the future. Admittedly, they are very uncertain — but high uncertainty also means it could arrive *sooner* rather than later.

Why is this important? Gorillas are faster than us, stronger than us, and have a more powerful bite. But there are only 100,000 gorillas in the wild, compared to 7 billion humans, and their fate is up to us.[101] A major reason for this is a difference in intelligence.

Right now, computers are only smarter than us in limited ways (e.g. playing StarCraft), and this is already changing the economy. But what happens when computers become smarter than us in almost all ways, like how we're smarter than gorillas?

This transition could be hugely positive, or hugely negative. On the one hand, just as the Industrial Revolution automated manual labour, the AI revolution could automate intellectual labour, unleashing unprecedented prosperity and access to material resources.

But we also couldn't guarantee staying in control of a system that's smarter than us — it might be more strategic than us, more persuasive, and better at solving problems. So we need to make sure the AI system shares our goals.

This, however, is not easy. No one knows how to program moral behaviour into a computer. Within computer science, this is known as the *alignment problem*.

Solving the alignment problem might be hugely important, but today very few people are working on it.

We estimate the number of full-time researchers working directly on the alignment problem is around 300, making it over 10 times more neglected than biosecurity.

At the same time, there is momentum behind this work. In the last 10 years, the field has gained academic and industry support, such as Stephen Hawking, Stuart Russell (who wrote the most popular textbook in the field of AI), and Geoffrey Hinton (who pioneered the field of AI).[102] If you're not a good fit for technical research yourself, you can contribute in other ways — for example, by working as a research manager or assistant, or donating and raising funds for this research.

This will also be a huge issue for governments. AI policy is fast becoming an important area, but policymakers are focused on short-term issues like how to regulate self-driving cars and job loss, rather than the key long-term issues (i.e. the future of civilisation).[103]

Of all the issues we've covered so far, reducing the risks posed by AI is among the most important, but also the most neglected. Despite also being harder to solve, we think it's likely to be among the most high-impact problems of the coming decades.

This was a surprise to us when we first considered it, but we think it's where the arguments lead. These days we spend more time researching machine learning than malaria nets.

Dealing with uncertainty and "going meta"

Our views have changed a great deal over the last 12 years, and they could easily change again. We could commit to working on AI or biosecurity, but might we discover something even better in the coming years? And what might this uncertainty imply about where to focus now?

Global priorities research

If you're uncertain which global problem is most pressing, here's one answer: "more research is needed." Only a tiny fraction of the billions of dollars spent each year trying to make the world a better place goes towards research to identify how to spend those resources most effectively — what we call "global priorities research."

As we've seen, some approaches are far more effective than others. So this research is hugely valuable.

A career in this area could mean working at Open Philanthropy, the Global Priorities Institute, Rethink Priorities, economics academia, think tanks, and elsewhere.[104]

Broad interventions, such as improved politics

The second strategy is to work on problems that will help us solve lots of other problems. We call these "broad interventions."

For instance, if we had more enlightened governments, that would help us solve lots of other problems facing future generations. The US government in particular will play a pivotal role in issues like climate policy, AI policy, biosecurity, and new challenges we don't even know about yet. So US governance is highly important (if maybe not neglected or tractable).

Political action in your local community might have an effect on decision-makers in Washington. In the last chapter, we did an analysis of the simplest kind of political action — voting — and found that it could be really valuable.

On the other hand, issues like US governance already receive a huge amount of attention, which makes them hard to improve.

We generally favour more neglected issues with more targeted effects on future generations. For instance, fascinating research by Philip Tetlock shows that some teams and methods are far better at predicting geopolitical events than others.[105] If the decision-makers in society were informed by much more accurate predictions, it would help them navigate future crises, whatever those turn out to be.[106]

However, the category of "broad interventions" is one of the areas we're most uncertain about, so we're keen to see more research on it.

Capacity building and promoting effective altruism

If you're uncertain which problems will be most pressing in the future, a third strategy is to simply save money or invest in your career capital (which we'll get to in chapter 7), so you're in a better position to do good when you have more information.

However, rather than make personal investments, it can be even better to invest in a community of people working to do good.

In an earlier chapter we looked at Giving What We Can, a charity building a community of people who donate 10% of their income to whichever charities are most cost effective.[107] Every $1 invested in growing Giving What We Can has led to over $9 already donated to its top recommended charities, and a total of over $3 billion pledged.[108]

By building a community, Giving What We Can has been able to raise *much* more money than their founders could have donated individually — they've achieved a *multiplier* on their impact.

But what's more, the members donate to whichever charities are most effective at the time. If the situation changes, then (at least to some extent) the donations will change too.

This *flexibility* makes the impact *over time* much higher.

Giving What We Can is one example of several projects in the effective altruism community, a community of people who aim to identify the best ways to help others and take action based on their findings.[109]

80,000 Hours itself is another example.

Better career advice doesn't sound like one of the most pressing problems imaginable. But many of the world's most talented young people want to do good with their lives, and lack good advice on how to do so. This means that every year, thousands of them have far less impact than they could have.

We could have gone to work on issues like AI ourselves. But instead, by providing better advice, we can help thousands of other people find high-impact careers. And so (if we do a good job), we might hope to have thousands of times as much impact ourselves.

What's more, if we discover new, better career options than the ones we already know about, we can switch to promoting them. Just like Giving What We Can, this flexibility gives us greater impact over time.

We call the indirect strategies we've covered — global priorities research, broad interventions, and promoting effective altruism — "going meta," because they work one level removed from the concrete problems that seem most urgent.

The downside of going meta is that it's harder to know if your efforts are effective. The advantage is they're usually more neglected, since people prefer concrete opportunities over more abstract ones, and they allow you to have greater impact in the face of uncertainty.

How to work out which problems *you* should focus on

You can see our list of the world's most pressing problems, in appendix 9.

But that's just our list. What matters for your career is *your personal list.*

The assessment of problems greatly depends on value judgements and debatable empirical questions, and you might not share our answers. There are a number of key ways in which we might be wrong.[110]

Personal fit is also vital, and so are the particular opportunities you can find. We don't think everyone should work on the number one problem. If you're a great fit for an area, you might have over 10 times as much impact working there as you would in one that doesn't motivate you. So this could easily change your personal ranking.

Just remember there are many ways to help solve each problem, so it's often easier than it first seems to find work you enjoy that helps with problems you might not have yet considered working on. Moreover, it's easier to develop new passions than most people expect.

Despite all the uncertainties, your choice of problem might be the single biggest factor determining your impact.

If we rated global problems in terms of how pressing they are, we might intuitively expect them to look like this:

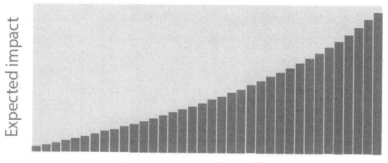

Problems, in order of impact

Some problems are more pressing than others, but most are pretty good. But instead, we've found that it looks more like this.

Problems, in order of impact

Some problems are *far* higher impact than others, because they can differ by 10 or 100 times in terms of how big, neglected, and solvable they are, as well as your degree of personal fit.[111] So getting this decision right could mean you achieve over 100 times as much with your career.

If there's one lesson we draw from all we've covered, it's this: if you want to do good in the world, it's worth at some point really taking the time to learn about different global problems, and how you might contribute to solving them. It takes time, and there's a lot to learn, but it's hard to imagine anything more interesting, or more important.

APPLY THIS TO YOUR OWN CAREER

You don't need to figure out which global problems you want to focus on right at the start of your career. Early on, the top priority is to explore to figure out what you're good at, and to build valuable skills. It's common to not directly tackle the problems you think are most pressing for many years.

However, it is useful to at least have a rough idea of which problems you'd like to work on in the future, since this can greatly affect which kinds of skills seem most useful to build. For instance, if you guess that reducing risks from AI is in your shortlist, that could suggest gaining some pretty different skills and experience to global health (though some skills are useful in both, such as management). So, even if you're right at the start of your career, we'd suggest spending at least a couple of days thinking about this question.

Here's an exercise:

1. Using the resources above, write down the three global problems that you think are most pressing for you to work on. Your personal list will depend on your values, empirical assumptions, and personal fit with the areas.
2. What are you most uncertain about with respect to your list? How might you learn more about those questions? (For example: Is there something you could read? Someone you could talk to?)

You can find summaries of our evaluations of different problem areas in appendix 9, and our complete and up-to-date evaluations at: https://80k.link/VEK/.

This list of problems is just a starting point. The next step is to find concrete career options that will make a difference within the area (which we cover in the next chapter), then to find an option with excellent personal fit (which we cover in chapter 8).

CHAPTER 6

Which jobs help people the most?

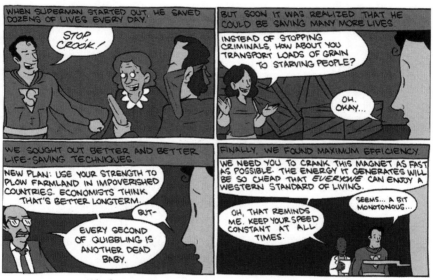

Why Superman was wrong to fight crime – comic from SMBC.

Many people think of Superman as a hero. But he may be the greatest example of underutilised talent in all of fiction. It was a blunder to spend his life fighting crime one case at a time; if he'd thought a little more creatively, he could have done far more good. How about delivering vaccines to everyone in the world at superspeed? That would have eradicated most infectious disease, saving hundreds of millions of lives.

Here we'll argue that a lot of people who want to "make a difference" with their career fall into the same trap as Superman. College graduates imagine becoming doctors or teachers, but these may not be the best fit for their particular skills. And like Superman fighting crime, these paths are often limited in the amount they could potentially contribute to solving a problem.

In contrast, Nobel Prize winner Karl Landsteiner discovered blood groups, enabling hundreds of millions of lifesaving operations. He would have never been able to carry out that many surgeries himself.

Below we'll introduce five ways you could use your career to help tackle the social problems you want to help work on (which we identified in the previous chapter). The five ways are: earning to give, communication, research, government and policy, and organisation-building. We'll make concrete recommendations on how to pursue each approach.

To get even more ideas, take a look at the summaries of our career reviews in appendix 8.

Approach 1: Earning to give

Would Elton John have done more good if he'd worked at a small nonprofit? We don't normally think of becoming a rock star as a path to doing good, but (quite apart from the value of his music!) Elton John has saved the lives of thousands of people by reducing the spread of HIV/AIDS.[112]

So here's one way of doing more good that's not normally put on the table: *earning to give.*

We often meet people who are interested in taking a higher-earning job, like software engineering, but are worried they won't make a difference. Part of the reason is that we don't usually think of earning more money as a path for people who want to do good. However, there are many effective organisations that have no problem finding enthusiastic staff, but don't have the funds to hire. People who are a good fit for a higher-earning option can donate to these organisations, making a large *indirect* contribution.

We define "earning to give" as working in a job with a neutral or positive direct impact, which pays more than what someone would have done otherwise, and while donating a large fraction of the extra earnings (typically 20–50% of the total salary) to organisations they think are highly effective.

Earning to give is not just for people who want to work in the highest-paying industries. Anyone who aims to earn more in order to give more is on this path. But if you're a good fit for a higher-earning path, it could be one of your higher-impact options.

Consider the story of Julia and Jeff, a couple from Boston with three children. Through his relationship with Julia, Jeff became interested in using his career for good. Jeff used to work as a research technician. He decided to train up to become a software engineer, and eventually got a job at Google. The couple were able to earn more than twice as much, so started to donate about half their income to charity each year.[113]

By doing this, they may have had more impact than they could by working directly in a nonprofit. Compare Jeff's impact to that of the CEO of a nonprofit:

	Google software engineer	Nonprofit CEO
Salary	$250,000	$65,000
Donations	$125,000	$0
Money to live on	$125,000	$65,000
Direct impact of work	Neutral	Very positive

Jeff could live on about two times as much as he would have earned in the nonprofit sector, and still donate enough to fund the salaries of about two nonprofit CEOs.[114] Jeff's guess is that the direct impact of his job was approximately neutral. He *also* thinks he became happier in his work because he enjoys engineering.

Moreover, Jeff and Julia could switch their donations to whichever organisations were most in need of funds at any given time based on their research, whereas it's harder to change where you work. This flexibility is particularly valuable if you're uncertain about which problems will be most pressing in the future.

Making this much difference is possible because (as we saw earlier) we live in a world with huge income inequality — it's possible to earn several times as much as a teacher or nonprofit worker, and vastly more than the world's poorest people. At the same time, hardly anyone donates more than a few percent of their income,[115] so *if you are* willing to do so, you can have an amazing impact in a very wide range of jobs.

Earlier, we also saw that any college graduate in a developed country can have a major impact by giving 10% of their income to an effective charity. The average graduate earns $77,000 per year over their life, and 10% of that could save about 40 lives if given to Against Malaria Foundation, for example.

If you could just earn 10% more, and donate the extra, then that's twice as much impact again. And if you think there are better organisations to fund than Against Malaria Foundation — perhaps working on different problems, or doing research, or communicating important ideas — the impact is even higher.

Since we introduced the concept of "earning to give" in 2011, hundreds of people have taken it up and stuck with it. Some give around 30% of their income, and a few even give more than 50%. Collectively, they'll donate tens of millions of dollars to high-impact charities in the coming years. In doing so, they are funding passionate people who want to contribute directly, but who otherwise wouldn't have the resources to do so.

One of the people we advised in 2011, Matt, donated over $1 million while still in his 20s, and was featured in the *New York Times*.[116] He found his new job more enjoyable too.

Should you earn to give?

Earning to give has been one of our most memorable and controversial ideas, attracting media coverage in the BBC, Washington Post, Daily Mail, and many other outlets.[117]

For this reason, many people think it's our top recommendation. But it's not.

We see earning to give mostly as a baseline. It's a path that many could pursue and do a lot of good — on the scale of saving 100 lives or more, as we just argued.

But we think that most of our readers can have an even greater impact again by pursuing one of the other approaches below. Overall, for people we speak to one-on-one, we only think about 10% should earn to give.

In fact, in 2022, Jeff left his high-paying job at Google. He's now a researcher at the Nucleic Acid Observatory, building a wastewater monitoring system that he hopes will help detect pandemics before they start. Jeff and Julia are still going to donate over 30% of their income — but given Jeff's lower salary, they expect most of their positive impact to come directly from their work.

When *is* earning to give especially promising?

- **You're a good fit for a higher earning option**, like Jeff was for software engineering, and you're not a good fit for other impactful options. (Definitely don't become a software engineer if you'd hate it!)
- **There's a particular job you really want to do for other reasons** where you think you can make significant donations. For instance, you might be someone who's always wanted to be a doctor, or you

might need a higher-earning job to support your family.

- You think a higher-earning option will be good for building skills (for use in more direct work later on), and earning to give could help you to stay engaged with social impact while you do so. For example, working at a tech startup can help you learn organisation-building skills that are useful when running nonprofits. (In the next chapter we explain why it's important to gain "career capital.")
- You're very uncertain about which problems are most pressing. Earning to give provides flexibility because you can easily change where you donate, or even save the money and give later. (Though money isn't the only thing that's transferable! Many skills — including those we cover below — can easily be transferred across problem areas.)
- You want to contribute to an area that is particularly funding-constrained rather than primarily talent constrained.

Common objections to earning to give

Don't many high-earning jobs cause harm?

We don't recommend taking a job that does harm in order to donate the money, and we've written an entire article about why — which you can find in appendix 5.

In practice, most people who earn to give work in the fields of technology, asset management, medicine, or consulting, and we think there are many positions in these industries that have roughly neutral or a small positive impact. For instance, many (but not all) financial traders make profits at the expense of other traders, so they're moving money around, mostly from rich people to other rich people.

Of course, *some* high-earning jobs can cause a lot of harm. A particularly stark illustration is Sam Bankman-Fried. Sam founded a cryptocurrency exchange with the stated goal of earning to give. In fact, we featured him on our website as an example of someone pursuing a positive career! But Sam ended up being charged with fraud.[118]

We've written more about Sam below, but here's the bottom line: while we think you can do a lot of good through earning to give, we think doing harm for the greater good is *almost never* a good idea, even if you think the donations *might* outweigh the costs of a harmful career.

Can people actually stick with it?

Won't people earning to give end up being influenced by their peers to spend the money on luxuries rather than donating? We were worried this would happen when we first introduced the idea, but it hasn't happened as often as you might think. Hundreds of people are pursuing earning to give, and while some have left because they thought they could do more good elsewhere, surprisingly few (that we know of) have simply given up their plans to donate. In part, this is because many people pursuing earning to give made public pledges of their intentions to donate, often through Giving What We Can. The existence of a community that earns to give also makes it much easier to stick with today.

But if you try to earn *vast sums* of money, there's a much more substantial risk: that power corrupts. For this reason, we're more concerned about people who try to earn as much as possible, to the exclusion of all else. We'd suggest publicly precommitting to making donations. And, if you do end up with a lot of money, you should set up safeguards to help make sure you use the money responsibly — such as a board, formal governance structures, and advisors who can keep you in check

What if I wouldn't be motivated doing a high-earning job?

In that case, don't do it. We only recommend earning to give if it's a good fit.

Just bear in mind, as we covered previously, that you can become interested in more jobs than you might think.

Approach 2: Communication

Consider the following options:

1. Earn to give yourself.
2. Persuade two friends to earn to give.

The second path does more good — in fact, probably about twice as much. This illustrates the power of communication careers.

Many of the highest-impact people in history have been communicators and advocates of one kind or another — people who spread important ideas and solutions to pressing problems.

Take Rosa Parks, who refused to give up her seat to a white man on a bus, sparking a protest which led to a Supreme Court ruling that segregated buses were unconstitutional. Parks was a seamstress in her day job, but in her spare time she was very involved with the civil rights movement. After she was arrested, she and the NAACP worked hard and worked strategically, staying up all night creating thousands of fliers to launch a total boycott of buses in a city of 40,000 African Americans, while simultaneously pushing forward with legal action. This led to major progress for civil rights.

There are also many examples you don't hear about, like Viktor Zhdanov, who was arguably one of the highest-impact people of the 20th century.

In the 20th century, smallpox killed around 400 million people — far more than died in *all* the century's wars and political famines. Credit for the elimination often goes to D.A. Henderson, who was in charge of the World Health Organization's smallpox elimination programme. However, the programme already existed before he was brought on board. In fact, he initially turned down the job. The programme would probably have eventually succeeded even if Henderson hadn't accepted the position.

Zhdanov single-handedly lobbied the WHO to start the elimination campaign in the first place. Without his involvement, it would not have happened until much later, and possibly not at all.[119]

So why has communicating important ideas sometimes been so effective?

First, ideas can spread quickly, so communication is a way for a small group of people to have a large effect on a problem. A small team can launch a social movement, lobby a government, start a campaign that influences public opinion, or just persuade their friends to take up a cause. In each case, they can have a lasting impact on the problem that goes far beyond what they could achieve directly.

Second, spreading important ideas in a careful, strategic way is neglected. This is because there's usually no commercial incentive to spread socially important ideas. Instead, advocacy is mainly pursued by people willing to dedicate their careers to making the world a better place. Moreover, the ideas that are most impactful to spread are those that aren't yet widely accepted. Standing up to the status quo is uncomfortable, and it can take decades for opinion to shift. This means there's also little personal incentive to stand up for them.

Communication is also an area where the *most* successful efforts do *far* more than the typical efforts. The most successful advocates influence millions of people, while others might struggle to persuade more than a few friends. This means if you're an exceptionally good fit for communication, it's often the best thing you can do, and you're likely to achieve far more by doing it yourself than you could by funding someone to engage in communication or advocacy on your behalf.

Communication careers can be pursued as a full-time job (such as many jobs in the media), as part of a wider role (like an academic who does science communication), or alongside almost any job (like Rosa Parks).

Communication careers are defined by their focus on spreading ideas on a big scale, but it's also possible to have a similar impact on a more person-to-person level as a community builder.

For instance, the American women's rights activist Susan B. Anthony hated writing. So while her cofounder at the Women's Loyal National League, Elizabeth Cady Stanton, was a powerful communicator — writing long books and editing their weekly newsletter — Anthony primarily focused on organising and building a community.

Anthony's work running events, talking to activists, and building the suffragist community in the United States eventually led to the 19th amendment to the US Constitution, guaranteeing all adult women the right to vote — it's often called the "Anthony Amendment" in her honour.

Example: Community building often works well as a part-time position. For instance, Kuhan was a student at Stanford when they came across 80,000 Hours, and realised the importance of reducing existential risks. However, they also saw there were no organisations on campus focusing on that idea. So they founded the Stanford Existential Risk Initiative, which runs courses and conferences about the topic to build a community of students aiming to work on these risks.

Approach 3: Research

People often pan academics as Ivory Tower intellectuals whose writing has no impact. And we agree there are many problems with academia that mean researchers achieve less than they could. However, we still think research is often high impact, both within academia and outside it.

Along with communicators, many of the highest-impact people in history have been researchers. Consider Alan Turing. He was a mathematician who developed code-breaking machines that allowed the Allies to be far more effective against Nazi U-boats in World War II. Some historians estimate this enabled D-Day to happen a year earlier than it would have otherwise.[120] Since World War II resulted in 10 million deaths per year, Turing may have saved about 10 million lives.

And he invented the computer.

Turing's example shows that research can be both theoretical and high impact. Much of his work concerned the abstract mathematics of computing, which wasn't initially practically relevant, but became important over time.

On the applied side, we saw lots of examples of high-impact medical research in chapter 2.

Of course, not everyone will be an Alan Turing, and not every discovery gets adopted. Nevertheless, we think that in some cases, research can be one of the best ways to have an impact. Why?

First, when new ideas are discovered, they can be spread incredibly cheaply, so it's a way that a single career can change a field. Moreover, new ideas accumulate over time, so research contributes to a significant fraction of long-run progress.

However, only a relatively small fraction of people are engaged in research. Only 0.1% of the population are academics,[121] and the proportion was much smaller throughout history. If a small number of people account for a large fraction of progress, then *on average* each person's efforts are significant.

Second, because there's little commercial incentive to do research relative to its importance, if you *do* care more about social impact than profit, then it's a good opportunity to have an edge. Most researchers don't get rich, even if their discoveries are extremely valuable. Turing made no money from the discovery of the computer, whereas today it's a multibillion-dollar industry. This is because the benefits of research come a long time in the future, and can't usually be protected by patents.

In fact, the more fundamental the research, the harder it is to commercialise, so, all else equal, we'd expect fundamental research to be more neglected than applied research, and therefore higher impact. On the other hand, applied issues can be more urgent — breakthroughs like the microscope can let us make fundamental breakthroughs faster — so it's hard to say whether applied or fundamental research has a higher impact on average.

So in theory, research can be very high impact. But does research actually help with the most pressing problems facing the world today?

We think it does. When you look at the problems we're most concerned about — like preventing future pandemics or reducing risks from AI systems — many are mainly constrained by a need for additional research.

For example, research could help us develop ways to decrease the time it takes to go from a novel pathogen to a safe, widely distributed vaccine. Alternatively, technical machine learning research could help us build safeguards into AI systems to prevent dangerous behaviour. [122]

Like communication, research is especially promising when you're a very good fit, because the best researchers achieve much more than the median. Most papers only have one citation, whereas the top 0.1% of papers have over 1,000 citations.[123] And when we did a case study on biomedical research,[124] remarks like this were typical:

> *"One good person can cover the ground of five, and I'm not exaggerating."*

If you might be a top 20% researcher in a topic that's relevant to a pressing problem area, then it's likely to be one of your most impactful options. And if you might be *exceptional* in an academic field (maybe, top few percent), even if you can't see now how it'll be useful, that's an option you should probably seriously consider.

As we saw earlier, Dr Nalin helped to save millions of lives with a simple innovation: giving patients with diarrhoea water mixed with salt and sugar.

While lots of research happens in academia, there are also many research positions elsewhere. For example, many private companies develop crucial technology — BioNTech is now famous for developing the first COVID vaccine[125]— while think tanks often do important research in policy.

Example: Neel was doing an undergraduate degree in maths when he decided that he wanted to work in AI safety. Our team was able to introduce Neel to researchers in the field, and helped him secure internships in academic and industry research groups. This helped him see AI safety as a concrete career path and that, despite scepticism of longtermism, AI posed a major risk to even people alive today. Neel didn't feel like he was a great fit for academia — he hates writing papers — so he applied to roles in commercial AI research labs. He's now a research engineer at DeepMind. He works on *mechanistic interpretability* research which he thinks could be used in the future to help identify potentially dangerous AI systems before they can cause harm.

DON'T FORGET SUPPORTING POSITIONS

Becoming an academic administrator doesn't sound like a high-impact career, but that's exactly why it is. Research requires administrators, managers, grantmakers, and communicators to make progress. Many of these roles require very capable people who understand the research, but because they're not glamorous or highly paid, it can be hard to attract the right people. For this reason, if a role like this *is* a good fit for you, then it can be promising. What ultimately matters is not who does the research, but that it *gets done*.

A hero of ours is Seán Ó hÉigeartaigh. He studied for a PhD in comparative genomics, but ultimately decided to pursue academic project management. He became a manager at the Future of Humanity Institute, which undertakes neglected research into emerging existential risks, like risks from AI and engineered pandemics. He did a huge amount of work behind the scenes to keep things running as funding rapidly grew. When there was an opportunity to start a new research group in Cambridge, he used what he'd learned to lead efforts there too — at one point managing both groups. The field would have moved much more slowly without his management.

If you're interested in positions like these, the best path is usually to pursue a PhD, pick a field, then apply to research groups. If you want to enable great research, you need a combination of familiarity with the field and operations skills. [126]

Approach 4: Government and policy

When we think of careers that "do good," we might not first think of becoming an unknown government bureaucrat. But senior government officials often oversee budgets of tens or even hundreds of millions.[127] If you could enable those budgets to be spent just a couple of percent more effectively, that would be worth millions of extra dollars spent on those programmes. And more broadly, the scale of the influence in government positions can be enormous.

For instance, Suzy Deuster wanted to become a public defender to ensure disadvantaged people have good legal defence. She realised that in that role she might improve criminal justice for perhaps hundreds of people over her career, but by changing policy she might improve the justice system for thousands or even millions. Even if the impact per person is smaller, the numbers involved give her the chance of making a greater impact. She was able to use her legal background to enter government, and now works in the Executive Office of the President of the US on criminal justice reform, and from there she can explore other areas of policy in the future.

Government is often crucial in addressing many of the issues we most recommend people work on, because they are the only institutions that create and enforce laws and regulation.

For example, only governments can do something like ban battery cages for egg-laying hens.

They can also act to solve coordination problems that are difficult for individual actors to tackle. When the COVID-19 pandemic hit, contact tracing was essential to slowing its spread, but it wasn't in any individual's self-interest to participate. Governments stepped in to provide contact tracing services, benefiting society as a whole.

Positions in policy require a wide range of skill types, so there should be some high-impact options for nearly everyone.

Approach 5: Building organisations

When most people think of careers that "do good," the first thing they think of is working at a charity.

The thing is, lots of jobs at charities just aren't that impactful.

Some charities focus on programmes that don't work, like Scared Straight which caused kids to commit *more* crimes. Others focus on ways of helping that don't have much leverage, like Superman fighting criminals one-by-one, or Dr Landsteiner focusing on performing surgeries rather than doing the work to discover blood groups.

Another problem is that many want to work at organisations that are more constrained by funding than by the number of people enthusiastic to work there. This means if you don't take the job, it would be easy to find someone else who's almost as good. Think of a lawyer who volunteers at a soup kitchen. It may be motivating for them, but it's hardly the most effective thing they could do. Donating one or two hours of salary could pay for several other people to do the work instead. Or they could do pro bono legal work, and contribute in a way that makes use of their valuable skills.

However, there are plenty of other situations when working for a nonprofit *is* the most effective thing to do.

Nonprofits can tackle issues that other organisations can't. They can carry out research that doesn't earn academic prestige, or do political advocacy on behalf of disempowered groups such as animals or future generations, or provide services that would never be profitable within the market.

And there are lots of nonprofits doing great work that really need more people to help build and scale them up. There are also lots of niches that aren't being filled, where we need new nonprofits set up to tackle them.

More broadly, helping to build an organisation can be a route to making a big contribution, because organisations allow large groups of people to coordinate, and therefore achieve a bigger impact than they could individually. Moreover, if you help build or start an effective organisation, it can continue to have an impact even after you leave.

And if you can help make an already existing and impactful organisation somewhat more effective, that can also be a route to a big impact.

Clare joined Lead Exposure Elimination Project (LEEP) as its third staff member. She thought that joining LEEP would help build her career capital — especially her skills and connections — and, more importantly, that lead exposure in low- and middle-income countries is an important, solvable, and highly neglected problem. Since joining, Clare has developed LEEP's programmes and managed the team implementing them, as well as led the hiring for crucial new staff. LEEP has since started working with governments and industry in 16 countries, and has successfully advocated for the government in Malawi to monitor levels of lead in paints.

These organisations don't even *need* to be nonprofits — some social impact projects are better structured as businesses, and could also include think tanks, research groups, advocacy groups, and so on.

For instance, Sendwave enables African migrant workers to transfer money to their families through a mobile app for fees of 3%, rather than 10% fees with Western Union. So for every $1 of revenue they make, they make some of the poorest people in the world several dollars richer. Within three years, they'd already had an impact equivalent to donating millions of dollars, and they've grown even more since then. The total size of the market is hundreds of billions of dollars — several times larger than all foreign aid spending. If they can continue to slightly accelerate the rollout of cheaper ways to transfer money, it'll have a big impact.

Organisation-building careers are a good fit for people who can develop skills in areas like operations, people management, fundraising, administration, software systems, and finance.

Pursuing this path usually means first focusing on building some of these skills (which can be done at any competent organisation), and then later on using them to contribute to the organisations you think are most impactful.

To find impactful organisations, think about which problems you think are most pressing, and then try to identify the best organisations addressing those problems. (In our problem profiles, we list recommended organisations to give you some ideas.[128]) Finally, try to identify those that have a pressing need for your skills and a role that might be a great fit for you.

WHAT ABOUT IF YOU WANT TO FOUND AN ORGANISATION?

One mistake people make is trying to work out which organisations should be founded from their armchair, or by choosing an issue that they've happened to come across in their own lives.

Instead, go and learn about big, neglected social problems. Take a job in the area, do further study, and speak to lots of people working on the problem to find out what the world really needs. You need to get near the edge of an area before you'll spot the ideas others haven't, and have the connections you'll need to execute.[129]

More ideas for impactful careers

These categories aren't intended to be comprehensive. There are lots of impactful options that don't naturally fit into them.

For example, experts in information security are sorely needed by organisations working to prevent AI-related and biological catastrophes. There aren't very many trained information security experts to begin with, and only a few are trying to use their careers to solve these urgent problems.

To see a much longer list of ideas (which still isn't exhaustive), check out appendix 8.

A WORD OF CAUTION:
POWER, HARM, AND CORRUPTION

Sam Bankman-Fried founded the cryptocurrency exchange FTX with the stated goal of earning to give. He briefly became the world's richest person under 30, and made large donations to pressing causes.[130] We previously featured him across our site as a positive example of someone pursuing a high-impact career.

Sam is now charged with fraud, FTX collapsed into bankruptcy, and billions of dollars of customer funds went missing.[131]

This has done a lot of harm to individual depositors and society, both through the money lost and the indirect harms of criminal activity. It may have also harmed the reputation of the causes he was supporting, and the idea of earning to give in general. For our part, we felt betrayed and shaken when we found out what had happened, and ashamed about our past promotion of him.[132]

It now seems clear that even if Sam told himself that the rewards justified the risks, that was totally wrong.

How might this be relevant to you? Each of the five paths covered in this chapter offers ways to substantially increase the amount that you can contribute to solving a problem.

But generally, the greater your ability to contribute, the greater your ability to do harm — whether by making a substantial mistake, supporting the wrong issues, or acting unethically.

Moreover, as you gain more ability to affect the world, you may face more temptations to act badly. "Power corrupts" is a cliché for a good reason.

This might be hard to imagine if you're at the start of your career, but if you end up in a powerful position in government, running a large organisation, with a degree of fame, or with lots of money, you may face situations where acting ethically will pose a risk of losing the large influence you have — like a politician lying to stay in office. This can be true even if you didn't originally seek power for your own benefit.

You may also face difficult ethical tradeoffs, such as taking roles you think involve an element of harm in order to achieve a potentially greater positive impact.

And typically, the more influence you have, the harder it will be for people to disagree with you, because they'll fear the consequences, so you'll become less able to make good decisions just at the point you most need to.

Working on problems that are unusually important and neglected also further raises the stakes, because if you slip up, you've set back a more important issue, and the fact that few other people are working on the issue magnifies your potential for harm.

One key point is that we don't generally recommend taking jobs or actions you think are harmful for the greater good.[133] We talked about that in the section on earning to give above, but it can come up with whatever approach you choose to take.

It's also one reason why we see building good character as an important part of career capital, which is coming up in the next chapter.

Which is the right approach for you?

We've now seen that by thinking broadly — considering earning to give, communication, research, government and policy, and organisation building — there are many ways to make a big contribution to solving pressing problems.

If you want to choose between these broad categories, how might you approach it?

What's most crucial is your degree of fit: any of these categories can be an impactful career, if you're good at it.

Throughout this chapter, there is a vital general principle to bear in mind: *the most successful people in a field have far more impact than the typical person.* For instance, a landmark study of expert performers found:[134]

> *"A small percentage of the workers in any given domain is responsible for the bulk of the work. Generally, the top 10% of the most prolific elite can be credited with around 50% of all contributions, whereas the bottom 50% of the least productive workers can claim only 15% of the total work, and the most productive contributor is usually about 100 times more prolific than the least."*

Just as we saw with choosing a problem, this means the most effective approach *for you* will be something you enjoy, that motivates you, and is a good fit for your skills.

We sometimes come across people tempted to do a job they'd hate in order to have more impact. That's likely a bad idea, since they'll just burn out. Their example could also discourage others from using their careers to do good.

An outstanding charity worker will likely do more good than a mediocre engineer earning to give, and the reverse is also true.

We cover the importance of personal fit and how to work out which career is best for you in chapter 8.

But don't worry if you feel unsure — that's normal. Finding a career that fits often takes many years. If you're at the start of your career, it's fine to just have some vague ideas about where you're aiming, and make them more specific over time.

And while personal fit is important, it's also important not to narrow down too early. As we've seen, people often underestimate how easily they can become interested in new jobs. So it's important to explore widely, giving yourself a chance to become interested in new approaches, but then to focus on what's going well.

You also don't need to limit yourself to your background so far. 80,000 hours is a long time, so you have a lot of scope to learn new skills.

Putting personal fit aside, note there is no single best approach for every problem. Rather, focus on the approaches that are most needed by the problems you want to solve. For instance, breast cancer doesn't need more advocacy to promote awareness, because almost everyone is aware that breast cancer is a problem. Instead, it probably needs more skilled researchers to develop better treatments. If you just focus on raising awareness, then your efforts won't go as far.

Also consider that these approaches are not mutually exclusive, and you can do more than one at the same time. For instance, a teacher helps their students (direct impact), but could also develop new educational techniques (research), or tell their students about pressing problems (communication). We know a teacher who did private tutoring in order to donate more (earning to give). As we've seen, often your impact is more about how you use your position than the position itself.

Conclusion: in which job can you help the most?

There are many more paths to helping others in your career than we normally talk about. Elton John started as a singer, and saved thousands of lives through earning to give. Rosa Parks was a seamstress, and helped to trigger the civil rights movement in America through communication and advocacy. Alan Turing was a mathematician who helped to end World War II through research, as well as inventing the computer.

Most people aren't born rockstars, but even at a normal graduate salary, anyone can have an astonishing impact through earning to give, literally saving hundreds of lives. And it's often possible to do even more through communication, research, government and policy, or building organisations.

By expanding the range of options you consider, it's often possible to find a path that's not only higher impact, but also a better fit and more satisfying too.

In this way, even if you don't want to be a doctor or a teacher, it's possible to do far more good with your career than is normally thought.

APPLY THIS TO YOUR OWN CAREER

Before we move on, make an initial shortlist of high-impact careers you could work towards in the long run. Here's some ways to generate ideas:

1. Go over each approach in this chapter. Try to generate 2–3 more specific paths within each that *might* be a good fit for you and meet your other personal criteria.
2. Take your list of pressing problems from earlier. What do those problems most need? Can you think of any career paths you might be able to take that could help address those needs?
3. See our list of career reviews and note down any other ideas there: https://80k.info/CRV.
4. Are there any other paths you're aware of that you might excel at, or are unique opportunities open only to you? Add them to your list too.
5. Imagine your ideal working day, hour by hour. What jobs might fit with that? What job would you do if money were no object, or if you only had 10 years left to live? Does that give you any other ideas for fulfilling longer-term career paths?

The aim at this point is just to come up with more options. We'll explain how to further narrow down in chapter 8.

In generating options, err towards including more rather than less. In particular, we often talk to people who only ever really think about jobs that are closely related to their past experience, and that's often a mistake. For example, you don't need to have studied anything to do with politics in order to work in government and policy.

It's often possible to get a job in a new area without specific experience, and even if it takes a couple of years to transition, that can easily be worth it in the context of the rest of your career. This is especially true if you're an undergraduate — what you've studied so far has little bearing on what you might do in the future.

Recap of our career guide so far

Back in chapter 1, we saw that an enjoyable and fulfilling job:

- Helps others
- Is something you're good at
- Has the right supportive conditions (e.g. engaging work, supportive colleagues, fit with the rest of your life)

We've now also seen that the jobs that most help others:

1. Are focused on the most pressing problems — those that are big in scale, neglected, and solvable – as we covered in chapter 4.
2. Take an approach that might let you make a big contribution, such as research, communication, earning to give, government and policy, and building organisations. That's what we covered in this chapter.
3. Provide you with the chance to excel. We'll explain how to work out where you have the best personal fit later on.

Should you sacrifice to do more good?

People often ask us whether they should sacrifice what they enjoy in order to have a greater impact. But as we discussed above, doing good involves less sacrifice than it first seems. A personally satisfying job involves helping others, because that's fulfilling. And a high-impact job will also need to be personally satisfying — because if you don't like your job, you probably won't be good at it and you'll burn out. So there's a lot of overlap.

We've also seen there are lots of ways to have a big impact, and some of these probably won't involve much sacrifice. Rather than making sacrifices, the key thing to focus on is finding these highly effective ways to help.

That's not to say there's no tradeoff at all. It's unlikely that the very best career for you personally is also the one that most benefits the world. Ultimately, you'll have to make a value judgement about how to weigh helping others against your own interests. But fortunately, the tradeoff is less than it first seems.

How can I put myself in the best position to get a high-impact job?

Some people can just walk into their dream job — one that matches all the criteria above — right away. And if you *can* do that, go for it! But for many others, you'll need to build your skills, connections, credentials, and character — what we call "career capital." By doing this, you can open up a wider range of options than just those you think you have today.

In the next chapter, we'll look at how to build career capital and best position yourself for long-term success.

THE BOTTOM LINE:
IN WHICH CAREER CAN YOU HELP PEOPLE
THE MOST?

- Once you've chosen a problem, as we covered in the previous article, the next step is to work out how best to contribute to solving it.
- Think broadly about the paths where you can make the biggest contribution, including research, communications and community-building, taking high-earning jobs to donate to charity, government and policy, and organisation-building.
- Focus on the approaches that are most needed in your problem area. Some problems are best solved through changing policy. Others most need research, while others require funding, and so on.
- Ultimately, in the long term you want to find the option that does best on a combination of (i) how pressing the problem is, (ii) how large your contribution will be, (iii) your degree of personal fit, and (iv) fit with your other personal goals.

CHAPTER 7
Which jobs put you in the best long-term position?

People like to lionise the Mozarts, Malala Yousafzais, and Mark Zuckerbergs of the world — people who achieved great success while young — and there are all sorts of awards for young leaders, like the *Forbes* 30 Under 30.

But these stories are interesting precisely because they're the exception.

Most people reach the peak of their impact in their middle age. Income usually peaks in the 40s, suggesting that it takes around 20 years for most people to reach their peak productivity.[135]

Similarly, experts only reach their peak abilities between age 30 to 60,[136] and if anything, this age is increasing over time.[137]

Field	Age of peak output
Theoretical physics, lyric poetry, pure mathematics	Around 30
Psychology, chemistry	Around 40[138]
Novel writing, history, philosophy, medicine	Around 50
Business - average age of S&P500 CEOs	55[139]
Politics - average age of first-term (US) president	55

When researchers looked in more detail at these findings, they found that expert-level performance in established fields usually requires 10 to 30 years of focused practice.[140] K. Anders Ericsson, a leader in this field of research, said after 30 years of research:

> *"I have never found a convincing case for anyone developing extraordinary abilities without intense, extended practice."*

For Mozart to succeed so young, he needed to start young. Mozart's father was a famous music teacher, and trained him intensely as a toddler.

All this may sound like a bit of a downer: being successful takes a lot of time. But consider the flip side: you can become much more skilled than you are today.

Lots of people come to us saying, "I'm not sure I have any useful skills to contribute." And that's often true. If you've just graduated, you've probably spent the last four years studying Moby Dick, quantum mechanics, and Machiavelli, and your future job is unlikely to involve any of those things.

However, Ericsson's research also suggests that anyone can improve at most skills with focused practice. Sure, other factors are important too: if you're seven feet tall it's going to be a lot easier to get good at basketball — but that doesn't mean short people can't improve their game.

This means even if you don't feel you have much to contribute now, you can become much more skilled in the future, and probably keep improving for decades — this should normally be the top priority early in your career.

Why career capital is so important

Chantelle[141] wanted to make a difference straight out of university, and even managed to land an exciting job as a programme manager at a nonprofit working to prevent pandemics. But the small team made it tricky to find time to develop her skills, and she wasn't able to have the impact she had hoped for in the role. After a few months, she was stressed, sleeping badly, and burned out.

Chantelle decided to go to graduate school instead. Not only is she enjoying it much more, she also feels like she's learning things that could really support her future career.

While it sucks to delay doing something meaningful, it's rare to have a big impact right away.

Early in your career, it's more important to ensure you invest in your skills and get the training you need to maximise your long-term impact.

This is especially true because it's possible to become *far* more productive over the course of your career. Consider the potential impact of a scientist, politician, or CEO at the peak of their influence (age 40–50) compared to the influence they had as a fresh undergraduate.

In our advising, we've seen lots of examples of people becoming far more successful, happy, and capable by investing in themselves — often in surprising areas that they never thought they'd be good at.

Focusing on impact too much too early can even be shortsighted, because it can preclude being in an even better position later.

This means that for most people, the top priority early in their career is to build what we call *career capital*. So what is career capital?

Five components of career capital

By "career capital," we mean anything that puts you in a better position to make a difference or secure a fulfilling career in the future.

We normally break it down into the following components, which you can use to compare your options in terms of career capital:

- **Skills and knowledge**: What will you learn, how useful will it be, and how fast will you learn? A job will be best for learning when you are pushed to improve and get lots of feedback from mentors and colleagues. Ask yourself: "Where will I learn fastest?"

- **Connections:** Who will you work with and meet? Will they include potential future collaborators on impactful projects, supportive friends and mentors, people who are influential, or people who will help you expand into new circles?

- **Credentials:** We don't just mean formal credentials like having a law degree, but also your achievements and reputation — or anything else that acts as a good signal to future collaborators or employers. If you're a writer, it could be the quality of your blog. If you're a coder, it might be your GitHub. If you're interested in doing good, how can you show you've cultivated that interest?

- **Character:** Will this option help you cultivate virtues like generosity, compassion, humility, integrity, honesty, good judgement, and respect of important norms? In particular, will you be able to work alongside people with good character (since that has a huge influence)? These traits are vital to being trusted, working with others, and not doing harm. They also determine whether, when faced with a high-stakes decision, you'll be able to do what's best for the world.

- **Runway:** How much money will you save in this job? Your "runway" is how long you could comfortably live with no income. It depends on both your savings and how much you could reduce your expenses by. We recommend aiming for at least six months of runway to maintain your financial security, while 12–18 months of runway gives you the flexibility to make a major career change. It's usually worth paying down high-interest debt before donating more than 1% per year or taking a big pay cut for greater impact.

How can you get the best career capital? Get good at something useful.

If we were going to summarise all our advice on how to get career capital in one line, we'd say: *get good at something useful.*

In other words, gain abilities that are valued in the job market — making it easier to bargain for the ingredients of a fulfilling job — as well as those that are needed in tackling the world's most pressing problems.

Once you have valuable skills, you also need to learn how to sell those skills to others and make connections. This can involve deliberately gaining credentials, such as by getting degrees or creating public demo projects, or it can involve what's normally thought of as "networking," such as going to conferences or building up a Twitter following. So it's true all these kinds of activities build your career capital too. But all of these activities become *much* easier once you have something useful to offer, which is why we put the emphasis on building skills first.

Getting good at something useful usually involves a combination of the following four ingredients:

1. **Choose valuable skills to learn** — we covered some broad skill types that we think are valuable for doing good in the previous chapter: organisation building, communication and community building, research, earning to give, and government and policy.[142]
2. **Find skills that are a good fit for you** — those that match your talents and that you can learn fastest — which we'll cover in the next chapter.
3. **Practice** — getting good at most jobs takes years, if not decades. You shouldn't expect to excel right away. This also makes it vital to find good mentorship, and to do something you can stick with for a long time.
4. **Increase your chances of being in the right place at the right**

time — for example, it's much easier to get to the top of a brand new field that's growing rapidly than an established area like law, since there are far fewer people to compete with. Likewise, being part of the right scene can be a huge factor, so if you've stumbled across a community, person, or organisation with momentum, sticking with that may pay off.

In short, try to maximise your rate of useful learning.

In the next section, we cover some concrete types of jobs that people we've worked with have often found useful for improving their career capital.

There's also a lot you can do *within* your existing job to invest in yourself and improve your career capital. We cover it in appendix 2, which includes advice on building character, networking, saving money, and becoming more generally effective. We also cover how to sell your existing career capital effectively in chapter 10, on how to get a job.

WHAT SKILLS WILL BE MOST VALUABLE IN THE FUTURE?

Thinking of becoming an illustrator, legal clerk, or medical technician? These jobs might soon be gone.

A 2020 analysis looked at the effects of three kinds of automation on the labour market over the past few decades: standard software, robots, and AI.[143] The author found that advances in IT and standard software have reduced the number of people working in highly routine or administrative jobs, while advances in robotics have replaced many manual jobs, but not those requiring social intelligence or creativity.

But it's the rapid recent advances in AI — in particular machine learning — which we think could have the biggest impact on your career.

To date, machine learning has worked best when you can gather lots of data to train an algorithm on a specific test. So we're already seeing automation in places like running power plants or analysing medical tests.

As we saw in chapter 5, in the last few years, we've seen huge advances in far more general, and more creative, AI systems. The most advanced AI systems can pass complex academic exams better than most humans,[144] generate extremely realistic images from text,[145] and solve some difficult coding problems.[146] None of this was possible even a year ago.

A paper from 2013, which we've written about in the past, speculated that tasks involving creativity would be among the hardest to automate, but generating ideas is one of the strengths of the latest AI systems.[147] For instance, they can generate hundreds of images in the style of Dali crossed with Pollock nearly instantly, or endless ideas for attention-grabbing headlines.

The types of tasks that seem hardest to automate likely involve:

- **Decision making and problem solving**. For example, choosing from a variety of AI-generated images, especially decisions where it's important for a human (perhaps for legal reasons) to stay in the loop.
- **Social intelligence and relationship building.**
- **Difficult motor skills.** Robots are lagging behind generative AI systems, so jobs from plumbing to surgery are likely to be less affected (at least for now).
- **High-level expertise.** AI systems are still not as accurate as

top human experts within their area of expertise (though it's not clear how long this will last).

It's very hard to predict how this will affect the labour market over the next 10 years.

The 2020 analysis discussed above argued that jobs between the top 70th percentile and the 99th percentile in terms of income will be most affected by advances in AI, and are likely to see lower relative income. The list of jobs most likely to be affected includes chemical engineers, optometrists, and dispatchers. In contrast, the list of the least affected jobs includes entertainment performers, food preparation workers, and college instructors. (This analysis is just one model — so we shouldn't fully trust it).

It's not that the jobs most affected by automation will see reduced employment or income. If each chemical engineer you hire can do the work that two could previously, that *could* lead to hiring half as many engineers, or it could lead to hiring *more* engineers, because now each produces twice as much value as before. It all depends on how the economics of the situation works out.

What's clearer is that jobs will shift to involve more of the harder-to-automate tasks, and fewer of those that can be done by AI systems.

So this means that if you want your skills to stay relevant in the future, focus more on learning the hardest-to-automate skills (perhaps such as the ones above) and also focus heavily on learning how to use AI to augment your productivity. The workers who do best in the future will probably be those most able to make use of AI and automation to solve important problems.

Beyond the next 5–10 years, it becomes near impossible to know what will happen. Ultimately it seems like AI systems will be able to do basically all jobs better than humans, and who knows how the economy will look at that point.

Concrete steps for gaining career capital

Which career capital is best for you to focus on depends on where you're aiming to end up longer term, which we encouraged you to think about in the last chapter.

It's worth asking yourself: "If I want to end up working in a particular position, what next step would *most* accelerate me in that path?" (We'll talk about this more in chapter 9, on career planning.)

But it's also worth thinking about which options will most boost your capabilities in general.

To help you come up with ideas for that, below are some steps that our readers have found to be good for gaining career capital in general. Note down any that could be a good fit for you — you can add these to your list of ideas for next steps that we'll make later in the guide.

1. **Work at a growing organisation that has a reputation for high performance in your path**

If you've just graduated, you're probably not very good at doing real work.

In college, you're told to answer well-defined problems with clear answers over short timeframes, which are possible to master. In the world of work, much of the challenge is working out what the problem is in the first place and prioritising what to work on. Projects don't (automatically) have well-defined scopes or success criteria. Great performance might not be possible, or could take many years.

You probably don't know how to do the basics, like run a weekly check-in meeting, read financial statements, give good presentations, or speak to a boss.

So, often one of the most useful things you can do after college is to go and work with any high-performing, high-integrity team, where you can be mentored in the highly useful skill of *generally getting stuff done at work*.

If the organisation also has a good reputation, then you'll also get the credential of saying you've worked there. And you'll probably be able to meet lots of other ambitious people, building your connections.

If it's rapidly growing, you'll have more opportunities for promotions, morale will be better, and your future achievements will be more impressive.

It's hard to meet all of these criteria in one job, but they're all worth looking out for. Here are some more considerations in choosing where to work:

Should you work in the private sector or at a nonprofit?

The private sector might actually be a better place to learn productivity, because the clear feedback mechanism of profit weeds out ineffective work faster. Our impression is that many conventional nonprofits are pretty dysfunctional, which is one reason why nonprofit leaders often recommend training up elsewhere.[148]

Another big factor is there are far more jobs in the private sector, and the higher pay can help you build up your runway.

That said, there are lots of great organisations and teams across all sectors, including nonprofits, government, and academia.

Even putting impact aside, working in an organisation with a social mission can offer major advantages, such as getting to learn about a pressing global problem, meeting and being around other people who want to do good, and more motivation and meaning.

Should you work for a small or large organisation?

In smaller organisations, you can usually learn a wider variety of skills and potentially get more responsibility faster. Larger organisations are usually more well known, so offer good credentials for your CV, and have roles with lower variance, and often have more capacity for training and mentorship.

More speculatively, small organisations may have better feedback loops between performance and success, while succeeding in large organisations becomes more about navigating politics and bureaucracy (though those can be valuable skills too!).

If you want to work in the nonprofit sector longer term, many of the organisations are small, so working at a smaller organisation may give you more relevant skills. However, if you want to work in government and policy, large organisations could be better preparation.

What will the people be like?

There's a lot of cultural variance between organisations, and even between teams within the same organisation.

If your goal is career capital, you should prioritise working somewhere you'll get good mentoring and feedback on your work. It's hard to learn without good teaching or role models. Likewise, the character of the people you work with will rub off on you.

Which concrete options seem best?

One option to especially consider is working in a promising tech startup, which can potentially combine many of the benefits above: high-performing teams with strong incentives to produce results, rapid growth, and the opportunity to gain a generalist skillset. If the startup succeeds, you'll also get a good credential and money. Bonus points if you can find a company where you can learn skills relevant to a top global problem.

Of course, a lot of startups are terribly run, and likely to fail. But you can take steps to increase your chances of working at a good one.[149]

Another option to consider is working at top AI labs such as OpenAI or DeepMind. These are high-performing organisations that can let you learn about and make connections within AI research, while also gaining great backup options. This would ideally be in a role directly working on

AI safety or policy, as simply boosting the development of AI capabilities could easily be harmful, due to their potential risks — we don't recommend taking harmful roles to gain career capital.[150] However, not all experts agree on the size of those risks.[151]

Within the private sector, some options people commonly consider include working in big tech, top financial firms, consulting (which can also let you experience several industries), professional services (like working at one of the Big Four accounting firms), and law. You should eliminate options you think are harmful and focus on those where you might have the best fit.

2. Go to graduate school in carefully chosen subjects

People often drift into expensive graduate programmes that don't offer good backup options even if they're not sure about academia. This is often not a good move.

Bilal did a research project in cosmology at the end of his undergraduate degree. Continuing into a PhD just seemed like the natural next step. But once he started his PhD, he concluded that it wouldn't be good at teaching him much except how to do academic cosmology — and he didn't think a career in academic cosmology would be an especially good way for him to make a difference. While it would have been easy to simply continue with the path he was on, he decided to leave early, and retrain in a different skill.

However, some graduate school programmes can boost your career a lot. If we had to pick, the most attractive grad programmes might be economics or machine learning PhDs:

- Almost all economics and machine learning PhDs can get jobs involving economics or machine learning if they want, which is not the case with most doctorate degrees.
- Machine learning is directly related to one the world's most pressing problems — risks from artificial intelligence — while economics

prepares you to work on a variety of important problems, including AI policy, global priorities research, international development, and many more.

- You can go from economics into the rest of the social sciences or into important positions in policy. Likewise, machine learning skills can be applied in many other fields of study.
- They both have high-earning backup options.

Besides economics and machine learning, some other useful subjects to highlight, given our list of pressing problems, include:

- Other applied quantitative subjects, like computer science, physics, and statistics
- Security studies, international relations, public policy, or law school, particularly for entering government and policy careers
- Subfields of biology relevant to pandemic prevention (like synthetic biology, mathematical biology, virology, immunology, pharmacology, or vaccinology)
- Studying China (or another emerging global power like India or Russia)

Of course, many people should study options that aren't on this list. For instance, we've written about how we'd like to see more of our readers study history,[152] and many of the team at 80,000 Hours have a background in philosophy. However, these subjects are more competitive and have worse backup options, so require a higher degree of personal fit.

And other options can make sense depending on your situation (e.g. doing an MBA if you're in the corporate sector).

Which subjects are best also depends on your longer-term career goals. We aim to discuss which kinds of graduate study are most useful to particular longer-term paths within our career reviews and problem profiles (see appendices 8 and 9 for summaries).

How can you compare graduate subjects?

Weigh up your options in terms of:

- **Personal fit** — will you be good at the subject? If you're good at the area, it's more likely that you'll be able to pursue work in that area later on, you'll enjoy it more, and you'll do the work more quickly.
- **Flexibility** — does it open up lots of options, both inside and outside academia? If you're uncertain about academia, watch out for programmes that mainly help you with academic careers (e.g. philosophy PhD, literature PhD). And if you do a maths PhD you can transfer into economics, physics, biology, computer science, and so on, but the reverse is not true. Also, some graduate programmes give you better odds of landing academic positions (e.g. more than 90% of economists can get research positions, whereas only about 50% of biology PhDs do).
- **Relevance to your long-term plans** — does it take you towards the options you're most interested in? Lots of people are tempted to do graduate study even when it doesn't particularly help with their longer-term plans. For instance, potential entrepreneurs are tempted to do MBAs when they're not particularly helpful to entrepreneurship; lots of people are tempted to do a random master's degree when they're not sure what to do; some people consider doing a law degree when they're not confident they want to be a lawyer.

Which programmes are best within a subject?

There's a huge amount of variation between schools and specific programmes within a subject. Pay attention to:

- Will you get good mentorship? Learning how to do good research is a craft that gets passed down mainly via hands-on training, so this is vital. Getting good mentorship helps hugely with motivation and your future opportunities in academia. It often comes down to the specific person you'll be working with and your fit with them.
- Will the particular university be an environment where you can flourish? For example, in terms of location and culture?
- What's the reputation of the professor and university? Your supervisor's reputation in the field will impact your future opportunities in academia. Being at a well-known university is useful for opportunities outside of academia (e.g. as a communicator or in policy).
- Will you get funding?

It could easily be better to do a subject you think offers fewer options in general if you find a particular opportunity that's strong in these criteria.

Should you do graduate study?

It's not a decision to be taken lightly. In particular, PhD programmes are often demoralising and people doing them often struggle with mental health or don't complete them, and master's degrees can cost a lot of money. Both take substantial time.

It's also not a question we can answer in the abstract — it depends on your other options.

For now, if any graduate school options seem plausible, add them to your list of ideas for next steps. Then later in the guide we'll come back to narrowing them down. (Or if you want to think about it now, you could compare graduate school to your best other options using our career decision process in appendix 4.)

Example: Dillon couldn't imagine studying anything except philosophy. Then he found out about the research that shows that our interests can easily change. Convinced, he decided to try out economics and computer science as minor courses, because he thought these would open up more options than philosophy. He liked them more than he expected, and is now doing a PhD in Economics.

3. Take an entry-level route into policy careers

Example: Tom Kalil spent 16 years working for the Clinton and Obama administrations. He worked to foster the development of the internet, then nanotechnology, and then cutting-edge brain modelling, among other things.

But the way he first got involved was his decision to volunteer for Michael Dukakis's campaign for the presidency in 1988. Dukakis lost, but some of the people Kalil worked for also wound up working for Bill Clinton in 1992 — and Clinton won.

As we saw in the previous chapter, careers in government and policy can be very high impact. There's also a very wide range of roles in this area, which often share common entry routes. That means these entry routes can open up a lot of impactful options, while potentially also giving you a general professional training, knowledge and connections in the policy world, and credentials.

The options differ slightly depending on the country you're in. We focus on the US here because it's the country where we have the largest number of readers — but there are often similar options available in other countries, and we highlight a few.

- **Executive branch fellowships and leadership schemes** — like the President Management Fellowship in the US or the Civil Service Fast Stream in the UK (among other possibilities. There are other options in the US depending on your background: the AAAS fellowship for people with science PhDs or engineering master's, or the TechCongress fellowship for mid-career tech professionals. If you are a STEM graduate, also consider the National Security Innovation Network's Technology and National Security Fellowship. These are especially good options if you want to work anywhere in the policy world or social sector.
- **Working for a politician** — for example, as a researcher or staffer is often the first step into political and policy positions. It's also demanding, prestigious, and gives you lots of connections. Our impression is that the very top staffers often have graduate degrees, sometimes including degrees from top law schools. From this path it's also common to move into the executive branch, or to seek elected office.[153]
- **Working on a political campaign** — some of the top people who work on winning campaigns eventually get high-impact positions in the executive branch. This is a high-risk strategy: it only pays off if your candidate wins, and even then, not everybody on the campaign staff will get influential jobs or jobs in the areas they care about. Running for office yourself involves a similar high-risk, high-

reward dynamic.

- **Think tank research roles** — these can help you learn about social issues, are reasonably prestigious, and open up options in policy and the social sector.[154]
- **Entry-level roles in the executive branch** — in the US, you could take an entry-level role as a federal employee, ideally working on something relevant to a problem you want to help solve. Elsewhere, look for relevant entry-level roles in the executive branch, like the UK civil service.

As with all options, whether these roles are a good option for building career capital depends on the specific job and people you'll be working with: Will you get good mentorship? What's their reputation in the field? Do they have good character? Does their policy agenda seem positive? Will the culture be a good fit for you?

Some people we know have entered promising policy positions, but later felt like the culture was a terrible fit for them. There's also a risk of doing harm if you get things wrong. So it's important to think about each specific opportunity, whether it's a job, a degree, or something else, and think carefully about your fit.

4. Develop a useful skill

Any option that gives you a provable, useful, transferable skill can be a good move. Some concrete options here include (in no specific order):

- **Software engineering** — We know lots of people who started with no technology background, and within six months ended up with highly paid programming jobs they enjoy far more than their old jobs. Programming is also an in-demand skill that can be used in many areas, including on some of our top problems. Even if you don't have much background in software engineering or even a quantitative background, it's often possible to learn rapidly through self-study or programming bootcamps, which can take you from zero experience to having a job in 6–12 months.[155]

- **Machine learning (ML) and applied AI** — ML will probably continue to become increasingly relevant to the world over the next few decades as AI becomes more widely applied. So besides preparing you to work on reducing risks from AI, you'll be able to apply ML to many other pressing problems, and likely earn over $100,000 a year. If you're currently at college, you might be able to take an ML course even if you're not majoring in computer science. Or, if you want to self-study, we list some places you might start in appendix 7.
- **Management** — a skill that increasingly becomes required in a very wide range of positions as you move further along your career, whether it's managing people, long and complex projects, or both. There are lots of ways to become better as a manager. Most importantly, find ways to start managing on a small scale. Ideally, work under a great manager or find a mentor or coach who is, and then regularly check in with them about what is and isn't working. Make sure to collect feedback from the people you manage. There are also lots of concrete habits and processes that can make you better as a manager, which you can practise applying while doing the above. To learn more, we have a list of resources in appendix 7.
- **Information security** — protecting organisations from cyberattacks that could compromise their mission, data, or assets. Some organisations need help protecting information that could be hugely dangerous if it was known more widely, such as harmful genetic sequences or powerful AI technology. Breaches in areas like these could have disastrous consequences — which makes information security a great option for people who want to have a high-impact career. And because it's an in-demand skill with high

salaries, it provides great backup options.[156]

- **Data science and applied statistics** — Data science is a cross between statistics and programming. The bootcamps are a similar deal to programming, although they tend to mainly recruit science PhDs. If you've just done a science PhD and don't want to continue with academia, this is a good option to consider, but we'd probably recommend ruling out programming first. Similarly you can learn data analysis, statistics and modelling by taking the right graduate programme, as discussed above.[157]

- **Marketing** — Learning to market toilet paper doesn't seem like the most socially motivated option. But almost all types of organisations need marketing, and demand for the skill is growing. You can learn the skillset, then transfer into an organisation with a social mission. Failing that, you'll have a lot of backup options and you could earn to give instead. You can learn marketing skills by taking an entry-level position at a top firm or working under a good mentor in a business. We'd especially recommend focusing on the style of marketing that's more data and technology driven, rather than traditional creative advertising.[158]

- **Sales and negotiation** — Similar to marketing and management, sales skills can be hugely useful, whatever your job (and whether or not it has "sales" in the title). If you want to hire people, promote an important cause, rent an office, get a job, or do almost anything, you'll need to "sell". Sales can feel adversarial — like you're trying to persuade people to do something against their interest. But the best kind of sales is collaborative: it's about finding ways to meet the needs of both parties. Much of good selling comes from genuinely trying to benefit and build good relationships with people. We give you some practical advice on how to build connections in appendix 2, and a list of some of the best resources we've found to develop these skills in appendix 7.

- **Develop expertise in China or another important emerging economy** — China has grown rapidly into an important global power, and is increasingly an important player in many of our top global problems, as well as the economy more broadly. However, very few people outside China have much knowledge of it. For these reasons, becoming a China specialist may be a very impactful career path, especially with a focus on global catastrophic risks. Knowledge of China could also open up other positions in business and policy. (With the caveat that recent tension between the US and China could mean that spending significant time in China could exclude you from certain government positions in other countries.) You can make a similar case about India, and to a lesser extent about Russia, the Arabic world, and Brazil.[159]

5. Do anything where you might excel (even if it's a bit random)

We came across someone who had a significant chance of becoming a magician and maybe landing a national TV show in India, and was deciding between that and... consulting. It seemed to us that the magician path was more exciting, since the skills and connections within media would be more unusual and valuable for work on the world's most pressing problems than those of another consultant.

A common mistake is to think that building career capital always means doing something that gives you formal credentials, like a law degree, or is prestigious, like consulting.

It's easy to focus on "hard" aspects of career capital, like having a well-known employer, because they're concrete. But the "soft" aspects of career capital — your skills, achievements, connections, and reputation — are equally important, if not more so. The very best career capital comes from impressive achievements.

You can build these "soft" aspects of career capital in almost any job if you perform well. Doing great work builds your reputation, and that allows you to make connections with other high achievers. If you push yourself to do great work, then you'll probably learn more too.

This is why doing something less conventional, like starting a new organisation, can sometimes be the best path for career capital. If you succeed, it'll be impressive. But even if you don't succeed, you'll learn a lot and meet interesting people.

Doing anything that will give you a concretely visible project that seems impressive can also be helpful, such as writing a successful blog or doing a project that appears in the media.

For someone who wants to make a difference, it can even be worth doing something that seems a bit random, if you're going to be great at it.

Earlier in the guide we talked about how it's possible to have a big impact through communication, community building, and donations. This means that excelling at almost any path can set you up to have a big impact, since it'll give you connections, influence, money, and credibility, which can be used to support you working on pressing problems.

So if you want to build career capital, it's worth considering any area where you have a good fit, even if it doesn't seem like a good option in general.

Bodybuilding isn't usually how to advance your career, but Arnie made it work.

6. Do what contributes

When I (Benjamin) founded 80,000 Hours, we hadn't yet come up with the concept of career capital. But if we had, it's likely I would have concluded working in finance would have been better career capital than starting a nonprofit. But I think that would have been a mistake. I gained better career capital from working at 80,000 Hours, because I learned more, achieved more, and met great people.

Learning by doing is often the most effective way to learn. Most people can't see a route to having a significant positive impact right at the start of their career, but if you *do*, just pursuing that might well be your best option for career capital.

This could look like joining a startup social impact project you think you could succeed over 5–10 years, or it could mean directly entering one of the career paths you think are most impactful. If you succeed, it'll be impressive, benefiting your career capital. And if you're someone who cares about doing good, you'll probably find it more motivating to work on something meaningful, making you more likely to succeed.

In addition, if you want to tackle pressing global problems, then at some point you need to learn about those problems, and meet others who want to work on them too. This is usually easier to do if you work in those areas than if you (for instance) work in a random corporate job.

And of course you might have a positive impact! Although career capital should probably be your top priority early on, any positive impact you can have early in your career matters too.

All these pros can make up for other weaknesses of this path (e.g. often you'll receive less training).

Whether to take the plunge and try to do something impactful early on is a difficult decision. It'll depend on the chances of success of the project, who you'll be working with, what kind of training you might get, and so on. But if you can see a way to significantly help with one of the most pressing global problems right away, it's certainly worth considering — even just from the perspective of gaining useful skills, achievements, and connections.

As we saw in the chapter on job satisfaction, doing what contributes is a good strategy both for helping others and being personally satisfied. But also, if you try to do what's most important for the world, it can sometimes be the best strategy for career capital too.

TRANSFERABLE VS SPECIALIST CAREER CAPITAL

One tradeoff you might face is between the following two types of career capital:

- *Transferable* career capital is relevant in lots of different options. For example, social skills, productivity and management skills (which are needed by almost every organisation), or achievements that are widely recognised as impressive.
- *Specialist* career capital prepares you for a narrow range of paths, like knowledge of malaria or information security.

Which should you focus on?

All else equal, when you're earlier in your career, you should focus more on transferable career capital. At the start of your career you're more uncertain about what's best, so it's more useful to have flexibility. And more generally, the more uncertain you are about what roles you want in the longer term, the more you should focus on transferable career capital.

Unfortunately, however, all else is often *not* equal. While specialist career capital gives you fewer options, it's often necessary to enter the most impactful jobs, so it's still probably worth focusing on at some point.

Should you wait to have an impact?

If you could work as an AI safety engineer today, should you still do a PhD to try to open up potential research positions you think might be higher impact?

If you do the PhD, not only do you give up the impact you would have had early on, you're also delaying your impact further into the future. Most researchers on this topic agree that, all else being equal, it's better to put resources towards fixing the world's most pressing problems sooner rather than later — for instance, once transformative AI systems have been built, your work might be too late!

Moreover, in the meantime, there's a risk you give up on trying to have an impact, and informal polls suggest the annual risk of this might be quite high.[160]

This means the boost in career capital you gain from doing the PhD needs to be *substantially* more than the career capital you'd gain as someone working directly on AI safety — say, a software engineer in a safety team — to be worth those costs.

But often it *is* worth it. It's not out of the question that you could have twice as much impact as a researcher than a software engineer. And, as we saw above, it's plausible that some people become 10 times more productive over their career by gaining particularly good career capital.

We have seen people take on projects they weren't equipped for early in their careers — like starting a new nonprofit — when they would have been better off getting some good mentorship in a well-respected firm.

So, while gaining career capital should be a significant priority for most people *early* in their careers, as your career progresses, it becomes harder to strike the right balance between impact and career capital.

Ultimately, getting this balance right will often come down to the quality of the opportunities you've found, as well as your beliefs about the urgency of global problems, and how old you are (the earlier you gain career capital, the longer you have to use it).

How can you get career capital in any job?

You don't need to change jobs to build career capital. Just as you can have an impact in any job through donations or advocacy, you can build career capital in any job if you use your time well.

We explain how in appendix 2.

Conclusion

You may not be sure how to best contribute today, and you may suspect that you have few valuable skills, but that's fine.

Although we like stories of people who achieved apparently instant fame and early success, like the *Forbes* 30 Under 30, they're not the norm. Besides those who just got lucky, behind most great achievements are many years spent diligently building expertise.

We've seen people transform their careers by doing things like learning to program, being mentored by the right boss, and going to the right graduate school.

If you build valuable career capital, then you'll be able to have a more impactful, satisfying career too.

We've now explored which options to aim for long term and how to work towards them. In the next chapter, we'll explain how to narrow them down.

APPLY THIS TO YOUR OWN CAREER

1. Given the longer-term paths you'd most like to take, what steps might most accelerate you toward them?
2. Go over all the six paths to career capital and ways to gain career capital in any job, and note down three next steps you could take to gain career capital. A few ideas to get you started:
    - Can you think of any opportunities to work at a high-performance, growing organisation?
    - Do any graduate study options make sense?
    - Are there any options in policy to consider?
    - Can you do something where you can learn a useful, transferable skill?
    - Is there an option where you might achieve something impressive?
    - Could you make a contribution right away?
3. What's the most valuable career capital you already have? Identifying this can give you clues about what you'll be best at, and help you convince employers to hire you. Review each of the categories:
    - Skills and knowledge
    - Connections
    - Credentials
    - Character
    - Runway

If you're stuck, list out 2–5 achievements you're most proud of, and ask yourself what they have in common.

We've now explored which options to aim for long term and how to work towards them. In the next chapter, we'll explain how to narrow them down.

THE BOTTOM LINE:
WHICH JOBS PUT YOU IN THE BEST POSITION
FOR THE FUTURE?

Career capital is anything that puts you in a better position to make a difference in the future, including skills, connections, credentials, character, and financial runway.

To get career capital, we suggest *getting good at something useful*. To do that, you need to:

- Focus on learning *valuable* skills.
- Learn skills that *are a good fit for you.*
- Practice for many years with good mentorship.
- Increase your chances of being in the right place at the right time (e.g. by working in new and rapidly growing fields).

Gaining career capital, especially early in your career, is vital, because it's what will allow you to become far more productive over your life. In your first couple of jobs, it's rare to have a big impact, and typically gaining career capital should be a greater priority.

Here are some common routes to gaining career capital, which can help you get ideas for next steps:

- Working with organisations or people that have a reputation for high performance in your field. We often highlight jobs in technology startups or top AI labs, but you can find good teams and organisations in any sector. [161]
- Undertaking certain graduate studies — especially

subjects relevant to our priority paths, like economics, machine learning, or synthetic biology — that provide good backup options outside of academia.

- Taking entry routes into policy careers, such as certain congressional staffer positions, joining a congressional campaign, or working in certain executive branch positions.
- Doing jobs that build useful skills for working on a pressing problem and also provide good backup options — such as management, software engineering, data science, information security, knowledge of China, or other emerging economies, or marketing.
- Taking opportunities that allow you to achieve anything impressive — e.g. founding an organisation, anything where you might excel or reach the top of a field.
- If you're fortunate enough to do something with significant positive impact in the next five years, that can often be a great choice — not only is it impressive, but it also gives you connections and skills that are highly relevant to solving the problem you're working on.

While career capital is usually the top priority in your first couple of jobs, after that it becomes difficult to know how much to prioritise career capital versus impact — it depends on the specific opportunities in question. Likewise, the question of how much to prioritise specialist versus transferable career capital depends on the circumstances.

There are also lots of ways to gain career capital *within* your existing job, which we cover in appendix 2.

CHAPTER 8
How to find the right career for you

Everyone says it's important to find a job you're good at, but no one tells you how.

The standard advice is to think about it for weeks and weeks until you "discover your talent." To help, career advisers give you quizzes about your interests and preferences. Others recommend you go on a gap year, reflect deeply, imagine different options, and try to figure out what truly motivates you.

But as we saw in the last chapter, becoming really good at most things takes decades of practice. So to a large degree, your abilities are *built* rather than "discovered." Darwin, Lincoln, and Oprah all failed early in their careers, then went on to completely dominate their fields. Albert Einstein's 1895 schoolmaster's report reads, "He will never amount to anything."

Asking "What am I good at?" needlessly narrows your options. It's better to ask: "What could I *become* good at?"

That aside, the bigger problem is that these methods aren't reliable. Plenty of research shows that while it's possible to predict what you'll be good at ahead of time, it's difficult. Just "going with your gut" is particularly unreliable, and it turns out career tests don't work very well either.

Instead, you should be prepared to *think like a scientist* — learn about and try out your options, looking outwards rather than inwards. Here we'll explain why and how.

Being good at your job is more important than you think

Everyone agrees that it's important to find a job you're good at. But we think it's *even more* important than most people think, especially if you care about social impact.

First, the most successful people in a field account for a disproportionately large fraction of the impact. A landmark study of expert performers found that:[162]

> *"A small percentage of the workers in any given domain is responsible for the bulk of the work. Generally, the top 10% of the most prolific elite can be credited with around 50% of all contributions, whereas the bottom 50% of the least productive workers can claim only 15% of the total work, and the most productive contributor is usually about 100 times more prolific than the least."*

So, if you were to plot degree of success on a graph, it would look like this:

Workers in a field, in order of success

It's the same spiked shape as the graphs we've seen several times before in this guide.

In the chapter on high-impact jobs, we saw this in action with areas like research and advocacy. In research, for instance, the top 0.1% of papers receive 1,000 times more citations than the median.

These are areas where the outcomes are particularly skewed, but our review of the evidence suggests that the best people in almost *any* field have significantly more output than the typical person.[163] The more complex the domain, the more significant the effect, so it's especially noticeable in jobs like research, software engineering, and entrepreneurship.

Now, some of these differences are just due to luck: even if everyone were an equally good fit, there could still be big differences in outcomes just because some people happen to get lucky while others don't. However, some component is almost certainly due to skill, and this means that you'll have much more impact if you choose an area where you enjoy the work and have good personal fit.

Second, as we argued, being successful in your field gives you more career capital. This sounds obvious but can be a big deal. Generally being known as a person who gets shit done and is great at what they do can open all sorts of (often surprising) opportunities.

For example, many organisations will hire someone without experience of their area, if that person has done something impressive elsewhere (e.g. many AI companies have hired people without a background in AI). Charity and company board members are often successful people recruited from other fields. Or you might meet someone in another field who admires your work and wants to work together.[164]

Moreover, being successful in any field — even if it seems a bit random — gives you influence, money, and connections, which, as we've also covered, can be used to promote all sorts of good causes — even those unrelated to your field.

 **Example:** Isabelle Boemeke started out as a fashion model. But after speaking to experts who said nuclear energy was needed to tackle climate change, she pivoted to using her social media following to promote it. Becoming a fashion model isn't normally one of our recommendations, but it could still be the right choice if your fit is high enough.

Third, being good at your job and gaining a sense of mastery is a vital component of being satisfied in your work. We covered this in the first chapter.

All this is why *personal fit* is one of the key factors to look for in a job. We think of "personal fit" as your chances of excelling at a job, if you work at it.

If we put together everything we've covered so far in the guide, this would be our formula for a perfect job:

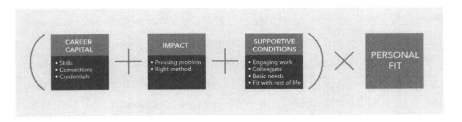

You can use these factors to make side-by-side comparisons of different career options (learn more about how to do this in appendix 4).

Personal fit is like a multiplier of everything else, which means it's probably more important than the other three factors. So, we'd never recommend taking a "high-impact" job that you'd be bad at. But how can you figure out where you'll have the best personal fit?

Hopefully you have some rough ideas for long-term options from earlier in the guide. Now we'll explain how to narrow them down, and find the right career for you.[165]

Why introspection, going with your gut, and career tests don't work

Performance is hard to predict ahead of time

When thinking about which career to take, our first instinct is often to turn inwards rather than outwards: "go with your gut" or "follow your heart."

People we advise often spend days agonising over which options seem best, trying to figure it out from the armchair, or through introspection.

These approaches assume you can easily work out what you're going to be good at ahead of time. But in fact, you can't.

Here's the best study we've been able to find so far on how to predict performance in different jobs over the next couple of years. It's a meta-analysis of selection tests used by employers, drawing on hundreds of studies performed over 100 years.[166] Here are some of the results:

Type of selection test	Correlation with job performance (r)
IQ tests	0.65
Interviews (structured)	0.58
Interviews (unstructured)	0.58
Peer ratings	0.49
Job knowledge tests	0.48

Integrity tests	0.46
Job tryout procedure	0.44
GPA	0.34
Work sample tests	0.33
Holland-type match	0.31
Job experience (years)	0.16
Years of education	0.10
Graphology	0.02
Age	0.00

Almost all of these tests are fairly bad. A correlation of 0.6 is pretty weak. And the accuracy for *longer-term* predictions is probably even worse.[167] So even if you try to predict using the best available techniques, you're going to be wrong much of the time: candidates that look bad will often turn out good, and vice versa.

Anyone who's hired people before will tell you that's exactly what happens (and there is some systematic evidence for this).[168] And because hiring is so expensive, employers *really* want to pick the best candidates. They also know exactly what the job requires — if even *they* find it really hard to figure out in advance who's going to perform best, you probably don't have much chance.

Don't go with your gut

If you *were* to try to predict performance in advance, "going with your gut" isn't the best way to do it. Research in the science of decision-making collected over several decades shows that intuitive decision-making only works in certain circumstances.[169]

For instance, your gut instinct can tell you very rapidly if someone is angry with you. This is because our brain is biologically wired to rapidly warn us when in danger, and to fit in socially.

Your gut can also be amazingly accurate when trained. Chessmasters have an astonishingly good intuition for the best moves, and this is because they've trained their intuition by playing lots of similar games, and built up a sense of what works and what doesn't.

However, gut decision-making is poor when it comes to working out things like how fast a business will grow, who will win a football match, and what grades a student will receive. Earlier, we also saw that our intuition is poor at working out what will make us happy. This is all because our untrained gut instinct makes lots of mistakes,[170] and in these situations it's hard to train it to do better.

Career decision-making is more like these examples than being a chess grandmaster.

It's hard to train our gut instinct when:

1. The results of our decisions take a long time to arrive.
2. We have few opportunities to practise.
3. The situation keeps changing.

This is exactly the situation with career choices: we only make a couple of major career decisions in our life, it takes years to see the results, and the job market keeps changing.

Your gut can still give you *clues* about the best career. It can tell you things like "I don't trust this person" or "I'm not excited by this project." But you can't simply "go with your gut."

Why career tests also don't work

Many career tests are built on "Holland types" or something similar. These tests classify you as one of six interest types, like "artistic" or "enterprising." Then they recommend careers that match that type. However, we can see from the table above that "Holland-type match" is only weakly correlated with performance. It's also only weakly correlated with job satisfaction (studies find correlations of around 0.1 to 0.3). So that's why we don't pay much attention to traditional career tests.

What *does* work in predicting where you'll excel, according to the research?

In the table above, interviews rank near the top, which suggests the following method: talk to people who have experience recruiting in the field, and ask them how you'd stack up compared to other candidates. This makes a lot of sense — experts are probably pretty good at making this sort of judgement call.

The cluster of job tryout procedures, job knowledge tests, and work samples also do well, and that suggests another intuitive method: try to get as close to *actually doing* the work as possible, and then see how that goes. We talk about some ways to do that below.

Surprisingly, IQ tests correlate the most, but they're not so useful for helping you figure out which kind of job is the best fit for you *relative* to other jobs (and that's setting aside the question of what IQ tests actually measure!).

All this said, it's important to keep in mind that none of these methods work that well. It's just hard to say where you might be able to excel or not in the future, and this means you should keep an open mind and give yourself the benefit of the doubt — you probably have more options than it first seems!

And ultimately, the only way to find out is to take the plunge and actually try things.

How can you find a job that fits? Think like a scientist.

If it's hard to predict where you'll perform best ahead of time, and going with your gut intuition doesn't work, then we need to take an empirical approach:

1. Make some *best guesses* (hypotheses) about which options seem best.
2. Identify your *key uncertainties* about those hypotheses.
3. *Go and investigate* those uncertainties.

And even when your investigation is complete and you start a job, that *too* is another experiment. After you've tried the job for a couple of years, update your best guesses, and repeat.

Finding the right career for you isn't something you'll figure out right away — it's a *step-by-step* process of coming to better and better answers over time.

Here are some more tips on each stage.

Make a big list of options

The cost of accidentally ruling out a great option too early is much greater than the cost of investigating it further, so it's important to start broad.

And since it's so hard to predict where you'll excel, that also means it's hard to rule out lots of paths!

This can also help you avoid one of the biggest decision-making biases: considering too few options.[171] We've met lots of people who stumbled into paths like PhDs, medicine, or law because those options felt like the default at the time — but if they'd considered more options, they could easily have found something that fit them better.

We also meet a lot of people who think they need to stick narrowly to their recent experience. For example, they might think that because they studied biology, they should mainly look for jobs that involve biology. But what major you studied rarely matters that much.

So start by making a long list of options — longer than your first inclination. We'll look more about how to do this in chapter 9.

Figure out your key uncertainties

You don't have time to try or investigate every job, so you need to narrow down the field.

To start, just make some rough guesses: roughly rank your options in terms of personal fit, impact, and supportive conditions for job satisfaction (plus career capital if you're comparing next steps rather than longer-term paths)

Then ask yourself: "What are my most important uncertainties about this ranking?"

In other words, if you could get the answers to just a few questions, which questions would tell you the most about which option should be top?

People often find the most important questions are pretty simple things, like:

1. If I applied to this job, would I get in?
2. Would I enjoy this aspect of the job?
3. Would the pay be high enough given my student loans?
4. What's the day-to-day routine actually like?

We have some more tips on how to predict your fit below.

Do cheap tests first

Now that you have a list of uncertainties, try to resolve them!

Start with the easiest and quickest ways to gain information first.

We often find people who want to, say, try out economics, so they apply for a master's programme. But that's a huge investment. Instead, think about how you can learn more with the least possible effort: "cheap tests."

In particular, consider how you might be able to eliminate your top option. Or consider what you might need to find out to move a different option to the top slot.

When investigating a specific option, you can think of creating a 'ladder' of tests.

After each step, reevaluate whether the option still seems promising, best or if you can skip the remaining steps and move on to investigate another option.

One such ladder might look like this:

1. Read our relevant career reviews, all our research on a given topic, and do some Google searches to learn the basics. (1–2 hours)
2. Speak to someone in the area. (2 hours)
3. Speak to three more people who work in the area and read one or two books. (20 hours)
4. Consider using some of the additional approaches to predicting success below.
5. Given your findings in the previous steps, look for a relevant project that might take 1–4 weeks of work — like applying to jobs, volunteering in a related role, or doing a side project in the area — to see what it's like and how you perform.
6. Only then consider taking on a 2- to 24-month commitment — like a work placement, internship, or graduate study. Being offered

a trial position with an organisation for a couple of months can be ideal, because both you and the organisation want to quickly assess your fit.

If you're choosing which restaurant to eat at, the stakes aren't high enough to warrant much research. But a career decision will influence decades of your life, so it could easily be worth weeks or months of work making sure you get it right.

Try something (and iterate)

You'll never be certain about which option is best, and even worse, you may never even feel *confident* in your best guess.

So when should you stop your research and try something?

Here's a simple answer: when your best guess stops changing.

If you keep investigating, but your answers aren't changing, then the chances are you've hit diminishing returns, and you should just try something.

Of course, some decisions are harder to reverse or higher stakes than others (e.g. going to medical school). So all else equal, the bigger the decision, the more time you should spend investigating, and the more stable you want your answers to be.

Once you take the plunge and start a job, it helps to remember that *even this* is just an experiment. In most cases, if you try something for a couple of years and it doesn't work out, you can try something else.

With each step you take, you'll learn more about what fits you best.[172]

ADVANCED: WHAT ARE THE BEST WAYS TO PREDICT CAREER FIT, ACCORDING TO THE RESEARCH?

Our key advice on predicting fit is to define your key uncertainties and go investigate them in whatever way seems most helpful.

But it's also true that, based on the research and our experience, some approaches to predicting fit seem better than others.

You can use these prompts to better target your efforts to gain information, and to make better guesses before you start doing lots of investigation.

1. **What is the job actually like?** We often meet people who speculate on their fit for, say, working in government, but have little idea what civil servants actually do. Before you go any further, try to get the basics down: Can you describe what a typical day might look like? What tasks create value in the job? What does it take to do them well?

2. **What do experts say?** If you can, ask people experienced in the field about how well you'd perform — especially people with experience recruiting for the job in question. But be careful — don't put too much weight on a single person's view! And try to find people who are likely to be honest with you.

3. **What's been working for you so far?**[173] One simple method to predict your success is to project forward your track record. If you've been succeeding in a path, that's normally a good reason to continue. You can also try to use your track record to make more precise estimates of your chances. For

instance, if you're at grad school, roughly the top half of your class will go into academia, so if you're in the top 25% of your class at grad school, you could roughly guess you'll be in the top 50% of academia.[174] To get a better sense of your potential over the long term, you should try to look at your *rate of improvement* rather than just recent performance.[175]

4. **What drives success in the area, and how do you stack up?** Your answers to steps 1–3 give you a starting point, but then you can then modify that up or down depending on specific factors that could increase or decrease your chances of success. The aim is to develop a model of what's needed for success. You can try to do this by asking people in the field about what's most needed, and trying to understand what causes people to succeed or not. Then try to assess how you stack up on these predictors. This is how (good) job interviews work: they try to identify the traits most important for the job, and then ask you about evidence that you've displayed those traits in the past.

5. **Does the job match your strengths?** One useful way to find your strengths is to look for activities that don't feel like work to you, but do for most people. We have an article with an evidence-driven process to assess your personal strengths.[176]

6. **Do you feel excited about it?** Gut-level motivation *isn't* a reliable predictor of success. But if you *don't* feel motivated, you probably won't be able to put in the effort you'd need to to perform well. So a lack of excitement should definitely give you pause; it might be worth exploring what precisely you find uninspiring.

7. **Will you enjoy it?** This matters even if you mainly care about

social impact: to stick with *any* career for long enough to make a difference, it'll need to be reasonably enjoyable and fit with the rest of your life. For example, if you want a family, you'll probably want a job without extreme working hours.

8. **Combine all these perspectives.** Predicting career success is hard, and there's no single approach that's reliable. So it's useful to consider all of the perspectives above, and focus on options that seem good from several of them.

See our individual career reviews in appendix 8 for more advice on how to assess your fit with a specific job.

Making good predictions in general is difficult. But it's also very useful if your aim is to do good, so we also have an article on how to get better at making decisions and predicting the future.[177]

How much should you explore in your career?

Suppose you've decided to try a job for a few years. You now face a tradeoff: should you stick with it, or quit with the hope of finding something better?

Many successful people explored a lot early in their career. Tony Blair worked as a rock music promoter before going into politics. Maya Angelou worked as a cable car conductor, a cook and a calypso dancer before she switched into writing and activism, while Steve Jobs even spent a year in India on acid, and considered moving to Japan to become a zen monk. That's some serious exploration.

Examples of people who specialised early, like Tiger Woods, often stand out to us — but it doesn't seem *necessary* to specialise that early, and it's probably not even the norm. In the book *Range: Why Generalists Triumph in a Specialized World,* David Epstein argues that most people try several paths, and that athletes who try several sports before settling on one tend to be more successful — holding up Roger Federer as a foil to Tiger.[178]

A 2018 study in *Nature* found that "hot streaks" among creatives and scientists tended to follow periods of exploring several areas.[179]

And today, it's widely accepted that many people will work in several sectors and roles across their lifetime. The typical 25- to 34-year-old changes jobs every three years,[180] and changes are not uncommon later too ("Employee Tenure Summary").

And if personal fit is as important as we've argued, it could be worth spending many years finding the job that's best for you.

But of course, exploring is also costly. Changing career paths can take years, and if you do it too often it can look flaky. Also, some paths can be hard to reenter once you've left them.

Steve Jobs liked to say you should "never settle." But that's not realistic advice. The real question is how to balance the costs of exploration with the benefits.

Fortunately, there's been plenty of research in decision science, computer science, and psychology about this question. We interviewed Brian Christian, author of *Algorithms to Live By: The Computer Science of Human Decisions* about how to summarise this research.[181]

These are some of the key findings.

Explore more when you're young

Everyone agrees that the earlier you are in your career, the more exploratory you should be.

This is because the earlier you discover a better option, the longer you have to take advantage of it.

If you discover a great new career at age 66 and retire at age 67, you've only benefited for one year. But if you discover something new at age 25, you may have decades to enjoy it.

In addition, early on you know relatively little about your strengths and options, so you learn a lot more from trying things.

Society is also structured to make it easier for younger people to explore — for instance, many internships are only available to people who are still at college — so the costs of trying other paths are also lower when younger.

Consider trying several paths (with careful ordering)

One exploration strategy is to try several paths, and then commit to whichever seems best at the end. This is similar to the solution to the (anachronistically named) "secretary problem" in computer science, which is about how long to spend searching for the best candidate to hire from a pool of applicants.

This strategy is most suitable while an undergraduate or in your first couple of jobs, when exploration is easiest and most valuable, and when your uncertainties are greatest.

The main downside of this strategy is that it's costly to try out several paths. However, it's often possible to reduce the costs significantly by carefully ordering your options. For example, you can try out a surprising number of paths between undergraduate and graduate school, during summer breaks, or by putting more reversible options first.

Here's some more detail on how to order your next steps:

1. Explore *before* graduate school rather than after (and put other reversible options first)

In the couple of years right after you graduate, you're not expected to have your career figured out right away — generally, you have licence to try out something more unusual, like starting a business, living abroad, or working at a nonprofit.

If it doesn't go well, you can use the "graduate school reset": do a master's, MBA, law degree, or PhD, which lets you return to a standard path.

We see lots of people rushing into graduate school or other conventional options right after they graduate, which makes them miss one of their best opportunities to explore.

It's especially worth exploring before a PhD rather than after. At the end of a PhD it's hard to leave academia. This is because going from a PhD to a postdoc, and then into a permanent academic position — you're unlikely to succeed if you don't focus 100% on research. So, if you're unsure about academia, try out alternatives before your PhD if possible.

Similarly, it's easier to go from a position in business to a nonprofit job than vice versa, so if you're unsure between the two, take the business position first

2. Choose options that let you experiment

An alternative approach is to take a job that lets you try out several areas by:

- Letting you work in a variety of industries. Freelance and consulting positions are especially good for this.
- Letting you practise many different skills. Jobs in small companies are often especially good on this front.
- Giving you the free time and energy to explore other things outside of work.

3. Try something on the side

If you're already in a job, think of ways to try out a new option on the side. Could you do a short but relevant project in your spare time, or in your existing job?

If you're a student, try to do as many internships and summer projects as possible. Your university holidays are one of the best opportunities in your life to explore.

4. Consider including a wildcard

One drawback of the strategies above is that your best path might well be something you haven't even thought of yet.

This is why in computer science, many exploration algorithms have a random element — making a random move can help avoid settling into a 'local optimum.' While we wouldn't recommend literally picking randomly, the fact that even computer algorithms find randomness helpful illustrates the value of trying something very different.

That could mean trying something totally outside your normal experience, like living in a very different culture, participating in different communities, or trying different sectors from the ones you already know (e.g. nonprofits, government, corporate).

For instance, I (Benjamin) went to learn Chinese in China before I went to university. I didn't have any specific ideas about how it would be useful, but I felt I learned a lot from the experience, and it turned out to be useful when I later worked to create our resources for people working on China-Western coordination around emerging technologies.[182]

Jess – a case study in exploring

Here's a real-life example: when Jess graduated from maths and philosophy, she was interested in academia and leaned towards studying philosophy of mind, but was concerned that it would have little impact.

So the year after she graduated, she spent several months working in finance. She didn't think she'd enjoy it, and she turned out to be right, so she felt confident eliminating that option. She also spent several months working in nonprofits, and reading about different research areas.

Most importantly, she spoke to loads of people, especially in the areas of academia she was most interested in. This eventually led to her being offered to study a PhD in psychology, with a focus on how to improve decision-making by policymakers.

During her PhD, she did an internship at a think tank that specialised in evidence-based policy, and started writing about psychology for an online newspaper. This allowed her to explore the 'public intellectual' side of being an academic, and the option of going into policy.

At the end of her PhD, she could have either continued in academia, or switched into policy or writing. She could also have gone back to finance or the nonprofit sector. Most importantly, she had a far better idea of which options are best.

A rational reason to shoot for the stars

Young people are often advised to "dream big," "be more ambitious," or "shoot for the stars" — is that good advice?

Not always. When asked, more than 75% of Division I basketball players thought they would play professionally, but only 2% actually made it.[183] Whether or not the players in the survey were making a good bet, they overestimated their chances of success… by over 37 times.

Telling people to aim high doesn't make sense when people are so overconfident in their chances of success.

But when you're more calibrated, it often *is* good advice.

Suppose you're comparing two options:
- Earning to give as a software engineer
- Research in AI safety

Imagine you think your chances of success in research aren't very high, so *most likely* you have more impact earning to give. But, if you *do* succeed in research, it would be much higher impact.

If you only get one shot to choose, you should earn to give.

But the real world isn't normally like that. If you try the research path, and it doesn't work out, you can most likely go back to earning to give. But if it *does* work out, then you'll be in a much higher-impact path for the rest of your career.

In other words, there's an asymmetry. It means that if you can tolerate the risk, it's better to try research first.

More generally, you stand to learn the most from trying paths that:

- Might be really, really good...
- But that you're very uncertain about.

In other words, long shots.

In this sense, the advice to shoot for the stars makes sense, especially for young people.

An aggressive version of this strategy is to rank your options in terms of upside — that is, how good they would be if they go unusually well (say in the top 10% of scenarios) — then start with the top-ranked one. If you find you're not on track to hit the upside scenario within a given time frame, try the next one, and so on.

This is usually only suitable if you have good backup options and the fortunate position of being able to try lots of things.

A more moderate version of this strategy is to use it as a tiebreaker: when uncertain between two options, pick the one with the bigger potential upside.[184]

If unsure, quit

The sunk cost bias[185] leads us to expect people to:

- Continue with their current path for too long.
- Want to avoid the short-term costs of switching.
- Be averse to leaping into an unknown new option.

This all suggests that if you're on the fence about quitting your job, you should quit.

This is exactly what an influential randomised study found. Steven Levitt recruited tens of thousands of participants who were deeply unsure about whether to make a big change in their life. After offering some advice on how to make hard choices, those who remained truly undecided were given the chance to flip a coin to settle the issue — 22,500 did so.[186]

Levitt followed up with these participants two and six months later to ask whether they had actually made the change, and how happy they were on a scale of 1 to 10. It turned out that people who made a change on an important question gained 2.2 points of happiness out of 10!

Of course, this is just one study, and we wouldn't be surprised if the effect were smaller on replication. But it lines up with what we'd expect.

APPLY THIS TO YOUR OWN CAREER

In the earlier chapters, you should have made a list of some ideas for longer-term career paths to aim towards.

Now you could start to narrow them down.

1. Make a rough guess at which longer-term paths are most promising on the balance of: impact, personal fit, and job satisfaction.
2. What are some of your key uncertainties about this ranking? List out at least five.
3. How might you be able to resolve those key uncertainties as easily as possible? Go and investigate them. Consider doing one or two cheap tests.
4. Which option do you think has the most upside potential?
5. If you were going to try out several longer-term paths, what would be the ideal way to order those tests?
6. How confident do you feel in your longer-term options? Do you think you should (i) do more research into comparing your longer-term options? (ii) try to enter one (but with a backup plan)? (iii) plan to try out several longer-term paths? or (iv) just gain transferable career capital and figure out your longer-term paths later?

If you want to think more about your longer-term options, try our full process for comparing a list of career options, which you can find in appendix 4.

Conclusion

We like to imagine we can work out what we're good at through reflection, in a flash of insight. But that's not how it works.

Rather, it's more like a scientist testing a hypothesis. You have ideas about what you can become good at (hypotheses), which you can test out (research and experiments). Think you could be good at writing? Then start blogging. Think you'd hate consulting? At least speak to a consultant.

If you don't already know your "calling" or your "passion," that's normal. It's too hard to predict which career is right for you when you're starting out, and even sometimes when you're many years in.

Instead, go and try things. You'll learn as you go, heading step by step towards a fulfilling career.

Next, we'll show how to tie together everything we've covered in the guide and avoid some common planning mistakes.

THE BOTTOM LINE:
HOW TO FIND THE RIGHT CAREER FOR *YOU*

- Your *personal fit* for a job is the chance that — if you worked at it — you'd end up excelling.
- Personal fit is even more important than most people think, because it increases your impact, job satisfaction, and career capital.
- Research shows that it's hard to work out what you're going to be good at ahead of time. Career tests, trying to introspect, or just "going with your gut" seem like poor ways of figuring this out.
- Instead, think like a scientist: make some best guesses (hypotheses) about which careers could be a good fit, identify your *key uncertainties* about those guesses, then *go and investigate* those uncertainties.
- Look for the cheapest ways of testing your options first, creating a 'ladder' of tests. Usually this means starting by speaking to people already working in the job. Later it could involve applying to jobs or finding ways to do short projects that are similar to actually doing the work.
- It can take years to find your fit, and you'll never be certain about it. So even once you take a job, see it too as an experiment. Try it for a couple of years, then update your best guesses.
- Early in your career, if you have the security, it can be worth planning to try out several career paths, aiming high, and being ready to quit if something is going so-so rather than great. You can make this easier by carefully considering which order to explore your options, and making good backup plans.

CHAPTER 9
How to make your career plan

People often come to us trying to figure out what they should do over the next 10 or 20 years. Others say they want to figure out "the right career" for them.

The problem with all of this is that, as we've seen, your plan is almost certainly going to change:

- You'll change — more than you think.
- The world will change — many industries around today won't even exist in 20 years.
- You'll learn more about what's best for you — it's very hard to predict what you're going to be good at ahead of time.

In a sense, there is no stable "right career for you." Rather, the best option will keep changing as the world changes and you learn more. Many people we've advised would never have predicted the job they've ended up doing.

Long-term planning could even be counterproductive. There's a risk of becoming fixated on a specific plan, and failing to change your plans as your situation changes.

All that said, giving up on planning and setting goals probably isn't wise either. As Eisenhower said, "Plans are useless but planning is essential."

Having *some* idea of where you'd like to end up can help you spot much better opportunities to advance. In fact, if you want to have a big positive impact, we'd argue that planning is *even more* important. Many of the highest-impact roles require specialist career capital you're unlikely to get by accident, such as connections to people in biosecurity or expertise in particular technical skills. Likewise, getting to the top of many fields often requires decades of focused effort.

This is the planning puzzle — most 'plans' will radically change long before they're completed, but we still benefit from having them.

Given all this, how should you make a good career plan? Here are our main tips.

Don't "keep your options open"

A very common response to the planning puzzle is to try to "keep your options open."

There is some wisdom in this idea: if you gain transferable career capital, you'll have more options in the future. And if you're extremely uncertain what to do, just building transferable career capital and coming back to your plan later is a reasonable course of action.

But through advising thousands of people with their careers, we've seen that it can have some serious pitfalls. Deciding to just "keep your options open" can:

- Lead to you spending far too long working in a generally prestigious job (like consulting) that you know you don't want to do long term and just isn't that relevant to your longer-term goals.
- Stop you committing, so you end up pursuing a middle-of-the-road job that gives you some flexibility, rather than going for something that might be *outstanding* for career capital, and so ultimately give you better options.
- Turn into an excuse to not think hard about what's best.

So what should you do instead?

The three key stages to a career

Move through the following three stages:

1. **Explore:** take low-cost ways to learn about and test out promising longer-term roles, until you feel ready to bet on one for a few years. (Most likely to be the top priority ages 18–24.)
2. **Build career capital:** take a bet on a longer-term path that could go really well by building the career capital that will most accelerate you in your chosen path, but with a backup plan. (Age 25–35.)
3. **Deploy:** use the career capital you've built to tackle pressing problems and bargain for a job you find personally satisfying. (Age 36 and up.)

And then keep updating your plan every 1–3 years as you continue to learn more and the world changes.

Career capital, exploration, and of course the impact of your work are always going to be relevant to every career decision you face, throughout your career. But your *focus* should change over time.

The stages last different amounts of time for different people:

- If you're especially uncertain about what to do longer term but feel like you're learning a lot about where to focus, you might stay focused on exploration for longer (or just build transferable career capital and figure out your vision later). (Or someone mid-career who's made a dramatic career change might shift back to exploration.)
- If you've already hit diminishing returns on career capital, you might move to the deploy stage faster, and vice versa.

- If you think work on your chosen problems is especially urgent — which many people think is the case for AI safety — and the opportunities around today are better than those that will be around in 10 years, that's a reason to skip to the deploy stage even *if* you'll be less well-prepared for it.

Next, we'll look at some more ways we recommend going about career planning — while taking the uncertainty involved seriously.

Have a longer-term vision

Although the future is very uncertain, we think for most people, it's helpful to have at least a *vague* idea of where you'd like to end up longer term. This is your *vision*.

Your vision should be broad enough that it won't constantly change, but narrow enough to provide some direction.

Your vision should include:

1. A list of 2–5 global problems you'd most like to work on longer term, as covered in chapter 5.
2. A list of 1–5 roles or types of work you'd like to aim towards, as covered in chapter 6.

Types of work you could aim for include the categories of high-impact careers we looked at earlier, like being an entrepreneur, writer, or organisation builder. "Longer term" could mean anything from five to 25 years — just pick a timeframe that makes sense to you. If you've done the exercises in previous chapters, you should have a shortlist already.

Here's an example: Megan was studying in Beijing when someone suggested she take a look at 80,000 Hours. After reading our guide, she decided that she wanted to work on reducing existential risks, and in particular the risks from AI and nuclear war.

She had spent some time doing research in academia, but she felt that academic work in her field — international relations — was unlikely to provide her with a high-impact career path. So her best guess was to aim for a career path in government and policy. Her vision, if all went well, was that she could become an expert in multilateral relations, and then advise key players on multilateral agreements around AI.

Your vision may feel much more uncertain than this, though, and that's fine. You only need a rough idea to help spot opportunities and guide your exploration.

As we've covered, finding the best career for you is a step-by-step process, so you'll update your vision every couple of years: adding or removing options from your list, and making the items more specific (e.g. you might start out looking at organisation-building roles, and later focus on becoming a PR specialist).

A common mistake is to obsess about which longer-term options seem best in the abstract. So once you have a rough idea of longer-term options, turn your attention to generating ideas for concrete *next steps*.

Spend longer planning your next steps

Ultimately, the decision you need to make is what to do *next*. Thinking about your vision is useful, but only because it helps to guide that decision.

Your next step could be a new job, but it could also be a course or a new project. Typically, it'd be something you might do for a couple of years, though it could be from a few months to 5+ years. For example: accepting a job at Oxfam, spending a summer studying Chinese, or starting a blog while continuing in your current job.

Trying to work out whether you should (for instance) be a researcher (like Dr Nalin) or a communicator (like Rosa Parks) longer term is hard because it's abstract.

It's often a lot easier to work out which concrete job or graduate programme to take. Sometimes it makes the decision really obvious: for instance, if you don't get into any good graduate programmes, that'll be off the table.

It's also even possible to skip having a vision and *only* focus on next steps. With each step, you'll ideally gain some career capital, learn more about what fits you best, and increase your impact — putting yourself into a better and better position and having more and more impact over time. In this way you can build a great career *step by step*, even if you have no idea where you're going to end up.

Hopefully, this feels like a relief. Even if you have *no idea* what you want to do longer term, you can still build a great career iteratively. And if you *do* have some good ideas for your vision, that's a bonus.

So, while we recommend most people spend some time thinking about their longer-term vision, most people should spend even more time identifying and comparing concrete next steps.

Working backwards: if you know your long-term vision, work out how to get there

To come up with next steps, there are two broad approaches.

The first is to *work backwards* from your vision: think about where you'd like to end up, and then identify the most direct routes to get there.

The best way to do this is to ask people in the field how someone with your background can advance most quickly. For example, ask: "If I wanted to be in role X in five years, what would I need to do?"

Also, look for examples of people who have advanced unusually quickly and figure out how they did it.

Think about which types of career capital will be most important. For example, Bill Clinton knew that to succeed in politics, he'd need to know a lot of people, so even as an undergraduate, he kept a list of everyone he'd met on a paper notepad.

We do some of this analysis in our career reviews, but there's no substitute for getting personal advice on the best next steps *for you*.

If you're feeling uncertain about a longer-term option, another question to consider is: "How might I eliminate that option?" Is there something you could do that would decisively tell you whether pursuing that longer-term path made sense or not?

Working forwards: look at the opportunities immediately in front of you

That said, it's important not to get wedded to a particular pathway.

Most great careers also involve *working forwards* — being alert to the opportunities that happen to be in front of you, following your nose, and going with what's working, even if you're not sure where it'll eventually lead.

One reason is the inherent unpredictability of career success.

Another reason is because next steps vary so much in how promising they are, so the variation between specific jobs can trump the variation between broad career paths.

For example, maybe you think biorisk policy is more pressing than nuclear risk policy *on average* — but if you find a job in nuclear policy with an unusual amount of responsibility, or that's an unusually good fit for you, or where you work with a great mentor, it could easily be better to work in nuclear policy.

To go back to Megan, when she was figuring out what to do after her master's, in order to work backwards, she considered ways she might most rapidly advance in a government and policy path. She put common options, like getting a job at a think tank, on her list of options.

But she also realised her current position, living and studying in China, could open up some additional opportunities off the standard path. She saw an ad for a job working for the US Department of State in Beijing as a Chinese social media analyst — and got it. She's since managed to find a role at the Department of Homeland Security, towards her vision of working on reducing the risk posed by AI systems.

When you're working forwards, it helps to make a big list of interesting jobs and training opportunities, even if they don't obviously feed into your current longer-term plans. Here are steps you could use:

- Earlier in the guide, we covered a list of next steps to gain general career capital, so you might have some ideas from there.
- Ask your friends, colleagues, people working on pressing problems, and people you admire what opportunities they know about. The best opportunities are usually found through people you know.
- Check out the jobs listed on our job board — do any of them seem interesting?[187]
- Are there any opportunities, areas to learn about, side projects, or people you feel especially excited about right now?
- Is anything you're doing right now going better than expected? Could you spend more of your time on that?

Many opportunities also only emerge after you start looking. So one of the most useful strategies is to simply pursue lots of specific jobs and make lots of applications.

We often come across people agonising about different longer-term paths, whereas if they'd simply made applications, the next step would have become obvious.

We'll look at how to manage the job application process in the next chapter.

Have backup options: the ABZ plan

Startup founders have a broad vision for the company, but face enormous uncertainties in the details of their product and strategy. To overcome this, they test lots of approaches, and gradually improve their plan over time.

You face similarly large uncertainties in your career, so we might be able to borrow some of the best practices in entrepreneurship and apply them to career strategy. This is the premise of *The Startup of You*, a book by the founder of LinkedIn, Reid Hoffman. One of his tips is making an "A/B/Z plan," which we've also found useful while giving one-on-one advice to our readers.[188]

Writing an ABZ plan helps you think about specific alternatives and backup plans, putting you in a better position to adapt when the situation changes.

1. Plan A: your ideal scenario

Your Plan A is your best guess at the route you'd most like to pursue.

This could be a particular vision you're going to bet on, and the next step that would imply.

For example: *Try to become an academic economist who works on global priorities research or AI policy (vision) by studying these extra maths courses at undergrad (next step).*

If you're more unsure about your vision, you could also plan to try out several longer-term paths, by taking a couple of carefully ordered next steps, as we covered in the chapter on personal fit.

Or your Plan A could be just to build some valuable transferable career capital (e.g. learn people management, get a degree in statistics), and then reevaluate your plan later.

2. Plan B: nearby alternatives

These are promising alternatives that you could switch to if your Plan A doesn't work out. Writing them out ahead of time helps you to stay ready for new opportunities.

To figure out your Plan B, ask yourself:

- What are the most likely ways your Plan A wouldn't work out? If that happens, what will you do?
- What other good options are there? List any promising nearby alternatives to Plan A, which may be other promising longer-term paths, or different entry routes to the same paths.

Then come up with two or three alternatives. For instance:

- If you're already in a job and applying to master's programmes, one possibility is that you don't get into the programmes you want. In that case, your Plan B might be to stay in your job another year and to assess later, or to apply for a master's in another discipline.
- If your Plan A is to work in policy by getting a job in the executive branch, your Plan B could be to try think tank internships or working on a political campaign.

3. Plan Z: if it all ****s up, this is your temporary fallback

Your Plan Z is what you'll do if this all goes wrong.

In other words, if your A and B plans don't work out, what will you do to pay the bills until you get back on your feet?

Having a Plan Z can not only help you avoid unacceptable personal outcomes, but it can help you get more comfortable with taking risks — knowing you'll ultimately be OK makes it easier to be ambitious.

Your Plan Z can be very short if you're comfortable with the risk you're taking, or are in a secure position. If you're in a higher-stakes situation (e.g. you have dependents) you might want to do more careful planning.

Some common examples are sleeping on a friend's sofa while paying the bills through tutoring or working at a café, living off savings, going back to your old job, moving back in with your family, or taking a job you find relatively undemanding.

It could even mean something more adventurous, like going to teach English in Asia — a surprisingly in-demand, uncompetitive job that lets you learn about a new culture.

Then ask yourself: "Is this Plan Z acceptable?" If not, you might need to revise your Plan A, or prioritise building your safety net for a while.

OPTIONAL: FURTHER WAYS TO REDUCE RISK

Sometimes you need to take risks in order to have a big impact. Thinking about them ahead of time can make this easier.

First, clarify what a realistic worst-case scenario really is if you pursue your Plan A. It's easy to have vague fears about "failing," and research shows that when we think about bad events, we bring to mind their worst aspects, while ignoring all the things that will remain unchanged. This led Nobel Laureate Daniel Kahneman to say:[189]

> "Nothing in life is as important as you think it is, while you are thinking about it."

Often, when you think through the worst realistic scenario, you'll realise it's not so bad, and is something you could overcome in the long term.

The risks to pay most attention to are those that could

permanently reduce your happiness or career capital, such as burning out, getting depressed, or ruining your reputation. You might also have dependents who rely on you.

Second, is there anything you could do to make sure that the serious risks don't happen?

Many people think of entrepreneur college dropouts like Bill Gates as people who took bold risks to succeed. But Gates worked on tech sales for about a year part-time as a student at Harvard, and then negotiated a year of leave from study to start Microsoft. If it had failed, Gates could have gone back to study computer science at Harvard — in reality, he took hardly any risk at all. Usually, with a bit of thought, it's possible to avoid the worst risks of your plan.

Third, make a plan for what you'd do if the worst case scenario *does* happen. Think about what you'll do to cope and make it less bad (as well as having a fallback Plan Z job, as above).

If it helps, remember you'll probably still have food, friends, a soft bed, and a room at the perfect temperature — better conditions than most people have faced in all of history.

Fourth, if at this point the risks are still unacceptable, then you may need to change your Plan A. For instance, you might need to spend more time building your financial runway.

Going through these exercises makes risk less scary, and makes you more likely to cope if the worst does happen.

Set a review point

Your plan should change as you learn more, but it's very easy to get stuck on the path you're already on. Not changing course when a better option exists is one of the most common decision-making mistakes identified by psychologists, and can be caused by the *sunk cost fallacy* or *status quo bias*.[190]

To help avoid this mistake, you need to set a review point. Here are some options:

- **Pick a timeframe to review your plan**, typically 6–24 months. (Go for shorter timeframes when you're more uncertain and learning a lot, and longer ones when you're more settled.) Around the new year is often a nice time.[191]
- **Review your plan when you next gain significant information about your career.** For example, publishing lots of papers in top journals is key to advancement in academic careers, so you could commit to reassessing whether you want to be an academic if you don't publish a certain number of papers by the end of your PhD.

When you do the review, the most important question to ask is: what have I learned since I last made a plan, and what might that imply about which longer-term paths and next steps are best?

Then go and discuss your thinking with someone else. Other people are better able to spot the sunk cost fallacy, and having to justify your thinking to someone else has been shown to reduce your degree of bias.[192]

If you have more time, it can be helpful to start from a blank slate: if I were making a career plan today, which vision and next steps would seem best? This can help you step out of your current situation and see things afresh.

APPLY THIS TO YOUR OWN CAREER

Bringing all this advice together, here are the seven steps to building your own career plan:

1. **What's your career stage?** Exploring, building career capital, or deploying your existing career capital?

2. **What's your vision?** If you haven't already, sketch out your best-guess shortlist of longer-term paths to aim towards and global problems to work on: your vision.

3. Now clarify: what's the very next decision you need to make? Then **generate a big list of ideas for next steps.** You should already have some ideas from the chapter on career capital. Lean towards including more rather than less, including some that seem like a stretch.
   • Work backwards: what steps would most accelerate you towards your vision?
   • Work forwards: what other interesting opportunities are you aware of?

4. **Now, make an initial guess at which 5–10 next steps are most promising.** If you're struggling to narrow them down, you can also use our decision process to help. Look at the lists of questions for comparing options in terms of career capital and in terms of personal fit from earlier in the guide.

5. Then make an initial guess at your:
   • **Plan A**: your top longer-term plan
   • **Plan B**: nearby alternatives
   • **Plan Z**: fallback options

6. **What are your most pressing *key uncertainties* about all the above?** We introduced the idea of a key uncertainty in

chapter 8, but it can be applied to all aspects of your plan — vision, strategy, next steps, and ABZ options. What information would most change your rankings of options or your Plan A?

7. **How might you best resolve those key uncertainties?** If you have time, go and do that. Ideally keep investigating until your best guesses stop changing.

At this point, often what seems best is to simply pursue your list of next steps, and then reevaluate your plan after you have concrete options on the table. We'll talk about how to get jobs in the next chapter.

Now is also a good time to consider applying to speak to our team one-on-one — just go to 80000hours.org/speak-with-us/. They can help you check your plan, decide which next steps to prioritise, and start toward them.

Once you have concrete job offers on the table, you can use our career decision process to choose between them. It's the same process for comparing longer-term paths, but it can also be applied to next steps. You can find it in appendix 4.

Finally, once you start your job, set a review point.

It could well be worth spending a whole weekend on career planning. If you'd like to do that, we've created a planning worksheet covering all the key exercises from the guide so far.

https://80k.link/NCP

If you fill it out, you'll have a complete career plan. (Try getting a friend to do it with you for moral support and to discuss options.)

THE BOTTOM LINE:
HOW TO MAKE YOUR CAREER PLAN

Your career should move through three stages:
1. **Explore** to find the best longer-term options for you.
2. **Build career capital** towards those options.
3. **Deploy** the career capital you've built to tackle pressing problems and bargain for a job you find personally satisfying.

Your plan will change, and most people can't predict what job they'll be doing in 10–20 years. But it's still useful to have a broad longer-term vision: 2–5 global problems you might try to solve, and 1–5 potential roles you'll steer towards longer term.

It's even more important to devote time to finding your best concrete next step — a specific job, educational opportunity, or project you're going to do in the next 1–3 years that will increase your impact or career capital.

Generate a long list of ideas for next steps by:
- Working backwards: look for options that accelerate you towards your longer-term vision.
- Working forwards: look at the opportunities right in front of you, even if you're not sure where they'll lead.

Then create an ABZ plan:
- Plan A is the top option you'd like to pursue, or a series of paths you want to try out.
- Plan Bs are the promising nearby alternatives you can switch into if Plan A doesn't go as intended.

- Plan Z is your temporary fallback in case everything goes wrong — it helps you feel more comfortable taking chances.

Identify key uncertainties with your plan, then investigate them. If you need help narrowing down your vision or your next steps, take a look at appendix 4.

Finally, set a time to review your career, typically within 6–24 months. You can use our tool to help – available at 80000hours.org/career-planning/annual-career-review/.

CHAPTER 10

All the best advice we could find on how to get a job

When it comes to advice on how to get a job, most of it is pretty bad.

1. CollegeFeed suggests that you "be confident" as their first interview tip, which is a bit like suggesting that you should "be employable."
2. Many advisors cover the "clean your nails and have a firm handshake" kind of thing.
3. One of the most popular interview videos on YouTube, with over 8 million views, makes the wise point that you *definitely* mustn't sit down until you're explicitly invited to do so by the interviewer.[193]

Who could ever recover from taking a seat a few seconds too early?

Over the years, we've sifted through a lot of bad advice to find the nuggets that are actually good. We've also provided one-on-one coaching to thousands of people who are applying for jobs, and hired about 30 people ourselves, so we've seen what works from both sides. Here, we'll sum up what we've learned.

Let's be blunt. You're not entitled to a job, and hiring is rarely fair. Rather, getting a job is, at root, a sales process. You need to persuade someone to give you responsibility and a salary, and even put their reputation on the line, in exchange for results.

We'll list key advice for each stage of the "sales" process:

1. Finding opportunities (leads).
2. Convincing employers (conversion).
3. Negotiating.

The common theme is to think from the employer's point of view, and do whatever they will find most convincing. That means instead of sending out lots of CVs, focus on getting recommendations and proving you can do the work.

While the rest of this guide is about working out which job is best for you and the world, here we focus on the practicalities of taking action on your plans. Just bear in mind there's no point using salesmanship to land a job that you wouldn't be good at — you won't be satisfied, and if your performance is worse than the next-best applicant, you'll have a negative impact.

But we wrote this chapter to prevent the opposite situation: we've seen too many great candidates who want to make a difference failing to live up to their potential because they don't know how to sell themselves.

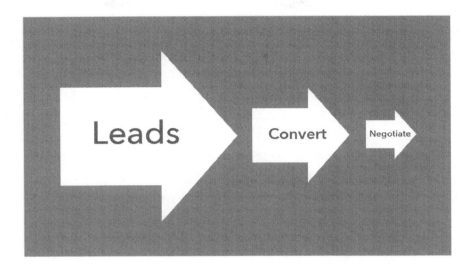

STAGE 1: LEADS

A lead is any opportunity that might turn into a job, like a position you could apply for, a friend who might know an opportunity, or a side project you might be able to get paid for.

You need a lot of leads

We interviewed someone who's now a top *NPR* journalist. But when he started out, he applied to 70 positions and got only one serious offer.[194]

This illustrates the first thing to know about leads: *you probably need a lot of them.* Especially early in your career, it can easily take 20 to 100 leads to find one good job, and getting rejected 20 times is normal.

In fact, the average length of a spell of unemployment in the US is six months, so be prepared for your job hunt to take that long.[195]

This is especially true if you're applying to jobs that are especially desirable and competitive, which are normally more selective, and therefore require more leads.

This includes most jobs directly working on the pressing problems we talk about — in part because we focus on neglected problems, so there just aren't that many jobs available. For instance, if you want to work on preventing catastrophic pandemics, but can only find 10 leads, that's (normally) not enough to make it likely you'll find a job. You might need to apply to jobs in other areas or career paths until you've got at least 30 leads.

To compound the problem, there's a huge amount of luck involved. Most employers are not only looking for general competence, they're also looking for someone who will fit that particular team and organisation, and the specific requirements of the job. They also have to make decisions with very little information, which means they'll make a lot of mistakes. You can be very talented but simply not find a match through bad luck.

While bad luck can derail even the best candidates, many people struggle in their job search through a lack of confidence. We know a lot of people who thought they'd never get a certain job, but went on to not only land the job, but also to excel within it.

Others are overconfident. We've met people whose backup option was to work at an effective altruism organisation — but those roles are also super competitive, so they aren't really a backup at all.

Unfortunately it's hard to know whether you're underconfident or overconfident. So it's important to pursue *both* backup and stretch positions:

- Backup positions are those that are less attractive but you think you're likely to land. Applying to them reduces the risk of not ending up with anything, and having offers can improve your negotiating position.
- Stretch positions are those you think you're unlikely to get, but would be great if you do, so offer a lot of upside.

Making all these applications is a lot of work. It helps to bear in mind that it's also one of the best ways to assess your fit with a career path — indeed, job applications are specifically designed to assess fit as quickly as possible. This means you stand to learn a lot from applying –– you might even discover a totally new career path.

Pursuing lots of jobs is also one of the best ways to find even more opportunities. Maybe one employer doesn't have any openings, but they know someone else who does.

How to get leads: don't just cold email your CV, use connections

Many large organisations have a standardised application process, such as the UK Civil Service and Teach for America. They want to keep the process fair, so there isn't much wiggle room. In these cases, just apply.

But what do you do in all the other cases? The most obvious approach is to send your CV to lots of companies and apply to the postings on job boards. This is often the first thing career advisors mention.[196]

We would recommend doing this sometimes — and have our own job board[197] — but the problem is that sending out your CV and responding to lots of internet job ads has a low success rate.

Richard Bolles — the author of *What Color is Your Parachute?*, the bestselling career advice book of all time — estimates that the chance of landing a job from cold emailing your resume to a company is around 1 in 1,000.[198] That means that (unless your application is much stronger than average) you need to send out 100 resumes just to have a 10% chance of landing a job. We'd guess responding to a job listing on a job board has about a 1% chance of success.

Moreover, the positions on job boards need to be standardised and are mainly at large companies, so they don't include many of the best positions.

The best opportunities are less competitive because they are hidden away, often at small but rapidly growing companies, and personalised to you. You need a different way to find them.

Consider the employer's point of view. Employers prefer to hire people they already know, or failing that, to hire through *referrals* — an introduction from someone they know.

Which would you prefer: a recommendation from someone you trust, or 20 CVs from people who saw your job listing on indeed.com? The referral is more likely to work, because the person has already been vouched for. It's less effort — screening 20 people you know nothing about is hard. Referrals also come from a better pool of applicants — the most employable people already have lots of offers, so they rarely respond to job listings.

For these reasons, many recruiters consider referrals to be the best method of finding candidates.[199]

But job seekers usually get things backwards — they start with the methods that recruiters *least* like.

Many if not most employers hunt for job-seekers in the exact opposite way from how most job-seekers hunt for them.

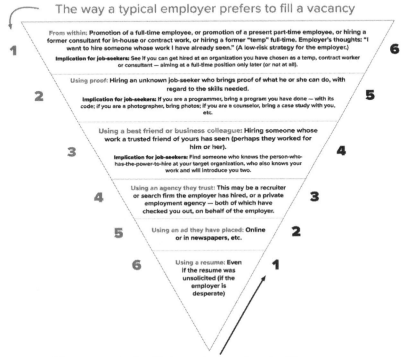

The way a typical employer prefers to fill a vacancy

1 — **From within:** Promotion of a full-time employee, or promotion of a present part-time employee, or hiring a former consultant for in-house or contract work, or hiring a former "temp" full-time. Employer's thoughts: "I want to hire someone whose work I have already seen." (A low-risk strategy for the employer.) — **6**

Implication for job-seekers: See if you can get hired at an organization you have chosen as a temp, contract worker or consultant — aiming at a full-time position only later (or not at all).

2 — **Using proof:** Hiring an unknown job-seeker who brings proof of what he or she can do, with regard to the skills needed. — **5**

Implication for job-seekers: If you are a programmer, bring a program you have done — with its code; if you are a photographer, bring photos; if you are a counselor, bring a case study with you, etc.

3 — **Using a best friend or business colleague:** Hiring someone whose work a trusted friend of yours has seen (perhaps they worked for him or her). — **4**

Implication for job-seekers: Find someone who knows the person-who-has-the-power-to-hire at your target organization, who also knows your work and will introduce you two.

4 — **Using an agency they trust:** This may be a recruiter or search firm the employer has hired, or a private employment agency — both of which have checked you out, on behalf of the employer. — **3**

5 — **Using an ad they have placed:** Online or in newspapers, etc. — **2**

6 — **Using a resume:** Even if the resume was unsolicited (if the employer is desperate) — **1**

The way a typical job-seeker prefers to fill a vacancy

SOURCE: "What Color Is Your Parachute?" (2015 edition)

Applicants find around 50% of jobs through connections,[200] and many are never advertised. So if you don't pursue referrals, you'll miss many opportunities.

Moreover, speaking to people in the industry is the best way to get information about how to present yourself and how to approach opportunities. It's also among the best ways to assess your fit, helping *you* to focus on the best opportunities.

How to get referrals

You need to master the art of asking for introductions. We've put together a list of email scripts you can use:

80000hours.org/articles/email-scripts/

To get referrals, here's a step-by-step process. If you're not applying for a job right now, skip this section until you are.

1. First, update your LinkedIn profile (or personal website, etc.). This isn't because you'll get great job offers through LinkedIn — that's pretty rare — it's because people who are considering meeting you will check out your profile. Focus your profile on your most impressive accomplishments. Be as concrete as possible — e.g. "ranked third in the nation," "increased annual donations 100%." Cut the rest. It's better to have two impressive achievements than two impressive achievements and three weak ones. Add links to any portfolio projects relevant to the job.

2. Search yourself on Google and do anything you can to make the results look good (e.g. delete embarrassing old blog posts). Take a look at the extra resources for this chapter in appendix 7 for a guide.

3. If you already know someone in the industry who can hire people, then ask for a meeting to discuss opportunities in the industry. This is close to going directly to an interview, skipping all the screening steps. Plus, you'll be able to ask them really useful information about how to best apply, and learn more about which positions might be your best fit. Remember, there doesn't need to be an open position — employers will often create positions for good people. Before you take the meeting, use the advice on how to prepare for interviews below.

4. If you know them less well, ask for a meeting to find out more about jobs in the industry: *an "informational interview"*. If it goes

well, ask them to introduce you to people who may be able to hire you, which is effectively getting a referral from this person. *Do not ask them* for a job if you promised it was an informational interview.

5. When asking for introductions, *prepare a one-sentence, specific description of the types of opportunities you'd like to find.* A good example is something like: "an entry-level marketing position at a technology startup in education." Two bad examples are: "a job in software" or "a job that fits my skills." Being concrete makes it easier for people to come up with ideas, so lean towards too narrow rather than too broad.

6. Failing the above steps, *turn to the connections of your connections.* If you have a good friend who knows someone who's able to hire you, then you could directly ask that friend for a referral. The ideal is to ask someone you've worked for before where you performed really well.

7. If your connection is not able to refer you, then ask them to introduce you to people in the industry who *are* able to hire. Then we're back to informational interviews as in step 2.

8. To find out who your connections know, use LinkedIn, Twitter, or other social networks. Say you want to work at Airbnb. Go to LinkedIn and search "Airbnb." It'll show a list of all your contacts who work at Airbnb, followed by connections of connections who work at Airbnb. Pick the person with the most mutual connections and get in touch.

9. Remember, if you have 200 LinkedIn connections, and each of them has 200 connections that don't overlap with the others, then you can reach at least 10,000 people using these methods.

10. There are lots of people in the 80,000 Hours LinkedIn group (linkedin.com/groups/5057625) who are happy to give advice on applications, and may be able to make introductions.

11. If you still haven't got anywhere, then it may be worth spending

some time building your connections in the industry first. Read our advice on how to network in appendix 2. Go back to our advice in the last chapter on how to network. Start with people with whom you have some connection, such as your university alumni, and friends of friends of friends (third-order connections). Your university can probably give you a list of alumni who are willing to help in each industry. There are probably some good groups you can join and conferences to attend. Otherwise you can resort to cold emailing. (Take a look at the extra resources for this chapter in appendix 7 for guides to getting jobs with no connections, and to finding anyone's email address.)

Recruiters and listings

We prefer the above tactics, but recruiters can be worth talking to, and are often more effective than just making cold applications. Look for those who have a good network in the industry you're interested in.

You can also browse job listings, which does sometimes work, and is also a useful way to get ideas. In particular, check out our job board,[201] which lists the best jobs we can find to put you in a better position to tackle the world's most pressing problems.

STAGE 2: CONVERSION

When you're speaking to someone who has the power to hire you, how do you convince them?

Again, think about it from their point of view. Once at 80,000 Hours, we were trying to hire a web engineer. Most applicants just filled out our application form, while one sent us a redesigned version of our old career quiz. Which application is more convincing? The person who sent the quiz was immediately in the top 20% of applicants, despite having very little formal experience.

Employers are looking for several qualities. They want employees who will fit in socially, stick around, and not cause trouble. But most importantly, the employer wants to be sure that you can solve the problems they face. If you can prove that you'll get the results the employer most values, everything else is much less important.

So how can you go about doing that?

When the process is highly standardised

In these cases, like Teach for America or many government jobs, you have to jump through the hoops. Maximise your chances by finding out exactly what the process involves, and practising exactly that. For instance, if it's a competency interview,[202] find out which competencies they look for, then have a friend ask you similar questions. Some public service organisations publish the rubrics they use to assess candidates.

The most useful thing you can do is find someone who recently went through the process, ask them how it works, and, if possible, practise the key steps with them. Sometimes there are books written about exactly how to apply.

Most employers, however, don't have a fully standardised process. What do you do in those cases?

If you've already done the same work before, then you just need to practise telling your story. Skip ahead to the interview tips. But what if you don't have much relevant experience?

The basic idea is: *just do the work.*

Just do the work

The most powerful way to prove you can do the work is to actually do some of it. And as we saw, doing the work is also a great way to figure out whether you're good at it, so it'll help you avoid wasting your own time too.

Here are four ways to put that into practice.

Do a portfolio project

For example, if you want to become a writer or a journalist, try to keep a blog or Twitter feed about a relevant topic. If you want to become a software engineer, put projects on your GitHub.

Include these projects on your personal web page and/or LinkedIn profile. Mention them in your applications or during interviews.

The pre-interview project

The pre-interview project is what the web engineer did with our career quiz. To do your own project:

1. Find out what you'd be doing in the role (this already puts you quite a way ahead).
2. In particular, work out which problems you will need to solve for the organisation. To figure this out, you'll probably need to do some desk research, then speak to people in the industry. (There's a link to a simple guide on how to research a company in the resources for this chapter in appendix 7.)
3. Spend a weekend putting together a solution to these problems, and send a 1 page summary to a couple of people at the company with an invitation to talk more.
4. If you don't hear back after a week, follow up at least once.

5. Alternatively, write up your suggestions, and present them at the interview. Ramit Sethi calls this "the briefcase technique."[203]

Speaking from personal experience, we've overseen four years' worth of competitive application processes at 80,000 Hours, and doing either of these projects would immediately put you in the top 20% of applicants (if your suggestions made sense). It demonstrates a lot of enthusiasm, and most people hardly know anything about the role they are applying for.

Trial period

If the employer is on the fence, you can offer to do a two- to four-week trial period, perhaps at reduced pay or as an intern. Make it clear that if the employer isn't happy at the end, you'll leave gracefully.

Only bring this out if the employer is on the fence, or it can seem like you're underselling yourself.

Go for a nearby position

If you can't get the job you want right away, consider applying for another position in the organisation — like a freelance position, or a position one step below the one you really want.

Working in a nearby position gives you the opportunity to prove your motivation and cultural fit. When your boss has a position to fill, it's much easier to promote someone they already worked with than to start a lengthy application process.

Just check that the position *can* actually lead to the one you want. For example, we often see people apply to operations positions at research organisations with the hope of later becoming a researcher. The paths require very different skillsets, so are treated as separate tracks, but lots of people would prefer to do research. This means that while it does sometimes work out, it's rare, and can be frustrating for both sides.

How to prepare for interviews

If you can *show* an employer you can solve their problems, you're most of the way there, and you probably don't need to *ace* the interview. However, there's more you can do to become even more convincing.

Here's some of the best advice we've found on preparing for interviews. It's also useful for getting leads while networking. **If you're not actively looking for a job right now, skip this section for now.**

1. **When you meet an employer, ask lots of questions to understand their challenges**. Discuss how you might be able to contribute to solving these challenges. This is exactly what great salespeople do. A survey of research on sales concluded "there is a clear statistical association between the use of questions and the success of the interaction." Moreover, when salespeople were trained to ask more questions, it made them more effective.[204]

2. **Prepare your three key selling points ahead of meetings.** These are the messages you'll try to get in during the discussion. For instance: 1) I have done this work successfully before, 2) I am really excited about this company, and 3) I have suggestions for what I could work on. Writing these out ahead of time makes it more likely you'll mention what's most important, and three points is about the limit of what your audience will remember. That's why this is standard advice when pitching a business idea. If you're not sure what you have to offer, look back at the exercise at the end of chapter 7.

3. **Focus on what's most impressive.** What sounds better: "I advised Obama on energy policy" or "I advised Obama on energy policy, and have worked as a high school teacher the last three years"?

Many people fill up their CVs with everything they've done, but it's usually better to pick your one or two most impressive achievements and focus on those. It sounds better, it makes it more likely you'll cover it, and it makes it more likely that your audience will remember it.

4. **Prepare 1–2 concrete facts and stories to back up your three key messages.** For instance, if you're applying to be a web engineer, rather than "I'm a hard worker," try "I have a friend who runs an organisation that was about to get some press coverage. He needed to build a website in 24 hours, so we pulled an all-nighter to build it. The next day we got 1,000 signups." Rather than say "I really want to work in this industry," tell the story of what led you to apply. Stories and concrete details are far more memorable than abstract claims.[205]

5. **Work out how to sum up what you have to offer in a sentence.** Steve Jobs didn't sell millions of iPods by saying they're 30% better than mp3 players, but rather with the slogan "1,000 songs in your pocket." Having a short, vivid summary makes it easy for other people to promote you on your behalf. For instance something like "He's the guy who advised Obama on climate policy and wants a research position" is ideal.

6. **Prepare answers to the most likely questions.** Write them out, then practise saying them out loud. The following three questions normally come up: (1) Tell me about yourself — this is an opportunity to tell the story of why you want this position and mention one or two achievements, (2) Why do you want this position? and (3) What are your questions for us? Then usually the interviewer will add some behavioural questions about the traits they care most about. These usually start "Tell me about a time you…" then are finished with things like: "exhibited leadership." "had to work as a team," "had to deal with a difficult situation or

person," "failed," or "succeeded."

7. **Practise the meeting, from start to finish.** Meet with a friend and have them ask you five interview questions, then practice responding quickly. If you don't have a friend to help, then say your answers out loud and mentally rehearse how you want it to go. Ask yourself what's most likely to go wrong, and what you'll do if that happens.

8. **Learn.** After each interview, jot down what went well, what could have gone better, and what you'll do differently next time.

Improve and adapt your process

Applying to jobs is a difficult skill that takes time to learn.

After every interview or other important interaction with an employer, jot down what went well, what could have gone better, and what you'll do differently next time.

If you've done 5–10 interviews and didn't make it through to the next stage, then it's time to do a more thorough reassessment. You might be making a mistake in how you present yourself. Ask someone in the area (ideally someone with hiring experience) to check over your materials, and do a mock interview with them (or explain what happened in the interviews).

Similarly, if you've made 20+ applications and haven't been invited to any interviews, ask someone in the area to review your application materials.

If you can't find a mistake, then you might be applying to jobs that aren't a good fit, and should consider a different area or position.

If you've done 10 interviews and have made it through to the later stages a couple of times, but haven't yet had any offers, then keep going. Often 3–10 people make it through to the final stages, so you'll probably have to do at least five final-stage interviews before you get an offer.

On the other hand, if you're getting offers relatively easily, then apply to more stretch positions.

STAGE 3: NEGOTIATION

Negotiation begins after you have an offer, once the employer has said they'd like to hire you.

Most people are so happy to get a job, or awkward about the idea of negotiating, that they never try. But 10 minutes of negotiation could mean major benefits over the next couple of years. So the key message here is to *actually consider doing it.*

For instance, you could ask the employer to match your donations to charity. That could mean thousands of dollars of extra donations per year, making those 10 minutes you took to negotiate among the most productive of your life.

You could also negotiate to work on a certain team, have more flexible hours, work remotely, or learn certain skills. All of these could make a big difference to your day-to-day happiness and career capital, and are often easier to ask for than additional salary.

Negotiation is not *always* appropriate. Don't do it if you've landed a highly standardised offer, like many government positions — they won't be able to change the contract. Also don't do it if you're only narrowly better than the other candidates or have no alternatives. And definitely don't negotiate until the employer has made an offer — it looks bad to start negotiating during the interview.

However, we think negotiation should be tried in most cases once you have an offer. Hiring someone takes months and consumes lots of management time. Once an employer has made an offer, they've invested many thousands of dollars in the process. The top candidate is often significantly better than the next best. This means it's unlikely that they'll let the top candidate get away for, say, a 5% increase in costs.

It's even more unlikely that they'll retract their initial offer because you tried to negotiate. Stay polite, and the worst case is likely that they'll stick to their original offer.

Negotiation should be most strongly considered when you have more than one good offer, because then you have a strong fallback position.

How to negotiate

The basic idea is simple: explain the value you'll give the employer, and why it's justified to give you the benefits you want. Then look for objective metrics and win-win solutions — can you give up something the employer cares about in exchange for something you care about? For instance:

- Other people with my level of experience in this industry are usually paid $50,000 and can work at home two days per week. But I'd prefer to work with you. Can you match the other companies?
- I'm really motivated to learn sales skills, so I'd like to work alongside person X. This will make me much more effective in the role in six months.

If your position is weaker, you could negotiate about a future promotion or salary increase:

- I'd like to work towards this [insert position name]. What would I need to do in the next six months to make that happen?

Then ask them to commit to it if you hit their conditions.

Negotiate after you've started

Once you start the job, try to perform as well as possible, and then negotiate again. Most employers will be very unwilling to lose someone who's already doing excellent work.

Just bear in mind, most companies have a standard performance review process, so wait until then to make your request.

Lots has been written about salary negotiation, so this hardly scratches the surface. Appendix 7 contains a list of resources to learn more.

Have a plan to stay motivated

Your first job search may be one of the hardest things you've ever done — you've probably never been rejected 30 times in a row before. It can involve months of work. And you may have to do most of it alone. It can make online dating look easy.

This means that you'll need to throw every motivational technique you know at the job hunt. Here are some tips:

1. Perhaps the most useful single tip our readers have found is pairing up with someone else who's also job hunting. Check in on progress, and share tips and leads. Alternatively, find someone who was recently successful at a similar hunt and is willing to meet up and give you tips.

2. Set a really specific goal — like speaking to five people each week until you have an offer — publicly commit to the goal, and promise to make a forfeit if you miss it.

3. Make it easier to face rejections. Maybe make yourself a loyalty card that you stamp every time you get a rejection, and reward yourself with an ice cream once the card is filled up!

4. Treat it like a job. You're most likely going to be doing the job for years at 40 hours per week, so it makes sense it might take 5%+ of that time to secure the position, and that's already 1–2 months of full-time work. The more time you can put into it, the better the results are probably going to be. And if you're not in a job right now, treating your job search as a job itself can help a lot with motivation. Turn up at 9am, and work till 5pm.

5. Apply other tips on how to motivate yourself. For example, check out the book *The Motivation Hacker* by Nick Winter,[206] and the advice on productivity in appendix 2.

Never job hunt again

Your job hunts will get easier and easier as you build career capital.

The most important thing you can do to put yourself in a better position is to gain more connections, so you can get better referrals. We have tips on that in the next chapter.

Once you're in a job, focus on developing strong skills and excel in your work. The best marketing is word of mouth — employers seeking you out rather than the other way around. If you're great at your job, then people will actively want to refer you to employers, because it's doing them a favour as well as you.

Conclusion

Getting a job can be an unpleasant process, but if you go through the steps in this chapter, you'll give yourself the best chance of success. And that will make sure you fulfil your potential to find a satisfying career and contribute to the world.

APPLY THIS TO YOUR OWN CAREER

What are the most important three steps to take in order to get into *your* top options?

Try to be as specific as possible. Some good examples:

- Follow up with my boss at my last internship.
- Write 10 applications.
- Meet three people in the industry.
- Find someone to job hunt with.

The key steps probably involve speaking to people.

When are you going to do each of these? Many studies have shown that writing down *when* you'll do a task makes it much more likely you'll actually do it — it's called an "implementation intention."[207]

THE BOTTOM LINE:
HOW TO FIND A JOB

- Getting a job is a sales process. Think of it from the employer's point of view, and do what the employer will find most convincing.
- Get lots of leads, especially by asking for introductions.
- Prove you can do the work by actually doing it. Do a project before the interview, explain exactly how you can solve their problems, or seek a related position first.
- Once you get an offer, actually negotiate.
- Do whatever it takes to keep yourself motivated, such as make a public commitment to apply for one position per day, or find a job-search partner.

CHAPTER 11
One of the most powerful ways to improve your career — join a community.

Not many students are in a position to start a successful, cost-effective charity straight out of a philosophy degree. But when Thomas attended an "effective altruism" conference in London in 2018, he discovered an opportunity to start a nonprofit that could have a major impact on factory farmed animals.

Through the community, he received advice and funding, and ended up in an incubation programme. Today, Thomas's charity, the Fish Welfare Initiative, has reduced the suffering of around one million factory farmed fish, and has an annual budget of over half a million dollars.[208]

If Thomas had just added loads of people on LinkedIn, this would have probably never happened. And this illustrates what many people miss about networking: the value of joining a great community.

Finding the right community can help you gain hundreds of potential allies in one go.

In fact, getting involved in the right community can be one of the best ways to make friends, advance your career, and have a greater impact. Many people we advise say that "finding their people" was one of the most important steps in their career, and life in general.

What's more, a group of people working together can have more impact than they could individually.

In this chapter, we'll explain how joining a community can help, and how to get involved.

Why joining a community is so helpful

There are lots of great communities out there. We've enjoyed being part of Y Combinator's entrepreneur community — it made us more ambitious and more effective at running a startup... hopefully. We've also enjoyed participating in the Oxford philosophy 'scene,' the World Economic Forum's Young Global Shapers, and many others.

Joining any good professional community can be a great boost to your career. In part, this is because you'll get all the benefits of having more connections: finding jobs, gaining up-to-date information, and becoming more motivated.[209] But it goes beyond that.

Let's suppose I want to build and sell a piece of software. One approach would be to learn all the skills needed myself — design, engineering, marketing, and so on.

A much better approach is to form a team of people who are skilled in each area, and then build it together. Although I'll have to share the gains with the other people, the size of the gains will be much larger, so we'll all win.

One thing that's going on here is specialisation: each person can focus on a specific skill, and get really good at it, which lets them be more effective.

Another factor is that the team can also share fixed costs — they can share the same company registration, operational procedures, and so on. It's also not three times harder to raise three times as much money from investors. This lets them achieve economies of scale.

In sum, we get what's called the "gains from trade." Three people working together can achieve more than three times as much as an individual working alone.

It's the same when doing good. Rather than have everyone try to do everything, it's more effective for people to specialise and work together.

An especially good thing about trade is that you can do it with people who *don't* share your goals. Suppose you run an animal rights charity and meet someone who runs a global health charity. Now also suppose you don't think global health is a pressing problem, and the other person doesn't think animal rights is a pressing problem, so neither of you think the other's charity has much impact. But maybe you know a donor who might give to their charity, and they know a donor who might give to your charity. You can trade: if you both make introductions, which is a small cost, you might both find a new donor, which is a big benefit.

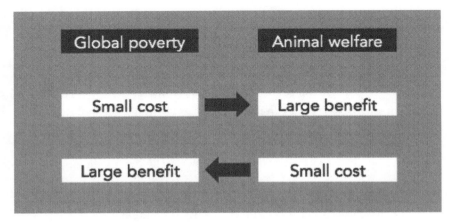

This shows it can be valuable to join a community even if the people in it have different aims from your own.

That said, it's far better again to join a community of people who *do* share your goals. Which brings us to...

Finding the right community for you

The people you spend the most time with have a big effect on what feels normal. If you spend time around generous people, you'll see generosity as the norm. If you're around people who regularly bend the truth, you're likely to become less honest, because it'll feel ubiquitous and acceptable.

So, choose your communities carefully.

Every community has a unique culture, so we recommend trying out several and seeing which are best for you.

And it's healthy to spend time in several communities, so your sense of your identity and connections aren't too dependent on one group or set of ideas, which can make the views of the group hard to question and have an 'echo chamber' effect.

As an exercise, make a list of several communities you might join, meet a variety of people and attend events within each one, and then get more involved in those (ideally more than one) that you think are most supportive for you at this time.

By "community," we mean something very broad. It could be anything from a casual group of friends who are interested in the same thing, to larger movements, like animal welfare, with conferences and websites.

So when thinking about the communities you'd like to join, don't only think about formal organisations. Rather, think about the types of people you'd most like to be around, and then think how you might achieve that. This could even involve setting up your own small "community," by getting together a group of friends, starting a reading group or Slack, and so on.

Here are some categories to help you generate ideas:

- If you're interested in working on a specific global problem, such as biosecurity or factory farming, there is probably at least one community (or several) in that field.
- If you're focused on a particular way of doing good — such as research, writing, journalism, or entrepreneurship — there are probably communities around that.
- There are relevant political and ideological communities dedicated to broad ways of doing good, such as social entrepreneurship, progress studies, animal welfare, socialism, libertarianism, and social justice.
- Many of our readers also join communities that aren't directly about doing good, but are supportive for personal development — e.g. nonviolent communication, rationality, and religious communities that promote important virtues.

Finally, there's the effective altruism community, which we count ourselves as a part of.

How can the effective altruism community boost your career?

Effective altruism is the project of finding better ways to have a positive impact — for example, by looking for issues that are big in scale, highly neglected, and tractable.

It's both a *research field* that aims to identify the world's most pressing problems and the best solutions to them, and a *practical community* that aims to use those findings to do good. We helped to start the community back in 2011, along with several other groups.

Applying effective altruism means aspiring to apply four key values:

- Doing more to prioritise more effective ways of helping others.
- Striving to treat others more equally.
- Trying harder to question our beliefs.
- Working cooperatively with high integrity.

Anyone who shares these values and is trying to find better ways to help others is participating in the project of effective altruism, and has good reason to get involved in the community.

In fact, we know people who have been involved with Harvard Business School, the Fulbright Scholarship, the World Economic Forum, and other prestigious networks — but many of them say they find it more useful to meet people in the effective altruism community. Why?

One reason is that this community has a lot of amazing people (such as many of the people we interview on our podcast).

Another reason is that (as we've argued) you can increase your impact by working on issues and solutions that are more neglected — but if you're working on something neglected, then (by definition) you won't find many others who want to work on these issues in most conventional networks.

Likewise, we'd argue it's important to focus much more on comparing different options in terms of impact than is standard.

The effective altruism community is useful because you can find lots of people working on these neglected issues and applying these norms gathered in one place.

Behind this is an even more fundamental reason: the power of shared aims. You can work with people who don't share your values because you can still trade with them — but if you *share* aims with someone else, then you don't even need to trade.

In the effective altruism community, people share a common goal: to help others more effectively. So, if you help someone else to have a greater impact, then you increase your own impact too. You both succeed.

This means you don't need to worry as much about getting favours back to break even. Just helping someone else is already impactful. This unleashes far more opportunities to work together than would be possible in a community where people don't share one another's aims as much. And because there are so many ways we can help each other, this makes it possible to achieve far more.[210]

Earning to give can actually be an example of that kind of collaboration. In the early days of 80,000 Hours, I (Benjamin) and my friend Matt had to choose between running the organisation and earning to give. We realised that Matt had higher earning potential, and I would be better at running the organisation. In part, this is why I became the CEO, and Matt became our first major donor, as well as a seed funder for several other organisations.

The alternative would have been for both of us to earn to give, in which case, 80,000 Hours wouldn't have existed. Or, both of us could have worked at 80,000 Hours, in which case it would have taken much longer to fundraise (plus the other organisations Matt donated to wouldn't have gotten those donations).

Within the community as a whole, some people are relatively better suited to earning money, and others to running nonprofits. We can achieve more if the people best suited to earning money earn to give and fund everyone else.

There are lots of other examples of how we can work together. For instance, some people can go and explore new areas and share the information with everyone else, allowing everyone to be more effective in the long term. Or people can specialise rather than needing to be generalists.

For instance, Dr Greg Lewis did the research into how many lives a doctor saves that we saw earlier. After realising it was fewer than he thought, he decided not to focus on clinical medicine. Instead, he's studied public health with the aim of becoming an expert on the topic within the community, particularly on issues relevant to pandemics. He actually thinks risks from artificial intelligence might be more urgent overall, but as a doctor, he's relatively best placed to work on health-related issues.

For all these reasons, if you share the aims of the effective altruism community, it can be a powerful community to join.

But we'd be remiss if we didn't mention some of the downsides here too.

Effective altruism is still an unusual idea, and that means it attracts some unusual people. Even if you agree with its values, you might find you don't gel with the people who have joined in practice.

Some find being part of the effective altruism community stressful — because of the focus on driving up positive impact, it can feel "totalising" to people. Others don't like how tight-knit it is, or other aspects of the culture.

Try out getting involved (ideally with more than one group), and then reduce your involvement if it's not supportive (while keeping a foot in some other communities to make this easier).

Effective altruism has also faced its fair share of controversy — especially since the collapse of FTX, which has many questioning the community's organisations, culture, and even underlying ethos.[211]

You can see some of the most common critiques of effective altruism over its history on its Wikipedia page and on the FAQ at effectivealtruism.org.

All that said, if you liked this guide, then you'll probably share aims with lots of people in the community, and get a lot out of it. We certainly have. If you want to try getting involved, check out the resources in appendix 7.

Other communities you may want to consider joining

There are many other great communities that can help you have more impact or be more successful. What matters is that you find people you can learn from and work with.

We know less about these communities, but we've got a few ideas about where to start.

First, we'd generally recommend getting involved in some communities especially focused on the global problems you're most interested in.

For instance, if you want to work on reducing the existential risks posed by the development of AI, you could consider getting involved with the AI alignment community.

If you're focused on factory farming, we'd recommend getting involved in the animal welfare community; if biorisk, the biosecurity community; if global health, the international development community (especially those focused on more evidence-based approaches like the 'randomistas'); if nuclear war or great power conflict, then part of the international relations community.

Lots of academic fields have associated communities — if you're starting out a career in academia, or are currently in college or grad school, talk to your professors to find out the best conferences to go to. These are usually worth getting involved in.

Finally, there's been some overlap between effective altruism and the rationality community, and many of our readers have found benefits in both. The online hub of the rationality community is LessWrong.[212]

Next up, let's wrap up our entire career guide.

The end
A cheery final note – imagining your deathbed

We're about to summarise the whole guide in one minute. But before that, imagine a cheery thought: you're at the end of your 80,000-hour career.

You're on your deathbed looking back.

What are some things you might regret?

Perhaps you drifted into whatever seemed like the easiest option, or did what your parents did.

Maybe you even made a lot of money doing something you were interested in, and had a nice house and car. But you still wonder: what was it all for?

Now imagine instead that you worked really hard throughout your life, and ended up saving the lives of 100 children. Can you really imagine regretting that?

To have a truly fulfilling life, we need to turn outwards rather than inwards. Rather than asking "What's my passion?," ask "How can I best contribute to the world?"

As we've seen, by using our fortunate positions and acting strategically, there's a huge amount we can all do to help others. And we can do this at little cost to ourselves, and most likely while having a more successful and satisfying career too.

The entire guide, in one minute

To have a good career, do what contributes. Rather than expect to discover your passion in a flash of insight, your fulfilment will grow over time as you learn more about what fits, master valuable skills, and use them to help others.

To do what contributes, build useful skills and apply them to meaningful problems. Here's the three key stages to focus on over time:

1. **Explore** and investigate your *key uncertainties* to find the best options, rather than "going with your gut" or narrowing down too early. Make this your key focus until you have enough confidence in some longer-term options to bet on one.
2. **Build career capital** to become as great as you can be. This means looking for jobs that let you generally improve your skills, reputation, connections, and character, and that most accelerate you towards your vision, as well as investing in your personal development. Do this until you've taken the best opportunities to invest in yourself. Then, use your career capital to...
3. **Deploy.** Use your career capital to effectively help others. Do this by focusing on the *most urgent social problems* rather than those you stumble into — those that are big in scale, neglected, and solvable.

To make the largest contribution to solving those problems, *think broadly*: consider earning to give, research, communications, community building, organisation building, and government and policy careers, as well as the direct helping careers that first come to mind. And focus on the paths that have the best personal fit. Although many efforts to help others fail, the best can be enormously effective, so be ambitious. But don't forget you can have a big impact in any job.

While doing the above, **keep adapting your plan to find the best**

personal fit. Think like a scientist testing a hypothesis: make your best guess, clarify your key uncertainties, then investigate those uncertainties. Have some ideas about the best longer-term vision, but then put a lot of attention into finding the best next step (both working backwards and forwards). Eliminate any jobs that do significant direct harm, even if it seems like they might let you have a greater impact. If you keep learning more and improving your skills with each step, you can build a better and better career over time. Seek community to be more successful.

By working together, in our lifetimes, we can prevent the next pandemic and mitigate the risks of AI, we can end extreme global poverty and factory farming, and we can do this while having interesting, fulfilling lives too. So let's do it.

You have 80,000 hours in your career.

Don't waste them.

What now?

If you still need to make a career plan, try out our planning template:
https://80k.link/NCP

If you've found this guide useful, and know someone else in the midst of planning their career, we've created a simple tool to give them a free copy:
80000hours.org/gift

The rest of this book

As you may have noticed, you're not at the end quite yet. In the rest of the book, we include:

- Some additional articles that further explore our key ideas.
- Summaries of our career reviews.
- Summaries of our top problem area profiles.

If you'd like more reading after that (we admire your stamina!), check out our advanced series:

80000hours.org/advanced-series/

Appendix 1 – The meaning of making a difference

Definition

We define "making a difference" or "having a social impact" as follows:

> *"Social impact" or "making a difference" is (tentatively) about promoting total expected wellbeing — considered impartially, over the long term.*

Our definition is tentative — there's a good chance we're wrong and it might change. Its purpose is practical — it aims to cover the most important aspects of doing good to help people make better real-life decisions, rather than capture everything that's morally relevant.

Why did we choose this definition?

Many people disagree about what it means to make the world a better place. But most agree that it's good if people have happier, more fulfilled lives, in which they reach their potential. So, our definition is narrow enough that it captures this idea.

Moreover, as we argue, some careers do far more to improve lives than others, so it captures a really important difference between options. If some paths can do good equivalent to saving hundreds of lives, while others have little impact at all, that's an important difference.

The definition is also broad enough to cover many different ways to make the world a better place. It's even broad enough to cover environmental protection, since if we let the environment degrade, the future of civilisation might be threatened. In that way, protecting the environment improves lives.

Importantly, having a broad scope also allows us to include nonhuman animals, as well as potential future sentient beings that might be entirely digital — which is why we have profiles on factory farming, wild animal welfare, and artificial sentience.[213]

That said, the definition doesn't include everything that might matter. You might think the environment deserves protection even if it doesn't make people better off. Similarly, you might value things like justice and aesthetic beauty for their own sakes.

In practice, our readers value many different things. Our approach is to focus on how to improve lives, and then let people independently take account of what else they value. To make this easier, we try to highlight the main value judgements behind our work. It turns out there's a lot we can say about how to do good in general, despite all these differences.

Why "promoting"?

When people say they want to "make a difference," we think they're primarily talking about making the world better — i.e. 'promoting' good things and preventing bad ones — rather than merely not doing unethical actions (e.g. stealing) or being virtuous in some other way.

Why "wellbeing"?

We understand wellbeing as an inclusive notion, meaning anything that makes people better off. We take this to encompass at least promoting happiness, health, and the ability for people to live the life they want. We chose this as the focus because most people agree these things matter, but there are often large differences in how much different actions improve these outcomes.

Why do we say "expected" wellbeing?

We can never know with certainty the effects that our actions will have on wellbeing. The best we can do is try to weigh the benefits of different actions by their probability — i.e. compare based on 'expected value.' Note that while the action with the highest expected value is best in principle, that doesn't imply that the best way to find the best action is to make explicit quantitative estimates. It's often better in practice to use rules of thumb, our intuition, or other methods, since these maximise expected value better than explicit expected value calculations.[214]

Why "considered impartially"?

We mean that we strive to treat equal effects on different beings' welfare as equally morally important, no matter who they are — including people who live far away or in the future.[215] In addition, we think that the interests of many nonhuman animals, and even potentially sentient future digital beings, should be given significant weight, although we're unsure of the exact amount. Thus, we don't think social impact is limited to promoting the welfare of any particular group we happen to be partial to (such as people who are alive today, or human beings as a species).

Why do we say "over the long term"?

We think that if you take an impartial perspective, then the welfare of those who live in the future matters. Because there could be many more future generations than those alive today, our effects on them could be of great moral importance. We thus try to always consider not just the direct and short-term effects of actions, but also any indirect effects that might occur in the far future.[216]

How can you measure social impact?

We are always uncertain about how much impact different actions will have — but that's OK, because we can use probabilities to make comparisons. For instance, a 90% chance of helping 100 people is roughly equivalent to a 100% chance of helping 90 people. Though we're uncertain, we can quantify our uncertainty and make progress.

Moreover, even in the face of uncertainty, we can use rules of thumb to compare different courses of action. For instance, later in this career guide we argue that, all else equal, it's higher impact to work on neglected areas. So, even if we can't precisely *measure* social impact, we can still be *strategic* by picking neglected areas. We cover many more rules of thumb for increasing your impact across this guide.

Is social impact all that matters?

No.

We don't know the ultimate truths of moral philosophy, but in the real world we think it's really important not to **only** focus on impact.

In particular, it's normally better — even from the perspective of social impact — to always act with good character, respect the rights and values of others, and to pay attention to your other personal values.

We don't endorse doing something that seems very wrong from a common-sense perspective, even if it seems like it might let you have a greater impact — read more about this in appendix 5.

Further reading

For more, read our in-depth article
at 80000hours.org/articles/what-is-social-impact-definition/.

Appendix 2 – All the evidence-based advice we found on how to be more successful in any job

The trouble with self-help advice is that it's often based on barely any evidence.

For example, how many times have you been told to "think positively" in order to reach your goals? It's probably *the* most popular piece of personal guidance, beloved by everyone from high school teachers to bestselling careers experts. One key idea behind the slogan is that if you visualise your ideal future, you're more likely to get there.

The problem? Recent research found evidence that fantasising about your perfect life actually makes you *less* likely to make it happen. While it can be pleasant, it appears to reduce motivation because it makes you feel that you've already hit those targets.[217] We'll cover some ways positive thinking *can* be helpful later in the appendix.

Much other advice is just one person's opinion, or useless clichés. But at 80,000 Hours, we've found that there are a number of evidence-backed steps that anyone can take to become more productive and successful in their career, and life in general. And as we saw in chapter 7, people can keep improving their skills for decades.

So we've gathered up all the best advice we've found over our last 10+ years of research. These are things that anyone can do in any job to increase their career capital, personal fit — and, therefore, their positive impact.

In many cases, the evidence isn't as strong as we'd like. Rather, it's the best we're aware of. We've tried to come to an all-considered view of what makes sense to try, given (i) the strength of the empirical evidence, (ii) whether it seems reasonable to us, (iii) the size of the potential upside, (iv) how widely applicable the advice is, and (v) the costs of trying. The details are given in the further reading we link to and the footnotes.

We've put the advice roughly in order: the first items are easier, more widely applicable, and do better on the factors listed above, so start with them, then move on to the more difficult areas later.

Much of what follows is about building new habits — regular behaviours and routines that become almost automatic. So if you get better at building habits, everything else will be faster.

And there's research on how to do exactly that. *Atomic Habits* is a bestselling book that turns the basic behavioural science on forming habits into a very practical guide.[218] If you'd prefer a more academic vibe, take a look at BJ Fogg's *Tiny Habits*.[219]

It takes about 30 days to ingrain a new habit. That's hard enough without starting five at once! So, skim through the list below, pick *one* area that you think might make the most difference to your life with the least effort, and pick *one* habit or exercise from there to start.

Typically you might focus on an area for 3–12 months, using each month to build one habit or do one exercise.

As you gain momentum, you can take on bigger challenges.

Throughout this appendix, we're going to hit you with a lot of further reading and other resources. We'll include the most relevant URLs in the text so you can really easily access anything that catches your interest. As always, to find out more, check out the endnotes and bibliography.

1. Don't forget to take care of yourself

Before we go onto more complex advice, a reminder: ambitious people often don't take care of themselves. This can make them burn out and ultimately be less successful.

In fact, even if you *only* care about helping others, it's important to look after yourself. Professor Adam Grant did research that suggested that altruists who also looked out for their own interests were more productive in the long term, and so ultimately did more to help.[220]

To look after yourself, the most important thing is to focus on the basics: getting enough sleep, exercising, eating well, and maintaining your closest friendships.

This is common sense, and research seems to back it up. These factors can have a big impact on your day-to-day happiness, not to mention your health and energy.[221] In fact, as we've seen, they probably matter much more than other factors people tend to focus on, like income.

So, if there's anything you can do to significantly improve one of these areas, it's worth taking care of it first. A lot has been written about how to improve them. Sometimes there are small technical tricks (e.g. some people find they sleep far better if they wear an eyemask), but it often comes down to building better habits (e.g. scheduling a weekly call with your best friend).

Here are some quick tips and places to learn more:

- The best guide we've found on how to get better sleep is by Lynette Bye, which aims to summarise all the research.[222]
- Within exercise, try to at least hit the guidelines set out by the UK's National Health Service at 80k.info/NHS-exercise. If you want to optimise further, I listed some of my favourite resources at 80k.info/HUB.
- Within diet, the main point of agreement is to avoid processed foods, and to eat lots of plants. Beyond that, experiment with what makes you feel best (e.g. I found I gained a lot of energy from having only coffee and no food in the morning, but others find the opposite).
- Perhaps the biggest thing you can do to maintain close friendships is to schedule regular time for them. We have more advice on this later in the article.
- A list of life hacks by Alex Vermeer (alexvermeer.com/life-hacking).
- The *Huberman Lab* podcast (hubermanlab.com) is by a Stanford professor, and tries to summarise the scientific research on topics like getting better sleep, exercise, diet, and energy management.

2. If helpful, make mental health your top priority

About 30% of people in their 20s have some kind of mental health problem.[223]

If you're suffering from a mental health issue — be it anxiety, bipolar disorder, ADHD, depression, or something else — then it's often best to prioritise dealing with it or learning to cope better. It's one of the best investments you can ever make — both for your own sake and your ability to help others.

We know many people who took the time to make mental health their top priority and who, having found treatments and techniques that worked, have gone on to perform at the highest level.

Many of our staff have also made taking care of their mental health a major priority, including our CEO, who spoke about it on our podcast.[224]

If you're unsure whether you have a mental health issue, it's well worth investigating. We've also known people who have gone undiagnosed for decades, and then found their life was far better after diagnosis and treatment.

And don't get hung up on whether you satisfy the criteria for a formal diagnosis. Many mental health conditions appear to lie on a spectrum (e.g. from good mood to 'normal' unhappiness to depression), and the point at which a formal diagnosis is made is ultimately arbitrary. What matters is not the label that's applied, but whether you can find helpful ways to feel better.

Mental health is not our area of expertise, and we can't offer medical advice. We'd recommend seeing a doctor as your first step. If you're at university, there should be free services available.

This said, we've collected some of the resources we've personally found most helpful for you to explore.

Probably the most evidence-based form of therapy is cognitive behavioural therapy (CBT), and has been found to help with many different conditions.

Moreover, managing your emotions is just a vital life skill for everyone, and CBT is one of the main evidence-based ways of getting better at that.

- On our podcast, we interviewed a CBT therapist, Tim LeBon, about what CBT involves and why it might be useful to our readers (80k.info/tim-lebon).
- A classic book is *Feeling Good* by David Burns — reading the book has even been tested in randomised controlled trials and found to reduce the symptoms of depression.[225]
- Spencer Greenberg (who has also been on our podcast — 80k.info/SG-podcast) developed an online CBT app that we like (uplift.app).
- We've also written up a list of simple CBT-inspired questions you can ask yourself whenever something bad happens in your life — from struggling to find your keys to being in a car accident — and which will probably help you feel better and move on more quickly (80000hours.org/2018/12/dealing-with-setbacks).
- See the STOPP process for a quick CBT-based technique you can use to work with any difficult emotion (anjclearview.co.uk/stopp).

You could also explore other therapies broadly in the CBT tradition, such as dialectical behavioural therapy, acceptance and commitment therapy, behavioural activation, compassion-focused therapy, exposure therapy, and more. Some of our readers have also found focusing, meditation (see below) and internal family systems therapy useful for general emotional management.

Here are some additional resources by condition:

- The UK's National Health Service publishes useful, evidence-based advice on treatments for most conditions at nhs.uk/mental-health/. That's usually a good starting point.
- Depression and low mood — in addition to CBT, see Siskind, 2021 for a summary of treatments for depression. We'd also recommend *It's Not Always Depression* by Hilary Hendel.[226]

- Anxiety — see Alexander, 2015 for a summary of treatments for anxiety and Mind Ease (mindease.io), another app created by Spencer Greenberg.
- ADHD — check out *Cognitive-Behavioral Therapy for Adult ADHD* by Mary Solanto [227] and *Taking Charge of Adult ADHD* by Barkley and Benton.[228]
- Perfectionism — this seems very common among our readers, and is the focus of the first part of our podcast episode with CBT therapist Tim LeBon.[229]
- Imposter syndrome — this is also extremely common, which is why one of our team wrote her own guide to overcoming it (80000hours.org/2022/04/imposter-syndrome/).

Beyond the self-help resources above, for many conditions, speaking with a therapist is extremely beneficial. A key step is finding a therapist who's a good match. Match is crucial — some research has suggested that the degree of 'therapeutic alliance' can even be more important than the *form* of therapy. This is often difficult, but here are some tips:

- Ask for referrals from your friends whose judgement you trust.
- Don't feel like you need to stick with the first therapist you find. Most therapists will be happy to do an initial consultation or trial session, so you can do several of these and go with whoever has the best match.
- Therapy can be roughly divided into two very different forms: those in the tradition of psychoanalysis, which aims to identify patterns of counterproductive behaviour starting in childhood, and those that are in the tradition of CBT, which tends to be practical and solution focused, and to have a clearer evidence base. Both forms can be useful, but our sympathies lie with the CBT tradition, so that's what we'd suggest trying first. Make sure not confuse the two types.
- If you're interested in effective altruism, you might like to check

out Mental Health Navigator (mentalhealthnavigator.co.uk) or the Slate Star Codex Psychiat-List (psychiat-list.slatestarcodex.com).[230]
- There's a longer guide on how to find a therapist at 80k.info/get-a-therapist.[231]

Just as with your mental health, it also pays to focus on your physical health...

3. Deal with your physical health (not forgetting your back!)

Lots of health advice is snake oil. But it's probably also the area where the most evidence-based advice exists. Besides your doctor, you can find easy-to-use summaries of the scientific consensus on how to treat different health problems on websites like the NHS's Health A to Z and the Mayo Clinic. Read more about how to get evidence-based health advice at 80k.info/health-questions.[232]

We were surprised to learn that the biggest risk to our productivity is probably back pain: it's a major cause of ill health globally, at least by some measures.[233]

Our cofounder, Will, was suddenly taken out for months by chronic lower-back pain. Will spoke to over 10 health professionals about his back pain before he got any useful advice. This isn't uncommon either, since the causes of much back pain are widely varied, and it can be hard to treat.

Repetitive strain injury (RSI) is also a hazard of modern workplaces, and can even permanently damage your ability to type or use a mouse.

Nevertheless, you can reduce your chances of back pain and RSI in a few ways:

1. Correctly set up your desk (read more at 80k.info/desk) and maintain good posture (read more at 80k.info/back).[234]
2. Regularly change position (the pomodoro technique is useful).
3. Exercise regularly, probably including some strength training for

the whole body (especially the posterior chain).

These steps sound trivial, but statistically, it's pretty likely you'll face a bout of bad back pain at some point in your life, and you'll thank yourself for making these simple investments.

If you do get any symptoms, treat them immediately before they get worse. Read more about how to treat back pain and RSI at nhs.uk/conditions/back-pain and nhs.uk/conditions/repetitive-strain-injury-rsi.

4. Set goals

There is plenty of debate about the best ways to set goals. Should you focus more on outcomes or the process? Should your goals be ambitious or achievable?

These differences don't matter too much. The key point is that setting goals works: people who set goals tend to achieve more.

So, what most matters is to get in the habit of setting goals for your personal development.

Longer-term goals

One place to start is to get clearer about what an ideal life would look like to you.

For example, how would your life ideally look in 10 years' time? If money were no object, or you knew you couldn't fail, how would you spend your time?

Don't only think about what you'd like to achieve (many external achievements don't seem to affect happiness that much), also think about your ideal 'mundane Wednesday'.[235] What exactly would you do from waking to falling asleep?

In doing this, it's useful to keep in mind the ingredients that are normally most important for fulfilment:

- Satisfying relationships

- Contributing to a goal beyond yourself
- Craft — something you feel competent in and find engaging (where you can enter a state of 'flow')
- Some fun and positive emotion
- A lack of major negatives, such as financial stress, health problems, or interpersonal conflicts

And that leads on to another useful exercise to clarify your direction. Write out your 5–10 most important values for guiding your life. You can pick some from an online list (maybe jamesclear.com/core-values), do a full life compass exercise (see Harris, 2014 for a worksheet), or use the Intrinsic Values Test by Clearer Thinking (80k.info/ivt).

Goals for the year

In addition to (or instead of) your longer-term goals, consider setting 1–2 professional and 1–2 personal goals for the next year or quarter. I (Benjamin) like to do an "annual life review." A template for doing this that many on the 80,000 Hours team have found helpful is Alex Vermeer's '8,760 Hours' document (no relation), at alexvermeer.com/8760hours. I've also published a slightly over-the-top document I created for doing these, which you can find at 80k.info/BTAR.

For your career, we also made a quick tool to help you reflect on your work once a year (80000hours.org/articles/annual-career-review/).

Learn to prioritise

A common pattern is that often most of the results come from the top couple of priorities. This is sometimes called the 80/20 principle — because about 80% of the results come from 20% of your activities.

This most likely applies to your goals, so it's vital to put them in order of priority, and to focus all your attention on those at the top.

But life constantly throws more options at you, so this is an ongoing practice.

One exercise to help you do this is to make a list of your goals, pick the top couple, and then put everything below that on a *do not* do list (read more at jamesclear.com/buffett-focus).

(If you want to think more about prioritisation, Bye, 2020 explains five different prioritisation frameworks.)

It's normal to always feel like you're not doing enough. But if you've prioritised, and focus on your top priorities, then you'll know you're doing the best you can.

Now, once you've set some goals, how can you actually achieve them?

5. Try out this list of ways to become more productive

You can find lots of articles about which skills are most in-demand by employers — is it marketing, programming, or data science? But what people don't talk about so often are the skills that are useful in *all* jobs; that make you more effective at *everything*.

We've already covered several examples: how to build habits, prioritising, and taking care of yourself. Here we'll cover another: building the habits of personal productivity.

Here's an example: implementation intentions. Rather than saying "I will exercise every day," define a specific trigger, such as: "When I get home from work, the first thing I'll do is put on my trainers and go for a run." This surprisingly simple technique has been found in a large meta-analysis to make people much more likely to achieve their goals — in many cases about twice as likely (effect size of 0.65).[236]

This section will also help you implement the rest of the advice in this appendix. Want to socialise more? Use a commitment device. Want to be more focused when you study? Batch your time. Want to take up gratitude journaling? Add it to your daily review.

What follows is a list of productivity techniques that have seemed most useful to the people we've worked with. This section is not particularly evidence-based, but we think that's OK, because you can quickly try the techniques yourself and see if you get more done. Work through them one at a time for about a week each. Then spend several weeks on the ones that work for you until you've built the new habits.

Sticking to your goals

If you're having trouble getting going, start here.

1. Use "implementation intentions," as we covered above.
2. You can make implementation intentions even more effective by: (i) imagining you fail to achieve the goal, (ii) working out why you failed, then (iii) modifying your plan until you're confident you'll succeed. In this case, it's negative thinking that's most effective. You can read more in Rethinking Positive Thinking by Professor Gabriele Oettingen.[237]
3. We know lots of people who swear by commitment devices, like Beeminder (beeminder.com) and stickK (stickk.com).[238]
4. To go more in-depth on how to become more motivated, check out The Motivation Hacker — a short popular summary of the research by Nick Winter, and The Procrastination Equation by Professor Piers Steel.[239]

Productivity processes

1. **Set up a system to track your tasks, especially small tasks** like a *simplified* version of the Getting Things Done system (hamberg. no/gtd — most people find the full system over the top, so you might want to first try something like Daniel Kestenholz's Minimalist Productivity System at 80k.info/MPS). This helps you avoid forgetting things, and provides (some) peace of mind. Todoist (todoist.com) is a popular tool for managing tasks; some

people in the 80,000 Hours team swear by Asana (asana.com).[240]

2. **Do a five-minute review at the end of each day.** You can put all kinds of other useful habits into this review, such as gratitude journaling, tracking your happiness, and thinking about what you learned each day. You can also use it to set your top priority for the next day: many people find it useful to focus on this first thing (a technique that's been called "eating a frog").[241]

3. **Each week, take an hour to review your key goals, and plan out the rest of the week.** (And the same monthly and annually.) There's an example at 80k.info/week.

4. **Share your to-do list.** At the start of each day, try sending your to-do list to a friend or colleague. We find that just telling someone else is enough to give some motivation — even if there's no formal accountability.

5. **Batch your time.** For example, try to have all your meetings in one or two days, then block out solid stretches of time for focused work; and clear your inbox once a week. Paul Graham discusses this in his essay, "Maker's schedule, manager's schedule" (paulgraham.com/makersschedule.html). This approach reduces the costs of task switching and attention residue. More detail on this can be found in our podcast episode with Cal Newport (at 80k.info/cal-newport), or in his book *Deep Work*.[242] Also, consider defining a fixed number of hours for work (for example, have a hard limit of stopping work by 6:00pm). Many people have found this makes them more productive during their work hours, while also reducing the chance of burning out and neglecting their social life. Read more at 80k.info/fsp. Toggl (toggl.com) and HourStack (hourstack.com) are useful tools for tracking your time.

6. **Be more focused by using the pomodoro technique.** Whenever you need to work on a task, set a timer, and only focus on that task for 25 minutes. It's hard to imagine a simpler technique, but

many people find it helps them to overcome procrastination and be more focused, making a major difference to how much they can get done each day. Professor Barbara Oakley recommends it in her course, *Learning how to learn*. Another step would be to do this with someone else: tell each other what you're each going to do in the 25-minute focus time, and then hold each other accountable at the end. Focusmate (focusmate.com) is a helpful platform for finding people to co-work with.

7. **Build a regular daily routine**, which you can use to complete tasks automatically — for example, always exercise first thing after lunch. Many people find having a good morning routine is especially important, because it gets you off to a good start.[243]

8. **Set up systems to take care of day-to-day tasks** to free up your attention, like eating the same thing for breakfast every day.

9. **Block social media**. It's designed to be addictive, so it can ruin your focus. Changing tasks a lot makes you less productive due to attention residue. For this reason, many people have found tools that block social media during work hours, or for a certain amount of time each day, to majorly boost their productivity. We've found News Feed Eradicator to be effective at limiting the time we spend on Twitter. You may also want to consider: Rescue Time (rescuetime.com), Freedom (freedom.to), or OFFTIME (offtime.app). Or reward yourself for focused work with apps like Forest (forestapp.cc).

Further reading on productivity

A huge amount has been written about all of these ideas. Hopefully, this gives you an idea of what's out there and some ways to get started. When you've spent a few months incorporating some of these habits into your routines, move on to the next step.

Here are some systems and over-the-top reflections from highly productive people:

- *Deep Work* by Cal Newport[244]
- "Productivity" by Sam Altman (blog.samaltman.com/productivity)
- "Pmarca guide to personal productivity" by Marc Andreessen (pmarchive.com/guide_to_personal_productivity.html)
- "Seeking the productive life" by Stephen Wolfram (80k.info/swp)
- "Productivity 101 for beginners" by Peter Wildeford (80k.info/productivity-101)
- Interviews with productive people in the effective altruism community by Lynette Bye.[245]

Want help implementing the above? We've worked with Lynette Bye, who does productivity coaching with a focus on those interested in effective altruism, and has a great blog with lots more ideas — at lynettebye.com.

6. Improve your basic social skills

Social skills are useful for almost everything in life, and although there's surprisingly little good advice on how to improve them, there are some really basic things that everyone can learn. Small habits, like how to make smalltalk and changing how you think about social situations, can make it much easier to make friends, get on with colleagues, and generally deal with people.

The most popular guide to learning basic social skills is probably *How to Win Friends and Influence People* by Dale Carnegie.[246] It's full of advice like "A person's name is to that person, the sweetest, most important sound in any language." We think the advice is a bit dated and simplified, and sometimes sounds a bit manipulative, but many people find it helpful. Find summary of the book by Bryan Caplan that highlights the best ideas at www.econlib.org/how-to-win-friends-and-influence-people-book-club-round-up/.

Our favourite guide is *Succeed Socially* (succeedsocially.com), which is now available as a book, by Chris MacLeod.[247]

If you're looking to develop more advanced social skills, then you might find *The Charisma Myth* by Olivia Fox Cabane useful.[248] It makes at least some attempt to use the limited research that exists. Other people have found things like improv and Toastmasters (toastmasters.org) helpful.

Finally, much comes down to practice, and getting comfortable talking to new people. So it's useful to work on this area while also following the steps in the next section...

7. Surround yourself with great people

Everyone talks about the importance of networking for a successful career, and they're right. A large fraction of jobs are found through connections — and many are probably never advertised, so are *only* available through connections.[249]

But the importance of your connections goes far beyond finding jobs. It may be an overstatement to say that "you become the average of the five people you spend the most time with," but there is certainly some truth in it. Your friends set the behaviour you see as normal, and directly influence how you feel (through emotional contagion). Your friends can also directly teach you new skills and introduce you to new people.

Researchers have even measured this influence, as reviewed in the book *Connected* by Christakis and Fowler.[250] One study found that if one of your friends becomes happy, you're 15% more likely to be happy. And if a friend of a friend becomes happy, you're 10% more likely to be happy.[251]

Your connections are also a major source of personalised, up-to-date information that is never published. For instance, if you want to find out what job opportunities might be a good fit for you in the biotech industry, the best way to find out is to speak to a friend in that industry. The same is true if you want to learn about the trends in a sector, or the day-to-day reality of a job.

If you ever want to start a new project or hire someone, your connections are the best place to start, because you already know and trust them.

Finally, if you care about social impact, then your connections are even more important. Partly this is because you can persuade people in your network of important ideas, such as global health or animal welfare. But it's also because your behaviour will help to set the social norms in your network, spreading positive behaviours in the way we just described above. For instance, if you start donating more, there's a good chance more than one other person will join you.

Practical tips on how to build connections

Networking sounds icky, but at its core, it's simple: meet people you like, help them out, and build genuine friendships. If you meet lots of people and find small ways to be useful to them, then when you need a favour, you'll have lots of people to turn to. However, it's best just to help people with no expectation of reward — that's what the best networkers do and there's evidence that it's what works best.[252]

You don't have to meet people through networking conferences. The best way to meet people is through people you already know — just ask for an introduction and explain why you'd like to meet (you can find some email scripts at 80000hours.org/articles/email-scripts). Alternatively, you can meet people through common interests — things you *actually* enjoy doing.

When you meet a new person, a useful habit is the "five-minute favour." Think of what you can do in just five minutes that would help this person, and do it. Two of the best five-minute favours are to make an introduction, or tell someone about a book or another resource. The right introduction can change someone's life, and costs you almost nothing.

But it still takes effort to reach out to people. In the long term, it's even better to develop habits that will let you build connections automatically. For instance, join a group that meets regularly, or live with people who have lots of visitors. Starting a side project can also work well — it gives you a good reason to meet people and work alongside them, building more meaningful connections.

Of all the social media, Twitter currently stands out as the one that we've found most useful for making professional connections and becoming more known in your industry. It's relatively easy to end up talking to amazingly successful people you'd struggle to meet in any other way.

Twitter only works if you have good content, but there are some relatively straightforward ways to do that. One option is to pick a niche topic you know about (that's professionally relevant!) and try to make your feed into a key place to follow for people interested in that topic. Another option is to post summaries of recent research or news within an area (e.g. Ethan Mollick has built a huge following by posting summaries of psychology papers). Posting thoughtful replies to people you'd like to connect with can also work.

You can also apply similar tactics to a newsletter (e.g. one of our readers, Jeffrey Ding, set up the ChinAI newsletter[253]) — there's a guide to setting one up at 80k.info/ps-newsletter.

Don't forget that you want both depth and breadth in your connections — it's useful to have a couple of allies who know you really well and can help you out in a tough spot, but it's also useful to know people in many different areas so you can find diverse perspectives and opportunities — there's evidence that being the 'bridge' between different groups is what's most useful for getting jobs.[254]

Draw up a list of your five most important allies, then make sure to stay in touch with them regularly. But also think about how to meet totally new types of people for breadth.

In chapter 11, we covered the very best way to improve your connections: join a community.

More reading:

- Chapter 4 of *The Startup of You* by the founder of LinkedIn,

Reid Hoffman.[255]

- *Give and Take*, by Professor Adam Grant, is about how the most successful people are those with a giving mindset, in part because it helps them to build more connections.[256]
- *Never Eat Alone*, by Keith Ferrazzi. The tone isn't for everyone, but it shares the same approach as the above, and also has lots of tactical tips.[257]
- "How to become insanely well-connected" is a classic article with great practical networking advice (review.firstround.com/how-to-become-insanely-well-connected).
- "How to make friends as an adult" is a short essay on *Barking Up the Wrong Tree* (bakadesuyo.com/2017/02/how-to-make-friends-as-an-adult).

Consider changing where you live

Should you move to the hub of your industry?

Another way to greatly improve your connections is to change cities.

Despite the rise of remote working, it's still true that industries still cluster in certain areas. Go to Silicon Valley for technology, LA for entertainment, New York for advertising / fashion / finance, Boston or Cambridge (UK) for science, London for finance, and so on.

In these clusters, it's much easier to build deeper professional connections, meet new people serendipitously, and find more jobs. Indeed, in some industries, the top positions only exist in certain regions — three-quarters of US entertainers and performers live in LA.[258] There are also significant pay differences between regions, which are often larger than the differences in the cost of living.

But that's only part of what's special about these regions. As of 2008 (and we expect the broad pattern holds true today), the world's 10 largest urban economic regions hold only 6.5% of the world's population, but account for 57% of patented innovations, 53% of the most cited scientists, and 43% of economic output.[259] This suggests that, in terms of innovation and economic output, the people in these regions are about eight times more productive than the average person.

These regions in 2008 were: (1) Greater Tokyo, (2) Boston-Washington corridor, (3) Chicago to Pittsburgh, (4) Amsterdam-Brussels-Antwerp, (5) Osaka-Nagoya, (6) London and South East England, (7) Milan to Turin, (8) Charlotte to Atlanta, (9) Southern California (LA to San Diego), and (10) Frankfurt to Mannheim. Silicon Valley, Paris, Berlin, and Denver-Boulder also deserve a mention as having some of the highest rates of innovation per person.

It's unclear exactly why these areas are so productive, but at least part of it seems to be that innovation comes from being in close communication with other innovators. Culture and social norms might be important too. If that's true, then it suggests you'll be more likely to make a breakthrough if you move to these regions. We've certainly advised people who saw major boosts to their careers after moving cities. (Read more about this in *Triumph of the City* by Edward Glaeser.[260])

Should you move to Thailand?

The opposite strategy is to move somewhere fun and cheap. This is easier than ever due to the rise of remote work, and could be good for quality of life. It's also good if you want to make your savings last longer to start a new project or study. However, due to the reasons above, someone ambitious early in their career might be better served by moving to their industry hub. Read more at 80000hours.org/2014/09/should-you-move-to-thailand/.

Location and your personal life

Your location is important in many other ways. One survey of 20,000 people in the US found that satisfaction with their location was a major component of life satisfaction.[261]

This is because where you live determines many important aspects of your life:

- The types of people you'll spend time with.
- Your day-to-day environment and commute.
- And even your security in retirement, as most people's biggest financial investment is in their house, and different regions have different property markets.

The main cost of changing cities is to your personal life. It takes a long time to build up a network of friends, and you'll probably leave behind relatives. Since close relationships are perhaps the most important ingredient of life satisfaction, this is not a trivial cost.

We moved 80,000 Hours to the San Francisco Bay Area, to be closer to an "industry hub" of people trying to do good — but after a couple of years, we decided to move back to the UK, in significant part for this reason.

If you don't feel like a good fit with the social life in your hometown, then you're more likely to gain from moving cities. Another option is to move for a period of years to build your connections, then return home later. Or if you can't move, you can periodically visit the cluster for your industry.

If you're unsure where to live, the ideal is to spend at least a couple of months living in each location.

If you'd like to learn more about this topic, we recommend the book *Who's Your City* by Richard Florida.[262] In the Appendix, he has a scorecard you can use to rate different cities based on the predictors of location satisfaction. Though note that we don't put much stock in his actual rankings of locations (e.g. see Soma, 2013 for criticism) and the data is from 2008. We also enjoyed Paul Graham's essay "Cities and Ambition" — paulgraham.com/cities.html.

8. Apply scientific research into happiness

Although most advice about being happier isn't based on anything much, the last few decades has seen the rise of "positive psychology" — the science of the causes of wellbeing — as covered in chapter 1.

Researchers in this field have developed practical, easy exercises to make you happier, and tested them with rigorous trials to see whether they really work. We think this is one of the best places to turn for self-help advice.

Partly, this research emphasises the importance of the basics — sleep, exercise, family and friends, and mental health. But they've made lots of other useful discoveries too.

Being happier is not only good in itself, but it can also make you more productive, a better advocate for social change, and less likely to burn out.[263]

Below is a list of techniques recommended by Professor Martin Seligman, one of the founders of the field. Most of these are in his book, *Flourish*.[264] Some of these techniques have been successfully replicated[265] and multiple recent meta-studies have found statistically significant positive effects of all of these techniques.[266] Test them out, and keep using them if they're helpful.

1. **Rate your happiness at the end of each day.** You'll become more self-aware and be able to track your progress over time. Moodscope (moodscope.com) is a good tool.

2. **Start gratitude journaling.** Write down three things you're grateful for at the end of each day, and why they happened. Other ways of cultivating gratitude are also good, like the gratitude visit.[267]

3. **Use your signature strengths.** Take the VIA Character Strengths survey (viacharacter.org/character-strengths), then make sure you use one of your top five strengths each day.[268]

4. **Learn some basic cognitive behavioural therapy (CBT)**. The key insight of CBT is the kernel of truth within the idea of "positive

thinking": much unhappiness is caused by unhelpful beliefs, and it's possible to change your beliefs. CBT has developed lots of techniques for doing exactly this. A simple exercise is the ABC of CBT which you could do at the end of each day — read more at 80k.info/ABC-CBT.[269]

5. **Try out a mindfulness practice** — usually meditation. There's a significant amount of evidence from trials that meditation helps with wellbeing, stress, mental health, focus, empathy, and more. You can see a review of some of this literature in *Altered Traits* by Goleman and Davidson, and some large studies in the footnotes.[270] More importantly, it's cheap to try doing 20 minutes per day for a couple of months, and see if you feel better afterwards. A good place to start is the *Waking Up* app (wakingup.com), created by Sam Harris. It has an introductory course, and also features courses from 20+ other teachers, which you can try to see which style makes you feel best (e.g. I (Benjamin) found Loch Kelly's courses especially helpful). The book *Mindfulness* by Penman and Williams, is also a great introduction, and is organised into an eight-week course.[271] The course is similar to "mindfulness-based stress reduction" which is a widely available evidence-based weekly programme, which you might be able to find on offer near you.

6. **Do something kind each day**, like donating to charity, giving someone a compliment, or helping someone at work.

7. **Practise active constructive responding** to celebrate successes with others
   (gostrengths.com/what-is-active-and-constructive-responding).

8. **Craft your job.** In chapter 1 we explored the ingredients of a satisfying job. Often it's possible to adapt your job so that it involves more of the satisfying ingredients, like 'flow' states, and less of what you don't enjoy. It could be as simple as trying to spend more time with a friend at work. It can also be possible to find more meaning

in your work. Adam Grant did a study of fundraisers for university scholarships. He found that introducing the fundraiser to someone who had benefited from the scholarships made them dramatically more productive.[272] This is especially important if you're pursuing a more abstract way of doing good, like earning to give. How can you make it seem more vivid? Job crafting exercises have been evaluated in trials and found to have positive effects. Berg et al., 2007 provides review of some of the research, or Wrzesniewski et al., 2010 is a more practical introduction.

To get more exercises, check out the free courses on *Clearer Thinking* (clearerthinking.org), and read *The How of Happiness* by Sonja Lyubomirsky.[273]

9. Use these tips to save more money

We recommend aiming to save enough money that you could comfortably live for at least six months if you had no income, and ideally 12 months (depending on how long it would take you to find another job). Besides the security, it also gives you the flexibility to make big career changes and take risks. The standard advice is also to save about 15% of your income for retirement.

So how can you go about saving money?

- Save automatically. Set up a direct debit from your main account to a savings account, so you never notice the money.
- Focus on big wins. Rather than constantly scrimping (don't buy that latte!), identify one or two areas of your budget you could cut that will have a big effect. Often cutting rent by moving somewhere smaller or sharing a house with someone else is the biggest thing.
- But beware of swapping money for time. Suppose you could save $100 per month by moving somewhere with an hour longer commute. Instead, maybe you could spend that time working

overtime, making you more likely to get promoted, or earning extra wages. You'd only need to earn an extra $5/hour to break even with the more expensive rent.

- Until you have six months' runway, cut your donations back to 1%.
- For more tips, check out *Mr. Money Mustache* (mrmoneymustache. com) and Ramit Sethi's book, *I Will Teach You to be Rich*.[274] Unfortunately, the tone of these is not for everyone, but they have some of the best advice we're aware of.

Bear in mind that it might be more effective to focus on earning more rather than spending less, especially through negotiating your salary.

Once you're saving 15% and have at least 6–12 months' runway, move on to the next step.

(For more reading on personal finance for people who want to donate to charity, see an introductory guide at benkuhn.net/giving-101 and an advanced guide at Tomasik, 2021.)

10. Learn how to learn

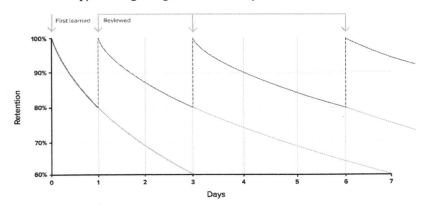

Typical forgetting curve for newly learned information

Spaced repetition learning takes advantage of the forgetting curve.

Another skill that will help you in every job is learning how to learn.

Perhaps surprisingly, you can become much faster at learning. One example is spaced repetition. If you're trying to memorise something, like a word in a foreign language, research shows that there's an optimal frequency to review the word. If you use this frequency, you'll be able to memorise it much faster. There are now tools that will do this for you, like Anki for making your own flashcards (ankisrs.net). (Take a look at an essay on using Anki at augmentingcognition.com/ltm.html.)

There are lots more techniques. Our top recommendation in this area is the *Learning How to Learn* course on Coursera by Professor Barbara Oakley,[275] which is now the most viewed online course of all time. You can also read the book it's based on, A Mind for Numbers.[276]

If you're interested in learning about a specific topic in detail, or forming a new opinion in an area that's important, it could be helpful to try learning by writing (see cold-takes.com/learning-by-writing for more).

Finally, *Peak* by Professor K. Anders Ericsson is a fascinating (if polemical) book about the importance of practice in developing expertise, and how to practise most effectively.[277] In brief, you need to have:

- Specific goals for your practice, focused on improving your weaknesses.
- Rapid feedback on how well you're performing.
- Intense focus on the task.
- A good coach or teacher.

Many people have spent thousands of hours driving, but they're not expert drivers. This is because they don't practise with all these ingredients, and their skill quickly tops out. This is the same for many people in many jobs.

"Deliberate performance" is a great paper by Fadde and Klein about how to turn any activity into practice that improves your skills.[278] See a summary at 80k.info/deliberate-performance.

When you've learned the basics, go on to learning more narrowly applicable skills, as we cover in the next two steps.

11. Be strategic about how to perform better in your job

How can you perform better in your job? As we covered in chapter 8, being good at your job brings all kinds of other benefits:

- You'll have better achievements and connections, boosting your career capital.
- You'll gain a sense of mastery, making you more satisfied.
- You'll have more positive impact.

Working harder helps — if you can go 10% beyond what everyone else is doing, that's often all that's needed to stand out. But it's better to work smarter rather than harder.

One key question to ask is: "What is *really* required for advancement in this position?" It's easy to get distracted, but there are often only a few things that really matter. For a salesperson, it's the revenue they bring in. For an academic, it's how many good papers they publish.

Talk to people who have succeeded in the area, and try to identify what this key thing is. Don't just trust what they say; work out what they actually did. Then, using the material in the earlier section on learning how to learn, figure out how to master it. Try to cut back on everything else.

To learn more, we recommend Cal Newport's work:

- *So Good They Can't Ignore You*[279]
- *Deep Work*[280]
- The *Top Performer* online course (top-performer-course.com). You can see some of the key ideas in this series of posts by the course co-creator Scott Young:
  - "Why most people get stuck in their careers" (www.scotthyoung.com/blog/2017/01/16/career-stuck)
  - "Four principles for decoding career success in your field"

(www.scotthyoung.com/blog/lesson-2-four-principles)
- "How do you 'deliberately practise' your job?" (www.scotthyoung.com/blog/lesson-3-how-do-you-deliberately-practice-your-job)

12. Use research into decision-making to think better

Another example of a skill that's useful in every job, but often not explicitly taught, is clear thinking. Research suggests that intelligence and rationality are distinct (perhaps that's why smart people make so many dumb decisions), but fortunately, rationality is easier to train.[281]

Clear thinking is also especially important if you want to make the world a better place. As we show in the rest of this guide, having a big social impact requires making lots of tough decisions and overcoming our natural biases — and it means doing that in areas where there are no clear answers, and our judgement is all we have to rely on.

So, how can you become more rational?

Broadly, it's about having the right *mindset*, building the right *habits* of thinking, and *practice*.

We think some of the best research about learning to think better is Philip Tetlock's research on forecasting.[282] He had people make predictions about difficult-to-predict things — like who would win the next election, or whether Russia would declare war on Ukraine — and measured who performed best. He then identified the traits of the best forecasters, and used this to develop a forecasting training programme. Finally, he tested that programme and found some good evidence that it really does help people make better predictions!

Drawing from this research, we wrote an article about how to improve your judgement, which summarises the mindset and techniques of good forecasters. It also explains how you can test your skills by doing calibration training or through making your own forecasts. You can find the article at 80k.info/good-judgement.

What else can help with learning to think better more broadly?

On developing the right mindset, we'd recommend the book Scout Mindset by Julia Galef (who we also interviewed on our podcast — listen at 80k.info/julia-galef).[283]

Partly it involves building up better habits of thinking. Decades of research have shown that we often make bad decisions due to cognitive biases (see appendix 3).

Being aware of these biases is unfortunately not enough to overcome them, but it can motivate us to improve our thinking, and research has found there are habits of thinking you can instil that make you more resistant to these biases.

For instance, several studies of decision-making found that "whether or not" decisions — those that only consider one option — were much less likely to be judged successful than those where several options were simultaneously compared. This suggests it may be helpful to develop a simple habit of always considering at least three options when you make decisions. This and much more advice is covered in Decisive by Chip and Dan Heath.[284] We also incorporate some of these techniques into our career decision process, which you can find in appendix 4.

To accurately understand the world or predict the future, it's important to update your opinions in the right way (i.e., in line with Bayes' theorem) each time you encounter a new piece of evidence. This is such an important idea we made an episode of our podcast all about it (80000hours.org/podcast/episodes/spencer-greenberg-bayesian-updating).

Finally, you can become better at thinking by building up your toolkit of concepts and mental models. This means understanding the big ideas in every field.

Former 80,000 Hours staff member, Peter McIntyre, created a list of 52 key concepts, which you can sign up to learn over a year via a weekly email at conceptually.org.

It's particularly important to understand basic statistics and decision analysis. A great book about taking a rational approach to messy problems is *How to Measure Anything*, by Douglas Hubbard.[285]

If you want to go into even more depth on improving your thinking, check out our notes on good judgement and how to develop it at 80k.info/good-judgement, as well as the free courses on Clearer Thinking (clearerthinking.org).

13. Consider teaching yourself these useful work skills

Having set up the basics, learned the skills that make you more effective at everything, and thought about how to best perform in your job, it's time to turn your attention to classic work skills, like management and marketing.

The best way to improve these skills is to apply them in the course of your job, while getting feedback from someone more experienced.

So rather than self-study, try to incorporate new skills into your day-to-day work, or start a side project. For instance, if you want to learn web design, then volunteer to design a page for a group you're involved with. Doing projects is also much more motivating than trying to learn in the abstract. (And don't forget to apply all the advice in the earlier section on how to learn.)

However, self-study is also easier than ever before thanks to the huge growth in cheap online courses, like Udacity (udacity.com), Coursera (coursera.org), and EdX (edx.org).

Which skills are best to learn?

We did an analysis of which transferable work skills are most useful[286] in the most desirable jobs, finding broadly that the best are:

1. **Analysis** — including decision making, critical thinking and problem solving.
2. **Learning** – new skills and information.
3. **Social skills** — including spoken communication, active listening,

social perceptiveness, and persuasion.

4.   **Management** — including time management, monitoring performance, monitoring personnel, and coordinating people.

We could broadly classify these as "leadership" skills. And, as we saw earlier, they still look to be among the most valuable skills in the age of GPT.

We've covered many ways to improve these skills already in the sections above on good thinking, learning how to learn, and improving your social skills.

The problem with leadership skills is that, while you can make some improvements, after learning the basics your rate of improvement tends to slow up quite a bit.

Consider the contrast with computer programming: you can go from having zero knowledge to having useful abilities in a year or two of practice, and advanced expertise beyond that.

So what to do? Our suggestion is to take any concrete ways you can see to noticeably improve the leadership skills listed, and then focus on concretely useful but faster-to-learn skills after that, such as technical and quantitative skills, or other specialist skills that seem especially useful to your career plans.

You also need to consider your personal fit. Some skills will be faster for you to learn than others, and this will make your efforts more effective. And you need to consider which skills will be most useful in the options you want to take in the future.

In other words, you want to look for the skills that have the best combination of: (i) future value to your career, and (ii) being quick for you to learn.

Here are some lists of skills to consider learning

You could pick one and make it your focus for three months (and perhaps longer if you decide to specialise in it).

We list some valuable transferable work skills and resources for learning more in chapter 7 including: machine learning, software design, data science, information security, applied statistics, management, marketing, sales, and knowledge of China and other emerging economies.

In the section on graduate studies, we also argue for the value of knowledge of machine learning and economics, as well as other applied quantitative subjects (like computer science, physics, and statistics), subfields of biology relevant to pandemic prevention (like synthetic biology, mathematical biology, virology, immunology, pharmacology, or vaccinology), security studies, international relations, public policy and law.

When it comes to social impact, you can also use the categories we highlighted in chapter 6, including: organisation building and entrepreneurship, communications and community building, research, and knowledge of government and policy.

Which *combinations* of skills are best?

Consider whether to focus on one main skill, or explore lots of skills. In some areas, success is more a matter of being exceptional at one thing — for example, academic career progression mainly depends on the quality of your publications. In that case, just focus on getting good at that one thing. Having one impressive achievement is also usually more useful for opening doors than several good but more ordinary achievements.

However, in other areas, it's useful to have an unusual combination of skills and become the best person within that niche. For instance, the creator of *Dilbert*, Scott Adams, attributed his success to being fairly good at telling jokes, drawing cartoons, and knowing about the business world. There are many people better than him on each dimension, but put all three together and he was one of the best in the world.

That said, not all combinations of skills are valuable. We can't give hard and fast advice about which combinations are best, or whether to focus on a single skill or a portfolio.

However, one combination that *does* seem valuable is the combination of quantitative and social skills. As technology improves, there's more and more demand for people who can work at the intersection of people and technology. And because people usually specialise in one or the other, there's a shortage of people who are good at both.[287]

14. Take these steps to master a field and make creative contributions

After you've taken the low-hanging fruit from the steps above, and explored different areas, one end game to consider is becoming a leader in a valuable skillset or global problem. This is where you gain the deep satisfaction of mastery, and can make a big impact on a field. However, while the previous points can be covered in years, becoming an expert usually takes decades.

So, how can you become an expert? This is a subject of huge debate.

A common belief is that in every area, some people are naturals, and can attain mastery with ease.

The most famous researcher in the study of expert performance, K. Anders Ericsson, however, mostly debunked this idea (as we covered in chapter 7 on career capital).

However, there is still debate about whether practice is the main thing you need, or whether talent is also important.[288] Given that there's not yet a consensus, we think the most reasonable position is to assume that both matter.

So this means that to become an expert you need four things:

1. Talent for the area.
2. The right training techniques and mentorship.
3. Five to 30 years of focused practice.
4. Luck.

How much practice is required depends on the area. There's evidence that it's most important in well-established, predictable domains, like running. In newer, more fluid areas, you can get to the forefront faster.

So how should you choose where to focus?

First, if you're going to put in (maybe) decades of work, you'll want to pick an area or skill that's valuable.

Second, you'll want to choose an area where you have a reasonable shot at attaining expertise. One shortcut here is to focus on a field that's new and neglected, since then it'll be much easier to get to the forefront. For instance, we think *GiveWell* established themselves as experts on charity evaluation in about five years, despite having little background in the area.

Beyond that, as we covered in the chapter on personal fit, it's hard to predict who's going to perform best ahead of time. So while it's possible to narrow down by, for instance, asking experts to assess your potential, ultimately it's important to try lots of areas.

Here's an overall process you could roughly work through for choosing what to focus on:

1. Consider a lot of options. Explore and try them out in small ways.
2. Narrow these options down based on: (i) where you think you'd have the best chances of success, (ii) what you think you'd enjoy, and (iii) what seems most valuable to master.
3. To assess your chances of success, you can consider: (i) where you're improving fastest, (ii) expert assessment of your potential, (iii) objective predictors of success (e.g. getting into a top PhD programme is predictor of success in research), and (iv) what's most motivating you — since staying motivated for many years is necessary for success. Apply the material on making better predictions that we covered above.
4. Consider committing for a couple of years, and then reassess. Use this as an opportunity to apply the research about how to learn

effectively that we covered above.

5. If that goes well, consider making a bigger commitment to the skill or area. Be prepared for years of hard work, but bear in mind that your interest in the area will probably grow as you gain mastery, and you start to use your skills to help others.

To learn more about how to develop expertise, we'd recommend *Peak* by K. Anders Ericsson (though bear in mind he's the strongest supporter of practice over talent).[289] We'd also recommend *Grit* by Angela Duckworth, which is about how to develop your passion and perseverance.[290]

Another key way experts contribute is by coming up with new solutions that no one has thought about before. Unfortunately, we're not aware of much good advice on how to be more innovative, but one recommendation is *Originals* by Professor Adam Grant.[291]

Once you become an expert, what then? Use your skills to solve the world's most pressing problems. Do what contributes.

You can learn more about what each problem most needs in our problem profiles — see appendix 9 for summaries.

15. Work on becoming a better person

Ultimately, everything above isn't worth much if you don't use it for good ends.

By becoming a better person, we mean coming to understand your own values, living your life in line with those values, and having a life of purpose.

Becoming a good person is a lifelong journey. Here are some steps to consider:

1. Take time to reflect on your values and goals. We find it useful to set aside some time each year to identify our values, consider whether we're living up to them, and work out what our top goals should be for the next year. We mentioned the idea of doing an annual

life review above. By "values" here, we mean ultimately what you think a good life consists of. To get clearer about them, ask yourself why you're pursuing your goals over and over again, until you can't think of any deeper reasons. Or, imagine you were going to die in a year, and think about what you'd do in the remaining time.

2. Learn about what else has been written about being a good person. People have thought about these questions for millennia, so don't just try to work it out by self-reflection. In particular, it's useful to know some basic moral philosophy — appendix 1 is particularly relevant. If you want to get more into theoretical philosophy, try *Being Good* by Simon Blackburn,[292] or for something more hardcore, *Reasons and Persons* by Derek Parfit.[293] You might want to explore some major spiritual traditions (personally, my pick would be to learn about meditation and secular Buddhism, such as the Coursera course on Buddhism and Modern Psychology at 80k.info/plb and *Waking Up* by Sam Harris).[294] Actively challenge your views, and look for ways in which you might be wrong.

3. Build character day by day. By this, we mean developing strengths like grit, self-control, courage, gratitude, kindness, helpfulness, curiosity, humility, prudence, justice, respect of important norms, honesty, integrity, and sincerity. These strengths are vital to having a fulfilling, successful life, as well as helping others. Moreover, weakness in character can easily flip your impact from positive to negative, whether you succumb to temptation to do something unethical to preserve your position, damage the reputation of your field, or make it harder to work together. This is why we see them as an important part of your career capital. Listen to our podcast with Tim LeBon at 80k.info/tim-lebon for more on why character matters and how to build it. Also see my thread on the importance of character to the project of effective altruism (80k.info/btchar), and see David Brooks' book, *The Road to Character*.[295]

You can build character by surrounding yourself with people you want to emulate, as well as by building up small habits of better behaviour. If you think that it's generally good to be honest, then practice being honest in low-stakes situations each day. That'll make it easier to do the right thing when you're really tempted. One exercise we like is picking 1–3 character virtues each year to especially focus on.

Which character strengths should you focus on? The list above is a good starting point. The VIA institute has a list of 24 signature strengths that are valued across many cultures and traditions (viacharacter.org/character-strengths). For those especially important to having a big positive impact, also see these articles: "Doing good together: how to coordinate effectively and avoid single-player thinking" (80000hours.org/articles/coordination), "Ways people trying to do good accidentally make things worse, and how to avoid them" (80000hours.org/articles/accidental-harm), "Reflecting on the Last Year — Lessons for EA" by Toby Ord (80k.info/ordeag23), "Integrity for consequentialists" by Paul Christiano (sideways-view.com/2016/11/14/integrity-for-consequentialists), "Virtues for real-world utilitarians" by Schubert and Caviola.[296]

4. Occasionally, really challenge yourself — change jobs to help others, give more, or take a stand for an issue. You could set yourself one big moral challenge each year.

How to be successful: the compounding benefits of investing in yourself

We've seen that even if you're not in the ideal job right now, there's still a huge amount you can do to make yourself happier, more productive, and better placed to have a positive impact on the world.

> *"Knowledge and productivity are like compound interest. Given two people of approximately the same ability and one person who works 10% more than the other, the latter will more than twice outproduce the former. The more you know, the more you learn; the more you learn, the more you can do; the more you can do, the more the opportunity."*
>
> –**Richard Hamming**, *You and Your Research.*[297]

If you apply the material on productivity and learning how to learn, you can learn everything else more quickly. Similarly, if you apply the material on positive psychology, you'll be happier, which helps you be more productive. If you surround yourself with supportive people, that helps with everything else too, and so on.

In this way, over the years, you can learn how to be successful, build your career capital, and achieve far more than you might first think.

So, pick one of these areas, and get started!

Appendix 3 – Four biases to avoid in career decisions

Over the last couple of decades, a large and growing body of research has emerged which shows that our decisions are far from rational.[298] We did a survey of this research to find out what it means for your career decisions.

It turns out that we likely don't know as much as we think we do, are overconfident, tend to think too narrowly and continue with paths that are no longer best for us. We need to be more sceptical of our decisions than we might be inclined to be; find ways to broaden our options; and take a more systematic and evidence-based approach to career choice.

In what follows, we summarise the main sources of irrational bias and outline what you can do about them.

1. Thinking narrowly

We often think too narrowly when considering what options are available to us, and what's important in comparing them.

What's the evidence for this?

There's evidence that in decision making, we "narrow frame" in two ways: first, we think too narrowly about what options are available to us. Second, we think too narrowly about what our objectives are in comparing those options.[299] This is supported both by direct studies, and by the existence of more general biases: the availability heuristic, causing us to focus on options that are readily available; anchoring, a tendency to overweight the first piece of information given; status quo bias, an irrational preference for the current state of affairs, and the sunk cost fallacy, the tendency to assign more weight to options we've already invested time and effort into.

Why is it a problem for careers?

If people consistently fail to think through all the opportunities available to them, it seems likely that many people could be in better-suited and higher impact careers than they are currently.

As explained above, it's not just about missing options: it's about how you compare them. If you neglect an important consideration when comparing options, you might end up favouring the wrong one for the wrong reasons. There's risk of a compound effect here: by first thinking too narrowly about what options are available to you, and then on top of this thinking too narrowly about how to evaluate this already limited set of options, your chances of choosing a sub-optimal career are greatly increased.

What can you do about it?

Take some time to broaden your horizons. Use frameworks to brainstorm new options, such as those suggested in our process for making tough career decisions (which you can find in appendix 4). Widen your perspective by talking to and comparing options with other people: the more diverse the range of people you consult, the better. As well as thinking through the pros of each of your options, think too about why they might not be so great: what are some reasons you might be wrong about this option?

2. Getting stuck

We often continue on paths or in careers for too long when it would actually be more beneficial to change.

What's the evidence for this?

A bias known as the sunk cost fallacy: a tendency to continue doing something that's no longer beneficial simply because we've already invested a lot of time or money in it.[300] This is irrational because the time or money is already spent, and therefore irrelevant to the decision you're now making: they are sunk costs.

Why is it a problem for careers?

Suppose you've spent years working and studying to get a dream job, only to realise you could be doing something completely different that would have much more impact. The thought of abandoning all those years' effort is hard, right? It's tempting to continue with what you've already invested in, hoping things will improve. But you can't get back the years you've already spent, and by continuing you're probably just wasting more. Abandoning sunk costs in your career can be incredibly difficult, but it's important if you want to make as much difference as possible. You need to be able to identify when your preference for a certain career is for a good reason, and when it's just because of past commitments.

What can you do about it?

The bad news is that it doesn't seem like simply knowing about the sunk cost fallacy, thinking hard about it, or talking it over with people, will help very much. The good news, though, is that sunk costs can be fought if you try hard enough and think about your decisions in the right way:

- **Ignore the past:** think about where you are now, the qualifications and experience you have, as if they just appeared from nowhere.
- **Think about the future:** make a list of the pros and cons of each of your alternatives from now on.
- **Justify your decision to someone else:** it's much harder to justify biassed decisions to someone else!

3. Misjudging our chances

We're likely to misjudge our chances of success in different career paths.

What's the evidence for this?

When judging our chances of success, we tend to use something called the representativeness heuristic: asking "how much do I seem like the sort

of person who would be successful in this field?" The problem with this approach is that, no matter how much you look like the kind of person who would be successful, if the chances of anyone succeeding in your field are low, you'll likely be overestimating your chances. This is known as base rate neglect: neglecting to consider the underlying probabilities or base rates. No matter how much you seem like the sort of person who would single-handedly find a cure for cancer, your chances of doing so are small simply because the chances of anyone doing so are so small.

There's also evidence from studies that we tend to be overconfident in general: most people think they're better than average, and underestimate the time it will take them to complete a given task.

Why is it a problem for careers?

Being successful in whatever you do is obviously crucial to making an impact. The existence of base rate neglect plus overconfidence suggest that we're likely to overestimate our chances of finding a cure for malaria, becoming head of the world's most cost-effective charity, or completely revolutionising academic incentives, to give a few examples. But this doesn't mean that no-one should do these things.[301] What we need is to be able to accurately judge our chances of success: aiming high, but not too high.

What can you do about it?

The suggested approach should help you judge your chances of success in a given field or career:[302]

1. Work out which factors (personality traits, skills and abilities) are most relevant to success in the field you're considering.
2. Find ways to objectively measure yourself on these factors.
3. Given this information, narrow down your reference class to those similar to you.
4. Get your "base rate" from this class.

4. Relying too much on your gut

Although conventional wisdom emphasises the importance of "going with your gut" in career decisions, we should be sceptical of at least some of our intuitive judgements.[303]

What can you do about it?

Double-check your intuitions against more systematic methods and get more evidence. You might, for example, try explicitly listing all the factors that are important for your decision, and then attempt to score different options on these factors and compare them. Even if you don't necessarily use this to determine your decision, it will likely highlight some factors that your first impressions miss, and flag the areas where you need to get more information.

Appendix 4 – How to make tough career decisions

Should I quit my job? Which of my offers should I take? Which long-term options should I explore?

These decisions will affect how you spend years of your time, so the stakes are high. But they're also an area where you shouldn't expect your intuition to be a reliable guide.[304] This means it's worth taking a more systematic approach.

What might a good career decision process look like? A common approach is to make a pro and con list, but it's possible to do a lot better. Pro and con lists make it easy to put too much weight on an unimportant factor. More importantly, they don't encourage you to make use of the most powerful decision-making methods, which can greatly improve the quality of your decisions.

SHOULD I DRINK BLEACH?

PROS

CONS

**CHEAPER THAN FOOD
ALREADY HAVE SOME
IT'S NICE TO TRY NEW
THINGS**

WOULD KILL ME

Pro and con lists make it easy to put too much weight on an unimportant factor.

In this appendix, we present a step-by-step process for making your next career decision, drawing on our impression of the most useful discoveries in decision-making research[305] and our experience advising thousands of people one-on-one.

Career decisions usually involve a huge amount of uncertainty. If you sometimes feel stressed or anxious, this is normal. We can't make your next decision easy, but if you work through this process, we think you'll be more likely to avoid common mistakes and take the best next step you can.

1. Clarify your decision

First, make sure you have a clear idea of exactly what decision you want to make. Are you choosing where to apply, between two specific offers, which medium-term options to focus on, or something else? When do you need to decide by?

Also note that this process is geared towards choosing between a list of specific options. (If you need help generating options — check out the rest of the guide, especially chapter 9 on career planning.)

2. Write out your most important priorities

Once you're clear about the next decision you need to make, write out your 4–7 most important priorities in making the decision. When making decisions, people usually focus on too narrow a set of goals.[306] Writing out your list of factors will help you stay focused on what most matters.

We typically recommend that people focus on these factors, which we think capture most of the key elements in high-impact careers:

- Impact potential – how pressing is the problem addressed and how large a contribution might the typical person in this career make to the problem (in expectation)?
- Personal fit – compared to the typical person in this career in the long-term, how productive do you expect to be?
- Personal satisfaction – how would this path satisfy other important personal priorities that aren't already covered?
- Career capital — does this option significantly accelerate you in a

long-term path, or otherwise open up better long-term options?
- Option value — if you pursue this option, how good are your back-up plans?
- Value of information — might this path be an outstanding long-term option that you're uncertain about and can test out?

If working with a community, you might also consider:
- Relative fit – how do your strengths compare to other community members focusing on these issues (which determines your comparative advantage)?
- Community capital — does this increase the influence of the community and its ability to coordinate?

This list of factors needs to be adapted depending on the decision you're making. For instance, if you're thinking about your long-term options, then focus on impact, personal fit and satisfaction. If you're considering which job to take next year, then also consider the value of information, career capital and option value.

Also try to make the factors more specific based on your situation. What type of career capital is most valuable? What signals best predict impact in the areas you're focused on? What exactly are your priorities in personal satisfaction? On the latter, it's important to try to be honest, even about your least noble motivations, or otherwise the path won't be sustainable.

There are also some other filters to consider:
- Do a significant number of people think this option is likely to have a negative impact in a top area? If so, can you modify the option to avoid the risk? If not, eliminate it.[307]
- Does this option pose a significant risk of a long-term negative impact on your happiness or career capital? If so, modify it or eliminate it.

3. Generate options

One of the most important mistakes when making career decisions is to consider too few options. Some research suggests that even just making sure you consider one extra option improves satisfaction with outcomes.

We looked at how to generate options — by working backwards from your long-term vision, and working forward from your current situation — in chapter 9.

Here are some prompts for working backwards:

- Which jobs / courses / projects will best help you get into your top long-term options?
- Which options will best help you test out your long-term options?
- Check our career reviews (see appendix 8) for more information on how to enter the paths we highlight.

Here are some prompts for working forwards:

- Speak to your friends, those working on interesting problems, and people you admire, and ask about what might be a good fit for you.
- Check out the jobs listed on our job board (jobs.80000hours.org) – do any of them seem interesting?
- What options might you be unusually good at?
- What options might help you learn the most?
- What 'open doors' are available right now? These are interesting opportunities that you happen to have come across and might not be around in the future.

Here are even more prompts to help you come up with more options. Pick and choose whichever seem most useful to think about:

- Career capital – What's the most valuable career capital you have right now? What are your greatest strengths? How could these be applied to having an impact?
- Ideal world – What would you do if money were no object? What

is your dream job?
- Combinations – are there any ways your top options could be combined to get the best of all worlds?
- Elimination – if you couldn't do any of your top options, what would you do instead?

4. Rank your options

Now you've got your options on the table, put them in a rough order according to how well they satisfy the factors you wrote down at step two. Don't worry too much about accuracy – we just want to get a rough idea at this stage to make it easier to do the next couple of steps.

5. List your key uncertainties

Try to identify the information that is most likely to change your ranking.

The questions people most commonly ask us are often not actually decision relevant. Frequently, people focus on big picture questions that are too hard to settle, so thinking about them is unlikely to change their ranking. It's also easy to get lost ruminating about the huge variety of issues that can be relevant. Try to focus on the questions that are most relevant.

Some useful questions to consider include:
- How could you most easily rule out your top option?
- If you had to decide your career tomorrow for the rest of your life, what would you do today?
- What were you most uncertain about in making your ranking? Do any of those uncertainties seem easy to resolve?

Some of the most common questions are things like:
- Would I enjoy this job?
- Could I get this job?
- What skills are required to get this job?

- How pressing is this problem compared to other issues you could work on?
- How much influence would you really have in this position?

Try to make the questions as specific as possible.

6. Go and investigate

Not every decision in life deserves serious research, but career decisions do.

We often find people get stuck analysing their options, when it would be better to go and gather information or test out their options. For instance, we encountered an academic who wanted to take a year long sabbatical, but wasn't sure where to go. They'd thought about the decision for a while, but hadn't considered going to visit their top choice for a week, which would have likely made the decision a lot easier.

We looked at how to investigate your options in chapter 8 — think of a **ladder of tests** that go in ascending order of cost, and aim to settle the key uncertainties you've identified.

We often encounter people considering taking drastic action – like quitting their job – before taking lower cost ways to learn more about what's best first.

One of the most useful, but often neglected, steps is to **simply apply to lots of jobs**. We often find people wondering whether one path is better than another, when if they'd applied, it would have been obvious which one to go for.

If you're lucky, at some point in these investigations, your next step will become clear.

If it doesn't, then you can keep going up the ladder of tests until you run out of time, or perceive that your best guess about which option is best is no longer changing (technically, when the value of information is less than the cost of the test). One other rule of thumb is that the higher the stakes of the decision, the more time it's worth investigating.

The aim is not confidence. You will likely always be uncertain about many aspects of your career. Instead, the aim is to find the best possible ranking using low-cost tests and basic research. Once you've done that, the most efficient way to learn more is probably to pick an option and try it out.

7. Make your final assessment

When you've finished investigating, it's time to make a decision. Here are some more decision-making tips to help make your ranking more accurate.

Consider scoring your options

It can be useful to score your short-list of options on each of the factors listed in your second step from one to ten. There's some evidence that making a structured decision like this can improve accuracy. It can be useful to add all your scores together and see what ranks highest. Don't blindly use the score to determine your decision — it's mainly a means of probing your thinking.

Upside-downside analysis

If you want to go into more detail in making your assessment, then also consider imagining an upside and downside scenario for your top options to get a sense of the full range of possibilities (instead of thinking narrowly, which is the norm, and is especially misleading in the world of doing good, where often most of your impact comes from the small chance of an outsized success).

A simple way to do that is to consider a 'success' and 'failure' scenario for each. A more complex option is to consider:

- The upside scenario – what happens in a plausible best-case scenario? (To be more precise, that could be the top 5% of outcomes.)
- The downside scenario – what happens in a plausible worst-case scenario? (E.g. the worst 5% of outcomes.)
- The median – what's most likely to happen?

In each scenario, consider how good or bad the option will be based on the factors you defined earlier – impact, career capital, learning and so on. One saving grace is that you often learn the most from failures, so the downside scenario is perhaps not as bad as it seems.

If you weight each scenario by their probability, you can make a rough estimate of the expected value of the option — this will often be dominated by the value of the upside scenario.

You may want to eliminate any options that have unusually large downsides. For instance, if you think pursuing an option might burn you out, bankrupt you, ruin your reputation, or holds another risk that could prevent you from making an impact in the future, it's probably best to eliminate it so that you can 'stay in the game' and continue to have opportunities to contribute in the future.

It's also worth being very cautious about any course of action that might significantly set back your field, especially because these are easy to underestimate, and eliminating any options that seem harmful from a common sense perspective (see appendix 5).

If you're trying to decide which job to focus on for a couple of years, then a big part of your decision should be learning about what might be the best fit for you in the long term (value of information). As we saw in chapter 8, this can mean it's best to focus on the path with the best upside scenario rather than the best expected value (provided the downsides are similar). This is because if the upside scenario is realised, you can stick with it, and if it isn't, you can switch to something else. This asymmetry means it's rational to be somewhat optimistic.

Check your gut intuition

After you've finished your assessments, take a break, and re-rank your options.

Once you've made a ranking, **notice if your gut intuition feels uneasy about something**. You can't simply go with your gut to make good career decisions, but you shouldn't ignore your gut either. Your intuition is good at aspects of the decision where you've had lots of opportunity to practise with relatively quick feedback, such as whether the other people involved are trustworthy. But your intuition is not good at assessing novel situations, as many career decisions are.

If your gut feels uneasy, try to pinpoint why you're having that reaction, and whether it makes sense to go with your gut or not in this instance. The ideal of good decision-making is to combine intuitive and systematic methods, and use the best aspects of each.

It's also a good idea to sleep on it. This may help you process the information. It also reduces the chance that you'll be unduly influenced by your mood at that moment.

More ways to reduce bias

If you want to go further, here are some other techniques to help reduce bias in your thinking:

- **Ask yourself why you're most likely to be wrong about your ranking.** This is one of the most useful tips to reduce bias.[308]
- **Pre-mortem and pre-party:** Imagine that you take an option, but two years later you've failed and regret the decision — what went wrong? Then imagine that instead the option was way better than you expected — what happened? This helps to expand your views about what's possible, which tend to be too narrow.
- **Change the frame.** Imagine you've already made the decision, how do you feel? How do you expect to feel one year later? What about 10 years later? What would you advise a friend to do?
- **Ask other people.** Having to justify your reasoning to someone else can quickly uncover holes. You can also ask people where they think you're most likely to be wrong.

More advanced decision-making techniques

There is much more to say about how to make good decisions. For instance, often decisions come down to predictions, especially about your likely chances of success in an area, and the expected impact of different interventions.

For instance, to make better predictions, you can make base-rate forecasts from many angles, combining them based on their predictive power.[309] You should try to update on your evidence in a 'bayesian' way. You can break down the prediction into multiple components as a 'fermi estimate'. And you can try to improve your calibration through training.

See the section on decision-making in appendix 4 for much more information.

8. Make your best guess, and then prepare to adapt

At some point, you'll need to make a decision. If you're lucky, one of your options will be clearly better than the others. Otherwise, the decision will be tough.

Don't be too hard on yourself: the aim is to make the best choice you can given the evidence available. If you've been through the process above then you have put yourself in a position to make a well-considered decision.

Here are some further steps you can take to reduce downsides.

Plan B

First, create a backup plan if your top choice doesn't work out.

- Why is your top option most likely not to work out?
- What will you do in this situation? List any promising nearby alternatives to plan A, and call them your 'plan B'. For instance, if you're already in a job and applying to a masters programme, one possibility is that you don't get into the programmes you want. In that case, your plan B might be to stay in your job another year.

Read the section on plan Bs in chapter 9 for more detail.

Consider how to order your options

When doing the above exercise, you might realise it's much easier to switch from option X to Y, than from Y to X i.e. that option X is more reversible than Y.

For instance, after completing a PhD, everyone in academia agrees that if you leave, it's hard to re-enter. This is because getting a permanent academic position is very competitive, and any sign that you're not committed will rule you out (especially in certain subjects). This means that if you're unsure about continuing with academia after your PhD, it's often best to continue.

If you haven't started a PhD, and want to try something else, then it's best to do that before you start.

It can sometimes be better to enter the more reversible option, even if you're less confident it's best. If you're right and it doesn't work out, you can go back to your top option later anyway.

Read the tips on ordering your options in chapter 8, then ask yourself whether thinking about ordering should cause you to rerank your options.

Plan Z

You may face unforeseen setbacks, so it's also useful to figure out a 'Plan Z'. Here are some questions to help you do that.

- If you take your top option, what might the worst case scenario be? Many risks are not as bad as they first seem, but pay attention to anything that could permanently reduce your happiness or career capital.
- How can you reduce the chances of the worst case happening? It's difficult to give general advice, but there are often ways to mitigate the risks.
- If the worst case scenario does happen, what will you do to cope?

Call this your 'Plan Z'. Some common options include: taking a temporary job to pay the bills, moving back in with your parents, or living off savings. What makes most sense will again depend a lot on your situation.

- Is your Plan Z tolerable? If not, then you should probably modify your plan A to build more career capital so that you're in a better position to take risks (e.g. take a job that lets you save more money). If it is, great – hopefully this exercise will make it easier to commit to your Plan A.

Read the section on plan Zs in chapter 9 for more detail.

Set a review point

A final point to bear in mind is that your next career step is probably only a commitment for 1–4 years — building a career is a step-by-step process, not a one-off decision — and if you plan ahead to that next revision point, you'll be better able to focus on your top option in the meantime, as well as be more prepared when it arrives. Here are some extra steps to consider:

1. Schedule in a time to review your career in six months or a year. We made a career review tool to make it easier.[310]
2. Set check-in points. Make a list of signs that would tell you you're on the wrong path, and commit to reassessing if those occur. For example, publishing lots of papers in top journals is key to success in academic careers, so you could commit to reassessing the academic path if you don't publish at least one paper in a top journal before the end of your PhD.

9. Take action

Once your plan is set, it's time to focus on execution. How to execute is not the main focus of this article, but here are some further resources.

First, translate your plan into very concrete next steps. Write out what you're going to do and when you'll do it. Setting 'implementation intentions' makes it significantly more likely you'll follow through.[311]

To get more ideas on how to increase your chances of success in a path:

- Check out our relevant career reviews, which sometimes have a section on how to succeed in a path. You can find some summaries in appendix 8.
- Appendix 2 covers how to become happier and more productive in any job (including how to network).
- Read our summary of advice on how to get a job in chapter 10.

One of the most useful steps you can take is to team up with others who want to have an impact. There are many great communities out there, often focused around specific problems. Your first step should probably be to try to meet people in the communities most relevant to you.

We also helped to found the effective altruism community, which is a group of people who use evidence and reason to work out the best ways to have a positive impact. This community is not for everyone, but through it we've met some of the most impressive people we know. Find out more about how to get involved in chapter 11.

Appendix 5 – Is it ever OK to take a harmful job in order to do more good? An in-depth analysis

Should you be willing to:

1. Work in a morally questionable part of finance in order to make large donations to charity (where you think the donations will have a greater positive impact than the harms done by the work)?
2. Work in a factory farm and make the conditions less bad, causing less suffering overall?
3. Join a political campaign you think might be harmful in order to gain connections (where you think the connections will let you have more positive impact than the harm done by working for the campaign)?
4. Work at a lab developing dangerous biotech so that you can blow the whistle if you see something particularly dangerous happening?

This appendix sets out 80,000 Hours's views on these issues.

We look at how to analyse these situations using moral philosophy, and then apply the results to some common options, like finance, law, and the oil industry. We assume you're capable of taking the harmful option, and focus on the question: "Is it *right* to take it?"

In summary:

- **We believe that in the vast majority of cases, it's a mistake to pursue a career in which the direct effects of the work are seriously harmful**, even if the overall benefits of that work seem greater than the harms. And within a job, we think you should avoid actions that seem very wrong from a commonsense perspective, even if you think it'll do more good overall.
- We think that this position is justified even if all you value, morally,

are the consequences of your actions. But we also think that we should put weight on the commonsense view that the ends don't always justify the means.

- Having said that, **it's important to bear in mind that *all* careers will involve some degree of negative impact**. So the question to think about is not whether your career involves making others worse off, but how much it does and in what way. We think you should be wary of treating classes of career paths monolithically, and instead should pay close attention to the specifics of the job in which you would be working. In the post, we'll outline a process you can use to judge individual cases.

Negative impact is unavoidable

For many, the first rule of ethics is "do no harm."

But this is not a good guide to career choice, because every career causes some negative impact.

For instance, imagine that you become a doctor with the aim of helping people. Everyone makes mistakes, so at some point you're going to mess up, and people might die as a result. In some cases, these mistakes will be your fault, plain and simple — maybe you had too little sleep, or maybe you could have studied a bit harder. But just because this scenario is extremely likely to happen doesn't mean that it's unethical to become a doctor.

Here's another example. Suppose you become vegan in order to avoid hurting animals. You'll still have to eat grains, and when those grains are harvested, typically some field mice will get killed in the process. In our modern economy, almost every action has some negative consequences.

To really minimise your negative impact, you could become a hermit and live alone in the woods. But that hardly seems like the most ethical life, because you're forgoing huge opportunities to help others (see chapter 2).

So, merely pointing out that a career path has negative effects doesn't mean much, because some negative effects are unavoidable.

Another problem is that it really matters exactly *how* you cause a negative impact.

These days when we think of harmful careers, finance is often the first that comes to mind.

But the financial sector employs almost 4% of the workforce, or 6 million people in the US.[312] These people do a huge variety of tasks, from legal compliance, to IT, to trading, to banking.

First, it's highly unlikely that all of these positions are net negative. Rather, some do harm, others do good, and many are roughly neutral.

Second, it matters exactly how the negative consequences come about. If a banker is overpaid, that may be socially wasteful and so in effect have a negative impact on others, but ethically it's very different from a banker who commits fraud.

When we get serious about the ethics of career choice, we cannot simply do no harm, or treat entire industries as a monolith. Rather, we should aim to:

1. Compare positive and negative impact, and seek to do far more good than bad overall.
2. Understand exactly what the harm consists of in the specific job at hand, and then distinguish between permissible negative impact, like the doctor making a mistake, and impermissible negative impact, like the banker committing fraud.

Career advice needs to be tailored to your situation, and that's even more true when there's a significant risk of doing harm.

This is what we'll cover in this appendix.

Why to avoid careers with significant negative impact, even if you think you'll do more good

As we've shown, entirely avoiding negative impact isn't possible. But that doesn't mean you should take a harmful option lightly, even if you think you'll do more good overall by donating or other means.

Our default position is: don't take a career *for the greater good* if that career directly causes significant harm.

And for very similar reasons, we'd oppose taking actions within a career that seem very wrong from a common sense perspective, even if you think they'll do a lot of good.

To see why, consider this question:

> *Is it ethical to kill one person, harvest their organs, and use those organs to save the lives of five people?*

Almost everyone agrees this isn't ethical, at least not in the actual world we live in. And this helps to explain why we would not generally recommend taking a career that causes significant negative impact in order to do more good.

There are five reasons not to take careers that cause significant harm:

1. It might violate rights (non-consequentialist reasons)

Many people think killing the one person is prohibited by the basic rules of moral behaviour, such as "do not kill," which is one of the Ten Commandments.

Early modern philosophers often also appealed to basic principles of morality that would rule this out, like Kant's categorical imperative.

Modern moral philosophers would probably focus on the person's right to life. Killing someone against their will violates their rights, and so is probably not permissible, even if it is for the benefit of more people overall.

Almost all ethicists agree that these rights and rules are not absolute. If you had to kill one person to save 100,000 others, most would agree that it would be the right thing to do (although you might still not be able to bring yourself to do it). However, they would say that such violations should only be made in exceptional circumstances.

Although they'd presumably fall short of literally killing people, jobs with a large negative impact might involve violating rights or other basic moral principles (such as truth-telling), which means that they will usually not be morally permissible on these grounds.

Even if you're sceptical of Kantian or other rules-based morality, it's hard to be confident these are wrong — more on this below.

Later, we'll consider which jobs in particular might be ruled out for these reasons.

2. It's probably not the highest-impact path due to hidden harms (consequentialist reasons)

Other moral philosophers think that what ultimately matters is only whether your actions produce good or bad effects overall. These are called "consequentialist" theories.

These philosophers think that *in principle* it would be justified to kill one person in order to save the lives of five. However, they generally don't think that in practice people should go around harvesting organs. That's usually because such activities would lead to indirect harms that would make everyone worse off in the long-term. So the means also affect the ends.[313]

Turning specifically to career choice, we think there are many ways that taking a harmful job could have overall negative consequences, even if it seems higher impact in the short run (and even if you think you'd be 'replaced' anyway). For instance:

1. **Reputation:** It'll harm your reputation and the reputation of the people you associate with. This makes it harder to achieve good in the future. This effect could be very significant if you're part of a social movement, such as effective altruism, veganism, feminism or environmentalism, because your actions could tar the

reputation of the whole group. (And note your reputation can be ruined merely by doing a job that's widely seen as harmful, even if it actually isn't.)

2. **Character:** Habit and norms are a huge driver of behaviour. Acting in ways that violate important ethical norms (even in small ways) and/or being around unethical people all today probably has a negative impact on your character, making you less able and likely to act morally in the future.

3. **Motivation:** Helping people is motivating, and a job that seems harmful day-to-day could be extremely demotivating, raising your chances of burning out.

4. **Career prospects:** The skills you learn will be less useful, because industries widely seen as harmful often shrink or perish. For instance, the earnings in investment banking went down significantly after new regulations were introduced after the financial crisis. Likewise, if you want to do good, it's helpful to make connections with other people who want to do good, and it will be hard to do this if you work in an industry that's widely seen as unethical.

5. **Signalling:** You'll implicitly make it more socially acceptable for other people to take these jobs, and they probably won't try to use the position for good (e.g. they probably won't donate a large fraction of their income). This effect is most significant when (i) you're doing something unusual and (ii) you have a large network or public platform.

There will probably be other harms, too,[314] and these harms will likely offset any indirect benefits. We think that commonsense moral intuitions often have important insights behind then, even if they're not immediately obvious. All of this means that it's usually better to avoid taking the harmful position even if you only care about the consequences of your actions.

3. You're probably wrong about the benefits

Suppose you've tried to weigh the harms against the benefits and have concluded the benefits are so great, that they outweigh the harms.

But not only might you be ignoring hidden harms (as above), your estimate of the benefits might be way off.

In particular, if you think the benefits of an action are particularly high, due to regression to the mean, you're probably too optimistic about them.

The problem gets worse if you throw in the natural human tendency for self-delusion and overconfidence.

And the track record of people who believed they were "breaking a few eggs" in order to promote "the greater good" seems terrible and includes many of the worst people in history. So taking an outside view should also give us pause.

All things considered, there's a good chance you're simply wrong, and the benefits don't actually outweigh the harms — even though you think they do.

You should be especially cautious in any circumstance where you also personally stand to benefit from the harm, such as via holding onto influence, money or status.

We think that in general, in real life, it's better to stick to simple rules — and just avoid doing anything that seems seriously wrong from a commonsense perspective.

4. Moral uncertainty and cooperation

Suppose you think only consequences matter, and you're convinced that the benefits of taking a job are larger than the harms, even taking into account all the hidden harms and all the arguments above that imply you're probably wrong. Should you do it?

It's very hard to settle ethical questions, so 100% confidence seems crazy. A survey of professional philosophers found they are very divided, and a majority are not consequentialist.[315]

Answer	Number of responses
Other	301 / 931 (32.3%)
Accept or lean toward: deontology	241 / 931 (25.9%)
Accept or lean toward: consequentialism	220 / 931 (23.6%)
Accept or lean toward: virtue ethics	169 / 931 (18.2%)

Even if you think consequences are likely all that matters, you should take into account the fact that there's some chance that it's unethical to ignore other considerations. And so, out of caution, you might still not want to take a harmful career. And, for non-consequentialist views, it's clearly morally wrong to take a career that does a lot of harm — potentially seriously wrong.

So, given our uncertainty, it seems morally safest to avoid significantly harmful careers, as long as there are other options that allow us to do a lot of good. (Will, one of the authors of this article, defended this form of argument at greater length in his PhD thesis.[316])

It's also good to take other moral views seriously so you can maintain cooperation and friendly relations with others who have those views. For instance, if you do something that lots of other people think is unethical, those people aren't going to want to work with you or support you in the future, reducing your long-term impact.

Instead, if you do things that seem good from lots of perspectives, you'll get more support and aid in the future. This is a form of indirect "moral trade."[317]

5. Better alternatives

When we look at real examples of harmful careers, there are often nearby options that are not harmful and almost as good on other dimensions. When this is true, you may as well just take the non-harmful option.

For instance, while some areas of finance might involve deceptively marketing financial products, other parts (like retail banking or venture capital) seem neutral or positive. Venture capital is also very high-earning, so if you're thinking of going into finance to earn to give, it seems better just to avoid the harmful areas.

There won't always be nearby alternatives, and sometimes you'll just face a sharp tradeoff. But our guess is that this won't happen very often.

When *might* it be justified to take a job that has significant negative impact?

We think putting the last five points together makes a good case for mostly avoiding jobs that have a significant negative impact. Doing so could mean violating rights and other moral principles, which should probably concern you even if you think consequences are all that ultimately matters (due to moral uncertainty). The net impact is also probably worse than you think due to hidden harms and because your estimates are wrong. Finally, there are probably better nearby alternative options to be considered.

That said, there might be *exceptional* circumstances in which you should take an option with serious negative impact, even if you're not a consequentialist. As an extreme example, Oskar Schindler ran munitions factories for the Nazis, producing mess kits and, later, ammunition for Nazi soldiers, but in so doing was able to earn enough money to ensure the safety of 1,200 of his Jewish workers. He also deliberately ran the factory inefficiently, so that fewer munitions were produced. It's hard to imagine a more unethical job than running a Nazi munitions factory, but Schindler is widely seen as a hero, and was celebrated in the movie *Schindler's List*.

In an emergency, like Schindler found himself in, it can be permissible to have a significant negative impact in order to achieve a greater positive impact.

There are also clearly cases where it's morally permissible to make individuals worse off. For instance, it's permissible to fire an employee who's performing badly, even though that will make their life worse. Earlier we also mentioned the example of a doctor who makes a mistake.

In what follows, we'll show how to think through these cases, and why it could be morally acceptable to work in finance, even if the industry causes a serious negative impact.

First, clarify exactly what situation you're in

When you're concerned about taking a job with negative impact, you could be in one of the four situations in the following table. Each situation requires a different response.

We've illustrated the four situations for the decision of whether to earn to give in an industry with some substantial negative impacts.

(We just focus on the direct impact of the work and the impact of the donations, whereas in reality you'd want to look at all the types of impact, including career capital and the indirect harms we mentioned earlier.)

Scenario	Impact of the work	Impact of donations	Should you do the job?	Analogy
1. Net harm.	Large negative and morally impermissible.	Small positive.	No. The net impact of taking the job is negative, so everyone agrees you shouldn't do it.	Killing 3 people to save 1 person.
2. Net positive, but arguably morally impermissible.	Small negative and violates a moral rule, e.g. against harming an innocent person.	Large positive.	No. Your net impact is positive, but taking the job may well still be morally impermissible.	Harvesting the organs of 1 person to save to lives of 5.
3. Net positive, permissible.	Small negative but morally permissible (e.g. the positive effects are sufficiently large that they outweigh the negative).	Large positive.	Maybe. It depends on your other opportunities. Maybe there's something even better.	Telling a lie to save 3 people's lives.
4. Industry isn't actually harmful.	Positive.	Positive.	Maybe. It also depends on your other opportunities.	Saving 3 lives when you could have saved 4.

If taking the job is net negative, then obviously you shouldn't take it. The job could also be net positive, but not worth taking because you have a better option.

The tricky part is deciding whether a path with net positive impact is morally impermissible or not — deciding between situations 2 and 3 above. This is what we explore in the next section.

Where's the line between permissible and impermissible negative impact? A step-by-step process for deciding.

Below are some of the key considerations that moral philosophers have proposed to decide between permissible and impermissible harms. We think they're a reasonable place to start when doing the analysis, although all of them are debated within the literature. If you favour non-consequentialism, you might interpret these as morally relevant rules of behaviour. If you favour consequentialism, you might interpret them as rules of thumb for when the indirect harms are relatively small.

These rules of thumb are roughly grouped into four categories.

1. **Emergency situations: are the benefits much larger than the harms?** Most agree that large enough benefits can *outweigh* harms. For instance, imagine an axe murderer came to your door and asked where your family is. You lie and tell him they're out of town. Deceiving people is (usually) wrong, so was that the wrong thing to do? No — almost everyone would agree that it's OK to lie to save the lives of your family. Protecting the lives of your family outweighs the wrong of lying. How large do the stakes have to be before it could be permissible to do harm, or violate someone's rights? There's no clear line, but our rough impression of the literature is that many people think it becomes permissible when the benefits are 100 times larger than the costs. Those with more consequentialist views might think that 10 times larger is already

enough, while those with more deontological views might think over 1,000 times is required. Almost everyone agrees that there is some point at which the harms are immediately outweighed.[318]

2. **Are the harms a means to achieving the good thing, or a side effect?** Deliberately causing harm in order to accomplish a greater good is widely thought to be wrong. For instance, killing innocent people to promote a cause (like in a terrorist bombing) is wrong, even if you expect to do more good in the long term. However, if the harm is an unintended consequence, it's more likely to be permissible. For instance, it could be justified to tolerate civilian casualties to win a just war as long as you make an effort to avoid them, because, unlike the terrorism case, you don't try to kill the civilians in order to achieve the end. If the harms are a side effect, then it's likely permissible to cause a negative impact if the benefits outweigh the harms substantially — even if by *much* less than 100x (e.g. 2–5x).

3. **Do the people involved consent to being made worse off?** Winning money from a friend in a poker game is not immoral, even though it makes your friend worse off. Part of this is because your friend consented to being in the game, knowing that they might lose. If you cheated, however, then this would be wrong, because the friend doesn't consent to play against a cheater. Or if your friend was addicted to poker, then they might not be able to give true consent. With the doctor who makes an error, their patients consent to be treated with full knowledge that the treatment might go wrong. Likewise, the ratio of benefits to harms can again be much lower if both parties consent. (A non-consequentialist might even think it's permissible to make *everyone* worse off if they all consent.)

4. **Is no one being exploited?** Is the arrangement just? Both parties might gain, but if the gains go disproportionately to one side

rather than another, and that side is much more powerful than the other, then it might be considered exploitation, and therefore impermissible. This is why many people consider it wrong to run a sweatshop factory, even if the jobs are better for the workers than what they would have had otherwise (among many other factors).

Based on the above, here's a step-by-step process for deciding whether a job is morally permissible or not:

1. Are the total benefits larger than the harms, including the hidden harms? If not, don't do it.
2. Are the (counterfactual) benefits 100 times larger than the harms with high-confidence (or 10–1,000 times larger, depending on your moral views)? If yes, the non-consequentialist factors are plausibly outweighed.
3. If the benefits are between 1 and 100 times larger than the harms, check the following:
    a. Would you be harming people as a means to your end?
    b. Do the people who get made worse off not consent?
    c. Is one group exploited?
    d. Is it unjust?

    If you answer yes to any of these, it's probably best not to do it (though it still depends on the situation).

Now we'll apply this process to a real case: finance.

Case study: earning to give in finance

We've promoted the idea of taking a highly paid job in finance in order to donate to effective charities — an example of a path we call earning to give.

Suppose you could take a job in finance where you'd expect to earn $200,000 per year, of which you'd donate $50,000 per year to GiveWell's recommended charities. Is this ethically permissible?

As we've said, finance is a huge sector, so it depends on exactly what you're doing. While some jobs in finance might have a negative impact, others are likely neutral or positive. A job that generally has a positive impact can end up having a negative impact if you do harmful or unethical actions within it.

Let's do a rough application of the steps above to finance to show how you might think through the case.

How large are the benefits compared to the harms?

If we define the value of giving $1 to a random American as one "unit" of impact, then we think each dollar donated to GiveDirectly creates at least 20 units of impact. This is mainly because GiveDirectly's recipients are about 100 times poorer, and money goes further the less you have. We're using 20 rather than 100 to be conservative, in case there are some spillover benefits of making rich countries wealthier.

On the basis of GiveWell's review in 2016,[319] we think Against Malaria Foundation is about four times more cost effective than GiveDirectly, and so creates 80 units of impact per dollar of donations.

This means that donations of $50,000 per year produce as much value as giving $4 million to randomly chosen Americans each year, and in concrete terms would be enough to save about seven lives per year. So the question is whether a single individual working in finance and earning $200,000 per year causes a comparable amount of harm.

In a 2013 article, we argued that for the financial sector on average, it's implausible that the harms are anywhere near this large. It would mean that the finance sector as a whole was doing harm on the scale of killing tens of millions of people each year.[320]

Moreover, since then we've seen other quantitative estimates, which generally find that the harms are smaller than the salary. For instance, we found a rough estimate that workers in finance cause negative externalities to the American economy of about 30% of their salary, which would be

~$70,000 per year.[321] And this seems more likely to be an overestimate than an underestimate, since, among other reasons, it doesn't fully take account of replaceability.

We also made a rough estimate of the damage caused by jobs in the financial sector that increase the chance of a financial crisis, and found a figure of $42,000 per year.[322]

This negative impact is large enough to make working in finance in a way that increases the chance of a financial crisis arguably ethically wrong if you don't donate to effective charities. But if you donate 25% of your income to Against Malaria Foundation, the benefits are over 50 times larger than the harms.

However, bear in mind some caveats:

First, the estimates are highly uncertain, and only apply to finance jobs *on average*. If you picked the *most* harmful jobs in finance, they could be much worse. For instance, in the leadup to the financial crisis, certain executives in investment banks who oversaw poor lending practices probably had a far greater negative impact than typical workers. It seems plausible that many caused more harm than the good they could have done by donating their income to charity (which, by and large, they didn't…).

This isn't, however, an argument against finance in general. It's possible to do huge amounts of harm in many professions, and obviously you should avoid this.

Second, a 50 times difference isn't *obviously* enough to put you in an outweighing scenario, and so we still need to consider whether the negative impact is ethically permissible, as we do in the next section.

Third, we've ignored hidden harms.

For instance, you could have an advocacy impact, such as making it more socially acceptable for others to take jobs like yours, causing additional harms. However, going into finance is relatively common, while donating a large fraction of your income to effective charities is not. So it seems likely the bigger effect is to encourage others to donate more.

A more difficult case is with reputation. The effective altruism community has to some extent become associated with earning to give in finance, which has discouraged some people from getting involved. This could have done more harm than good (though it seems like a relatively small factor going forward, since those costs have already been paid).

On the other hand, we've ignored the possibility that some jobs in finance have a positive impact. For instance, value investors like Warren Buffett do intense research to identify undervalued firms. This brings information into the market, helping to make the price of company shares more accurate. This means companies get investment in proportion to their needs, helping the economy to grow.

Moreover, Buffett often invests after major crashes. This helps to prop up falling prices, making markets less volatile. So, it's at least plausible that Buffett's impact is positive, though it's hard to say.

Are the negative impacts permissible or not?

Let's suppose the benefits of the donations are only 1 to 100 times larger than the negative impacts of finance, and that we don't count that as an outweighing situation. *Then*, would the path be morally permissible? Would we be in situation 2 or 3 from the table above?

We want to know:
- Are the harms intended?
- Are people used as means?
- Do the people who get made worse off not consent to it?
- Is one group exploited?

This depends on the details of what you're doing.

For instance, in the leadup to the financial crisis, some people in finance sold people mortgages that they knew they probably couldn't afford if there was a small increase in interest rates, but didn't make these risks clear. Moreover, sometimes this was done on the back of fraudulent income statements. Besides the large economic damage this caused, these activities involved intentionally deceiving people, making them morally impermissible. They were also illegal.[323] Leading banks have collectively paid over $100 billion in fines due to these activities,[324] and Goldman Sachs has admitted it defrauded investors.[325]

On the other hand, suppose you work at a hedge fund that trades the markets and makes large profits at the expense of other investors who trade frequently. This makes other people worse off, but it doesn't seem morally impermissible. Rather, it seems more like the example of winning money off your friend while playing poker, or haggling to get a cheap product.

Moreover, most of the wealth in financial markets is held by the top 1%. They understand the risks of trading the markets and consent to taking on these risks. So if you trade against them and win, it's hard to find a moral objection.

Some other jobs in finance are probably just socially wasteful. For instance, investors employ asset managers who don't beat the market on average, so don't produce any value for them. Many of these asset managers also probably don't create significant positive externalities by making the market more efficient (though perhaps some do, like Warren Buffett as we mentioned earlier). This is a shame, but it doesn't seem like it's morally impermissible to take the job if you're going to donate the money. If investors want to waste their money on useless managers, that's OK, so long as they're not being deceived. If you then redirect these funds into socially positive activities, that's for the better.

Are there better alternatives?

Suppose you restrict yourself to a part of finance that has neutral or small positive direct impact. In that case, we're in situation 4 from the table above.

We still think it's often not best to pursue finance to earn to give, because there are other options that have greater impact or career capital.

For instance, the expected earnings in tech entrepreneurship are similar (though higher risk), but tech entrepreneurship potentially has a greater direct impact, and likely gives you better career capital too. So, if you're a reasonable personal fit for both finance and tech entrepreneurship, then there's a good argument that tech entrepreneurship is better.

We also think many areas are more talent constrained than funding constrained, so if you have the skills to go into finance, it may well be better to work directly in a socially valuable organisation instead.

Overall, we don't currently rate investment banking as a "recommended" career, though we do sometimes recommend quant trading.

Conclusions on finance

It's hard to generalise, because there are so many different types of activities within finance. Some parts seem net harmful, some morally impermissible, and some are just outweighed by alternatives. However, there are probably also options that are reasonable contenders for someone with good personal fit.

Which jobs might get ruled out?

We made some guesses at jobs that involve causing a significant amount of negative impact.[326] In these jobs, the negatives are likely too great compared to the benefits, even if you donate. Some might also be morally impermissible for non-consequentialist reasons.

1. Marketing and R&D for compulsive behaviours such as smoking, alcoholism, gambling, and payday loans
2. Factory farming
3. Fraudulent medicine
4. Patent trolls
5. Lobbying for rent-seeking industries
6. Weapons development
7. Activities that make financial firms highly risky

8. Fundraising for a charity that's less effective than average
9. Forest clearing
10. Tax minimisation for the rich

Working in the oil and gas industries might also qualify, but we haven't looked into them much.

Bear in mind that the list isn't the result of thorough research, and any of the above could easily be wrong. Making good estimates of the size of the harms and benefits is very hard, as is analysing the ethics of the situation.

What actions are ruled out?

Doing an analysis at the level of jobs is still very broad — for most people, analysing specific actions will be more useful.

Unfortunately, it's hard to give clear guidelines that everyone can agree with. However, to give you a flavour, here are some examples of actions that could become possibilities in your career, which we think should be ruled out:

- Committing fraud or stealing money while 'earning to give' (this idea became particularly salient because of the charges against Sam Bankman-Fried)[327]
- Being dishonest (including withholding important negative information) in order to have a stronger pitch for a charity or an idea
- Covering up unethical behaviour committed by someone doing important work
- Acts of violence as a form of protest, even if you think it might be justified to draw attention to a crisis like climate change or a potential AI disaster

Should you go into a harmful industry in order to make it better?

For instance, could it be justified to work on a factory farm for a year in order to publicise the conditions, or develop better welfare standards that could be applied across the industry?

This is a tricky situation, and should not be pursued without a lot of thought. Our main advice is to be cautious and seek advice from people with an outside perspective.

When *might* it be justified? Applying what came earlier, one situation might be *outweighing* — if the benefits are expected to be much larger (such as 100 times) than the harms. This seems plausible with the example suggested above.

Second, it seems more acceptable if you can work in a position that doesn't directly harm the animals, since then the harm seems more like a side effect, rather than intentional.

Conclusion

If you're considering taking a career with a substantial negative impact (even if you think it'll be net positive), you probably shouldn't, for a few reasons:

1.   There are likely to be better alternatives.
2.   The option is probably less positive than it first looks, due to hidden harms.
3.   Even if it's net positive, you probably shouldn't violate common standards of morality. Even if you mainly care about the consequences of your actions, it's worth putting some weight on the commonsense position that the ends don't justify the means.

However, that doesn't mean you should *never* take a career that causes some harm. For one thing, all careers have some negative impacts. In exceptional circumstances, it might well be justified, such as when the benefits outweigh the harms by more than 100 times (or 10–1,000 times, depending on how consequentialist you are). It also might be justified to cause the negative impact even if the benefits outweigh the harms by a much smaller factor (say 2–5 times), if the harms aren't especially morally problematic, like being an overpaid asset manager.

We think a combination of these factors can apply in high-stakes areas such as national security, where it's very hard to guarantee you'll never do harm — even very significant harm — but you might also have opportunities to prevent a lot of harm, and the moral rules are pretty complicated.

For example, the national security establishment in the US has a big effect on the development of AI – and we think risks from AI are one of the world's most pressing problems. But it's important to take seriously the substantial harm that's sometimes been done in the name of national security. You will find yourself in an ethically complicated situation if you're professionally obligated to protect one country's national security — potentially at the expense of another's. Sufficient progress reducing those risks may well put you in an 'outweighing' situation, and if there are no other better options, the harms of a career in national security are also more likely to be permissible.

So, if you are considering taking a harmful job that causes some harm because you think overall it can help you make the world better, be really cautious, and explore all the arguments before you go ahead. Much comes down to the details of the situation, so you need to make a case-by-case analysis.

Further reading

- Ways people trying to do good accidentally make things worse, and how to avoid them
  (80000hours.org/articles/accidental-harm)
- Appendix 1, and the longer article "What is social impact? A definition"
  (80000hours.org/articles/what-is-social-impact-definition)
- Notes on good judgement and how to develop it
  (80000hours.org/2020/09/good-judgement/)
- Our interview with Will MacAskill on why our descendents will probably see us as moral monsters
  (80000hours.org/podcast/episodes/will-macaskill-moral-philosophy)
- "Considering considerateness: Why communities of do-gooders should be exceptionally considerate", which argues that people who want to do good should aim to be extremely considerate of others — and presumably as a corollary, not take jobs that are widely seen as harmful.
  (www.centreforeffectivealtruism.org/blog/considering-considerateness-why-communities-of-do-gooders-should-be)
- "Integrity for Consequentialists" by Paul Christiano
  (sideways-view.com/2016/11/14/integrity-for-consequentialists/)

Appendix 6 – College advice

Here is some tentative college advice about how to choose an undergraduate course, and what to do once you start studying. It's based on our general knowledge and the experiences of people we've advised. We haven't yet done in-depth research into this area, so our views could easily change.

Priorities

Clarify what you want to get out of college. Three common priorities include:

1. Studying – so you can get good grades or learn useful skills
2. Social – many people meet their most important friends and romantic partners through their college network
3. Preparing for your future career through work, side projects, or research
4. Generally learning about yourself and the world

On preparing for your future career, you're right at the start — so it usually makes sense to focus mainly on exploring promising future career options and building flexible career capital, rather than pursuing a single option (unless you've already identified something that seems clearly best). We discuss how to do that below.

It's worth asking yourself how much you want to focus on each of these priorities, or whether you want to prioritise something else.

It can help to make some guesses about potential longer-term career options to help inform this. For instance, if you're interested in research, then getting good grades is important to get into graduate school. We discuss how much time to spend studying below. You can use chapter 9 (on career planning) to reflect on longer-term career options.

Which degree subject?

Here are some key factors to consider when weighing your options:

Personal fit – Will you be good at the subject? If you're good at the subject, it's more likely you'll be able to pursue work in that area later on, you'll enjoy it more, you'll get better grades, and you'll do the work more quickly.

Flexibility of the programme – Does it open up lots of options, both inside and outside academia?

If you're unsure about personal fit, try out the subject (e.g. through an online course, or in a minor course).

Which subjects offer the most options and flexibility?

- One indicator is the earnings prospects. In general, more applied, quantitative subjects lead to the highest earnings, even if you adjust for the intelligence of the people studying different subjects.[328]
- However, some subjects only improve earnings at the expense of flexibility. Petroleum engineers have among the highest earnings, but their fate is tied to a single (declining?) industry. In general, more 'fundamental' subjects provide more flexibility. For instance, you can go from economics into the rest of the social sciences, but the reverse is harder. People with applied maths skills probably have the most flexibility – they can go into biology, physics, economics, computer science, psychology and many other areas. The worst options for flexibility are narrow applied options, such as nursing or education.
- Some subjects are more prestigious than others, especially those perceived as 'difficult', like maths, medicine, and philosophy. This is important because a lot of the value of a degree comes from the 'signal' it gives to future employers.
- Some majors at certain institutions are more prestigious than the same major at other institutions. For example, UC Berkeley is well

known for its business programme, so if you're already at Berkeley, that's an extra reason to consider pursuing that major.

Some other, less important, factors to consider include:

- **Relevance of the option to your longer-term plans** — If you want to e.g. become a medic, you'll need to study pre-med. Flexibility is usually more important than relevance, but it's also worth considering.
- **Difficulty of learning the subject outside of university** — Some subjects are hard to study by yourself, either because they require lots of feedback, discipline, or cumulative background knowledge. This is most pronounced with quantitative technical skills, like statistics or mathematical modelling. It also applies to skills like understanding law or accounting, or being good at writing.

Putting all this together, and holding all else equal:

- We think it's reasonable to aim for the most fundamental, quantitative option you can do, i.e. one of these in the following order: mathematics, economics, computer science, physics, engineering, political science/chemistry/biology (the last three are roughly equal).
- If you want to focus on something non-quantitative, then consider focusing on developing great written communication skills in philosophy, history, or English.
- If you want to do something more applied, then maybe choose business or accounting.
- A good combination seems to be a major in a quantitative subject and a minor in a subject that requires great written skills (e.g. a major in maths and a minor in philosophy). We say this because people who can both understand quantitative topics and communicate clearly seem to be in high demand in all kinds of areas.

But don't forget personal fit. For instance, if you'd be mediocre at mathematics — but great at political science or philosophy — then it's probably better to go for the subject you'd be great at.

How to spend your time while at college

How much time to spend studying

If you want to keep open the option of going into academia and to also keep open the option of pursuing some professional courses like law and medicine, then you need top grades (1st class honours in the UK, or a GPA over 3.6 in the US).

If you're learning something in your course you're likely to use in the future (e.g. how to write, engineering, programming, or statistics), then it can also be good to study hard and learn those skills. This is especially true for skills that are hard to study by yourself e.g. most people find it easier to learn mathematics in school, whereas reading history is easier to do in your spare time later on, and it's more effective to learn languages by spending time in the relevant country than in college classes.

However, most people never use 90%+ of what they learn in college. The main benefit of studying hard is to get the credential.[329]

You also don't need top grades in many career paths. For instance, many employers (e.g. many professional services positions) are satisfied with middling grades (2.1 in the UK, or GPA over 3.0 in the US), or you might want to be self-employed.[330]

In this case, it's probably more important to do internships and side projects – college is perhaps the best time in your life to pursue a side interest, since you have so much flexibility. Many important projects and startups were started while at university (which is also where we started 80,000 Hours). The right internship can often turn into a job offer, which can make a big difference to your first career step.

As we discussed in appendix 2, 'leadership' skills are extremely valuable, and your connections are also very important for your later success. This could mean that it's similarly important to do things like meet people and improve these skills, such as by managing a student society.

In fact, even in cases where good grades are useful to your future career, it could still be *even more* useful to pursue side projects, internships, running student societies, etc. Going from acceptable to great grades often takes a lot of extra time, and this time can often be better spent on other priorities.

We've been discussing the importance of good grades, but in the US, there's also the question of how *many* courses to take. While students sometimes take as many courses as they can, this leaves them with much less time for the valuable activities we mentioned earlier: getting good grades in the classes they do take, doing internships, doing side projects, meeting people, running student societies, etc. At the same time, taking more courses doesn't add much to the 'credential' value of your degree. For these reasons, we think undergraduates can usually do better by replacing several of their would-be classes with other valuable activities. (There can be exceptions, e.g. if extra classes let you learn concrete skills you'll actually use, if they open up graduate school options, or if they let you explore other potential career paths).[331]

If you need to write a thesis towards the end of your degree, the project Effective Thesis (effectivethesis.com) tries to help people choose the right question to research to advance their long-term career while hopefully also moving you closer to a socially impactful topic. If you find an opportunity to develop expertise in an important question, that would count in favour of studying more.

How to study effectively

By learning how to learn, you can probably study far faster than you do today.

And by keeping your goals clearly in mind, you might be able to be far more efficient in choosing what to study in the first place. Some classes you will only need to pass, rather than remember the material, and in those cases it makes sense to optimise for the exam. It's easy to instead get caught feeling like you need to do everything 'well', because that's what's expected of you, rather than to think about what you're actually trying to achieve.

Read more about this in appendix 2. We'd also recommend Cal Newport's book *How to Win at College*.[332]

How to explore future career options

In preparing for your future career, most people have not yet identified a standout option while at university, and instead the priority should be to explore options that might be standouts. This is especially true since college is one of your best opportunities to explore, because you have enormous flexibility and it's what society expects you to do — so you have lots of opportunities to explore that go away later (e.g. internships).

You can explore standout options by learning about them, or by trying out relevant next steps, which both helps you to assess your fit and to get relevant career capital.

In brief:

1. Draw up a long list of potentially great longer-term options. A common mistake is to explore 'standard' paths (e.g. finance and consulting) even if you're confident you don't want to do these after college, though these are sometimes worth doing purely as a credential.

2. See if you can 'try out' all of these paths while in college and right after.

3. Also explore some 'wild card' options, even if they seem like long shots. You don't want to narrow down too early, and trying something off the beaten path is more likely to surprise you.

You can consider all the following ways to try out potential paths, which also give you useful career capital:

1. Doing 1-2 internships or summer jobs.
2. Doing a research project as part of your studies or during the summer.
3. Going to lots of talks by people in different areas.
4. Getting involved in relevant student societies (e.g. student newspaper).
5. Doing side projects and self-study in your free time (e.g. building a website, learning to code, volunteering).
6. If you're interested in doing graduate school in a subject, attend lectures in that subject.
7. Before you start, seriously consider taking a gap year, where you work part of the time. This both helps you explore and be better prepared for college, and people rarely seem to regret it.
8. Near the end, you can apply to jobs in several categories as well as graduate school, and see where you get the best offers.
9. After college, you can keep exploring. In particular, you can do something unusual for ~2 years, and then go to graduate school, which helps you to 'reset' onto the standard path.

Read more about how to explore in chapter 8.

What else to do outside your degree?

1. Get involved with student societies to learn about important ideas, make friends, and build career capital. If you want to have a big impact with your career, we especially recommend getting involved with your university's effective altruism student group, if it has one.
2. Consider travelling, especially to somewhere with a very different culture, and/or to a very poor country.
3. Build lasting friendships. University is perhaps your single best opportunity to make lifelong friends, and they're extremely

important for your long-term happiness and success. It's also pretty common to end up marrying someone you met through college. Once you start work, you have far less time to hang out with new people, and you won't meet as many people similar to you. We know lots of people who regret not spending more time meeting people while at university.

4. Invest in your personal development. The flexibility of college makes it a great time to work on your routines (e.g. finding a form of exercise you like) and mental health, which can be one of the best investments you make for the long term. See appendix 2 for ideas.

5. Take up extracurricular options that build skills, that you enjoy, and that look good. For example, you can run a student society, start a microbusiness (read *The $100 Startup* by Chris Guillebeau),[333] or do anything you'll be good at and that allows you to get impressive achievements.

Should you go to college at all?

On average, in financial terms, college is a great investment. Researchers on this topic widely agree that going to college significantly boosts your income, even after you account for (i) lost earnings while studying (ii) the fact that the people who go to college are often more able, which means they'll earn more anyway.[334]

Our guess is that this boost reflects a general increase in your career capital – not only will you earn more, you'll also be more productive and influential. Moreover, the boost seems large enough that (i) college is likely to be better than whatever else you could be doing to boost your career capital, and (ii) it's likely to be better to make this investment in yourself rather than try to make a difference sooner.

We don't know what causes the boost. It's likely a combination of the skills you learn, the fact that employers value the credential, and the connections you make, but we're not sure which is most important.

What are the exceptions?

College is unlikely to offer great returns in the following cases:

- If you're likely to drop out. If you'd struggle with the academic demands, or really not enjoy it, then consider not going. If you think you wouldn't enjoy college, bear in mind that there are lots of different types of college and social scenes, which can provide very different experiences.[335]
- If you've found a more effective way to build your career capital. These opportunities seem rare, but they do exist. For instance, we've met people who learned to program and skipped college. This can work because the technology industry doesn't care so much about formal credentials (though you're still betting your career on one industry). Getting a Thiel Fellowship is another example.
- If you've found a time-sensitive opportunity to do good. In that case, it might be better to delay going to college to do good right away. For instance, if you have a startup project that's taking off.

However, in most cases, if you think you've found something better than going to college, it's best to start college, do the project on the side, then leave if it takes off (and ideally retain the option to return). This is what many famous dropouts like Bill Gates did.

For more on how to think about the decision, take a look at colah.github. io/posts/2020-05-University — a longer post by Chris Olah (a machine learning researcher who didn't attend college). We also interviewed Chris for our podcast, which you can listen to at 80k.info/chris-olah.

For a detailed analysis of the costs and benefits of going to college — and how to think it through in your own case — we'd recommend chapter 5 of Bryan Caplan's book, *The Case Against Education*.[336] This book is controversial, but we think the general approach to thinking about the question makes sense.[337]

Which type of university should you go to?

One famous study in the US found that students who were accepted to an 'elite' university but turned it down, went on to earn just as much. This suggests that elite universities are selecting more talented people, but not actually helping them be more successful (with the exception of low-income students, who did earn more).[338]

It could be that the benefits of elite universities are mainly offset by other costs, such as an increased chance of burning out. Or perhaps talented students at non-elite universities get more attention from professors. Given that elite universities also cost more, the choice is not obvious.

On the other hand, it could be that the main benefits of elite universities are not reflected in income.

We find it hard to believe that elite universities don't offer significant benefits. Attending an elite university is widely seen as a good credential by employers. Most importantly, there are more opportunities to meet other talented students at elite universities, helping you build better connections. Certain elite professions are also dominated by people from top colleges (e.g. judges).

Overall, we think it's still better to try to attend an elite university, but we're not sure.

You can get more information on how to compare different institutions using 'value-added' rankings, such as *The Economist*'s rankings of US universities (at 80k.info/economist-ur).

There's also evidence that an elite university degree is helpful if you do a liberal arts major or a business degree, but not if you major in science.[339] This could be because arts subjects are harder to evaluate, so employers resort to credentials to compare candidates. Your network might also be more important outside of science. So, if you want to study science, going to a good value state college is a decent option.

Finally, bear in mind that your choice of major is similarly important to your choice of university, so it could be better to do your preferred major at a less prestigious university.

Further reading

- Our podcast with 80,000 Hours advisors Michelle and Habiba, discussing the advice they'd have given their younger selves (80k.info/michelle-habiba).
- Our podcast with 80,000 Hours advisor — and former high school teacher — Alex Lawsen on his advice for students (80k.info/alex-podcast). This is aimed at high school students but we expect that the advice would also be useful for undergraduates.
- Our podcast with Holden Karnofsky on building aptitudes and kicking ass (80k.info/aptitudes-podcast).
- For some more provocative thoughts on the purpose of education, and how to estimate the returns of college, see Bryan Caplan's book *The Case Against Education*,[340] or our interview with him at 80k.info/bryan-caplan.
- For more practical advice on how to optimise your time at college, we'd recommend Cal Newport's book *How to Win at College*.[341]

Appendix 7 — Additional resources

Here we'll list some extra resources for various parts of the book. We'll include URLs in the text so you can easily find anything you're interested in. As always, you can find additional information on every source in the bibliography.

Resources for chapter 7

Machine learning

If you want to self-study, here are some places you might start:
- 3Blue1Brown's series on neural networks is a really great place to start for beginners (youtu.be/aircAruvnKk).
- *Neural Networks and Deep Learning* is good if you have a quantitative background (networksanddeeplearning.com).
- Online intro courses like fast.ai (focused on practical applications), *Full Stack Deep Learning* (fullstackdeeplearning.com), and the various courses at deeplearning.ai.
- For more detail, see university courses like MIT's *Introduction to Machine Learning* (openlearninglibrary.mit.edu/courses/course-v1:MITx+6.036+1T2019/course) or NYU's *Deep Learning* (atcold.github.io/pytorch-Deep-Learning).

Management

To learn more about management, we recommend:
- *The Great CEO Within*[342] summarises a lot of the best advice on all aspects of running a startup, including a lot of basics on management. *If there's one thing to read, this is it.*
- The *Manager Tools "Basics"* podcast (manager-tools.com/manager-tools-basics), which has also been turned into a book,[343] is also a

good introduction. It's geared towards big corporate environments.
- *Managing to Change the World* is geared towards management in nonprofits.[344]
- Good management is based in part on coaching, and a good introduction to that is *Coaching for Performance* by John Whitmore.[345]
- There are lots of useful management processes, including *4 Disciplines of Execution* by Sean Covey and colleagues,[346] and *Running Lean* by Ash Maurya.[347]
- For more academic, evidence-based advice, check out the *Handbook of Principles of Organizational Behaviour*, by leading management researcher Edwin Locke.[348] Google also has interesting research on successful teams.[349]

Sales and negotiation

Some of the best resources we've found to develop sales and negotiation skills include:
- *Spin Selling* by Neil Rackham. It sounds terrible, but it's actually the most evidence-based resource we found. Rackham studied top sales people, saw what techniques they used, trained people in those techniques, and did randomised controlled trials on the results. However, note that this advice is fairly old and widely known.[350]
- *Influence: The Psychology of Persuasion* by Robert Cialdini summarises psychology research about persuasion.[351]
- *To Sell is Human* by Daniel Pink also looks at what research can say about how to sell.[352]
- *Getting Past No* by William Ury is one of the classic books on negotiation techniques.[353] The techniques have not been rigorously tested, but we're not yet aware of any evidence-based negotiation advice.

Should you wait to have an impact?

If you'd like to explore this topic more, we'd recommend:
- "Should you wait to make a difference?" — an article we wrote in 2014 (80000hours.org/articles/should-you-wait/).
- "The timing of labour aimed at reducing existential risk" by Toby Ord (fhi.ox.ac.uk/the-timing-of-labour-aimed-at-reducing-existential-risk/).

Resources for chapter 10

How to get referrals

Some extra resources for our step-by-step process on getting referrals:
- "How to clean up your online presence and make a great first impression" by Alan Henry (lifehacker.com/how-to-clean-up-your-online-presence-and-make-a-great-f-5963864).
- "How to get a job without applying online" by Austin Belcak (cultivatedculture.com/how-to-get-a-job-anywhere-no-connections/) a guide to getting jobs with no connections:.
- "How to find email addresses" by Scott Britton (life-longlearner.com/find-email-addresses/).

Conversion

Some extra resources about stage 2 — conversion:
- "The ultimate guide to researching a company pre-interview" by Lily Zhang (themuse.com/advice/the-ultimate-guide-to-researching-a-company-preinterview).
- See some more examples of pre-interview projects in "How to get virtually any job you want" by Raghav Haran — it's an 8 minute

read, also where we got the term "pre-interview project" (medium.com/@RaghavHaran/how-to-get-virtually-any-job-you-want-even-if-you-dont-have-the-right-experience-a622149262d5).

Negotiation

Lots has been written about salary negotiation, so the section in chapter 7 hardly scratches the surface.

- "Salary negotiation: Make more money, be more valued" by Patrick McKenzie is a good 30 minutes guide (kalzumeus.com/2012/01/23/salary-negotiation/).
- Ramit Sethi (whose style won't fit every situation!) also has tips. There's a 14-minute video at youtu.be/XY5SeCl_8NE.
- If you want to get more advanced, check out the book *Getting Past No* by William Ury, who developed the negotiation course at Harvard Law School.[354]

Resources for chapter 11

How to get involved in effective altruism

The easiest thing to do right now is join the Effective Altruism Newsletter. You'll be sent a couple of emails that introduce the key ideas, a monthly update on new research, and be notified of the key conferences each year. https://www.effectivealtruism.org/get-involved

If you want to learn more about the ideas of the effective altruism community, you have a choice of introductions:

- Our podcast series: Effective Altruism: An Introduction (80000hours.org/podcast/effective-altruism-an-introduction/).
- A short introduction by our president and cofounder Benjamin Todd (effectivealtruism.org/articles/

introduction-to-effective-altruism).

- An academic article, *Effective Altruism*, by our other cofounder and Oxford philosopher Will MacAskill.[355]
- A book: *Doing Good Better*, also by Will MacAskill.[356]

Once you're up to speed, try to meet people in person, since this is how to find connections that can really help your career. The best way to do this is to attend an Effective Altruism Global conference.[357] The EAGx series are locally organised conferences aimed at people new to the community. EAGx conferences have taken place in cities around the world — including Nairobi, Norway, Hong Kong, Sydney, and Boston — as well as virtually.

If you've already had some involvement in the community, you could attend an EAG event. They usually take place annually in London and San Francisco, and there are travel grants available.

Alternatively, you can attend a local group event,[358] or you can join the discussion online on the Effective Altruism Forum (forum.effectivealtruism.org).

Once you've met a few people in the community, ask for more introductions.

Start by aiming to meet people in a similar situation to yourself, since there will often be opportunities to help each other. Then, try to speak to people who are one or two steps ahead of you in their career (e.g. if you want to start an organisation, meet people who started one last year).

When you're getting involved, look for "five-minute favours" — quick ways you can help someone else in the community. There are probably some small things you can do that will be a great help to someone else in the community, such as making an introduction or telling them about a book. This will both have an impact and let you meet even more people.

Another way to get more involved is to visit one of the hubs of the community. These are, roughly in descending order of size:

- San Francisco
- London / Oxford / Cambridge (UK)
- Boston and Cambridge, Massachusetts (especially for biorisk)
- Washington, DC for US policy
- Plus New York, Sydney, Melbourne, Berlin, and many other major cities

You can read even more in our career review and problem profile (see appendices 8 and 9).

Finally, here's a list of other in-person and online events: forum.effectivealtruism.org/events.

Appendix 8 — Career review summaries

As part of our research, we've evaluated different careers: how likely people are to succeed in them, how much good they could do in them, and how to enter them.

The following summaries reflect some of our career reviews as of May 2023, which can be found on our website. If any of them sound interesting, we strongly recommend that you go online to view the full and most up-to-date-reviews at:

https://80k.link/J3T

Some of these reviews are of ways you might gain career capital. Other reviews represent longer-term career paths (that you might follow for 3–10 years). We've ranked these paths roughly in terms of impact, assuming your personal fit for each is constant. There is a lot of variation within each path — so the best opportunities in one lower on the list will often be better than most of the opportunities in a higher-ranked one. Our top 10, as of May 2023, are:

1. AI safety technical research and engineering
2. Shaping future governance of AI
3. Biorisk research, strategy, and policy
4. Information security in high-impact areas
5. Helping build the effective altruism community
6. China-related AI safety and governance
7. Grantmaker focused on pressing world problems
8. Operations in high-impact organisations
9. Research into global priorities
10. Forecasting research and implementation

Note that this list changes frequently over time — you can find our up-to-date views on our website.

Academic research

To work on some important fields of research that are hard to fund commercially, academia is the natural place to go. A single outstanding researcher can move a field forward and make a significant contribution to solving key global problems. Beyond research, academics also have other avenues for impact, such as by influencing government policy, the priorities within their field, and the culture of society at large.

On the other hand, entering academia is a lengthy process, involving 5-15 years of study and post-docs, or even more. Most people who make the attempt – already a talented bunch – are rejected or give up getting a permanent position. While it has many positives, it's common for people to continue with academic research by default when they'd be better suited elsewhere, so we encourage you to be self-sceptical and consider other options before starting a PhD.

Raw intelligence, hard work and curiosity are the key indicators you may be able to beat the odds. Salaries are lower than elsewhere, though job satisfaction nevertheless seems high.

Choosing the right research questions is essential to maximise your expected social impact and we offer advice on how to do that, but PhD students often face a trade-off between working on the questions they think are most useful, and those which will best advance their career.

Pros:
- If you're a good fit, there's a large potential for social impact by working on pressing research questions
- Prestigious platform for advocacy
- Autonomy and job satisfaction

Cons:
- High competition for a limited number of positions

- Lengthy training time
- You often have to teach, and academic incentives remain imperfectly aligned with having social impact

Key facts on fit

High intelligence, conscientiousness and need for intellectual stimulation. Ability to work independently. Deep interest in the area and willingness to focus on particular questions for long periods.

Next steps

Explore different fields to find one you're interested in which can be used to work on important problems. Get very good grades at the undergraduate level. Look for PhD submission dates and search for an academic supervisor working on valuable questions at a prestigious university. Work hard to publish in good journals during your PhD or during postdocs.

Read more

See our article at 80000hours.org/career-reviews/academic-research/ for more.

Actuarial science

Actuarial science could be a good option for someone who wants to earn to give, has strong quantitative skills, and values security and work-life balance.

However, someone capable of pursuing an actuarial career should also consider quantitative finance, which offers higher expected earnings, spending a few years in management consulting, which offers superior flexibility and prestige, or training for data science, which offers more flexibility and opportunity for direct impact.

Pros:

- Reasonably high salary and reliable employment
- Moderate intensity of work allows for a long-lasting career and even side-projects
- High chances of career progression

Cons:

- Little opportunity for direct impact or advocacy, though we doubt actuarial careers are harmful
- Lower prestige and salary growth than some adjacent careers requiring similar skills
- Professional certification exams require impressive quantitative skills

Key facts on fit

Strong quantitative and computer skills, attention to detail, willing to have social impact mostly through donations.

Next steps

Admission to a Master's courses or trainee position will usually require having done well in a significant number of quantitative courses, such as mathematics, economics, or finance as an undergraduate.

Professional bodies in all major countries offer guides to becoming actuaries, and you should read them for details.

Read more

See our article at 80000hours.org/career-reviews/actuarial-science/ for more.

AI governance and coordination

Advanced AI systems could have a massive impact on the course of humanity, and they potentially pose global catastrophic risks. This emerging technology is increasingly drawing attention, but it's not clear how the world will respond and whether we'll be up to the task of managing the risks and benefits.

There are opportunities in AI governance and coordination around these threats — essentially, shaping how society responds to and prepares for the technological changes. Given the high stakes involved, pursuing this career path could be many people's highest-impact option. But they should be very careful not to accidentally exacerbate the threats rather than mitigate them.

Ideally, AI governance work would:

- Prevent the deployment of any AI systems that pose a significant and direct threat of catastrophe
- Mitigate the negative impact of AI technology on other catastrophic risks, such as nuclear weapons and biotechnology
- Reduce the risk of an "AI arms race," in which competition leads to technological advancement without the necessary safeguards and caution – between nations and between companies
- Ensure that those creating the most advanced AI models are incentivised to be cooperative and concerned about safety
- Slow down the development and deployment of new systems *if* the advancements are likely to outpace our ability to keep them safe and under control
- Guide the integration of AI technology into our society and economy with limited harms and to the advantage of all

Read more

See our article at 80000hours.org/career-reviews/ai-policy-and-strategy/ for more.

AI safety technical research

Artificial intelligence will have transformative effects on society over the coming decades, and could bring huge benefits — but we also think theres a substantial risk. One promising way to reduce the chances of an AI-related catastrophe is to find technical solutions that could prevent AI systems from carrying out dangerous behaviour.

Pros:
- Opportunity to make a significant contribution to a hugely important area of research
- Intellectually challenging and interesting work
- The area has a strong need for skilled researchers and engineers, and is highly neglected overall

Cons:
- Due to a shortage of managers, It's difficult to get jobs and might take you some time to build the required career capital and expertise
- You need a strong quantitative background
- It might be very difficult to find solutions
- There's a real risk of doing harm

Key facts on fit

You'll need a quantitative background, and it helps if you enjoy programming. If you've never tried programming, you may be a good fit if you have a willingness to teach yourself, ability to break problems down into logical parts and generate and test hypotheses, willingness to try out many different solutions, and high attention to detail.
　If you already:
- Are a strong software engineer, you could apply for empirical

research contributor roles right now (even if you don't have a machine learning background, although that helps).
- Could get into a top 20 machine learning PhD, that would put you on track to become a research lead.
- Have a very strong maths or theoretical computer science background, you'll probably be a good fit for theoretical alignment research.

Read more

See our article at 80000hours.org/career-reviews/ai-safety-researcher/ for more.

Biomedical research

Biomedical researchers investigate how the human body works with the aim of finding new ways to improve health. Biomedical research has likely produced large returns to society per researcher in the past; we expect it to continue to be a high-impact area in the future; and it appears to be constrained by good researchers. Its drawbacks are that it takes a long time to train, has high drop-out rates and leaves you relatively fixed in the biomedical field. You should strongly consider this path if you have an undergraduate degree from a top university with high grades (GPA 3.8+); you've tested your fit for research by doing a placement in a lab; and you have a place at a top 10 PhD program for your specialty. However, success in this path is very hard to predict, and so we encourage you to have a back-up plan.

Pros:
- Biomedical research is a promising cause area.
- The field seems to be constrained by good researchers.
- Highly interesting work for the intellectually curious.

Cons:
- Long time to train (4-12 years).
- Highly competitive; people drop out even in their late thirties and forties.
- Relatively narrow exit options.

Key facts on fit

Very high intelligence, intense intellectual curiosity and interest in biomedical research, grit, programming and statistics in demand.

Next steps

Contact lab managers during your sophomore (2nd) or junior (3rd) year at university to get a job as a research assistant in a lab to test your fit.

Read more

See our article at 80000hours.org/career-reviews/biomedical-research/ for more.

Biorisk research, strategy and policy

Advances in biotechnology could generate, through accident or misuse, pandemics even worse than those that occur naturally — and bad enough to threaten human civilization. COVID-19 demonstrated global preparedness and response to a major pandemic is inadequate in general, and the threat from pandemics arising from the misuse of biotechnology remains especially neglected. Efforts to reduce this danger are thus extremely valuable.

There are many promising interventions in this field, and you can make valuable contributions from different academic and professional backgrounds — including machine learning, social sciences, business development, and more — and while working in varied professional contexts, such as government, industry, civil society, or academia.

Working to prevent catastrophic pandemics seems very high value to us and can *easily* be your top option if you have a comparative advantage in this path (e.g. a background in medicine).

Key facts on fit

To assess if this path might be a good fit for you, consider these questions:
- Do you have an aptitude for, or already have experience in, a relevant research area? Relevant areas include: Synthetic biology, genetics, public health, epidemiology, international relations, security studies, political science/
- Do you have a chance of getting a PhD from a top 30 school in one of these areas? (This isn't required but can be a good indicator of your ability.)
- Are you able to be discreet about sensitive information concerning biorisks?
- If focused on policy contributions, might you be able to get and

enjoy a relevant position in government? In policy, it's useful to have relatively strong social skills, such as being happy to speak to people all day, and being able to maintain a robust professional network. Policy careers also require patience in working with large bureaucracies, and sometimes also involve facing public scrutiny, which many people find stressful and hard to navigate — so if you don't find this stressful, that's a good sign.

Read more

See our article at 80000hours.org/career-reviews/biorisk-research/ for more.

China-related AI safety and governance

Expertise in China and its relations with the world might be critical in tackling some of the world's most pressing problems. In particular, China's relationship with the US is arguably the most important bilateral relationship in the world, with these two countries collectively accounting for over 40% of global GDP.

China is one of the most important countries developing and shaping advanced artificial intelligence (AI). The Chinese government's spending on AI research and development is estimated to be on the same order of magnitude as that of the US government, and China's AI research is prominent on the world stage and growing.

Some promising career paths to aim for include:

- Technical AI safety research
- Safety policy advising in an AI lab
- Research at a think tank or long-term focused research group
- Translation and publication advising

Pros:

- Effective coordination between the US and China is imperative for avoiding dangerous conflicts and racing dynamics.

Cons:

- There are major risks and complexities involved in this career path.
- There's lots of luck involved in your ability to have an impact.
- You'll need excellent judgement and sufficient expertise to influence decisions in a positive direction.

Key facts on fit

People with strong Mandarin and English will have a greater chance of success in this area. Proficiency in French or German could also open up opportunities to support coordination between China and the EU. Beyond bilingualism, the ability to communicate and empathise across cultures is important.

Networking is important to career advancement in many cultures, and success in policy and strategy in particular require the ability to build and make good use of connections. You'll also need outstanding judgement to avoid doing harm.

Read more

See our article at 80000hours.org/career-reviews/china-related-ai-safety-and-governance-paths/ for more.

China specialist

China is becoming increasingly important in the solution of many of the global problems we prioritise, including biosecurity, factory farming, and nuclear security. A lack of understanding and coordination between China and the West means we might not tackle those challenges as well as we can (and need to).

This suggests that a high-impact career path could be to develop expertise in the intersection between China and pressing global issues. Once you have this expertise, you can use it to carry out research into global priorities or AI strategy, work in governments setting relevant areas of China–West policy, advise Western groups on how to work together with their Chinese counterparts, and other projects that we'll sketch below.

Key facts on fit

Focusing on this path seems most attractive if you have an interest in China and a humanities research skillset.

You need to be able to develop your expertise in China and a global problem to at least the point where Western organisations would want to seek your advice.

If you're not sure about your level of interest, then you could study in China for a month, or do some other kind of short visit or project, to see how interesting you find it. We may be able to help you find funding to cover this.

You could then pursue one of the more flexible paths listed in the full profile — such as graduate study (especially in economics), good early-career policy positions (think tank researcher, staffer, government leadership schemes), or work in technology companies — with the intention of focusing on China. If that doesn't work out, you'll have good backup options elsewhere in policy, research, earning to give, and so on.

Focusing on this path is also more attractive if you're more focused on issues around global catastrophic risks, emerging technology, and factory farming, rather than global health.

Read more

See our article at 80000hours.org/career-reviews/china-specialist/ for more.

Computer science PhD

A computer science PhD offers the chance to become a leading researcher in a highly important field with potential for transformational research. Especially consider it if you want to enter computer science academia or do high-level research in industry and expect to be among the top 30% of PhD candidates.

Most people qualified to do a computer science PhD should seriously consider doing a PhD focussed on Machine Learning, which we cover in another career review.

Pros:
- Potential for a large impact from your research
- Opportunity to become an expert in AI
- Freedom to pursue research topics that most interest you
- Very smart colleagues
- Helps you enter technical jobs in industry, providing a backup to academia (though if industry is your aim, it's probably better to enter directly)

Cons:
- Less than 10% end up with tenure-track jobs
- Takes a long time (5-7 years), with relatively low pay
- Doing highly open-ended research provides little feedback which can be unmotivating
- About half of those who enter industry afterwards don't end up with research positions

Key facts on fit

Strong quantitative skills (i.e. above 650 on quant GRE), want to enter high-level computer science research roles, extremely interested in computer science research.

Next steps

If you are interested, try out doing computer science research by doing a dissertation as an undergraduate or taking up research assistant jobs in a professor's lab.

Read more

See our article at 80000hours.org/career-reviews/computer-science-phd/ for more.

Congressional staffer

As a congressional staffer you'll be able to improve how the government uses its enormous power, while also building knowledge of how Congress works and the network to go with it. While some senior positions in the executive branch might be more impactful, Congress is a good place to start out, especially if you don't have a master's in policy, security studies or international relations.

Pros:
- Potential for large impact on pressing global problems
- Build deep knowledge of and strong network in government
- Exciting, stimulating work
- Potential for rapid career progression towards important political and policy positions

Cons:
- High pressure work environment with long hours
- An uncertain career path that depends on political conditions
- The need to work on policies you disagree with
- Generally lower salaries than the private sector or executive branch

Key facts on fit

US citizenship usually required, willing to join a political party and work on policies you might disagree with, able to develop strong networking skills, able to handle long hours, stress, and the frustrations of working in a slow moving system.

Next steps

Talk to congressional staffers to learn more. Start making connections as soon as possible, perhaps by moving to Washington DC. Apply for internships and fellowships in Congress, the White House, and relevant federal agencies.

Read more

See our article at 80000hours.org/career-reviews/congressional-staffer/ for more.

Data collection for AI alignment

To reduce the risks posed by the rise of artificial intelligence, we need to figure out how to make sure that powerful AI systems do what we want. Many potential solutions to this problem will require a lot of high-quality data from humans to train machine learning models. Building excellent pipelines so that this data can be collected more easily could be an important way to support technical research into AI alignment, as well as lay the foundation for actually building aligned AIs in the future. If not handled correctly, this work risks making things worse, so this path needs people who can and will change directions if needed.

Human data collection mostly involves hiring contractors to answer relevant questions and then creating well-designed systems to collect high-quality data from them.

This includes:

- Figuring out who will be good at actually generating this data (i.e. doing the sorts of tasks that we listed earlier, like evaluating arguments), as well as how to find and hire these people
- Designing training materials, processes, pay levels, and incentivisation structures for contractors
- Ensuring good communication between researchers and contractors, for example by translating researcher needs into clear instructions for contractors (as well as being able to predict and prevent people misinterpreting these instructions)
- Designing user interfaces to make it easy for contractors to complete their tasks as well as for alignment researchers to design and update tasks for contractors to carry out
- Scheduling workloads among contractors, for example making sure that when data needs to be moved in sequence among contractors, the entire data collection can happen reasonably quickly
- Assessing data quality, including developing ways of rapidly

detecting problems with your data or using hierarchical schemes of more and less trusted contractors

Being able to do all these things well is a pretty unique and rare skillset (similar to entrepreneurship or operations), so if you're a good fit for this type of work, it could be the most impactful thing you could do.

Key facts on fit

The best experts at human data collection will have:
- Experience designing surveys and social science experiments
- Ability to analyse the data collected from experiments
- Some familiarity with the field of AI alignment
- Enough knowledge about machine learning to understand what sorts of data are useful to collect and the machine learning research process
- At least some front-end software engineering knowledge
- Some aptitude for entrepreneurship or operations

Data collection is often considered somewhat less glamorous than research, making it especially hard to find good people. So if you have three or more of these skills, you're likely a better candidate than most!

Read more

See our article at 80000hours.org/career-reviews/alignment-data-expert/ for more.

Data science

If you have a PhD in a quantitative subject (or if you're the type of person who would enjoy a quantitative PhD), but are not sure you want to go into academia, consider data science. It can provide the intellectual satisfaction of research, but with more immediate, tangible results, and more team work. And you'll get a great skill-set that's increasingly in-demand in a wide variety of important areas.

Pros:
- Gain the ability to generate actionable insights from the increasing amount of data collected by humanity, opening the opportunity to contribute a wide range of causes.
- Develop undersupplied skills in programming, machine learning and statistics, for which demand is forecast to grow rapidly, opening many options.
- Cultures of learning and mentorship, often reasonable hours and flexible hours.
- High starting salaries; graduates of data science bootcamp Zipfian Academy earn $115K on average.

Cons:
- A large portion of time is spent on cleaning data, which most find unexciting.
- Pressure to find and deliver immediately actionable insights; less scope for longer term exploratory research.

Key facts on fit

Strong quantitative skills (i.e. above 650 on quant GRE), want to enter high-level computer science research roles, extremely interested in computer science research.

Next steps

You can enter either by self-learning, building a portfolio of projects on a blog and GitHub, and applying to companies directly, or you can take a data science bootcamp.

Read more

See our article at 80000hours.org/career-reviews/data-science/ for more.

Early-stage startup employee

Being an early employee at a startup is similar to being a startup founder, except (i) the impact and financial return are usually lower (ii) the risk is lower and (iii) the personal demands are lower. It's a promising path if you'd like to found a startup, but don't have a good idea and co-founder, or want a less demanding option.

Key facts on fit

If you can't come up with a promising idea and co-founder, then it's better to try to join a startup as an early employee.

It's also better to be an early employee if don't want to make the personal sacrifices needed to found or want lock yourself in for 3-10 years.

If you get the opportunity to join a startup that's taking off, you may have greater earnings and impact by joining it than founding your own e.g. the 100th employee of Dropbox still made about $10m, equivalent to a 10% stake in a $100m company. See a more in-depth version of this argument.

Next steps

The best startup jobs are found through referrals, so start by reaching out to everyone you know for leads. If that doesn't work, do something to build up your network in the technology sector for a year or two, such as software engineering at a large tech firm. You can also try Angel List – the largest directory of startup jobs. If you're an engineer, also try TripleByte. To find tech startups focused on important social problems, see our tips in the full profile.

Read more

See our article at 80000hours.org/career-reviews/startup-early-employee/ for more.

Economics PhD

An economics PhD is one of the most attractive graduate programs: if you get through, you have a high chance of landing an impactful research job in academia or policy. In particular, academic economics is one of the best ways of conducting and promoting global priorities research, one of our priority paths. You have back-up options in the corporate sector since the skills you learn are in-demand (unlike many PhD programs). You should especially consider an economics PhD if you want to go into research roles, are good at maths (i.e. quant GRE score above 165) and have a proven interest in economics research.

Pros:
- Decent chance of entering economics academia, which has potential for highly valuable research (such as contributing to global priorities research) and the option of working on topics in related social sciences.
- In demand by think-tanks, government departments and international organisations (e.g. IMF, World Bank).
- Gain a broad set of tools for understanding how the social world works and evaluating causes and interventions.
- High degree of autonomy when writing your dissertation.
- Backup options in the corporate sector.

Cons:
- Extremely competitive to enter.
- Takes a long time (5-7 years), with low pay.
- Doing highly open-ended research provides little feedback which can be unmotivating.

Key facts on fit

Strong maths skills (i.e. 165+ on quant GRE), want to enter high-level research roles, prepared to work long hours.

Read more

See our article at 80000hours.org/career-reviews/economics-phd/ for more.

Engineering

Many potential solutions to the top problems we recommend working on include developing and deploying technology — and this often needs engineers.

If you're an engineer, you can read through our article to see if any of these solutions appeal to you — and then aim to speak to some people in each area about how your skills could be applied and what the current opportunities are.

Engineers often have a systems mindset that can make them a particularly good fit for operations management or entrepreneurship. If that work interests you, it's worth considering whether to retrain and try to make a transition.

Some engineers may also excel at other options that require good quantitative ability.

Read more

See our article at 80000hours.org/career-reviews/engineering/ for more.

Executive assistant (for someone doing especially high-impact work)

Some people may be extraordinarily productive compared to the average.[359] But these people often have to use much of their time on work that doesn't take the best advantage of their skills, such as bureaucratic and administrative tasks. This may be especially true for people who work in university settings — as many researchers do — but it is also often true of entrepreneurs, politicians, writers, and public intellectuals.

Acting as an executive assistant for one of these people can dramatically increase their impact. By supporting their day-to-day activities and freeing up more of their time for work that other people can't do, you can act as a 'multiplier' on their productivity. We think that having a highly talented executive assistant can make someone 10% more productive, or perhaps more, which is like having one tenth (or more) as much impact as they have. If you're working for someone who is doing really valuable work, that's a lot.

In general, we think that helping others have a greater positive impact than they would have had otherwise is sometimes underappreciated, and that it's an important and valid way to do good. At least, that's the strategy we take here at 80,000 Hours!

Read more

See our article at 80000hours.org/career-reviews/executive-assistant-for-an-impactful-person/ for more.

Expert in AI hardware

Advances in hardware — such as the development of more efficient, specialised chips — have played an important role in improving the performance of AI systems and allowing them to be used economically.

There is a common-sense argument that if AI is an especially important technology, and hardware is an important input in the development and deployment of AI, specialists who understand AI hardware will have opportunities for impact — even if we can't foresee exactly what form they will take.

Some ways hardware experts may be able to help positively shape the development of AI include:

- More accurately forecasting progress in the capabilities of AI systems, for which hardware is a key and relatively quantifiable input.
- Advising policymakers on hardware issues, such as export, import, and manufacturing policies for specialised chips.
- Helping AI projects make credible commitments by allowing them to verifiably demonstrate the computational resources they're using.
- Advising on and fulfilling hardware needs for safety-oriented AI labs.

These are just examples of ways hardware specialists might be helpful. We haven't looked into this area very much. So, we are pretty unsure about the merits of different approaches, which is why we've listed working in AI hardware as only sometimes recommended, rather than as a part of the AI technical safety and policy priority paths.

We also haven't come across research laying out specific strategies in this area, so pursuing this path would likely mean both developing skills and experience in hardware and thinking creatively about opportunities to have an impact in the area.

If you do take this path, we encourage you to think carefully through the implications of your plans, ideally in collaboration with strategy and policy experts also focused on creating safe and beneficial AI.

Read more

See our article at 80000hours.org/career-reviews/become-an-expert-in-ai-hardware/ for more.

Forecasting and related research and implementation

Small groups of decision-makers in governments and other institutions sometimes have to make extremely difficult judgement calls on high-stakes matters, like global catastrophic risks or the development or deployment of emerging technologies. But human judgement is often biased, and decision-makers don't always follow the right processes. We've seen evidence that it's possible to use rigorous forecasting techniques to improve our ability to predict future events, and by extension, to make good decisions. We'd like to see more people doing research into forecasting and other methods for improving institutional decision-making, as well as putting those methods into practice at important institutions.

There are two main options in this path:

1. Developing better forecasting and decision-making techniques, and testing those that already exist.
2. Applying the most effective techniques in important organisations, especially those working on catastrophic risks.

Key facts on fit

To assess if this path might be a good fit for you, consider these questions:
- Might you be able to get a job in a relevant area of government?
- Do you know how to influence choices within a bureaucracy?
- On the research path, do you have a chance of getting into a relevant PhD at a top 30 school?
- On the research path, do you have a chance at making a contribution to one of the relevant research questions? For instance, are you highly interested in the topic, and sometimes have ideas for questions to look into? Are you able to work independently for many days at

a time? Are you able to stick with or lead a research project over many years?

Read more

See our article at 80000hours.org/career-reviews/forecasting/ for more.

Found a tech startup

Technology entrepreneurship is a very high-potential path, offering good career capital, with a chance of both high earnings and large direct impact. Overall, we think more people should try this path. However, it's also one of the most difficult paths, and only suits a relatively small number of people. Consider this career if you think you can develop strong technical skills, as well as the ability to deal with high risk of failure, work very long hours and do something unconventional.

Key facts on fit

Intelligent, risk-taking, able to work very long hours for 3-7 years, high grit, independent, can develop strong technical skills

Next steps

If interested, we recommend you prioritise testing your potential in this path while keeping your options open. This can be done by meeting entrepreneurs, reading more and learning technical skills such as programming. After that, the normal path is to find a co-founder, build a prototype product and apply to enter a 'seed accelerator'.

Read more

See our article at 80000hours.org/career-reviews/tech-entrepreneurship/ for more.

Founder of new projects tackling top problems

Founding a new organisation to tackle a pressing global problem can be extremely high impact. Doing so involves identifying an idea, testing it, and then helping to build an organisation by investing in strategy, hiring, management, culture, and so on.

Even a moderate chance of success could easily make this your highest-impact option.

Founding a project can also be among the best options for building your career capital, since it's impressive and you'll probably learn a huge amount.

Key facts on fit

An idea that's cost-effective and really motivates you; deep knowledge of the area; leadership potential; the ability to convince funders; good judgement; generalist skills; the ability, willingness and resilience to work on something that might not work out.

Next steps

If you have an idea, the next steps typically involve further testing out your idea, since getting started is often the quickest way to learn about whether funders and potential hires are interested, how quickly you can make progress, and what the main strategic uncertainties are. This could mean trying to pursue it on the side while you stay in your current job, or if you have the flexibility, you could aim to work on it exclusively for a few months.

If you don't have an idea yet, normally we'd recommend working within the problem areas that you might want to found something within. Working within the problem area will help you gain relevant knowledge and connections, and give you a chance to stumble across gaps you might help fill — especially if you explore ideas on the side at the same time.

Read more

See our article at 80000hours.org/career-reviews/founder-impactful-organisations/ for more.

Founding effective international development nonprofits

If you have gained expertise in a relevant area of international development, there are opportunities to found a nonprofit that seeks to efficiently and transparently implement an evidence-backed intervention which is not already the focus of an existing nonprofit. Organisations like this have the potential to receive tens of millions of dollars from funders like the Gates Foundation and GiveWell within a couple of years, achieving a large impact.

Pros:
- Potential to have a large direct impact within international development.
- Builds expertise in international development, as well as generally valuable career capital.

Cons:
- It seems to take several years to build up the necessary expertise.
- The people who take this path seem highly able, suggesting it's very difficult.
- We're very uncertain how easy it is to find and take these opportunities before they would be exploited by other non-profits or governments.

Key facts on fit

Well-rounded, risk-taking, very long hours, grit, independent, deep knowledge of relevant area.

Next steps

If you're at an early stage, focus on accumulating expertise and connections that put you in a better position to discover and take advantage of opportunities to found nonprofits (e.g. a postgraduate degree, working on the ground, doing project management), while keeping your options open. Find out which interventions are developing an evidence-base but don't already have a nonprofit focusing on them, and consider especially focusing your learning on these areas.

If you're considering founding, speak to GiveWell, the strategic development foundations such as Gates and CIFF, and other groups which are attempting this, such as Evidence Action and Charity Entrepreneurship. Aim to find out what conditions your organisation would need to satisfy in order to get funding.

Read more

See our article at 80000hours.org/career-reviews/founding-effective-global-poverty-non-profits/ for more.

Grantmaker focused on pressing world problems

There are many philanthropists interested in donating millions or even billions of dollars to tackle pressing world problems — but there currently aren't enough grantmakers able to vet funding proposals. Because a randomly chosen proposal has little expected impact, grantmakers can have a large impact by helping philanthropists distinguish promising projects from less promising ones.

Key facts on fit

This position requires a well-rounded skillset. You need to be analytical, but also able to meet and build relationships with lots of people in your problem area of focus.

You'll also need excellent generalist knowledge in the field in which you want to make grants.

To assess your potential fit for this position, ask yourself:

- Are you generally very proactive?
- Do you sometimes have ideas for grants that others haven't thought of, or only came to support later?
- Do you think you could persuade a major funder of a new donation opportunity?
- Can you clearly explain the reasons you hold particular views, and their biggest weaknesses?
- Could you develop expertise and strong relationships with the most important actors in a top problem area?
- Could you go to graduate school in a relevant area at a top 20 school? (This isn't needed, but is an indication of analytical ability.)

Read more

See our article at 80000hours.org/career-reviews/ai-safety-researcher/ for more.

Helping build the effective altruism community

The effective altruism community has lots of talented people who are motivated to work on whichever issues turn out to be most pressing in the future — even if that means switching careers or areas (see chapter 11). The community also has potential to grow substantially. Working at an organisation dedicated to growing, shaping, and supporting it — and thereby helping build capacity to address pressing global problems — could therefore be very impactful.

We realise this may seem self-promotional, since 80,000 Hours is itself an effective altruism organisation. However, if we didn't recommend what we ourselves do, then we'd be contradicting ourselves. We also wouldn't want everyone to work on this area, since then we'd only build a community and never do anything. But we think recommending it as one of several high-impact paths makes sense.

There are a variety of roles available in effective altruism organisations, including:

- Management, operations, and administration
- Research and advice
- Outreach, marketing, and community
- Systems and engineering

We'd like to especially highlight roles in operations management — there's a significant need for them, but these roles are often neglected, perhaps because they're seen as less glamorous.

Key facts on fit

Whether you are a good fit to work at an effective altruism organisation depends in large part on the type of role you're interested in. However, there are some common characteristics the organisations typically look for:

- A track record that demonstrates intelligence and an ability to work hard.

- Evidence of deep interest in effective altruism — for some roles, you need to be happy to talk about it for much of the day. This breaks down into a focus on social impact and a scientific mindset, as well as knowledge of the community.
- Flexibility and independence — these organisations are relatively small, so staff need to be happy to work on lots of different projects with less structure.
- Several years of experience in a relevant skill — although this isn't a requirement, it seems to be becoming difficult to get most of these jobs without it.

Read more

See our article at 80000hours.org/career-reviews/work-in-effective-altruism-organisations/ for more.

Historian of large societal trends, inflection points, progress or collapse

Historical research into the long-term arc of history — by looking at societal trends over time and key inflection points — could help us better understand what might cause important technological and social shifts in the future.

Studying subjects relevant to the long-term arc of history may shed light on the range of changes that are possible (or probable) in our future. These subjects may include things like economic, intellectual, or moral progress from a long-term perspective; the history of social movements or philanthropy; or the history of wellbeing. Historians in these areas can help us better understand long trends and key inflection points, such as the Industrial Revolution and other promising topics.

Our impression is that although many of these topics have received attention from historians and other academics some are comparatively neglected, especially from a more quantitative or impact-focused perspective.

How can you estimate your chance of success as a history academic? We haven't looked into the fields relevant to history in particular, but some of our discussion of parallel questions for philosophy academia or academia in general may be useful.

It may also be possible to pursue this kind of research in 'non-traditional' academia, or at nonprofits.

Read more

See our article at 80000hours.org/career-reviews/historian-of-societal-trends/ for more.

Information security in high-impact areas

Information security is vital to safeguard all kinds of critical organisations such as those storing extremely sensitive data about biological threats, nuclear weapons, or advanced artificial intelligence, that might be targeted by criminal hackers or aggressive nation states. Such attacks, if successful, could contribute to dangerous competitive dynamics (such as arms races) or directly lead to catastrophe.

Some infosecurity roles involve managing and coordinating organisational policy, working on technical aspects of security, or a combination of both. We'd be excited to see more altruistically motivated candidates move into this field.

Key facts on fit

A great way to gauge your fit for information security is to try it out. There are many free online resources that will give you hands-on experience with technical aspects of security.[360]

Some other ideas to get you started:

- Try out ethical hacking to understand how hacks work and gain an intuition for security loopholes. If you're studying at a university, it may be easy to join a Capture the Flag (CTF) team.
- Play around with security tools.
- Set up your own infrastructure. Host a virtual machine. Build a web server and secure it.

Having a knack for figuring out how computer systems work, or enjoying deploying a security mindset are predictors that you might be a good fit — but they are not required to get started in information security.

Read more

See our article at 80000hours.org/career-reviews/information-security/ for more.

Journalism

For the right person, becoming a journalist could be very impactful. Good journalists help keep people informed, positively shape public discourse on important topics, and can provide a platform for people and ideas that the public might not otherwise hear about.

But the most influential positions in the field are highly competitive, and journalists face a lot of mixed incentives that may detract from their ability to have a positive impact.

Pros:

- The opportunity to spread important ideas to a large audience and shape public debate and opinion
- Developing a strong network, versatile skills, and an understanding of the media that significantly increase your career capital
- Involves creativity and learning about a variety of areas

Cons:

- Competitive for most influential roles
- Shrinking industry in US, somewhat poor outlook
- Relatively low pay (and sometimes little job security)
- Fast pace with constant deadlines

Key facts on fit

- Ability to write engaging pieces for a large audience very quickly
- Comfort navigating an uncertain job market
- Willingness to work long hours and in a competitive environment
- A bachelor's degree from a top university is useful but not required

Read more

See our article at 80000hours.org/career-reviews/journalism/ for more.

Law school (in the US)

Going to law school in the United States may help you pursue careers in policy that can address some of the world's most pressing problems. Being a practising lawyer can also potentially have a high impact. The educational experience itself can offer meaningful career benefits.

However, there are substantial downsides to law school, and it may be a poor fit depending on your personal circumstances. It's worth fully exploring what aims law school would help you accomplish, whether there are more promising alternatives, and whether you would find pursuing a career in law or policy fulfilling.

Pros:
- You may have more access to impactful roles
- You can develop a deep understanding of critical aspects of US policy
- Law school imparts potentially valuable skills, connections, and opportunities

Cons:
- Law school can be expensive, competitive, and stressful
- There may be more promising alternative paths to achieving similar goals
- Some legal careers are demanding and onerous

Key facts on fit

Pursuing a law degree is best for people who have a clear idea of how they want to use a policy career to have a positive impact. People with strong verbal reasoning, writing, and analytical skills will have an advantage in this path. It may be difficult for people who can't spend 50+ hours per week on schoolwork or for whom prolonged periods of stress or frequent discouraging feedback are especially costly.

Next steps

Consider attending a law class, watching videos of classes online, or speaking to a law school student to better understand the process. You can even get an internship or an entry-level job in a legal or policy field to test out your aptitude and fit.

Read more

See our article at 80000hours.org/career-reviews/should-you-go-to-law-school/ for more.

Machine learning PhD

A machine learning PhD catapults you into a field of critical importance for humanity's future. You can use the skills you gain to help positively shape the development of artificial intelligence, apply machine learning techniques to other pressing global problems, or, as a fall-back, earn money and donate it to highly effective charities. It's open to people who have studied a quantitative subject, even if they haven't done computer science before.

Pros:
- Potential for a large impact from your research
- Build skills in what's plausibly one of the most important technologies of the coming decade
- High earning potential after graduation
- Intellectually stimulating work with capable colleagues

Cons:
- Extremely competitive to enter
- Takes 4-6 years, with relatively low pay
- Requires a lot of work alone without much feedback, which makes it demotivating for many

Key facts on fit

Strong maths skills (equivalent to having a undergraduate degree in a quantitative subject), want to do high-level research.

Read more

See our article at 80000hours.org/career-reviews/machine-learning-phd/ for more.

Management consulting

Consulting is a promising path, offering good career capital that keeps your options open and your earnings high. However, it's highly competitive and we have a limited understanding of its potential for direct impact.

Consider a job in consulting if you have strong academic credentials, aren't sure about your long-term plans and want to experience work in a variety of business environments, don't have a high-impact alternative immediately available, or you want to earn to give but are not a good fit for quantitative trading or technology entrepreneurship.

Before committing to management consulting, consider directly entering priority paths, policy, startups, and the other options for career capital we looked at in chapter 7.

Pros:
- Experience work in a wide variety of industries
- Network with impressive colleagues
- High earnings

Cons:
- Highly competitive
- Long hours
- Limited direct impact

Key facts on fit

Must be able to put up with 60 hour work weeks, frequent travel, lots of powerpoints. High academic achievement a predictor, but technical knowledge not required.

Next steps

College students with a strong interest in consulting should apply for a summer internship the year before they complete their studies. It's also common to enter after graduate programs, especially MBAs. Others should network with consultants and apply if interested.

Read more

See our article at 80000hours.org/career-reviews/management-consulting/ for more.

Also, take a look at our article about why you should consider other options before committing to management consulting, at 80000hours.org/articles/alternatives-to-consulting/.

Marketing

Spending a few years doing marketing in the private sector can teach you highly generalizable skills that can later be used in a wide range of industries and causes. You should consider marketing if you have good social and verbal skills, want a decent work life balance and want to keep your options open across causes.

Pros:
- Marketing is a valuable and highly transferable skillset that keeps your options open across industries and causes.
- A decent chance of reaching leadership positions in companies and good preparation for entrepreneurship.
- Better work-life balance than finance, law and consulting
- Reasonably well-paid (after a few years).

Cons:
- Some industries and marketing practices may be harmful.
- Corporate culture can reduce altruistic motivation.
- Not as prestigious or well-paid as finance, consulting, law.

Key facts on fit

Ability to communicate ideas very clearly, very social and able to get on well with a wide range of people, want decent work life balance.

Next steps

To get a sense of what's involved in marketing, you can buy and read case studies used for teaching marketing at business schools. Taking classes in business, economics or statistics can increase your chances of getting a position. The best way to get a full-time position is through internships –

large consumer-product companies and some tech-firms do on-campus recruitment at universities; for other industries use your network or contact firms directly.

Read more

See our article at 80000hours.org/career-reviews/work-in-marketing/ for more.

Medical careers

Medicine is a highly paid and highly satisfying career. However, working in medicine has a modest direct impact, and relative to the cost and time required for medical training, it has mediocre 'exit opportunities' to other career paths, and provides little platform for advocacy. It is also highly competitive.

Our view is that the people likely to succeed at medical school admission could have a greater impact outside medicine. We therefore recommend those contemplating medical school consider other opportunities instead. Within medicine, we believe the highest impact opportunities lie in the fields of (in order) biomedical research, public health and health policy, and healthcare management.

Pros:

- Generally doctors are very satisfied by their jobs, and enjoy high levels of life satisfaction and well-being
- They are amongst the highest paid professions, and reliably earn a high salary
- There is reasonable variety among medical specialties, and thus the ability to select a specialty that suits one's interests, personal characteristics, or a particular approach to having a large impact

Cons:

- The direct impact of being a doctor is modest, and smaller than 'conventional wisdom' may suggest
- Although medicine is a respected qualification, it has modest career capital for transitioning into other jobs relative to the amount of time and money it demands. It is also very hard to change careers in medicine after entering a training program for a given specialty

- Similarly, although doctors enjoy widespread public esteem, they do not have a great platform for advocacy given the costs involved

Key facts on fit

Strong academic achievement, particularly in science; a caring ethos; resilience to stress and distressing situations; tolerance of long hours and unpleasant bodily fluids.

Read more

See our article at 80000hours.org/career-reviews/medical-careers/ for more.

Non-technical roles in leading AI labs

Although we think technical AI safety research and AI policy are particularly impactful, having very talented people focused on safety and social impact at top AI labs may also be very valuable, even when they aren't in technical or policy roles.

For example, you might be able to:

- Shift the culture around AI toward safety and positive social impact by talking publicly about what your organisation is doing to build safe and beneficial AI.
- Recruit safety-minded researchers.
- Design internal processes to consider social impact issues more systematically in research.
- Help different teams coordinate around safety-relevant projects.

We're not sure which roles are best, but in general those involved in strategy, ethics, or communications seem promising. Or you can pursue a role that makes an AI lab's safety team more effective — like in operations or project management.

If you can find a position at a specifically AI safety–oriented organisation, then any role that helps them do their work better makes a contribution.

That said, it seems possible that some of these roles could have a veneer of contributing to AI safety, without doing much to head off bad outcomes. For this reason, it seems particularly important to continue to think critically and creatively about what kinds of work in this area are useful.

Some roles in this space may also provide strong career capital for working in AI policy by putting you in a position to learn about the work these labs are doing, as well as the strategic landscape in AI.

Read more

See our article at 80000hours.org/career-reviews/non-technical-roles-in-ai-labs/ for more.

Nursing

Nurses perform a very wide range of tasks to heal the sick and keep people healthy. Nurses, especially advanced practice nurses, can earn significant amounts in some countries, permitting 'earning to give'. The entrance requirements are lower than any careers that we strongly recommend.

Nonetheless, we don't recommend nursing to many people because i) specialising in nursing does not open up many if any options outside of medicine; ii) it appears higher salaries are available in other non-physician medical careers; iii) we estimate that the impact of further medical care on health in the developed world is small.

However, if nursing is particularly appealing to you, and you have already explored your other options and decided to specialise, there are opportunities to have a significant social impact by being a nurse.

Pros:

- Medium salaries in some countries, particularly the USA, and high salaries for advanced specialities
- High meaningfulness of work
- Relatively uncompetitive for a graduate profession, with a high likelihood of employment.

Cons:

- Little flexibility because the skills developed are not easily transferred outside nursing
- Difficult work and high rate of burnout
- Low potential for advocacy, and less prestige than medicine.

Key facts on fit

Social skills and compassion, ability to deal with physical work and high pressure situations (and for advanced practice: memory and attention to detail).

Next steps

While qualifications vary by country, becoming a registered nurse will usually require a three-year undergraduate degree at a nursing school. After practising as a nurse for a few years, you can then pursue a Master's course to become an advanced practice nurse.

Read more

See our article at 80000hours.org/career-reviews/nursing/ for more.

Operations management in high-impact organisations

People in operations roles act as multipliers, maximising the productivity of others in the organisation via building systems that keep the organisation functioning effectively at a high level. As a result, people who excel in these positions require significant creativity, self-direction, social skills, and conscientiousness. If you're a good fit, operations could be the highest-impact role for you.

Any of the nonprofits we recommend on our job board[361] — especially the rapidly scaling ones — could likely benefit from great operations work.

Key facts on fit

We often find that people think they'd be a poor fit for operations roles, when actually they seem to us like promising candidates.

People may think they need to have a background in operations to contribute. While such a background is useful, it's not required. As we've covered, being great at operations is ultimately about building systems. Someone smart and hardworking who has the right mindset can usually learn the specific knowledge they need for an operations role fairly quickly. What's more, best practices and software are always changing, so even people who already have a background need to keep learning.

The key skills you'd need are:
- Optimisation mindset.
- Systems thinking and going meta.
- Aesthetic pleasure in systems working smoothly.
- Planning skills.
- Prioritisation skills.
- Staying calm.
- Able to learn quickly.

- Communication skills.
- High attention to detail.
- Organisation and reliability.

Read more

See our article at 80000hours.org/articles/operations-management/ for more.

Philosophy PhD

Some of the most important questions that arise for people trying to make the world a better place are philosophical. What does it mean to live a worthwhile life? What are our obligations to future generations? And how do we decide what to do when we are uncertain about the answers to these questions?

In our view, investigating philosophical questions like these — as well as other questions in ethics, epistemology, and other subfields of philosophy — can be extremely valuable. Thus for some people it can be high-impact to pursue philosophical research as a career. Professional philosophers can sometimes also have a substantial impact via advocacy as public intellectuals.

However, the academic job market for philosophy is extremely challenging. Moreover, the career capital you acquire working toward a career in philosophy isn't particularly transferable. For these reasons we currently believe that, for the large majority of people who are considering it, pursuing philosophy professionally is unlikely to be the best choice. Almost all professional philosophers who have written publicly on this topic advise against aiming to become a professional philosopher unless "there is nothing else you can imagine doing."

Pros:
- Potential to do important research in a variety of neglected areas
- As an academic, potential for advocacy through teaching or public engagement
- If successful, a high degree of autonomy and intellectual satisfaction

Cons:
- Extremely competitive, and job prospects are often dim even for PhDs who graduate from top programmes

- The PhD takes a long time to complete (4-8 years), and has poor transferable career capital compared to other similarly competitive options
- Highly autonomous work and long timelines for projects can be stressful or demotivating for some people

Key facts on fit

All-consuming interest in important philosophical questions; strong writing, abstract thinking, and logical reasoning skills; ability to spend long periods of time autonomously doing research; ability to get into a top-15 philosophy PhD programme or write a high quality philosophy research paper.

Next steps

Because philosophy is so competitive, we would encourage most people to explore other career options before beginning a PhD. A high degree of personal fit for philosophy may suggest a good fit for other less professionally risky and potentially higher impact paths as well, such as a PhD in economics or a career shaping public policy.

If you do decide to get a philosophy PhD, you should probably have a bachelor's or a master's degree in philosophy. Learn about PhD programmes by reading about them online and by talking to professors and current graduate students at your home institution or the programmes you are considering.

Read more

See our article at 80000hours.org/career-reviews/philosophy-academia/ for more.

Product manager

Product management is one of the best non-programming roles in the tech industry, and tech is one of the most attractive industries to work in. It builds more widely-applicable skills than software engineering roles and has comparable pay. Programming experience isn't necessary, but it's also a great next step for software engineers.

Pros:
- Gain wide range of valuable skills, especially the soft skills needed for senior roles that are harder to develop in technical jobs
- Influence and responsibility early in your career
- Relatively highly paid (similar to software engineering, less than quant trading, high-end law, and consulting)
- Programming and university-level quantitative skills not required

Cons:
- Difficult to enter immediately from university
- Can be stressful and involves a lot of multitasking
- Can lose specialist skills

Key facts on fit

Experience working in a tech company; exceptional communication and people skills (e.g. you have successfully run teams before); ability to handle many conflicting demands on your time

Next steps

If you don't have experience, apply to a product management graduate scheme at a large company or go into software engineering or user experience design first. If you already work in tech, try moving into product management in your current company or apply for product management jobs in other companies.

Read more

See our article at 80000hours.org/career-reviews/product-manager-in-tech/ for more.

Program manager in international organisations

This means pursuing work at organisations like the World Bank, World Health Organisation, International Monetary Fund and United Nations. The influence of international organisations suggests working within them is an opportunity for substantial impact if you have good personal fit for the role and are strongly motivated by social impact.

It can be possible to enter these organisations directly from graduate studies (ideally in a relevant area), but it seems much more common to start by building a career elsewhere since these positions are highly competitive. A few common paths include: (i) the world of think-tanks and policy-oriented civil service, (ii) consultancy and MBAs, (iii) nonprofit management, (iv) economics academia, focusing on a high-priority area. Which of these is best for you depends on which international organisation you're aiming at, and what types of positions you're aiming for.

Pros:
- Gain wide range of valuable skills, especially the soft skills needed for senior roles that are harder to develop in technical jobs
- Influence and responsibility early in your career
- Relatively highly paid (similar to software engineering, less than quant trading, high-end law, and consulting)
- Programming and university-level quantitative skills not required

Cons:
- Difficult to enter immediately from university
- Can be stressful and involves a lot of multitasking
- Can lose specialist skills

Key facts on fit

Jobs in this area seem to require a well-rounded profile: good social skills, analytical skills and high motivation. Some roles are more tilted towards research, whereas others are more about management and negotiation. You'll also need to be comfortable working in a large and potentially bureaucratic organisation.

Next steps

We recommend first learning more about these roles by seeking an internship. You'll need to build up several years of relevant experience through doing graduate studies or working in policy or nonprofits, before you can make applications to paid positions.

Read more

See our article at 80000hours.org/career-reviews/program-manager-in-international-organisations/ for more.

Public intellectual

Some people seem to have a very large positive impact by popularising important ideas — often through writing books; giving talks or interviews; or writing blogs, columns, or open letters. Putting ideas on the map — and shaping their understanding among the public — can substantially impact social movements, policy, cultural change, and technological innovation.

However, it's probably even harder to become a successful and impactful public intellectual than a successful academic, since becoming a public intellectual often requires a degree of success within academia while also having excellent communication skills and spending significant time building a public profile. Thus this path seems to us to be especially competitive and a good fit for only a small number of people.

As with other advocacy efforts, it also seems relatively easy to accidentally do harm if you promote mistaken ideas, or even promote important ideas in a way that turns people off.

All that said, this path seems like it could be extremely impactful for the right person. We think it might be especially valuable to build awareness of certain global catastrophic risks, of the potential effects of our actions on the long-term future, or of effective altruism, as well as spreading positive values like concern for foreigners, nonhuman animals, future people, or others.

There are public intellectuals who are not academics — such as prominent bloggers, journalists, podcasters, YouTubers, and authors. However, academia seems unusually well-suited for becoming a public intellectual, because it requires you to become an expert in something and trains you to write (a lot), and the high standards of academia provide credibility for your opinions and work. For these reasons, if you are interested in pursuing this path, going into academia may be a good place to start.

Public intellectuals can come from a variety of disciplines — what they have in common is that they find ways to apply insights from their fields to issues that affect many people, and they communicate these insights effectively.

If you are an academic, you can experiment with spreading important ideas on a small scale through a blog, magazine, YouTube channel, or podcast. If you share our priorities and are having some success with these experiments, we'd be especially interested in talking to you about your plans.

Read more

See our article at 80000hours.org/career-reviews/public-intellectual/ for more.

Pursuing fame in art and entertainment

While there is the potential for huge earnings, advocacy power and direct impact, the odds are stacked against even very talented individuals. A very large number of people attempt to achieve success in the arts for reasons unrelated to its social impact, making it unlikely to be a neglected area. For most people, a career in arts and entertainment is unlikely to be the path with the highest potential to do good, so we suggest you consider your other options first.

However, as with all careers, if you think you could be truly exceptional and fulfilled within this career, but not in others, you should strongly consider it.

Pros:
- High levels of job meaningfulness and autonomy
- The possibility of obtaining very large amounts of money and social influence

Cons:
- The field is crowded and highly competitive
- Earnings are very unevenly distributed, making this a high-risk option, with the most likely outcome being little income or influence
- A large amount of high-quality art already exists for people to enjoy
- Sometimes low transferability of skills, and potentially low prestige in cases where your career doesn't take off

Key facts on fit

Much stronger verbal/social than quantitative skills; high risk tolerance; art is highly motivating on a day-to-day basis.

Next steps

We suggest that you seek frank feedback from masters in your art form on whether you show outstanding potential for someone at your stage in your career.

We suggest you try to reach checkpoints in your art form that indicate a higher likelihood of future success (e.g. getting into highly competitive programs such as the Iowa Writers' Workshop).

As you proceed, also aim to develop transferrable skills and contacts that will allow you to switch to other socially valuable careers if this becomes necessary.

Read more

See our article at 80000hours.org/career-reviews/pursuing-fame-in-art-and-entertainment/ for more.

Quantitative trading

Quantitative traders use algorithms to trade on the financial markets for profit, typically at hedge funds and proprietary firms.

We think most people's highest-impact options involve working directly on solving pressing global problems. But if you want to focus on having an impact by donating part of your income (earning to give) and will thrive in a quantitative trading role — which means having very strong mathematical skills, among other key qualifications — this is likely among your best options.

A number of people we've advised over the years have successfully taken this path and made large donations, while also gaining valuable skills in management, software engineering, research, and other areas. They also tend to enjoy a culture that's high-performing and more 'nerdy' than is stereotypically the case in finance.

One main caveat is that the industry faces many risks — these activities could become unprofitable due to regulation or competition — so it's important to make sure you also build strong career capital.

Key facts on fit

To assess if this path might be a good fit for you, consider the following:
- Would you be capable of finishing in the top half of the class at a top 30 school in mathematics, theoretical physics, or computer science at the undergraduate level?
- Top quantitative trading firms look for intelligence, good judgement, and rapid decision-making skills. One indication of these traits is that you like playing strategy games or poker.

- Do you have strong communication and teamwork skills? If you want to succeed in quantitative trading, you'll need to work closely with your colleagues hour-by-hour in potentially stressful situations.
- Would you be capable of reliably giving a large fraction of your income to charity? (If you're unsure about this, finding support in your giving though community or public commitments can help.)

Read more

See our article at 80000hours.org/career-reviews/quantitative-trading/ for more.

Research and advocacy promoting impactful climate solutions

We suspect that different ways of tackling climate change vary significantly in their impact. This means focusing on the most effective methods is likely much higher impact — especially if you focus on the most extreme risks from climate change.

We don't have well-developed career advice in this area. But here are some rules of thumb for choosing approaches we think can help maximise your impact:

1. **Focus on the most extreme risks where possible.** The worse the potential effects of climate change are, the more pressing it is to reduce their likelihood. We think that focusing on the ways in which climate change could increase other risks, like nuclear war or catastrophic pandemics, would be a particularly good way of having an impact.

2. **Pay attention to the best evidence on what kinds of interventions are the most cost-effective in the long term.** This can be hard — many people have differing strong opinions on what kinds of projects are important. Remember that majority of future energy demand will come from non-OECD countries, so solutions that aren't geared toward those countries are unlikely to be most effective, and that what's most cost effective in the long term could well differ from what seems like the best deal now.

3. **Focus on more neglected strategies.** As we argued in chapter 4, more neglected strategies tend to me much more impactful.

4. **Look for *leverage.*** Causing even a relatively small improvement in others' resources that might go toward climate change likely dwarfs anything you could do entirely on your own, because these other resources are so massive — government spending on climate change alone is in the hundreds of billions per year. This means it will probably be most effective to leverage these other resources.

We're not sure which career paths are best in this area, but here are a few ideas:

- Pursue a career in policy or policy research, and use your position to help develop low-carbon technology innovation, help institute 'market-pull' policies like carbon pricing or taxes, or develop frameworks for international coordination and cooperation — or whatever policy interventions look most cost-effective in the future.

- Become an advocate for 'technology agnosticism.' Many people focus on renewables like wind and solar — these are important but not enough on their own. Other technologies that are often more neglected can also contribute to climate change mitigation — e.g. carbon capture and storage, other methods for making carbon-neutral fuels, nuclear energy, and 'Super Hot Rock' geothermal energy. Each technology should be studied for its risks and benefits, but we can and should use whatever methods are best, which may mean using several methods at once instead of championing one or a few over the others.

- Help build the field of research on extreme climate change risks — in particular, focusing on any ways climate change might increase existential risks from other sources (an especially understudied area). This might mean becoming a researcher yourself and working with an eye toward helping shift the scientific community's attention toward the most important and neglected topics.

Read more

See our article at 80000hours.org/career-reviews/effective-altruist-approach-to-climate-change/ for more.

Research into global priorities

We've argued that one of the most important priorities is working out what the priorities should be. There's a huge amount that's not known about how to do the most good, and although this is one of the most important questions someone should ask, it has received little systematic study.

The study of which actions do the most good is especially neglected if you take a long-term perspective, in which what matters most are the effects of our actions on future generations. This longtermist position has only been recently explored, and we know little about its practical implications. With more research, we could easily see our current perspective on global priorities shifting, so these questions have practical significance.

We'd like to see global priorities research turn into a flourishing field, both within and outside of academia.

To make this happen, perhaps the biggest need right now is to find more researchers able to make progress on the key questions of the field. There is already enough funding available to hire more people if they demonstrate potential in the area — but demonstrating potential is hard in a nascent field with a lack of mentorship. However, if you are able to enter, then it's extremely high impact — you might help define a whole new discipline.

Key facts on fit

To assess if this path might be a good fit for you, consider these questions:

- Do you have a chance of getting into a PhD in economics or philosophy at a top 10 school? (This isn't required, but potential success on this path is an indicator of ability.)
- Do you have excellent judgement? For example, can you take on messy, ill-defined questions, and come up with reasonable assessments about them? This is not required in all roles, but it is especially useful right now given the nascent nature of the field and the questions that are being addressed.

- Do you have general knowledge or an interest in a wide range of academic disciplines?
- Do you have a chance at making a contribution to one of the relevant research questions? For instance, are you highly interested in the topic, and have ideas for questions to look into? Are you able to work independently for many days at a time? Are you able to stick with or lead a research project over many years?

Read more

See our article at 80000hours.org/career-reviews/global-priorities-researcher/ for more.

Research management

In general, we think that helping others have a greater positive impact than they would have had otherwise is sometimes underappreciated, and that it's an important and valid way to do good. Indeed, that's our strategy here at 80,000 Hours!

Research managers enhance the impact of others' work by prioritising projects within an institution, coordinating research, fundraising, and producing communications to make the institution more impactful. In some cases, research managers also help set strategy for an organisation — though this is usually in cases where they have previously been researchers themselves.

Being a research manager seems valuable for many of the same reasons working in operations management does — these coordinating roles are crucial for enabling researchers and others to have the biggest positive impact possible.

Read more

See our article at 80000hours.org/career-reviews/research-management/ for more.

Software engineering

Software engineering could be a great option for having a direct impact on the world's most pressing problems. There is a shortage of software engineers at the cutting edge of research into AI safety. We've also found that software engineers can contribute greatly to work aiming at preventing pandemics and other global catastrophic biological risks. Aside from direct work on these crucial problems, while working for startups or larger tech companies you can gain excellent career capital (especially technical skills), and, if you choose, earn and donate substantial amounts to the world's best charities.

Pros:
- Gain a flexible skillset.
- Make a significant direct impact, either by working on AI safety, or in otherwise particularly effective organisations.
- Have excellent working conditions, high pay, and good job security.

Cons:
- Late-stage earnings are often lower than in many other professional jobs (especially high-paying roles such as quantitative trading), unless you help found a successful startup.
- Likely only a small proportion of exceptional programmers will have a highly significant impact.
- Initially, it could be relatively challenging to gain skills quickly compared to some other jobs, as you need a particular concrete skillset

Key facts on fit

The best way to gauge your fit is to try it out. You don't need a computer science degree to do this. We recommend that you:

1. Try out writing code — as a complete beginner, you can write a Python program in less than 20 minutes that reminds you to take a break every two hours. Once you know the fundamentals, try taking an intro to computer science and programming class, or work through free resources. If you're in college, you could try taking CS 101 (or an equivalent course outside the US).
2. Do a project with other people — this lets you test out writing programs in a team and working with larger codebases. It's easy to come up with programming projects to do with friends — you can see some examples here. Contributing to open-source projects in particular lets you work with very large existing codebases.
3. Take an internship or do a coding bootcamp.

Some other indicators of fit: willingness to teach yourself, ability to break problems down into logical parts and generate and test hypotheses, willingness to try out many different solutions, high attention to detail, quantitative degree useful but not required.

Read more

See our article at 80000hours.org/career-reviews/software-engineering/ for more.

Specialist in emerging global powers

India and Russia seem likely to become increasingly important over the next few decades — politically, militarily, economically, and technologically. Because of this, we expect that helping Western institutions better cooperate with Russian and Indian actors might be highly impactful, especially if you're early in your career (and therefore able to spend the next decade developing relevant expertise and advancing your career).

This is likely to be a better option for you if you are from one of these countries, or have spent a substantial amount of time there. The best paths to impact here likely require deep understanding of the relevant cultures and institutions, as well as language fluency (e.g. at the level where you might be able to write a newspaper article about longtermism in the language).

If you are not from one of these countries, one way to get started might be to pursue area or language studies (one source of support available for US students is the Foreign Language and Area Studies Fellowships Program), perhaps alongside economics or international relations. You could also start by working in policy in your home country and slowly concentrate more and more on issues related to the country you want to focus on, or try to work in philanthropy or directly on a top problem there.

There are likely many different promising options in this area, both for long-term career plans and useful next steps.

Read more

See our article at 80000hours.org/career-reviews/emerging-global-power-specialist/ for more.

Teaching

Better teachers lead to better economic outcomes, higher attendance at better universities and lower teenage birth rates for the students they teach, and the benefits talented teachers provide to society are considerably greater than what is recouped by their salary. This is the common-sense and widely held view, though there are some dissenting voices on the impact of schooling, at least at the tertiary level.

However, we generally do not recommend teaching as the best career path to maximize your social impact: if you're working in a rich country, the impact you have as a teacher is by improving the lives of people who are almost all going to end up in the richest 15% of the world's population. Moreover, teaching is an area that is already extremely popular among the socially-motivated, so it's unlikely that you'll make as big a difference on the margin within education as you could elsewhere. Further, even the most talented classroom teacher can only impact around 30 students at a time, less than is possible using other approaches.

As with all careers, if you think you could be truly exceptional within this career, but not at others, you should strongly consider it.

Pros:
- Rewarding to be interacting directly with the beneficiaries of your work
- You may have the opportunity to advocate for important issues with your students
- Significant vacations, which allow you to pursue other projects on the side
- If you want to become a teacher, you are relatively likely to be able to do so, since there are so many teaching positions available

- If you are an outstanding teacher, you may get the opportunity to teach the next generation of your country's leaders, a group that it is very important have good values and strong skills

Cons:
- If working in a rich country, your direct impact accrues to people who are among the richest in the world
- It's perhaps the most common path for socially motivated people to pursue, so harder to make a big difference
- Weaker than other paths at building general-purpose skills that are in demand in other fields
- Salaries are low for the level of skill and commitment required to be a good teacher

Key facts on fit

Must be happy with constant social interaction; able to maintain control of the classroom; a positive disposition

Next steps

If you want to enter teaching, we'd recommend applying to TeachFirst in the UK, or Teach for America in the USA. These organisations enable you to get a taste for teaching over two years in a demanding position, while at the same time making you an attractive candidate for other careers in case you decide to move to a different career area.

Read more

See our article at 80000hours.org/career-reviews/teaching/ for more.

Think tank research

Working in a think tank for a few years early in your career is a plausible way to influence government policy for the better, and in the meantime gain skills and contacts to advance your future career in politics or elsewhere, while doing work that's often fulfilling.

Those with either great skills in quantitative analysis, or the ability to synthesize and communicate ideas clearly, should think carefully about how well it compares relative to their other opportunities, such as joining party politics.

Pros:
- Your colleagues are likely to be intelligent, desire to improve the world, and have similar interests to you.
- You have the potential to advocate on important issues that that are neglected elsewhere.
- You gain contacts in policy and an understanding of how the public policy ecosystem can be shifted.

Cons:
- Early on in your career it may be hard to find a think tank which will hire you and also matches your personal values.
- The number of think tank research projects on the most important, neglected and tractable problems directly is relatively small.
- It is likely you will work for significant periods of time, and potentially your entire career, without successfully influencing government policy.

Key facts on fit

Either good quantitative research or writing skills depending on the role; ability to synthesize and clearly communicate your and other people's research; personal interest in some area of government policy.

Next steps

Attend events put on by think tanks, network, discuss their work and get to know the people. Try to get on their radar by writing things that impress them. Being a research assistant is very relevant work experience. Some think tanks hire undergraduate as interns, and that is a great opportunity to see if it's a career in which you could excel. Read their reports and try to find a few that fit your temperament and beliefs.

If you are choosing your degree, the majors they hire from are wide-ranging depending on their field of interest, but often include economics, government, social sciences, law or further degrees in international relations.

Read more

See our article at 80000hours.org/career-reviews/think-tank-research/ for more.

Web designer

Web designers create the look and layout of web pages. Their skills are in-demand in many types of organisations, from charities to startups, giving you flexibility to work on high impact projects. As a backup, you can enter paths with good pay, like UX design ($80k median salary), and earn to give. However, good design is hard to measure, which makes it hard to prove your abilities to potential employers, meaning entry and progression can be difficult. You should consider web design if you studied graphic design or a related field, you've already spent several years developing good taste in web-design and you have strong persuasion skills that enable you to get a foot in the door when you're starting out. However if you have the technical skills to do web development, we recommend you do that instead, since it has higher pay, more jobs and entry and progression is easier.

Pros:
- Useful skillset that can be used to work directly on a wide range of important problems
- Freelance and remote work widely available
- Good outlook (similar to web-developers)
- Less competitive and uses more visual skill than our other recommended paths
- Fall back option to earn to give by transitioning into higher paid UX design (median salary ~$80,000)

Cons:
- Entry and progression can be difficult because good design is hard to measure
- Salaries, number of jobs and job growth rate lower than in web-development, so if that's open to you, consider going into web development

Key facts on fit

Visual arts background, well developed taste in web design informed by feedback from other designers, strong communication skills, good at persuasion and negotiation.

Read more

See our article at 80000hours.org/career-reviews/web-designer/ for more.

Working at effective nonprofits

Working at effective nonprofits lets you have a big impact, whilst doing rewarding, meaningful work. But it's crucial that you pick the right nonprofits — look for organisations working on urgent global problems, that are well-run and are short of staff. You should especially consider this option if you've already built up skills by working in the private sector or through graduate study.

Pros:
- Potential for large direct impact
- Build connections and expertise in high priority problem areas
- Significant influence and responsibility early in your career
- Rewarding and meaningful work

Cons:
- Less formal training than in large for-profit companies
- Salaries ~10-30% lower than in equivalent roles in private sector
- Less clearly defined job roles in smaller nonprofits

Key facts on fit

Deep interest in problem area the nonprofit works in, ability to quickly pick up new skills and knowledge, self-motivated, willing to earn less than one could in other areas.

Next steps

1. Find well-run nonprofits working on urgent global problems.
2. Test your fit by doing side-projects at nonprofits through volunteering, freelance work or internships.
3. If necessary, build relevant skills in the for-profit sector first (e.g. in consulting, finance, marketing, or tech), or through relevant graduate studies (e.g. economics, statistics).

Read more

See our article at 80000hours.org/career-reviews/effective-non-profits/ for more.

Appendix 9 — Problem profile summaries

As part of our research, we've evaluated different problem areas. We drew on work by other groups to assess them on scale, neglectedness and solvability — a framework we introduced in chapter 4.

We've included summaries of these problem profiles below, but we're always updating them. So to see the full and most up-to-date versions of the profiles, please go to:

https://80k.link/VEK

We've ranked these problems roughly by our guess at the expected impact of an additional person working on them, assuming your ability to contribute to solving each is similar (though there's a lot of variation in the impact of work within each issue as well). Our top 5, as of May 2023, are:

1. Preventing an AI-related catastrophe
2. Catastrophic pandemics
3. Nuclear war
4. Great power conflict
5. Climate change

We also prioritise issues that enable others to have a greater impact regardless of which issues turn out to be most pressing. These issues include:

- Building effective altruism
- Global priorities research
- Improve decision making (especially in important institutions)

Note that this list changes frequently over time — you can find our up-to-date views on our website.

AI-related catastrophe

There will be substantial progress in AI in the next few decades, potentially even to the point where machines come to outperform humans in many, if not all, tasks. This could have enormous benefits, helping to solve currently intractable global problems, but could also pose severe risks. These risks could arise accidentally (for example, if we don't find technical solutions to concerns about the safety of AI systems), or deliberately (for example, if AI systems worsen geopolitical conflict). More work needs to be done to reduce these risks.

Some of these risks from advanced AI could be existential — meaning they could cause human extinction, or an equally permanent and severe disempowerment of humanity. There have not yet been any satisfying answers to concerns about how this rapidly approaching, transformative technology can be safely developed and integrated into our society. Finding answers to these concerns is very neglected, and may well be tractable. We estimate that there are around 400 people worldwide working directly on this. As a result, the possibility of AI-related catastrophe may be the world's most pressing problem — and the best thing to work on for those who are well-placed to contribute.

Promising options for working on this problem include technical research on how to create safe AI systems, strategy research into the particular risks AI might pose, and policy research into ways in which companies and governments could mitigate these risks. If worthwhile policies are developed, we'll need people to put them in place and implement them. There are also many opportunities to have a big impact in a variety of complementary roles, such as operations management, journalism, earning to give, and more — some of which we list below.

Our overall view

Recommended — highest priority

We think this is among the most pressing problems in the world.

Scale

AI will have a variety of impacts and has the potential to do a huge amount of good. But we're particularly concerned about the possibility of extremely bad outcomes, especially an existential catastrophe. Some experts on AI risk think that the odds of this are as low as 0.5%, some think that it's higher than 50%. We're open to either being right. Views on our last staff survey ranged from 1–55%, with a median of 15%.[362]

Neglectedness

Around $50 million was spent on reducing catastrophic risks from AI in 2020 — while billions were spent advancing AI capabilities.[363] While we are seeing increasing concern from AI experts, we estimate there are still only around 400 people working directly on reducing the chances of an AI-related existential catastrophe (with a 90% confidence interval ranging between 200 and 1,000).[364] Of these, it seems like about three quarters are working on technical AI safety research, with the rest split between strategy (and other governance) research and advocacy.

Solvability

Making progress on preventing an AI-related catastrophe seems hard, but there are a lot of avenues for more research and the field is very young. So we think it's moderately tractable, though we're highly uncertain — again, assessments of the tractability of making AI safe vary enormously.

Read more

See our article at 80000hours.org/problem-profiles/artificial-intelligence/ for more.

Artificial sentience

AI systems in the future may be moral patients — that is, they could deserve moral consideration for their own sake. Why? The biggest reason we're concerned about this is because they could become sentient — and so feel conscious pleasure, suffering, or other good and bad feelings.

If so, then we will need to ensure that the future goes well not only for humans and animals, but for AI systems themselves.

It might sound a bit outlandish to think that AI systems could be sentient, and it's true that we don't have a great understanding of sentience/consciousness. However, many philosophers and consciousness researchers think there's no reason in principle that an artificial system made from silicon couldn't be sentient.

One way AI systems could be sentient is if they emulate the computational structure of the human brain. If we are conscious because of the computational structure of our brains (as is plausible), then digital people with the same computational structure would also be sentient. But AI systems that are very different from us might also have their own forms of sentience, in the same way that nonhuman animals like octopuses might.

Our overall view

Sometimes recommended

Working on this problem could be among the best ways of improving the long-term future, but we know of fewer high-impact opportunities to work on this issue than on our top priority problems.

Scale

Mistreating sentient systems or allowing them to suffer — whether intentionally or accidentally, perhaps because we don't know that they are sentient — could be a moral catastrophe, analogous to factory farming, but on a potentially much larger scale.

Unlike with nonhuman animals, we are actively engaged in the process of designing artificial systems. And it seems very important to get right — imagine if we mistakenly think that some huge number of systems we create are non-sentient, or feeling pleasure, when really they are suffering. As AI systems continue to grow in both scale and capability, this issue will grow more and more pressing.

Neglectedness

Despite longstanding interest in the question of whether AI systems could be conscious — dating back to the very beginning of the field of AI — rigorous work on artificial sentience is surprisingly neglected, in part because it falls at the intersection of several fields of inquiry.

Solvability

We're far from fully understanding this domain. Understanding when/ how artificial systems could be conscious is even more difficult than understanding which nonhuman animals are sentient, because artificial systems can be even more architecturally different to us than animals, do not share our biological substrate, and do not share our evolutionary history.

Read more

See our article at 80000hours.org/problem-profiles/artificial-sentience/ for more.

Atomically precise manufacturing

Atomically precise manufacturing is a form of particularly advanced nanotechnology. With atomically precise manufacturing we could build products out of individual atoms and molecules, allowing us to perfectly create a very wide range of products with very few flaws. Effectively, this would be like having perfect 3D printers that can produce anything.

Both the risks and benefits of advances in atomically precise manufacturing seem like they might be significant, and there is currently little effort to shape the trajectory of this technology. However, there is also relatively little investment going into developing atomically precise manufacturing, which reduces the urgency of the issue.

Our overall view

Sometimes recommended

Working on this problem could be among the best ways of improving the long-term future, but we know of fewer high-impact opportunities to work on this issue than on our top priority problems.

Scale

Ben Snodin, a researcher at Rethink Priorities, guessed there's something like a 4–5% probability of advanced nanotechnology arriving by 2040 (though he emphasises the guess is unstable).[365] There appear to be substantial (and perhaps even existential) risks associated with developing atomically precise manufacturing, including widespread ability to unilaterally produce things as destructive as nuclear weapons or catastrophic pandemics and the invention of new kinds of weapons.

Neglectedness

Snodin estimates that there is around one full-time equivalent person working on nanotechnology strategy as of 2022.[366] We think that at least 2–3 people should be working full time on this issue.

Solvability

We're not currently sure what the best things to do to reduce this risk might be — we think more research in this area would be valuable. It might be too early in the technology's development for work on this now to have any concrete impact on atomically precise manufacturing's ultimate trajectory. But it does seem plausible that there are things that could be done, particularly through developing better strategies for managing the development of nanotechnology. These include:

- Identifying and accelerating any particular areas of technical research that could make atomically precise manufacturing more likely to be beneficial overall.
- Researching policy recommendations around atomically precise manufacturing.

Read more

See our article at 80000hours.org/problem-profiles/atomically-precise-manufacturing/ for more.

Building effective altruism

Effective altruism is about using evidence and reason to figure out how to benefit others as much as possible, and taking action on that basis (see chapter 11). Building effective altruism can increase your impact many times over, through influencing other altruists to pursue the very best opportunities for doing good. Past efforts to build effective altruism from Giving What We Can have already caused over 8,000 people to pledge to donate at least 10% of their income to highly effective charities, with over $220 million donated so far and much more pledged in lifetime donations. Building effective altruism also builds a community that will work on whichever global problems turn out to be most pressing in the future, so it's a good option if you're unsure about which problem is most pressing.

Very few people are working on building effective altruism directly. The total staff at effective altruism-aligned organisations is probably about 500 — that includes many people who are not involved in building the effective altruism movement, but also excludes some that are (like local group leaders). The combined budgets of organisations that work on building effective altruism is around $25 million. In part because doing so is relatively neglected, we think building effective altruism is one of the most promising ways to improve the world.

80,000 Hours regards itself as an effective altruist organisation and also wrote this profile, so it should be taken with a grain of salt. On the other hand, if we weren't working on a problem we thought was pressing, we'd be hypocrites.

Our overall view

Recommended — capacity-building
This is among the most pressing ways to build capacity to solve global problems.

Scale

We think work on building effective altruism has the potential for a very large positive impact. It seems plausible that the effective altruism community could eventually save 100–1,000 million quality-adjusted life years (QALYs) per year by causing $10–100 billion per year to be spent on much more effective projects. As an alternative measure, it seems plausible that the effective altruism community could do good equivalent to reducing the risk of human extinction by between 1% and 10%. These estimates are extremely rough and uncertain.

Neglectedness

This issue is moderately neglected. Current spending is between $10 million and $100 million per year.

Solvability

Making progress on building effective altruism seems moderately to highly tractable. We expect that doubling spending on this issue could perhaps be expected to take us around 10% of the way toward seeing the full potential benefits of the effective altruism community.

Read more

See our article at 80000hours.org/problem-profiles/promoting-effective-altruism/ for more.

Catastrophic pandemics

Pandemics — alongside other global catastrophic biological risks, like bioterrorism or biological weapons — pose a substantial existential threat to humanity. As biotech progress continues, it looks increasingly plausible that it will become easier to manufacture extremely dangerous pathogens (whether deliberately or accidentally), potentially far worse than the SARS-CoV-2 virus that causes COVID-19.

We can prepare for the next pandemic — and hopefully head it off before it happens. We're excited about a number of approaches to reduce these risks. For example, we could find technological solutions that make it easier to prevent and treat infections, and policy solutions that ensure countries and institutions respond better to pandemics. While there's lots of work going on in this area, very little of this work is focused on the worst-case risks, and as a result, we think work to prevent potentially existential pandemics is highly neglected.

Our overall view

Recommended — highest priority
We think this is among the most pressing problems in the world.

Scale

Pandemics — especially engineered pandemics — pose a significant risk to the existence of humanity. We think there is a greater than 1 in 10,000 chance of a biological existential catastrophe within the next 100 years.[367]

Neglectedness

Billions of dollars a year are spent on preventing pandemics. Little of this is specifically targeted at preventing biological risks that could be existential — and we think that, if you care about future generations, it's particularly important to try to reduce existential risks. As a result, our quality-adjusted estimate suggests that current spending is around $1 billion per year. (For comparison with other significant risks, we estimate that hundreds of billions per year are spent on climate change, while tens of millions are spent on reducing risks from AI.)

Solvability

There are promising existing approaches to improving biosecurity, including both developing technology that could reduce these risks (e.g. better bio-surveillance), and working on strategy and policy to develop plans to prevent and mitigate biological catastrophes.

Read more

See our article at 80000hours.org/problem-profiles/preventing-catastrophic-pandemics/ for more. Alternatively, see our in-depth report (although it was written prior to COVID-19) at 80000hours.org/problem-profiles/preventing-catastrophic-pandemics/full-report/.

Climate change

Climate change is going to significantly and negatively impact the world. Its impacts on the poorest people in our society and our planet's biodiversity are cause for particular concern. Looking at the worst possible scenarios, it could be an important factor that increases existential threats from other sources, like great power conflicts, nuclear war, or pandemics. But because the worst potential consequences seem to run through those other sources, and these other risks seem larger and more neglected, we think most readers can have a greater impact in expectation working directly on one of these other risks.

We think your personal carbon footprint is much less important than what you do for work, and that some ways of making a difference on climate change are likely to be much more effective than others. In particular, you could use your career to help develop technology or advocate for policy that would reduce our current emissions, or research technology that could remove carbon from the atmosphere in the future.

Our overall view

Recommended

Working on this issue seems to be among the best ways of improving the long-term future we know of, but all else equal, we think it's less pressing than our highest priority areas.

Scale

We think work to materially reduce the probability of the worst outcomes of climate change would have a large positive impact. However, climate change seems hundreds of times less likely to directly cause human extinction than other risks we're concerned about, like catastrophic pandemics. As a result, if climate change does have catastrophic and potentially long-lasting consequences for human civilisation, this will likely be through aggravating other problems, such as conflict between great powers. This indirect risk brings the scale of climate change as a problem closer to other extinction risks, although it still seems more than 10 times less likely to cause extinction than nuclear war or pandemics. Our guess is that more people should seriously consider aiming at those issues directly.

Neglectedness

Overall, climate change is far less neglected than other issues we prioritise. Current spending is likely over $640 billion per year. Climate change has also received high levels of funding for decades, meaning lots of high-impact work has already occurred. It also seems likely that as climate change worsens, even more attention will be paid to it, allowing us to do more to combat its worst effects. However, there are likely specific areas that don't get as much attention as they should.

Solvability

Climate change seems more tractable than many other global catastrophic risks. This is because there is a clear measure of our success (how much greenhouse gas we are emitting), plus lots of experience seeing what works — so there is clear evidence on how to move ahead. That said, climate change is a tricky global coordination problem, which makes it harder to solve.

Read more

See our article at 80000hours.org/problem-profiles/climate-change/ for more.

Easily preventable or treatable illness

Every year around 10 million people in poorer countries die of illnesses that can be very cheaply prevented or managed, including malaria, HIV, tuberculosis, and diarrhoea.

Only around $100 per capita is spent annually on the healthcare of people living in low-income countries (adjusted for purchasing power). To put this in context: annual health spending in the EU is over $4,500 per capita, in the UK it's about $5,000 per capita, and in the US it's nearly $11,000.[368]

As a result, there remain many opportunities to scale up treatments that are known to prevent or cure common health conditions in low-income countries.

Options for working on the problem include serving as a donor to effective projects, working as an economist in intergovernmental organisations (such as the World Bank or World Health Organization), or starting or working in a nonprofit that scales up proven treatments.

Our overall view

Sometimes recommended
We'd love to see more people working on this issue. But you might be able to do even more good working on one of our top priority problem areas.

Scale

We think work to alleviate global health problems has the potential for a large positive impact. The damage done by easily preventable diseases in the least developed countries plus India amounts to between 200 million DALYs (disability-adjusted life years) and 500 million DALYs per year.[369]

Neglectedness

This issue is much less neglected than most others we prioritise. Current spending in the least developed countries plus India is about $300 billion per year.

Solvability

Making progress on alleviating global health problems seems highly tractable. It is mostly a matter of scaling up approaches that are known with near certainty to work if done correctly.

Read more

See our article at 80000hours.org/problem-profiles/health-in-poor-countries/ for more.

Factory farming

There are likely well over 100 billion animals living in factory farms at present.[370] Most experience serious levels of suffering. The problem is neglected relative to its scale — less than $200 million per year is spent via nonprofits trying to solve it.

There are promising paths to improving the conditions of factory farmed animals and supporting progress towards the abolition of factory farming.

Options for working on this problem include:

- Taking a high-earning job and donating to cost-effective organisations working on the problem.
- Working at effective animal advocacy nonprofits directly.
- Working at companies developing animal product alternatives.
- Advocating for action on the problem as an academic, journalist, or politician.

Our overall view

Sometimes recommended

We'd love to see more people working on this issue. But you might be able to do even more good working on one of our top priority problem areas.

Scale

We think work to reduce the suffering of present and future nonhumans has the potential for a large positive impact, given the large numbers that could be affected.

Neglectedness

This issue is moderately neglected. Current spending is likely between $100 million and $10 billion per year, depending on how you count commercial investments in animal product alternatives.

Solvability

Making progress on reducing the suffering of present and future nonhumans seems moderately tractable. There are some plausible ways to make progress, though some efforts have had disappointing results to date.

Read more

See our article at 80000hours.org/problem-profiles/factory-farming/ for more.

Global priorities research

Every year governments, foundations and individuals spend over $500 billion on efforts to improve the world as a whole. They fund research on cures for cancer, rebuilding of areas devastated by natural disasters, and thousands of other projects.

$500 billion is a lot of money, but it's not enough to solve all the world's problems. This means that organisations and individuals have to prioritise and pick which global problems they work on. For example, if a foundation wants to improve others' lives as much as possible, should it focus on immigration policy, international development, scientific research, or something else? Or if the government of India wants to spur economic development, should it focus on improving education, healthcare, microeconomic reform, or something else? How should it allocate resources between these options?

As we argued in chapter 5, there are vast differences between the effectiveness of working on different global problems. But of the $500 billion spent each year, only a miniscule fraction (less than 0.01%) is spent on global priorities research: efforts to work out which global problems are the most pressing to work on.

With a track record of already influencing hundreds of millions of dollars, future research into global priorities could lead to billions of dollars being spent many times more effectively. As a result, we believe this is one of the highest-impact fields you can work in.

Our overall view

Recommended — capacity-building
This is among the most pressing ways to build capacity to solve global problems.

Scale

We think work on global priorities research has the potential for a very large positive impact. It seems plausible that better prioritisation within international organisations, nonprofits, and governments could help lower extinction risk by between 1% and 10%, raise global economic output by more than 10%, or otherwise considerably improve the expected value of the future.

Neglectedness

This issue is highly neglected. Current spending might be between $5 million and $10 million per year.

Solvability

Making progress on global priorities research seems moderately tractable, though it varies a lot depending on the issues being investigated (with more applied and empirical questions often being more tractable). We'd guess that doubling the resources going toward this issue could take us something like 1% of the way toward the full benefits of better prioritisation.

Read more

See our article at 80000hours.org/problem-profiles/global-priorities-research/ for more.

Great power conflict

Economic growth and technological progress have charged the arsenals of the world's most powerful countries. As a result, the next war between them could be far worse than World War II, the deadliest conflict humanity has yet experienced.

Could such a war actually occur? The possibility can't be ruled out. Technical accidents or diplomatic misunderstandings could lead to accidental conflict that quickly escalates. Or international tension could lead decision-makers to start a conflict purposefully if they think they're better off fighting than negotiating.

It seems hard to make progress on this problem. It's also less neglected than some of the problems that we think are *most* pressing. There are certain issues, like making nuclear weapons or military artificial intelligence systems safer, which seem promising — although it may be more impactful to work on reducing risks from AI, bioweapons or nuclear weapons directly. You might also be able to reduce the chances of misunderstandings and miscalculations by developing expertise in one of the most important bilateral relationships (such as that between the United States and China).

Finally, by working on making conflict less likely, reducing competitive pressures on the development of dangerous technology, and improving international cooperation, you might be able to reduce the chances of many different kinds of other disasters, such as future pandemics.

Our overall view

Recommended

Working on this issue seems to be among the best ways of improving the long-term future we know of, but all else equal, we think it's less pressing than our highest priority areas, primarily because it seems relatively less neglected and also harder to solve.

Scale

There's a significant chance that a new great power war occurs this century. Although the world's most powerful countries haven't fought directly since World War II, war has been a constant throughout human history. There have been numerous close calls, and there are several flashpoints that are likely to cause diplomatic disputes in the years to come. As a result, by assessing various estimates and models, we'd suggest there's about a one-in-three chance that a new great power war breaks out in roughly the next 30 years.

Few wars cause more than 10,000,000 casualties, and it's most likely that a new great power war will remain smaller than that. However, there's some chance it could escalate massively. Modern great powers have much larger economies, more powerful weapons, and larger military budgets than they did in the past. An all-out war could kill far more people than even World War II, the worst war we've yet experienced. The chance of an existentially threatening war—one that could cause human extinction, or significantly damage the prospects of the long-term future—in the next century is very difficult to estimate. But it would be hard to justify an estimate lower than 1%.

Neglectedness

War is a lot less neglected than some of our other top problems. There are thousands of people in governments, think tanks, and universities already thinking about this problem and working to mitigate it. But some solutions or approaches remain neglected. One particularly promising approach is to develop expertise at the intersection of international conflict and another of our top problems. Experts who understand both geopolitical dynamics and risks from advanced artificial intelligence are sorely needed, for example.

Solvability

Reducing the risk of great power war seems very difficult. But there seem to be specific technical problems that can be solved to make weapons systems safer or less likely to trigger catastrophic outcomes. And in the best case, working on this problem can have a leverage effect, making the development of several dangerous technologies safer by improving international cooperation and making them less likely to be deployed in war.

Read more

See our article at 80000hours.org/problem-profiles/great-power-conflict/ for more.

Improving decision making (especially in important institutions)

Working to help governments and other important institutions improve their decision making in complex, high-stakes decisions — especially relating to global catastrophic risks — could potentially be among the most important problems to work on. But there's a lot of uncertainty about how tractable this problem is to work on and what the best solutions to implement would be.

Our overall view

Recommended — capacity-building

We think working on this issue may be among the best ways of improving prospects for the long-term future — though we're not as confident in this area as we are in others, in part because we're not sure what's most valuable within it.

Scale

We think this kind of work could have a large positive impact. Improvements could lead to more effective allocation of resources by foundations and governments, faster progress on some of the world's most pressing problems, reduced risks from emerging technologies, or reduced risks of conflict. And if this work could reduce the likelihood of an existential catastrophe — which doesn't seem out of the question — it could be one of the best ways to improve the prospects for the long-term future.

Neglectedness

Parts of this issue seem extremely neglected. For the sorts of interventions we're most excited about, we'd guess there are around 100–1,000 people working on them full-time, depending on how you count. But how neglected this makes the issue overall is unclear. Many, many more researchers and consultancies work on improving decision making broadly (e.g. by helping companies hire better). And many existing actors have vested interests in how institutions make decisions, which may cause them to resist certain reforms.

Solvability

Making progress on improving decision making in high-stakes situations seems moderately tractable. There are techniques that we have some evidence can improve decision making, and past track records suggest more research funding directed to the best researchers in this area could be quite fruitful. However, some of these techniques might soon hit a wall in their usefulness, and it's unclear how easy it will be to get improved decision-making practices implemented in crucial institutions.

Read more

See our article at 80000hours.org/problem-profiles/improving-institutional-decision-making/ for more.

Mental health

Improving mental health seems like one of the most direct ways of making people better off, since it's specifically targeted at their subjective experience — and it could be particularly effective in the developing world.

Our guess is that improving physical health in poor countries is still likely to have a bigger impact on welfare for the same resources, given that there are several common diseases we can treat easily with more funding — but we're not sure.

Our overall view

Sometimes recommended

We'd love to see more people working on this issue. But you might be able to do even more good working on one of our top priority problem areas.

Scale

Around one in every nine people lives with a diagnosable mental health disorder. These disorders are responsible for 5% of the global burden of disease, as measured in disability-adjusted life years (DALYs), and 15% of all years lived with disability.[371]

Neglectedness

Mental health in general gets much less attention than physical health from people thinking about how to make the world a better place because it's not as well understood. This means it's more neglected, but also likely means it's harder to make progress.

Improving mental health in the developing world might be an area where you can have a substantial impact, because it is particularly neglected by existing institutions and markets.

Solvability

There are several promising areas for research into mental health that appear to have not yet been adequately explored.

Read more

See our article at 80000hours.org/problem-profiles/neglected-mental-health/ for more.

Nuclear war

Nuclear weapons have the potential to kill hundreds of millions of people directly, and billions due to subsequent effects on agriculture. The potential for a 'nuclear winter' poses some unknown risk of human extinction, or of a social collapse from which we never recover.

There are many examples of moments in which the US or Russia appear to have come close to accidentally or deliberately using their nuclear weapons, so a nuclear war between global powers might not be as unlikely as it seems.

However, nuclear security is already a major topic of interest for governments, making it harder to have an impact relative to other global problems.

Most opportunities to influence the risk from nuclear weapons seem to be through work in the military or foreign policy institutions, or research in the think tanks that offer them ideas for how to lower the risk of nuclear conflict. Some less conventional approaches could involve working independently to improve relationships between people in the nuclear powers, or trying to improve the resilience of our food supply in the case of a serious agricultural collapse.

Our overall view

Recommended

Working on this issue seems to be among the best ways of improving the long-term future we know of, but all else equal, we think it's less pressing than our highest priority areas.

Scale

We believe work to reduce the probability of nuclear war has the potential for a large positive impact, as nuclear war would have devastating effects, both directly and also through secondary effects such as nuclear winter.

We think the chance of nuclear war per year is around 0.01–2%. Assuming this remains constant, the chance of a nuclear war is 10–85% in the next 100 years, although we expect this yearly chance will decrease over time. Estimates of existential risk from nuclear war within the next 100 years range from 0.005% to 1%.[372] We think the direct existential risk from nuclear war (i.e. not including secondary effects) is less than 0.01%. The indirect existential risk seems around 10 times higher.

Neglectedness

This issue is not as neglected as most other issues we prioritise. Current spending is between $1 billion and $10 billion per year (quality-adjusted).[373]

Solvability

Making progress on nuclear security seems somewhat tractable. While many routes to progress face significant political controversy, there may also be some more neglected ways to reduce this risk.[374]

Read more

See our article at 80000hours.org/problem-profiles/nuclear-security/ for more.

Space governance

Humanity's long-run future could be vast in scale and duration, because almost all of it could lie beyond Earth. As private interest in space increases, early work on space governance could positively shape that spacefaring future, and make it less likely that a future in space goes irreversibly wrong. Of course, it also matters that humanity avoids catastrophe in the meantime, and space governance focused on arms control and diplomacy can help here too — mostly by reducing the risk of great power conflict. However, the path to making a really important difference on these issues looks much less clear and robust than in some of our other top recommended areas.

Our overall view

Sometimes recommended

Working on this problem could be among the best ways of improving the long-term future, but we know of fewer high-impact opportunities to work on this issue than on our top priority problems.

Scale

Creating the right foundations for space governance today could end up being enormously valuable if that work positively influences how space is governed in the long run. In any case, the value of reducing the chance of conflict between spacefaring nations is large.

Neglectedness

Many aspects of space governance look significantly less neglected than other issues we prioritise, though still more neglected than most issues people focus on. Several think tanks already address legal- and defence-related issues in space, and there seem to be 400–500 people working directly on space governance.[375] However, at the time of writing, we think fewer than five people are working on researching space governance from a longtermist perspective — and maybe no more than the equivalent of one person working full-time.

Solvability

It should be feasible to make progress on some research areas within space governance, such as arms control and dealing with space debris. But other areas could be unusually speculative.

When it comes to influencing decisions, things look more difficult. It might be most feasible to get agreement on issues that aren't urgent, like questions about settling beyond the solar system. But deliberations about space governance are led by powerful actors (countries and companies) that are mostly guided by existing interests — in the majority of cases, it will probably be hard to shift the course of those deliberations. However, academics and think tank researchers are in some cases able to influence policymakers, and you could try to shape space governance by going into policy or private industry yourself.

Read more

See our article at 80000hours.org/problem-profiles/space-governance/ for more.

Stable totalitarianism

Economist Bryan Caplan has written about the worry that "stable totalitarianism" — i.e. a global totalitarian regime that lasts for an extremely long period of time — could arise in the future,[376] especially if we move toward a more unified world government or if certain technologies make it possible for totalitarian leaders to rule for longer.

Stable global totalitarianism would be an example of what Toby Ord calls an "enforced unrecoverable dystopia."[377] Ord categorises this as a form of existential risk: although humanity would not be extinct, an unrecoverable dystopia would mean losing out on the possibility of a good future for future generations.[378] In this way, a truly perpetual dystopia could be as bad as (or possibly even worse than) outright extinction.

We think that more attention should be paid to the technological changes that could make a perpetual totalitarian regime possible:

- More sophisticated surveillance techniques — which could either be developed to monitor the possession of potentially dangerous technologies, or for other less laudable ends — could greatly enhance the ability for totalitarian regimes to persist.
- Lie detection technology may soon see large improvements due to advances in machine learning or brain imaging. Better lie detection technology could improve cooperation and trust between groups by allowing people to prove they are being honest in high-stakes scenarios. On the other hand, it might increase the stability of totalitarian regimes by helping them avoid hiring, or remove, anyone who isn't a 'true believer' in their ideology.

We're also concerned about advances in AI making robust totalitarianism more likely to be possible.[379] AI-enabled totalitarianism would be even more concerning if we believe that we should have some concern for artificial sentience. This is because it seems plausible that it would be even easier to enforce a totalitarian regime over simulated beings, for example by resetting a simulation to a point before the leaders of the regime lose control.

Our overall view

Sometimes recommended

Working on this problem could be among the best ways of improving the long-term future, but we know of fewer high-impact opportunities to work on this issue than on our top priority problems.

Scale

Overall, Caplan thinks that there is a 5% risk of perpetual totalitarianism within the next 1,000 years.[380] We think the risk of this is much lower — most forms of long-lasting totalitarianism won't be truly *perpetual*. But any long-lasting totalitarianism would cause an immense amount of suffering and would be worth substantial effort to avoid.

Neglectedness

We're not currently aware of anyone working full-time on risks from stable totalitarianism, so we believe this area is highly neglected.

Solvability

We'd be excited to see further analysis and testing of Caplan's argument, as well as people working on how to limit the potential risks from these technologies and political changes if they do come about.

We're unsure overall on where the balance of risks from surveillance lies: it's hard to say whether the increase in safety from potentially existential catastrophes like advanced bioweapons is or is not worth risks to political freedom. As a result, it may be especially useful to develop ways of making surveillance more compatible with privacy and public oversight.

We'd also be excited about people working specifically on reducing the risks of stable totalitarianism that could arise as a result of the development of AI — though we're not sure exactly what this kind of work would look like.

Read more

See our article at 80000hours.org/problem-profiles/risks-of-stable-totalitarianism/ for more.

Wild animal suffering

It's easy for us to think of the natural world (without human intervention) as unambiguously positive: to imagine that wild animals live harmoniously with one another in a natural 'balance.'

But advocates for wild animal welfare argue that this attitude ignores the huge amounts of suffering present in nature. Moreover, the large, healthy, adult vertebrates we usually picture (like foxes, songbirds, or lions) are a very small proportion of the overall wild animal population — almost all wild animals are actually juvenile[381] invertebrates.[382]

This means that the actual day-to-day lives of wild animals are pretty different to how we'd expect. Animal lives are mostly quite short — in some species, only one in millions of juveniles survive to adulthood — and are filled with disease, parasitism, hunger, thirst, fear of predators, and suffering from heat or cold. Wild animals often die in very drawn-out, painful ways, and most die at a fraction of their possible lifespan.[383]

Our overall view

Sometimes recommended

We'd love to see more people working on this issue. But you might be able to do even more good working on one of our top priority problem areas.

Scale

There are huge numbers of wild animals. Collectively, wild land vertebrates probably number between 10^{11} and 10^{14}. Wild marine vertebrates number at least 10^{13} and perhaps a few orders of magnitude higher. Terrestrial and marine arthropods each probably number at least 10^{18}.[384]

We can't know for sure what it's like to be a wild animal, but we can observe that many or even most wild animals live in conditions that would be considered extremely cruel to inflict on a human, or a domesticated animal.

Neglectedness

Very little effort goes towards trying to reduce the suffering of wild animals, even within the broader field of animal welfare. There might be good reasons for this, because it seems so hard to solve — but at present the field is extremely neglected.

Solvability

Wild animal welfare seems much less tractable than, for example, farmed animal welfare, where we've seen lots of wins recently and where humans are the unambiguous cause of the suffering. In the comparatively much newer and smaller field of wild animal welfare, it's much less clear what exactly we should do.

It's also very hard to accurately predict the effects of our actions on ecosystems, because they're so complicated, so it seems like the interventions we can be confident won't do harm are currently limited.

This may point to additional reasons to build this research field: because the area is so neglected, there might be many opportunities to discover more ways of reliably helping wild animals in the future.

Read more

See our article at 80000hours.org/problem-profiles/wild-animal-welfare/ for more.

Notes

1. 80000hours.org/articles/job-satisfaction-research/
2. Bolles, 2014.
3. There has been an extensive programme of research into how good humans are at predicting the effects of future events on their emotional wellbeing. It began with Kahneman and Snell in the early 1990s, and was led in the 2000s by Harvard psychologist Daniel Gilbert. Much of the research is summarised in Gilbert's book *Stumbling on Happiness* (Gilbert, 2006). A 2009 review is in Gilbert et al., 2009. One takeaway is that we are bad at predicting how we will feel in the future, and we don't realise this.

    We're unsure how robust all of these findings are in light of the replication crisis, and haven't found any more recent work replicating these findings.

    In particular, we're concerned about Gilbert's prominent rejection of the existence of the replication crisis, published in Science in 2016 (Gilbert et al., 2016). A convincing response to Gilbert was also published in Science in 2016 (Anderson et al., 2016). Gelman, 2016 provides an excellent summary of the dispute by a Columbia statistician.

    So we expect Gilbert has overstated the findings. Nevertheless, we think the broader point that we can't simply trust our intuition about these matters is correct.

4. While many studies have found support for the "peak–end rule" — the idea that we judge experiences based on how we feel at the most intense point (i.e. the peak, and at the end) — some have cast doubt on it.

    For instance, Kemp et al., 2008 found that the peak–end rule was "not an outstandingly good predictor," and that the most memorable or unusual moments (not necessarily the most intense moments) were more relevant predictors of recalled happiness. This suggests the "peak" is more relevant than the end.

    > *"The peak–end rule predicts approximately the correct level of happiness, but the correlations of the peak–end average with the overall recalled happiness are generally lower than those obtained by considering the participants' happiness in the most memorable or most unusual 24-h period... Remembered overall happiness seems to be better predicted by end happiness than by peak or trough happiness, and the comparative failure of the peak–end rule appears to stem more from the peak than from the end."*

    That said, a 2022 meta-analysis looking at 58 independent studies, with a cumulative sample size of around 12,500 people, found "strong support" for the peak–end rule (Alaybek et al., 2022).

    > *"The peak-end effect on retrospective summary evaluations was: (1) large (r = 0.581, 95% Confidence Interval = 0.487–0.661), (2) robust across boundary conditions, (3) comparable to the effect of the overall average (mean) score and stronger than the effects of the trend and variability across all episodes in the experience, (4) stronger than the effects of the first (beginning) and lowest intensity (trough) episodes, and (5) stronger than the effect of the duration of the experience (which was essentially nil, thereby supporting the idea of duration neglect)."*

5. Gilbert, 2006.
6. CareerCast, 2015.

    We're using CareerCast's 2015 rankings because we want to compare these rankings with measurements of job satisfaction and meaningfulness. The most recent large survey on job satisfaction and meaningfulness that we could find was conducted by Payscale with data collected from 2.7 million people between 6 November 2013 and 6 November 2015 (Payscale, 2015).

    CareerCast's 2021 methodology is largely unchanged (Careercast, 2021).

7. CareerCast, 2015. Actuary was the top-ranked career in 2015. Actuary dropped to ninth place in the 2021 rankings (CareerCast, 2021).

8. The most recent national survey by the UK's Cabinet Office on life satisfaction by occupation was conducted in 2014 (and published by the University of Kent). The survey found "actuaries, economists and statisticians" ranked 64th out of 274 job titles, putting them in the top 23% (Easton, 2014).

9. Payscale's surveys cover millions of workers. The most recent survey which asked about job satisfaction and job meaningfulness was conducted from 2013 to 2015. The survey found that only 36% of actuaries found their work meaningful. Job satisfaction was also high at 80%, but a significant number of jobs were rated over 80%. (Payscale, 2015)

10. A Gallup survey in October 2021 asked 13,085 US employees what was most important to them when deciding whether to accept a new job offered by a new employer. 64% of people said that "a significant increase in income or benefits" was "very important," compared to 61% for "greater work-life balance and better personal well-being," 58% for "the ability to do what they do best" and 53% for "greater stability and job security." (Wigert, 2023)

    The survey was a self-administered web survey. There are a number of possible sources of bias. For example, if this survey was paid (it's unclear from the Gallup methodology), this may have introduced bias. That said, Gallup did weight samples to correct for nonresponse by adjusting the sample to match the national demographics of gender, age, race, Hispanic ethnicity, education, and region.

11. Judge et al., 2010:

    "When individuals are asked what would most improve the quality of their lives, the most common response is a higher income."

12. Take a look at 80000hours.org/articles/money-and-happiness/ for an overview of the evidence.

13. Kahneman et al., 2010.

14. A 2021 study found that wellbeing does rise with income, even above $75,000 a year (Killingsworth, 2021). However, it found that this, like life satisfaction, was approximately logarithmic — as an individual's income increases, their wellbeing increases at a slower and slower rate. As a result, above $75,000 a year, the wellbeing increases are very small. The study also found that, as income increased, wellbeing rose more slowly than life satisfaction (which was also approximately logarithmic).

    Hazell et al., 2021, provides a critical review of Killingsworth, 2021, and concludes:

    "Killingsworth's study has advanced our state of knowledge on the link between money and happiness through the use of a clever research design. The new data suggests that increases in happiness don't stop after an individual reaches an income of $75,000. Instead, the increases continue, and perhaps plateau, at a later point. However, this new insight doesn't significantly change the conclusions drawn after Kahneman and Deaton's 2010 study. It seems that chasing ever-increasing amounts of money is an ineffective way to find happiness for ourselves."

15. The average household in the US has 2.5 people, but of course this is just an average across a wide range of family structures. Larger households enjoy "economies of scale" by sharing houses, cars, and so on. This makes it tricky to say what the equivalent of a household income is for a single individual.

    Standard conversion rates are the following:

    A single individual has an equivalence score of 1.

    A single extra adult adds another equivalence score of 0.5.

    Adding a young child to this adds an equivalence score of 0.3, while a teenager costs another 0.5.

    As a result, a couple can achieve the same lifestyle as an individual with 50% more income; a couple with a young child can achieve the same lifestyle as an individual with 80% more income; a couple with a teenager require an income twice as high.

    These are approximations, but reasonable ones used by international organisations (Institute for Fiscal Studies, 2022). (The IFS table gives conversion rates from a childless couple to a household. Dividing by 0.67 — the conversion rate to a single individual — will give you the numbers we listed above.)

For the sake of simplicity we will assume that on average across their adult lives people are in a household with an adult couple and a child. This is just an average — some people will be single, while some will be supporting multiple children, at least for some of their lives.

Using this approximation means that a single individual requires about $1/1.9 = 53\%$ as much as a typical household, averaged over their adult lives, to achieve the same standard of living.

In this case, 53% of $50,000–$75,000 for a household represents $27,000–$40,000 for an individual.

16.   Carnevale et al., 2021:

"A bachelor's degree holder earns, at the median, $2.8 million during a lifetime, which translates into average annual earnings of about $70,000."

This figure was for 2021, but wages have grown since then. In January 2021, average wages per hour in the US were $29.92 and were $33.03 in January 2023. That's growth of 10%, which suggests that the average college graduate now earns $77,000. This is likely an overestimate, because college graduate earnings have been growing slower than average earnings since 2021 (FRED, 2023).

This growth matches roughly what we'd expect from inflation, which was about 10% over the period, and wages tend to lag inflation in high-inflation periods like 2021–23.

It's hard to find comparable data for just Ivy League graduates. Payscale found a median mid-career salary of over $135,000, where mid-career is defined as over 10 years (Payscale, 2021).

Our guess is that the Payscale data is too high, because people with higher incomes will be more likely to fill out the survey. On the other hand, income only peaks after 20–30 years, so the figure for 10+ years probably underreports the overall average. Moreover, the median will be less than the mean.

Overall, we're pretty confident that the mean lifetime average for Ivy League graduates is over $120,000.

If you want to estimate your future income, then you should also account for future wage growth (which has been about 2% historically). We ignore this here, and only estimate current income.

17.   See 80000hours.org/2016/02/should-you-look-for-a-low-stress-job/.

18.   Based on payscale.com surveys of over 2.7 million Americans. (Payscale, 2015)

19.   Curry et al., 2018 found that there is a causal link between performing acts of kindness and wellbeing. They included 27 experimental studies included in the review (of which 23 were randomised), with a total sample size of 4,045 people.

"These 27 studies, some of which included multiple control conditions and dependent measures, yielded 52 effect sizes. Multi-level modeling revealed that the overall effect of kindness on the well-being of the actor is small-to-medium ($\delta = 0.28$). The effect was not moderated by sex, age, type of participant, intervention, control condition or outcome measure. There was no indication of publication bias."

20.   Aknin et al., 2013.

However, there is some evidence that part of the reason for the correlation is that happier people give more (Boenigk et al., 2016).

For a more comprehensive review of the question, see Mogensen, 2017.

21.   Humphrey et al., 2007.

22.   Montini, 2014.

23.   Newport, 2012.

24.   Grant, 2014.

25.   You can get more accurate information on what you enjoy over time by rating your happiness at the end of each day. That way you don't need to rely on unreliable memory.

26.   Lewis, 2012.

27.   Lopez et al., 2006.

28. We used WHO data from 2004 (Mathers et al., 2008). Line is the best fitting hyperbola determined by nonlinear least square regression.

29. Reynolds, 2023.

30. Institute for Health Metrics and Evaluations, 2019.

31. Ingram, 2021:

    "Since the adoption of this inexpensive and easily applied intervention, the worldwide mortality rate for children with acute infectious diarrhoea has plummeted from around 5 million to about 1.5 million deaths per year. Lives Saved: Over 57,500,000."

    Very roughly, this means 50/40 = 1.25 million lives have been saved per year. So if Dr Nalin sped up the discovery by five months (just a guess), that means that (5/12)*1.25 = 0.52 million extra lives were saved by his actions. This is a highly approximate estimate and could easily be off by an order of magnitude. See more comments in the next footnote.

32. Kinney, 2011:

    "Every source quoted an amazing number of transfusions and potential lives saved in countries and regions worldwide. High impact years began around 1955 and calculations are loosely based on 1 life saved per 2.7 units of blood transfused. In the USA alone an estimated 4.5 million lives are saved each year. From these data I determined that 1.5% of the population was saved annually by blood transfusions and I applied this percentage on population data from 1950-2008 for North America, Europe, Australia, New Zealand, and parts of Asia and Africa. This rate may inflate the effectiveness of transfusions in the early decades but excludes the developing world entirely."

    If we assume a constant number of lives saved per year, then that's about 10 million lives per year. If he sped up the discovery by two years, then that's 20 million lives saved.

    This is a highly approximate estimate and could easily be off by an order of magnitude in either direction, and seem more likely to be too high than too low. We're a bit sceptical of the *Science Heroes* figures. Moreover, our attempt at modelling the speed-up is very simple. Since most of the lives were saved in the modern era once a large number of people had medical care, it's possible that speeding up the discovery wouldn't have had much impact at all. On the other hand, the discovery of blood groups probably made other scientific advances possible, and we're ignoring their impact. Nevertheless, the basic point stands: Landsteiner's impact was likely vastly greater than a typical doctor.

33. Aksenov, 2013.

34. We often say "helping people" here for simplicity and brevity, but we don't mean just humans — we mean anyone with experience that matters morally — e.g. nonhuman animals that can suffer or feel happiness, or even conscious machines if they ever exist.

35. This definition is enough to help you figure out what to aim at in many situations — e.g. by roughly comparing the number of people affected by different issues. But sometimes you need a more precise definition.

    The more rigorous working definition of social impact used by 80,000 Hours is:

    "Social impact" or "making a difference" is (tentatively) about promoting total expected wellbeing — considered impartially, over the long term — without sacrificing anything that might be of comparable moral importance.

    You can read about why we use this definition in appendix 1.

36. Of 174 patients with injuries of varying severity, 94% were first-time charity-parachutists. The injury rate in charity-parachutists was 11%, at an average cost of £3,751 per casualty. Sixty-three percent of casualties who were charity-parachutists required hospital admission, representing a serious injury rate of 7%, at an average cost of £5,781 per patient. The amount raised per person for charity was £30. Each pound raised for charity cost the NHS £13.75 in return. (Lee et al., 1999.)

    We've been told by skydivers that safety has improved significantly since the 1990s, so it might not be as bad of an idea these days. Nevertheless, it's still an example of ineffective do-gooding that was pursued by over 1,000 people, and we think you can probably do much better even than modern-day parachuting.

37.   Erickson, 2008.

38.   Stevenson et al., 2013. This chart only shows correlation, not causation — you can find more detail on causation on our website at 80000hours.org/articles/money-and-happiness/.

39.   GiveWell, 2020:

> "GiveDirectly does not routinely collect data on the absolute levels of poverty (i.e. average assets and consumption) of households enrolled in its program. Preliminary results from GiveDirectly's general equilibrium study indicate that households in the area targeted for that study (in Kenya) are very poor. Endline results from this study in July 2018 found that mean consumption per capita per day in the full population of the control villages was $0.79.
>   Control group households in Haushofer and Shapiro 2013 had a mean monthly non-durable consumption level of $157.40 USD PPP (Table 1, p. 49). In our [2018] cost-effectiveness model, we use this figure to roughly estimate baseline annual consumption per capita at $286 (nominal USD; see here for more detail). This translates to a daily consumption rate of approximately $0.78 (nominal USD)."

To convert $287 per day to a 'purchasing power parity' figure, we use the World Bank's record of the nominal KES to USD exchange rate from 2018 to convert this to 29,073.1 Kenyan Shillings.

We then use the World Bank's PPP conversion factors for 2018, which indicates that 42.55 KES buys the equivalent of $1 in the US. This suggests an effective consumption level of $683.27 in that year.

We then inflation-adjust that figure using the US Consumer Price Index from 2018 to January 2023, arriving at a figure of $810–$825, depending which months we use.

That's an equivalent of $2.25, PPP adjusted, per day.

This figure is, of course, imprecise. It's difficult to compare the purchasing power of people living in different countries and circumstances. (We discuss some of the problems at 80000hours. org/2017/04/how-accurately-does-anyone-know-the-global-distribution-of-income.) There are reasons it might be both too low and too high. However, we'd be surprised if it were off by more than a factor of five. Moreover, all the official estimates we've seen of the income of the poorest billion people agree that they are about 10 times poorer than almost everyone living in a rich country, and about 100 times poorer than someone living on an upper-middle-class salary in a rich country.

40.   Carnevale et al., 2021. To calculate post-tax income, we plugged $77,000 into the SmartAsset online income tax calculator for someone living in California, and it came out at $54,500 post-tax (SmartAsset, 2023). This includes federal income tax, FICA, and state tax, working out at an effective rate of 29%. California generally has higher taxes, so this post-tax income estimate is an underestimate.

41.   If the relationship between income and wellbeing is logarithmic, then doubling someone's income increases their wellbeing by a constant amount. That means if someone has an income of $54,500 and another has an income of $800, you'd need to increase the first person's income by $54,500 to increase their wellbeing as much as you would if you increased the second person's income by $800. $54500/$800 = 68. We explain why we think the relationship is logarithmic (or perhaps even weaker) in our evidence review on income and happiness at 80000hours.org/articles/ money-and-happiness/.

42.   GiveDirectly, 2015.

43.   GiveDirectly has had randomised controlled trials performed on their programmes (Haushofer et al., 2016, McIntosh et al., 2021, McIntosh et al., 2022, Egger et al., 2022,) and there is a wider literature showing benefits from cash transfers — see McGuire et al., 2021 and GiveWell, 2012.

44.   That's $55,000 in individual income, not household income.

45. Aknin et al., 2013.

46. Open Philanthropy — 80,000 Hours' biggest funder — was spun out of GiveWell, and the two share some leadership.

47. GiveWell's estimate of the cost to save a life through its top charities has varied over time between $1,000 and $10,000, and is typically around $3,000–5,000.

   GiveWell also reported how cost effective it thinks these charities are compared to GiveDirectly, considering a wider range of effects (e.g. also including improvements to education and income), and typically estimate that they're about 10 times more effective.

   10% of $77,000 is $7,700, which is enough to prevent at least one death per year.

   Of course, there is a lot more to say about how valuable these donations are when we try to consider *all* the possible effects. You can read more about the philosophical problem of cluelessness at 80000hours.org/articles/cluelessness. In general, we'd encourage you to consider which global problems you think are most pressing, all things considered (we take a longtermist perspective), and find the best organisations working to address those issues. We've written more about how to find a charity to support at 80000hours.org/articles/best-charity/.

48. The richest 10% of the global population currently takes 52% of global income, PPP-adjusted (Chancel et al. 2023). So, if the top 10% give 10%, then that's 5% of world income. World income in 2021 was about $96.5 trillion (according to the World Bank) so that's around $5 trillion donated.

49. The World Bank's poverty line is $2.15 per person per day, in 2017 USD, PPP-adjusted (World Bank, 2022). The poverty gap at $2.15 a day (2017 USD, PPP-adjusted) in 2019 was 2.6%, according to the World Bank. This means that people below the poverty line live off of $2.10 a day, on average. The poverty headcount ratio at $2.15 a day (2017 USD, PPP-adjusted) — i.e. the proportion of the world population below the extreme poverty line — was 8.4% in 2019, according to the World Bank. The global population in 2019 was 7.74 billion, according to the World Bank, which means 650 million people were in extreme poverty in 2019.

   This means it would cost only $36 million a day to bring everyone in extreme poverty up to the poverty line. That's $13 billion a year. This is probably an underestimate, because transferring all that money to people in poverty would raise prices, have substantial logistic costs, etc. Let's say it's a factor of 10 out, and it'd cost around $130 billion a year.

   Research and development expenditure as a percentage of GDP was about 2.6% in 2020.

   Assuming this proportion has stayed roughly constant, if world GDP is about $96.5 trillion annually, it would cost about $2.5 trillion per year to double global R&D.

   Globally an estimated 244 million children and youth are out of school (UNESCO, 2022). If we suppose it would cost $1,000 each per year to provide them with education — schools in the US spend around $13,000 per person (Hanson, 2022) — that would be $244 billion per year.

   In 2012, contributions to the arts totalled $31 billion annually (National Endowment for the Arts, 2012). Adjusting for inflation, that's $40 in 2023, so it would cost $31 billion to double it.

   According to Wikipedia, going to Mars has been estimated to cost $500 billion (Wikipedia, 2023). Though it suggests this is likely an underestimate, we also wouldn't have to pay for it all in one year, so will go with this figure for our purposes.

   Summing all the above with $1 trillion put toward mitigating climate change gets us to just under $4.5 trillion annually, meaning we'd still have nearly $1 trillion to spare. So, although all these figures are very imprecise (and budgets often blow up), we don't doubt the basic point that it would be a huge amount of resources directed to the most urgent problems.

   If this many resources were actually suddenly given to charity, it would take time for the economy to adapt, corrupt leaders might try to extract it from their citizens, and there might be other unpredictable effects — it certainly wouldn't be straightforward to use them effectively. However, these figures at least show there is the potential for enormous gains from greater and more effective charitable giving.

50. For a detailed discussion of the origins and accuracy of this graph, see https://80k.link/income. Briefly, the data for percentiles 1 to 79 were taken from PovcalNet: the online tool for poverty measurement developed by the Development Research Group of the World Bank (World Bank, 2016). Note that this is in fact a measure of *consumption*, which closely tracks income and is the standard way of tracking the wealth of people towards the lower part of the distribution. The data for income percentiles 80 to 99 were provided by Branko Milanović in private correspondence.

51. Giving What We Can, like 80,000 Hours, is a project of the Effective Ventures group — the umbrella term for Effective Ventures Foundation and Effective Ventures Foundation USA, Inc., which are two separate legal entities that work together.

52. According to the World Bank, US GDP was about $23.3 trillion in 2021, 0.2% of that is $47 billion (data retrieved March 2023). Over a four-year term, that's $187 billion.

53. Read more about these estimates at 80000hours.org/articles/is-voting-important/.

54. Whether or not this actually does more good depends on the *counterfactuals*: what exactly the other person would have done otherwise, what you'd do otherwise, and what would happen to all the other people whose careers would be affected (for example, the person you replace in the job that you then go on to do).

55. Open Philanthropy is 80,000 Hours' largest donor.

56. MacKay, 2015.

57. The average British person used about 120 kWh per day in 2008, when MacKay conducted his experiment (MacKay, 2009). Today, the average British person uses about 80 kWh per day (Our World in Data, 2022).

   Heating an uninsulated detached home takes about 53 kWh per day, while adding loft and wall insulation reduces that by 44% to 30 kWh per day. Assuming a single house contains 2.5 people, then compared to total energy use per person, that's a reduction of $33/(120*2.5) = 11\%$. If unplugging phone chargers when they're not in use reduces personal energy use by under 0.01%, then adding home insulation is 1,100 times more important. It can also cut your heating bill by 44%, which can mean you save money over the long term, depending on the cost of the insulation (MacKay, 2009).

58. World Bank data says that the United States has about 260 doctors per 100,000 people. With a population of approximately 330 million, that means there are over 850,000 doctors in the United States.

59. Centers for Disease Control and Prevention, 2017:

   "Neglected Tropical Diseases (NTDs) are a group of parasitic and bacterial diseases that cause substantial illness for more than one billion people globally. Affecting the world's poorest people, NTDs impair physical and cognitive development, contribute to mother and child illness and death, make it difficult to farm or earn a living, and limit productivity in the workplace. As a result, NTDs trap the poor in a cycle of poverty and disease."

60. There are *some* reasons to think about increasing returns, especially within organisations (Todd, 2015). But in general we think there are good reasons to think diminishing returns will be the norm.

61. Andreeva, 2011.

62. A meta-analysis by the Campbell Collaboration, a leading evaluator of the effectiveness of social policies, concluded (Petrosino et al., 2004):

   "The analyses show the intervention to be more harmful than doing nothing. The program effect, whether assuming a fixed or random effects model, was nearly identical and negative in direction, regardless of the meta-analytic strategy.

   We conclude that programs like 'Scared Straight' are likely to have a harmful effect and increase delinquency relative to doing nothing at all to the same youths. Given these results, we cannot recommend this program as a crime prevention strategy. Agencies that permit such programs, however, must rigorously evaluate them not only to ensure that they are doing what they purport to do (prevent crime) – but at the very least they do not cause more harm than good to the very citizens they pledge to protect."

A review of American social programmes made a cost-benefit analysis of the programme, concluding there were $203 social costs incurred per $1 invested in the programme (Aos, 2004 – see table 1). However, note that this estimate is quite old so could be out of date. Moreover, we're generally sceptical of very large differences between costs and benefits, so we doubt the true ratio is as high as this. Nevertheless, the programme looks to have been a terrible use of resources.

63.   Anderson, 2008.

64.   Giving USA, 2022:

> "In 2021, Americans gave $484.85 billion to charity, a 4.0% increase over 2020. Adjusted for inflation, total giving remained relatively flat, with -0.7% growth."

65.   According to the January 2023 Post-Secondary Employment Outcomes data (United States Census Bureau, 2023), one year after graduating:

21% of employed graduates are in health (this remains at 21% at 5 years and at 10 years after graduating)

17% of employed graduates are in education (this rises to 19% at 5 years and 21% at 10 years after graduating)

5% of employed graduates are in public administration (this rises to 6% at 5 years and 7% at 10 years after graduating).

Note that a large fraction of government spending goes into education and health, so those who go into government are also contributing to these areas.

We downloaded the raw data from the Post-Secondary Employment Outcomes page of the US Census Bureau website and aggregated these figures ourselves. See all the aggregated data at https://80k.info/pseo-data/.

The US Census Bureau notes: "The PSEO are made possible through data sharing partnerships between universities, university systems, State Departments of Education, State Labor Market Information offices, and the U.S. Census Bureau. PSEO data are available for post-secondary institutions whose transcript data have been made available to the Census Bureau through a data-sharing agreement."

We'd guess that a high enough proportion of colleges are involved for these figures to be roughly right, but there may be some systematic bias (e.g., state colleges may be more likely to share data than private colleges).

66.   Office of the Assistant Secretary for Planning and Evaluation, 2023.

67.   Giving What We Can, 2019.

68.   Our World in Data, 2021.

69.   How many live in poverty globally? Exactly where to draw the line is arbitrary, but in *Poverty and Shared Prosperity 2022*, the World Bank set the poverty line at $2.15 per day (in 2017 USD, purchasing parity adjusted), and estimated that in 2022, there were 667 million people living below this level. $2.15 is around $785 per year and most live below this level (World Bank, 2021).

70.   The US Census Bureau report "Poverty in United States: 2022" finds 37.9 million Americans living below the US poverty line (Creamer et al., 2022):

> "The official poverty rate in 2021 was 11.6 percent, with 37.9 million people in poverty."

The US poverty threshold varies depending on the size of the household (Department of Health and Human Service, 2023). For a single person, the threshold in 2022 was $13,950 (Office of the Assistant Secretary for Planning and Evaluation, 2023).

71.   Total ODA (overseas development assistance) spending in 2021 was $178.9 billion (OECD, 2022). Note official ODA only includes spending by the 31 members of the OECD Development Assistance Committee (DAC) (roughly, European and North American countries, the EU, Japan, and South Korea).

The OECD estimate of ODA-like flows from key providers of development cooperation that do not report to the OECD-DAC was $4 billion in 2020.

They note that:

> "Scholars have estimated that China's development aid is much larger [than the reported USD 3.2 billion in 2019 and USD 2.9 billion in 2020], standing at USD 5.9 billion in 2018 (see Kitano and Miyabayashi) or as high as USD 7.9 billion if one includes preferential buyers credits (see Kitano 2019). China's development co-operation is estimated to have decreased due to expenditure cuts to deal with COVID-19 (Kitano and Miyabayashi).

> The OECD measure of Total Official Support for Sustainable Development (TOSSD), which also includes loans, investments, and spending by many, but not all, other countries (including 'South-South' 'spending by developing countries in other developing countries) came to a total of $434 billion in 2021."

There is also international philanthropy, but we don't think adding it would more than double the figure. The US is the largest source of philanthropic funding at $400–$500 billion, but only a few percent goes to international causes. A Giving USA report estimated that US giving to "international affairs" was only $27 billion in 2021 (Giving USA, 2022).

Moreover, if we were to include international philanthropy, we'd need to include philanthropic spending on poor people in the US.

Estimates of welfare spending vary depending on exactly what is included. Total spending also varies from year to year. We used a representative figure from usgovernmentspending.com:

> "In FY 2022 total US government spending on welfare — federal, state, and local — was "guesstimated" to be $1,662 billion, including $792 billion for Medicaid, and $869 billion in other welfare."

72. GiveWell, 2010.

73. Ord, 2017.

Oral rehydration therapy, which rose to prominence during the 1971 Bangladesh Liberation War, cut mortality rates from 30% to 3%, cutting annual diarrhoeal deaths from 4.6 million to 1.6 million over the previous four decades.

All wars, democides, and politically motivated famines killed an estimated 160 million to 240 million people during the 20th century, or an average of 1.6 million to 2.4 million per year.

International humanitarian aid has contributed substantially to reductions in the number of annual deaths from disease. $500 million of the $1.5 billion spent on eliminating smallpox came from international funders.

Toby Ord is an advisor to 80,000 Hours.

74. Ord, 2017. International humanitarian aid has contributed substantially to reductions in the number of annual deaths from disease. $500 million of the $1.5 billion spent on eliminating smallpox came from international funders.

75. Jamison et al., 2006. See 80000hours.org/2023/02/how-much-do-solutions-differ-in-effectiveness/ for more on this data.

76. Ord, 2013:

> "[In the DCP2] in total, the interventions are spread over more than four orders of magnitude, ranging from 0.02 to 300 DALYs per $1,000, with a median of 5. Thus, moving money from the least effective intervention to the most effective would produce about 15,000 times the benefit, and even moving it from the median intervention to the most effective would produce about 60 times the benefit."

In private correspondence, Ord added that the mean intervention had an effectiveness of 24 DALYs averted per $1,000. Note that a DALY is a "disability-adjusted life year" i.e. a year of life lost to ill health — the opposite of a "quality-adjusted life year."

If you selected an intervention at random, then on average you'd pick something with the mean effectiveness. Most of the interventions are worse than the mean, but if you picked randomly you'd have a small chance of landing on the top one.

77. Berger, 2014.

78. Because, as we've discussed, the relationship between income and happiness is approximately

logarithmic. One potential complication is that making poor US or UK citizens better off could eventually have spillover benefits for the global poor (Shulman, 2014) which would cap the degree of difference. However, I (Benjamin) expect the spillover is less than 1/20, so this consideration doesn't have much effect on the 20-fold ratio.

79.   In 2018, GiveWell estimated that it cost $900 to do an amount of good equivalent to averting the death of an individual under five through the most effective global health intervention: Deworm the World. GiveWell estimates that it costs $11,300 to do an equivalent amount of good by giving cash to the global poor through donating to GiveDirectly. This would imply that the best global health interventions are 13 times more effective than giving cash to the global poor. To be conservative, we assume that global health interventions are only five times more effective.

GiveWell's cost-effectiveness analysis is available at https://80k.info/health-vs-cash/.

80.   Though if you could find a similarly leveraged way to do good in a rich country, that would bring the ratio back to more like 20 times. The 100-fold comparison is with a typical rich country social intervention.

81.   Below a most plausible ICER (incremental cost-effectiveness ratio) of £20,000 per QALY gained, the decision to recommend the use of a technology is normally based on the cost-effectiveness estimate and the acceptability of a technology as an effective use of NHS resources (UK NICE, 2022).

82.   Cotra, 2016.

83.   The 300-fold difference is when comparing health benefits against other health benefits in the short run. The economic benefits of helping people in rich countries may be larger because they are richer, so if we took into account both economic benefits and health benefits, the size of the difference might shrink.

For instance, making the US wealthier has spillover benefits to the developing world, such as increased foreign aid and improved technology. Very roughly, this might reduce the size of the difference by a factor of three (Shulman, 2014).

If we took into account further corrections, the difference would probably shrink still further (Todd, 2023). Nevertheless, if we made an all-considered comparison in terms of what most benefits the present generation, we'd still expect investing in global health to be over 20 times more effective than randomly selected US social interventions.

84.   Climate scientists disagree on exactly how much longer Earth will remain habitable. Their models generally predict that Earth will remain habitable for between the next few hundred million years and over a billion years. Kollipara, 2014, says:

"Two new modeling studies find that the gradually brightening sun won't vaporize our planet's water for at least another 1 billion to 1.5 billion years—hundreds of millions of years later than a slightly older model had forecast."

85.   It's possible that future generations would live for longer than 100 years. This would probably reduce the number of future generations, but wouldn't necessarily decrease the number of future people.

86.   We cover these ideas in more depth at 80000hours.org/articles/future-generations/.

87.   Obama, 2013.

88.   Schmall, 2019:

"Three in four Americans think climate change will eventually result in the extinction of humanity, according to new research.

A new survey of 2,000 Americans aiming to reveal just how much "climate anxiety" people carry found that nearly half of Americans think climate change will result in the end of the world within the next 200 years.

Not only that, but one in five millennials think climate change will trigger the end of the world in their lifetime."

89.   We argue more for the importance of reducing existential risks at 80000hours.org/articles/existential-risks/.

90. You can read more about the risk from climate change in appendix 9.
91. Randerson, 2006:

    "The DNA sequence of smallpox, as well as other potentially dangerous pathogens such as polio virus and 1918 flu are freely available in online public databases. So to build a virus from scratch, a terrorist would simply order consecutive lengths of DNA along the sequence and glue them together in the correct order. This is beyond the skills and equipment of the kitchen chemist, but could be achieved by a well-funded terrorist with access to a basic lab and PhD-level personnel.

    One study estimated that because most people on the planet have no resistance to the extinct virus, an initial release which infected just 10 people would spread to 2.2 million people in 180 days."

92. Giattino et al., 2023.
93. Read more about biosecurity in appendix 9.
94. Graph produced from Maddison, 2013, p. 379, table A.4.
95. In 2004, Frank Levy and Richard Murnane wrote that "executing a left turn across oncoming traffic involves so many factors that it is hard to imagine discovering the set of rules that can replicate [a] driver's behavior." (Levy et al., 2004).) Today autonomous vehicles are a common sight in five US states: California, Texas, Arizona, Washington, and Michigan.
96. Steinhardt, 2022.
97. Dyer, 2022.
98. Chow, 2023.
99. Reed et al., 2022.
100. Stein-Perlman et al., 2022 contacted 4,271 researchers who published at NeurIPS and ICML conferences in 2021. All the researchers who published were randomly allocated to either the Stein-Perlman et al. survey or a second survey run by others. They received 738 responses (a 17% response rate).

    Researchers were asked about "high-level machine intelligence" (HLMI). This was defined as:
    "When unaided machines can accomplish every task better and more cheaply than human workers. Ignore aspects of tasks for which being a human is intrinsically advantageous, e.g. being accepted as a jury member. Think feasibility, not adoption."

    Two other surveys, Zhang et al., 2022, conducted in 2019, and Grace et al., 2018, conducted in 2016, found similar results.

    For more information on these surveys, including information on their accuracy, see 80000hours.org/problem-profiles/artificial-intelligence/.
101. Over 100,000 western lowland gorillas are thought to exist in the wild, with 4,000 in zoos; eastern lowland gorillas have a population of under 5,000 in the wild and 24 in zoos. Mountain gorillas are the most severely endangered, with an estimated population of about 880 left in the wild and none in zoos. (Wikipedia, 2017)
102. The Puerto Rico conference in 2015 hosted by the Future of Life Institute was a watershed moment, leading to an open letter signed by many AI leaders within academia and industry (Future of Life Institute, 2015).

    In May 2023, Geoffrey Hinton resigned from his position at Google (Bisset, 2023):
    "Google computer scientist Geoffrey Hinton, who has made significant contributions to the development of artificial intelligence, has left the technology giant to warn the world of the "existential risk" posed by AI systems to humans."

103. You can find out more in appendix 9.
104. Read more in appendix 9.
105. Tetlock, et al., 2019.
106. Read more in appendix 9.
107. Giving What We Can, like 80,000 Hours, is a project of the Effective Ventures group — the

umbrella term for Effective Ventures Foundation and Effective Ventures Foundation USA, Inc., which are two separate legal entities that work together.

108. Townsend, et al., 2023.

109. See a summary of our profile on promoting effective altruism in appendix 9.

110. The most important and unusual driver of our views is probably that — as we've argued — we think you should especially focus on the impact different issues can have on all future generations (longtermism). This increases the importance we place on reducing existential risks and on shaping other events that could affect the long-run future.

   If we were to reject longtermism, issues that contribute to existential risk would stand out much less (including most of our top-recommended issues), while issues like ending factory farming, improving global health, speeding up economic growth, improving science, and migration reform would all be boosted.

   That said, even if we rejected longtermism, we still think positively shaping AI and reducing the chance of a catastrophic pandemic would be top problems for more people to work on due to their large near-term and medium-term effects, as well as their neglectedness.

   You can read about some counterarguments to longtermism at 80000hours.org/articles/future-generations/#objections.

   Another major worry we have about our list is that there's an important issue we haven't even thought of, but should be among our top-ranked issues. We sometimes call this the possibility of finding a 'cause X.' The possibility of finding cause X is one reason why we rate further research and capacity-building so highly.

   Finally, we could easily be wrong about any of the particular issues we list — maybe some are much bigger or smaller than we think, or turn out to be more or less solvable. For example, perhaps the development of AI will be largely safe by default. You can see some of our key uncertainties about each individual issue on our website, and we invite you to investigate these questions for yourself.

111. Because the three factors multiply together, if each can vary by a factor of 100, the overall variation could be up to six orders of magnitude. In practice, the factors anti-correlate, so it's not quite as large as this, and there are other reasons for modesty. See our advanced series article on how much your choice of problem area matters at 80000hours.org/articles/your-choice-of-problem-is-crucial/.

112. Elton John regularly tops lists of the most generous celebrities in the UK (Oppenheim, 2016). His money helped found the Elton John AIDS Foundation.

   But it's unclear how many lives he's saved.

   He gave £26.8 million to charity in 2016 (Ibid.), and likely gave similar amounts in other years, so we'd guess he's given hundreds of millions overall.

   How cost effective was this spending? Elton John's focus has primarily been HIV/AIDS interventions in the developing world. We'd guess that these interventions aren't as cost effective as the most cost-effective interventions in global health. GiveWell — an independent charity evaluator — found that (Givewell, 2010):

   > "HIV/AIDS is a leading cause of adult deaths in the developing world. Antiretroviral therapy can prolong and improve patients' lives, and potentially reduce the risk that they will infect others, for a cost of several hundred dollars per year. We are revisiting the question of how this compares to the cost-effectiveness of other global health interventions. There are other interventions (including preventative interventions) that may be more cost-effective. We have not found a charity we can confidently recommend that focuses on HIV/AIDS."

   GiveWell reviewed three specific interventions: condom promotion and distribution, drug treatment with Antiretroviral Therapy (ART), and prevention of mother-to-child transmission.

   GiveWell estimated that ART is approximately 1.4 times as cost effective as direct cash transfers (see https://80k.info/ART-CEA/ for the full cost-effectiveness analysis). GiveWell's funding bar (as of March 2023) is that it funds interventions that are around 10 times more cost effective than cash (Hassenfeld, 2022), which would make ART about seven times less cost effective than top interventions in global health. While GiveWell expects that preventative interventions may be more cost effective, they note that evidence for condom promotion and distribution reducing HIV/AIDS transmission, one of the most common interventions in the area, is weak (GiveWell, 2019).

Overall, we'd guess that spending on HIV/AIDS interventions in the developing world is around 10 times less cost effective than GiveWell's top charities.

GiveWell's estimate of the cost to save a life through its top charities has varied over time between $1,000 and $10,000, and is typically around $3,000–5,000.

As a result, we'd guess Elton John's AIDS spending saved a life for around $50,000.

113. In 2012, they donated to 80,000 Hours. They have also donated to related projects such as the Centre for Effective Altruism (where Julia now works) that, like 80,000 Hours, is a project of Effective Ventures Foundation.

114. Watkins Uiberall, 2012 found that:

> *"The median salary for executive directors/CEOs is between $50,000 and $75,000. CEO salaries correlate with organizational budget size. For small organizations, the median salary is between $30,000 and $50,000. Among medium-sized organizations, 36% of CEOs have salaries between $50,000 and $75,000, while 50.5% earn more than $75,000 and 13.5% earn less than $50,000. Among large organizations, 14.2% pay salaries of $100,000 or less; 38.1% pay between $101,000 and $150,000; and 47.7% pay more than $150,000."*

Note that this is significantly lower than the median figures reported by the prominent Charity Navigator Annual Survey (Charity Navigator, 2016). This is because Charity Navigator focuses on "mid to large" US charities, which pay substantially higher salaries.

115. National Center for Charitable Statistics, 2015:

> *"...those with income between $100,000 and $200,000 contribute, on average, 2.6 percent of their income, which is lower compared to those with income either below $100,000 (3.6 percent) or above $200,000 (3.1 percent)"*

Rates of charitable giving in the US are among the highest in the world.

116. Kristof, 2015.

117. Coughlan, 2011, Matthews, 2013, Daily Mail, 2013.

118. Southern District of New York, 2022. We've written more about Sam and the possible harm of high-earning careers at 80000hours.org/about/credibility/evaluations/mistakes/#ftx-2022.

119. Irlam, 2012.

120. Copeland, 2012 quotes a number of historians, concluding:

> *"If Turing and his group had not weakened the U-boats' hold on the North Atlantic, the 1944 Allied invasion of Europe — the D-Day landings — could have been delayed, perhaps by about a year or even longer, since the North Atlantic was the route that ammunition, fuel, food and troops had to travel in order to reach Britain from America."*

121. Price, 2011.

122. For more ideas, and to get a sense of what you might be able to work on in different fields, see this list of potentially high-impact research questions, organised by discipline: 80000hours.org/articles/research-questions-by-discipline/

123. Most scientific articles get little to no attention (Van Dalen et al., 2005). One study found that 47% of articles catalogued by the Institute for Scientific Information have never been cited, and more than 80% have been cited less than 10 times (Redner, 1998). Articles in the median social science journal, on average, get only 0.5 citations within two years of publication (Klamer et al., 2002). The mean number of citations per article in mathematics, physics, and environmental science journals is probably less than 1 (Mansilla et al., 2007).

By contrast, the top 0.1% of papers in the Institute for Scientific Information have been cited over 1000 times (Redner, 1998). Citations per paper are basically distributed by a power law, which means that only a few papers dominate. This trend seems to hold across fields, even when the average number of citations per article varies widely (Radicchi et al., 2008), and a similar distribution holds across individual researchers, not just articles (Petersen et al., 2010, Peterson et al., 2010).

124. Summarised in appendix 9.

125. Technically, it was the first vaccine cleared for use by a regulator recognised by the World Health Organization as a stringent regulatory authority (Bosel, 2020).

126. Read more about research management in appendix 8.

127. Based on interviews with UK civil servants. For more, see our review of UK civil service careers at 80000hours.org/career-reviews/policy-oriented-civil-service-uk/.

128. See https://80k.link/VEK/.

129. Read more about founding impactful organisations in appendix 8.

130. Sam Bankman-Fried donated to 80,000 Hours early in his career, and FTX donated funds to Effective Ventures group. 80,000 Hours is a project of the Effective Ventures group — the umbrella term for Effective Ventures Foundation and Effective Ventures Foundation USA, Inc., which are two separate legal entities that work together.

131. Saeedy, 2023.

132. We've written more about this on our mistakes page at 80000hours.org/about/credibility/evaluations/mistakes/#ftx-2022.

133. Appendix 5 goes into much more detail on why.

134. Simonton, 1988.

135. One large study in the US (Guvenen et al., 2015) found:

> "The average life-cycle profile is obtained from panel data or repeated cross sections by regressing log individual earnings on a full set of age and (year-of-birth) cohort dummies. The estimated age dummies are plotted as circles in Figure 3 and represent the average life-cycle profile of log earnings. It has the usual hump-shaped pattern that peaks around age 50.
>
> One of the most important aspects of a life-cycle profile is the implied growth in average earnings over the life cycle (e.g., from ages 25 to 55). It is well understood that the magnitude of this rise matters greatly for many economic questions, because it is a strong determinant of borrowing and saving motives. In our data, this rise is about 80 log points, which is about 127%."

We expect the figures to be similar in other countries. The peak could be 10 years lower, but that doesn't change the basic conclusion.

136. Simonton, 1988.

> "At one extreme, some fields are characterized by relatively early peaks, usually around the early 30s or even late 20s in chronological units, with somewhat steep descents thereafter, so that the output rate becomes less than one quarter the maximum. This agewise pattern apparently holds for such endeavors as lyric poetry, pure mathematics, and theoretical physics, for example (Adams, 1946; Dennis, 1966; Lehman, 1953a; Moulin, 1955; Roe, 1972b; Simonton, 1975a; Van Heeringen & Dijkwel, 1987). At the contrary extreme, the typical trends in other endeavors may display a leisurely rise to a comparatively late peak, in the late 40s or even 50s chronologically, with a minimal if not largely absent drop-off afterward. This more elongated curve holds for such domains as novel writing, history, philosophy, medicine, and general scholarship, for instance (Adams, 1946; Richard A. Davis, 1987; Dennis, 1966; Lehman, 1953a; Simonton, 1975a). Of course, many disciplines exhibit age curves somewhat between these two outer limits, with a maximum output rate around chronological age 40 and a notable

yet moderate decline thereafter (see, e.g., Fulton & Trow, 1974; Hermann, 1988; McDowell, 1982; Zhao & Jiang, 1986)"

137. Jones, 2014:
"For example, Nobel Prize winning research is performed at an average age that is 6 years older at the end of the 20th century than it was at the beginning."

138. The figure for chemistry is taken from the average age people do Nobel Prize–winning work in the field, which is 39 (Jones, 2014).

139. Average age of CEOs and presidents from Snow, 2016.

140. Ericsson shows that world-class performance usually requires 10 to 30 years of focused practice. It's debated whether this level of practice is enough to guarantee expertise, but everyone agrees that it's usually always *necessary* for expertise. Ericsson's research is summarised in Ericsson, 2018, or see the excellent, popular summary by the same author, *Peak* (Ericsson, et al., 2016).

Kaufman, 2013 points out some of the limits of deliberate practice.

A meta-analysis also found that deliberate practice explains a small amount of performance in professions and education. It also explains more performance in predictable areas rather than unpredictable ones (Macnamara et al., 2014).

141. Details of this story have been changed at the request of those involved to protect their anonymity.

142. We also have an article on which skills make you most employable, at 80000hours.org/articles/skills-most-employable/.

143. Webb, 2020.

144. OpenAI, 2023.

145. Midjourney, 2023.

146. Shinn, et al., 2023.

147. Frey et al., 2013. See also 80000hours.org/2015/02/which-careers-will-be-automated/.

148. MacAskill, 2015.

149. See more in the section on startup jobs in appendix 8.

150. See appendix 5 for more.

151. We asked 22 experts, and wrote up their answers anonymously. Take a look at 80000hours.org/articles/ai-capabilities/.

152. See the section in appendix 8 about being a historian.

153. Read more about becoming a congressional staffer in appendix 8.

154. Read more about working in think tanks in appendix 8.

155. Read more about software engineering in appendix 8.

156. Read more about working information security in appendix 8.

157. Read more about working in data science in appendix 8.

158. Read more about working in marketing in appendix 8.

159. Read more about developing expertise in China and other emerging powers in appendix 8.

160. Todd, 2020.

161. Find our list of organisations especially relevant to our pressing problems at jobs.80000hours.org/organisations/.

162. Simonton, 1988, p.251.

163. See our review of the evidence at 80000hours.org/2021/05/how-much-do-people-differ-in-productivity/.

164. You can hear more on the case for generally kicking ass in our podcast with Holden Karnofsky at 80000hours.org/podcast/episodes/holden-karnofsky-building-aptitudes-kicking-ass//

165. If you're working as part of a community, then your comparative advantage compared to other people in the community is also important. Read more in our advanced series at 80000hours.org/articles/comparative-advantage/.

166. Schmidt et al., 2016.

167. We're pretty confident this is true, because uncertainty compounds over time. For example, Ericsson has argued that the best predictor of expert performance over longer time frames is how much 'deliberate practice' someone has done.

        But a 2014 meta-analysis found that this only explained about 20% of the variance, and that was in fields like sport, chess, and music, where deliberate practice is comparatively more important. In the other professions, it was only 1% (Macnamara et al., 2014).

        This suggests that even the best predictor we have doesn't tell us that much.

168. Heath et al., 2013:

        "Career choices, for instance, are often abandoned or regretted. An American Bar Association survey found that 44% of lawyers would recommend that a young person not pursue a career in law. A study of 20,000 executive searches found that 40% of senior-level hires "are pushed out, fail or quit within 18 months." More than half of teachers quit their jobs within four years."

169. Read more about the research at 80000hours.org/articles/dont-go-with-your-gut-instinct/.

170. See appendix 3.

171. See appendix 3.

172. See our individual career reviews — summaries in appendix 8, and more at 80000hours.org/career-reviews/ — for more advice on how to assess your fit with a specific job.

173. If the outcome of a choice of career path is dominated by 'tail' scenarios (unusually good or bad outcomes), which we think it often is, then you can approximate the expected impact of a path by looking at the probability of the tail scenarios happening and how good/bad they are.

174. If we suppose that the 50% with the best fit continue to academia, then you'd be in the top half. In reality, your prospects would be a little worse than this, since some of your past performance might be due to luck or other factors that don't project forward. Likewise, past failures might also have been due to luck or other factors that don't project forward, so your prospects are a bit better than they'd naively suggest. In other words, past performance doesn't perfectly predict future performance.

175. More technically, you can try to make a base rate forecast. Read more at 80000hours.org/2012/12/how-to-judge-your-chances-of-success/.

176. Which you can find at 80000hours.org/articles/personal-strengths/.

177. Which you can find at 80k.info/good-judgement/.

178. Epstein, 2019.

179. Liu et al., 2018.

180. United States Bureau of Labor Statistics, 2022.

        "Median employee tenure was generally higher among older workers than younger ones. For example, the median tenure of workers ages 55 to 64 (9.8 years) was more than three times that of workers ages 25 to 34 years (2.8 years). Also, a larger proportion of older workers than younger workers had 10 years or more of tenure. For example, among workers ages 60 to 64, 53 percent had been employed for at least 10 years with their current employer in January 2022, compared with 9 percent of those ages 30 to 34."

181. And we have an advanced series article all about it at 80000hours.org/articles/career-exploration/.

182. See the sections on China careers in appendix 8.

183. New, 2015.

184. See a longer article on when to be more ambitious at 80000hours.org/articles/be-more-ambitious/.

185. See appendix 3.

186. Levitt, 2016.

187. You can find our job board at jobs.80000hours.org.

188. Hoffman, 2022.

189. Kahneman, 2011.

190. See appendix 3 for more on these biases.

191. We made an annual career review tool to make this easy, which you can find at 80000hours.org/career-planning/annual-career-review/.
192. Simonson et al., 1992, Fennema, et al., 2008.
193. See the whole video at youtu.be/wexzvClUcUk.
194. Find the interview at 80000hours.org/2014/10/tips-on-careers-in-journalism-from-npr-correspondent-david-folkenflik/.
195. The mean duration of unemployment is 20–30 weeks, or about six months (FRED, 2023).
196. For instance, the UK's national career advice service lists internet job listings and job boards as their first two tips (National Careers Service, 2022).
197. At jobs.80000hours.org.
198. Bolles, 2014. The 2015 edition of *What Color is Your Parachute?* mentions several studies which found success rates per resume of under 1 in 1,000. His best guess at the overall success rate of sending out your resume is under 10%, which would be consistent with a per-resume figure of 1 in 1,000 if the average job seeker sent out 100 resumes, which sounds reasonable. Unfortunately these are the best figures we're aware of for job hunting success rates.
199. Sam Altman is the former President of Y Combinator, the world's most successful startup accelerator. In his advice to startups on hiring, he says (Altman, 2013):
    "Focus on the right ways to source candidates. Basically, this boils down to "use your personal networks more". By at least a 10x margin, the best candidate sources I've ever seen are friends and friends of friends. Even if you don't think you can get these people, go after the best ones relentlessly. If it works out 5% of the time, it's still well worth it. When you hire someone, as soon as you're sure she's a star you should sit her down and wring out of her the names of everyone that you should try to hire. You may have to work pretty hard at this."
    We think this advice is reflective of best practice, at least in the technology industry. Swartz, 2013, in *The New York Times,* also describes how referrals are becoming more widely adopted as a key method of hiring across the business world.
200. Granovetter, 2013, Wolff et al., 2008.
201. Available at jobs.80000hours.org.
202. See wikijob.co.uk/interview-advice/interview-questions/competency-based-questions for more on competency interviews.
203. Sethi, 2017.
204. Rackham, 1995. Rackham's research is based on surveys of 35,000 salespeople, and draws from the existing literature, making it one of the most thorough reviews we know. Moreover, most advice is about low-value sales, which turn out to be quite different.
    Rackham not only found the techniques that the best salespeople use, he then trained people in these techniques and showed they made them more effective compared to a control group who received normal sales training.
205. For a popular summary of the research on how to do memorable communication, see Heath, 2013. It puts a major emphasis on using stories, analogies, and concrete facts to make ideas more memorable.
206. Winter, 2013.
207. Golwitzer et al., 2006, Toli et al., 2015.
208. Fish Welfare Initiative managed to fully fund their 2023 budget, which they estimated at $662,385 (Fish Welfare Initiative, 2023).
    They estimate that they have "potentially helped" approximately 1.13 million fish.
    They say:
    In "fish potentially helped," we include all the fish living in a fish farm where 1) we have implemented a welfare improvement that we believe otherwise would not have been implemented, and 2) we feel ≥80% confident that the welfare improvement made a positive impact on the fish.

They also note the following limitations:

"We don't (currently) assess magnitude. The numbers of fish potentially helped do not consider the degree to which they were helped. While our welfare improvements theoretically should improve fish welfare, given the on-the-ground implementation difficulties and our current lack of a rigorous impact analysis, we are still significantly uncertain about the magnitude of our per-fish impact. Thus, it is unfortunately possible that our improvements are currently only having a trivial impact. To address this uncertainty, we plan to conduct an impact assessment in the coming year.

We generalize. It is possible that some fish counted may not have suffered in the absence of our intervention. For example, water quality is dynamic depending on where fish are in the pond. Thus, we do not know with certainty that all individuals would have suffered under water quality levels we deem inadequate.

We only count the fish we know of. It is common for there to be fish within a pond that have not been intentionally stocked by the farmer, such as invasive fish who enter the system through in-flow or fish that were not successfully removed in previous harvests. We expect that in almost all cases our improvements will also positively improve these fishes' lives. However, we do not currently have a way to account for our impact on these individuals, so they are excluded.

209. Read more about this in appendix 2.

210. Read more in our article on coordinating with a community at 80000hours.org/articles/coordination.

211. For example, see Todd, 2023.

212. See an introduction at lesswrong.com/tag/introduction-to-lesswrong-subculture.

213. See appendix 9 for summaries of these problem profiles.

214. Read more at 80000hours.org/articles/expected-value.

215. See Jollimore, 2021 for more.

216. Read more at 80000hours.org/articles/future-generations.

217. This research is covered in Oettingen, 2015. Oettingen actually finds that also thinking about how you're most likely to *fail* makes you more likely to achieve your goals, so in a sense *negative* thinking is more effective in this context. However, there are other senses in which positive thinking is helpful. CBT, as we cover in this appendix, is based on the idea that many mental health problems are caused by unhelpful beliefs, which can be changed by disputing them, and other techniques. So "positive thinking" can work, but it depends on exactly what you mean and what the context is.

218. Clear, 2022.

219. Fogg, 2020.

220. "But, there's this other group of givers that I call "otherish." They are concerned about benefiting others, but they also keep their own interests in the rearview mirror. They will look for ways to help others that are either low cost to themselves or even high benefit to themselves, i.e., "win-win," as opposed to win-lose. Here's the irony. The selfless givers might be more altruistic, in principle, because they are constantly elevating other people's interests ahead of their own. But my data, and research by lots of others, show that they're actually less generous because they run out of energy, they run out of time and they lose their resources, because they basically don't take enough care of themselves. The "otherish" givers are able to sustain their giving by looking for ways that giving can hurt them less or benefit them more."

From an interview with Adam Grant, by Wharton, where he summarises his research (Knowledge at Wharton, 2010).

You can find more detail in his book *Give and Take* (Grant, 2014).

221. We think it's common sense that health, diet, exercise, and relationships all matter a great deal to day-to-day happiness. The literature on positive psychology — discussed in chapter 1 — also

points in favour of this idea (especially the importance of close relationships), or at least doesn't contradict it. There is also research specifically about the impact of sleep on mood.

Note that we haven't seen good direct evidence that a healthy diet improves mood, but we find it hard to believe that it doesn't improve health and energy, which will improve mood over the long term.

222. Bye, 2019.
223. Different surveys give different results, but 30% seems like a reasonable ballpark. For instance, the US National Institute of Mental Health (NIMH) says that 30.6% of 18- to 25-year-olds and 25.3% of 26- to 49-year-olds have "any mental illness." The NIMH also finds that 17% of people aged 18–25 experienced a major depressive incident in the last 12 months, compared to only 5.4% for those above 50. (National Institute of Mental Health)
224. You can find the podcast at 80000hours.org/podcast/episodes/depression-anxiety-imposter-syndrome/.
225. Burns, 2001.
226. Hendel, 2018.
227. Solanto, 2011.
228. Barkley, et al., 2010.
229. Which you can find at 80000hours.org/podcast/episodes/tim-lebon-self-defeating-altruistic-perfectionism/.
230. Private practitioners include Ewelina (ewelinatur.com), Daystar Eld (daystareld.com), and Tim LeBon (londontherapy.timlebon.com).
231. Donovan, 2014.
232. Belluz et al., 2015.
233. A major study published in *The Lancet* found the top-five causes of ill health (measured by percentage of disability-adjusted life years) were, among 25- to 49-year-olds:

   Road injuries (5.1%)
   HIV/AIDS (4.8%)
   Ischaemic heart disease (4.7%)
   Low back pain (3.9%)
   Headache disorders (3.7%)
   See figure 2 in Vos et al., 2020.
   According to HIV.gov, 2022:
   "The vast majority of people with HIV are in low- and middle-income countries. In 2021, there were 20.6 million people with HIV (53%) in eastern and southern Africa, 5 million (13%) in western and central Africa, 6 million (15%) in Asia and the Pacific, and 2.3 million (5%) in Western and Central Europe and North America."
   And according to NHS 2020:
   "Coronary heart disease (CHD) is usually caused by a build-up of fatty deposits (atheroma) on the walls of the arteries around the heart (coronary arteries). The build-up of atheroma makes the arteries narrower, restricting the flow of blood to the heart muscle. This process is called atherosclerosis. Your risk of developing atherosclerosis is significantly increased if you: smoke, have high blood pressure (hypertension), have high cholesterol, have high levels of lipoprotein (a), do not exercise regularly, have diabetes."
   While, for back pain, according to NHS, 2022:
   "Back pain can have many causes. It's not always obvious what causes it, and it often gets better on its own."
   This suggests that if you're not hit by a vehicle, don't live in a developing country, and don't have any of the major factors associated with ischaemic heart disease, the biggest risk to your health during your working life is low back pain.

234.   Mayo Clinic, 2023, Mayo Clinic, 2021.

235.   See waitbutwhy.com/2013/11/life-is-picture-but-you-live-in-pixel.html.

236.   Golwitzer et al., 2006. "Holding a strong goal intention ("I intend to reach Z!") does not guarantee goal achievement, because people may fail to deal effectively with self-regulatory problems during goal striving. This review analyzes whether realisation of goal intentions is facilitated by forming an implementation intention that spells out the when, where, and how of goal striving in advance ("If situation Y is encountered, then I will initiate goal-directed behavior X!"). Findings from 94 independent tests showed that implementation intentions had a positive effect of medium-to-large magnitude (d = .65) on goal attainment."

A later meta-analysis (Toli et al., 2015) supports these findings, and found an even larger effect of implementation interventions on goal achievement *for people with mental health problems*: "Excluding one outlying (very large) effect, forming implementation intentions had a large-sized effect on goal attainment (d+ = 0.99, k = 28, N = 1,636). Implementation intentions proved effective across different mental health problems and goals, and in studies with different methodological approaches."

237.   Oettingen, 2015,

238.   Read more at 80000hours.org/2013/04/how-to-finally-do-what-you-ve-been-putting-off/.

239.   Winter, 2013, Steel, 2012.

240.   Asana was founded by Dustin Moskovitz, who is the primary funder behind Open Philanthropy, which is 80,000 Hours' largest donor.

241.   Tracy, 2013. See a summary at njlifehacks.com/eat-that-frog-brian-tracy-summary.

242.   Newport, 2016.

243.   Read more at mymorningroutine.com (Spall et al., 2018).

244.   Newport, 2015.

245.   Bye, 2022.

246.   Carnegie, 2006.

247.   You can find MacLeod's guide at succeedsocially.com.

248.   Cabane, 2013.

249.   There have been several studies that show more workers find out about new jobs through their personal network than any other method (Granovetter, 2003). For example, a study of workers in the Quebec provincial government found that 42.7% of the 2553 people in the study had found the job through personal contacts despite the government's efforts to formalise the application process. An unpublished study of 1780 people in the Philadelphia area found that 56% of those who weren't self employed got their current job with significant help from another person (Ibid.).

A longitudinal study that questioned people on their networking behaviours and then recorded their salary over three years found that networking was related to salary growth. (Wolff, 2009) There is also some evidence that you're more likely to find a job through your acquaintances than through close friends(Granovetter, 2003). Also, often as you become more senior in an organisation, networking becomes more important as your productivity relies more on managing people and bringing in business through contacts.

Though more evidence is needed, this shows that networking is a key skill for career success.

250.   Christakis et al., 2011.

251.   Fowler et al., 2008. The researchers don't think this effect is caused by the fact that happy people tend to hang out with other happy people — they used a couple of smart techniques to separate causation from correlation. Negative behaviours like smoking spread in a similar way. Our guess is that who you spend time with is a major factor in your personal growth and character.

252.   In his book *Give and Take*, psychologist Adam Grant argues that *givers*, who help others without condition, are more likely to be successful (Grant, 2014).

253.   Which you can find at chinai.substack.com.

254. Read more at 80000hours.org/2013/05/how-important-is-networking-for-career-success/.

255. Hoffman et al., 2022.

256. Grant 2014.

257. Ferrazzi et al., 2014.

258. Florida et al., 2008.

259. Ibid. "The world's 10 largest mega-regions in terms of LRP house only about 416 million people, or 6.5 percent of the world's population, but account for 42.8 percent of economic activity ($13.4 trillion), 56.6 percent of patented innovations, and 55.6 percent of the most-cited scientists."

260. Glaeser, 2012.

261. Ibid. "The correlation coefficients between overall happiness and various factors are as follows: financial satisfaction (.369), job satisfaction (.367), and place satisfaction (.303). Compare with income (.153), home-ownership (.126), and age (.06)."

   We're not aware of much other research into the importance of location in life satisfaction, so we only have weak confidence in these correlation coefficients.

262. Florida, 2009.

263. Donaldson, 2019 performed a meta-analysis which looked at 22 different studies including thousands of participants, and found support for the idea that positive psychology techniques improve wellbeing and performance at work.

   They looked at the following kinds of interventions:

   Psychological capital (e.g. practising optimism and bouncing back from adverse situations)

   Job crafting (e.g. helping employees craft projects and objectives)

   Employee strengths (e.g. helping employees identify their strengths)

   Employee gratitude (e.g. asking employees to keep a log about what they are grateful for in their job)

   Employee wellbeing (e.g. spending time with people they care about, practising living in the moment)

   They found small-to-moderate effects of all these interventions (g=0.1 to 0.4).

   Again, the study found evidence of publication bias, and it's not clear to us that the effect sizes were appropriately reduced to account for this. Nevertheless, it still seems like there's pretty good evidence that these interventions work.

264. Seligman, 2011.

265. See, for example, Mongrain, 2012.

266. The largest, most recent meta-study of positive psychology interventions we could find is Carr et al., 2020. The interventions included:

   Practising gratitude

   Practising forgiveness

   Doing exercises that create an optimistic outlook (e.g. best possible self)

   Savouring by reminiscence, life review, recalling recent events, or appreciating the present moment

   Identifying and using signature strengths

   Being kind to others

   Writing about positive, meaningful or successful experiences

   Practising meaning making

   Humour (e.g. recalling three funny things)

   Setting highly valued goals (e.g. writing an obituary, eulogy, or legacy letter)

   Savouring

   Solution-focused coaching

   Relationship strengthening

Appreciating beauty/nature
Active constructive responding
Rehearsing positive statements
Volunteering
Practising humility
Finding flow
Temporarily having restricted access valued experiences (e.g. giving up chocolate)

They classified these into 10 types: savouring, optimism and hope, meaning-making, gratitude, using signature strengths, humour, kindness, positive writing, forgiveness, and goal setting. They tested effects on (among other things) increasing wellbeing, reducing depression, reducing anxiety, and reducing stress.

They found that the effects of forgiveness and goal-setting interventions on wellbeing were not statistically significant; the effect of kindness interventions on depression was not statistically significant; the effects of kindness and gratitude interventions on anxiety reduction were not significant; and the effects of forgiveness, kindness, and using signature strengths interventions on stress were not significant.

They found statistically significant effects of all other interventions, although correlations varied from around 0.2 to 0.7 depending on the intervention and the effect.

The study found evidence of publication bias, and it's not clear to us that the effect sizes were appropriately reduced to account for this. Nevertheless, it still seems like there's pretty good evidence that these interventions work.

267. To do a "gratitude visit", deliver a letter of gratitude to a person who had been particularly kind to you, but who you never properly thanked. See Tomasulo, 2011 for a review of the evidence.

268. We've written up an evidence-based process for identifying your personal strengths at 80000hours. org/articles/personal-strengths.

269. Walsh, 2012.

270. Goyal, et al., 2014 is a highly cited review article on the benefits of meditation:

"After reviewing 18,753 citations, we included 47 trials with 3515 participants. Mindfulness meditation programs had moderate evidence of improved anxiety (effect size, 0.38 [95% CI, 0.12-0.64] at 8 weeks and 0.22 [0.02-0.43] at 3-6 months), depression (0.30 [0.00-0.59] at 8 weeks and 0.23 [0.05-0.42] at 3-6 months), and pain (0.33 [0.03-0.62]) and low evidence of improved stress/distress and mental health–related quality of life. We found low evidence of no effect or insufficient evidence of any effect of meditation programs on positive mood, attention, substance use, eating habits, sleep, and weight. We found no evidence that meditation programs were better than any active treatment (ie, drugs, exercise, and other behavioral therapies)."

Note that most of the studies included were about mental health rather than wellbeing, which is a significant reason for the null result.

Lomas, 2019 conducted meta-analysis on mindfulness in the workplace and found:

"Mindfulness had moderate effects on deficit-based outcomes such as stress (SMD = –0.57), anxiety (SMD = –0.57), distress (SMD = –0.56), depression (SMD = –0.48), and burnout (SMD = –0.36), and moderate to small effects on asset-based outcomes like health (SMD = 0.63), job performance (SMD = 0.43), compassion and empathy (SMD = 0.42), mindfulness (SMD = 0.39), and positive wellbeing (SMD = 0.36), while no effects were observed for emotional regulation. However, the quality of the studies was inconsistent, suggesting more high-quality randomised controlled trials are needed."

271. Williams, et al., 2012.

272. Knowledge at Wharton, 2010, Grant, 2007.

273. Lyubomirsky, 2008.

274. Sethi, 2009.
275. You can find the course at coursera.org/learn/learning-how-to-learn.
276. Oakley, 2014.
277. Ericsson, et al., 2016.
278. Fadde et al., 2010.
279. Newport, 2012.
280. Newport, 2016.
281. Hambrick et al., 2016.
282. We interviewed Tetlock about his research. You can find the interview at 80000hours.org/podcast/episodes/prof-tetlock-predicting-the-future.
283. Galef, 2021. You can find our interview with Galef at 80000hours.org/podcast/episodes/is-it-time-for-a-new-scientific-revolution-julia-galef-on-how-to-make-humans-smarter.
284. Heath et al., 2013.
285. Hubbard, 2014.
286. Read our full analysis at 80000hours.org/articles/skills-most-employable/.
287. Deming, 2017. Torkington, 2016 summarises the results:

    "David Deming, associate professor of education and economics at Harvard University, argues that soft skills like sharing and negotiating will be crucial. He says the modern workplace, where people move between different roles and projects, closely resembles pre-school classrooms, where we learn social skills such as empathy and cooperation.

    Deming has mapped the changing needs of employers and identified key skills that will be required to thrive in the job market of the near future. Along with those soft skills, mathematical ability will be enormously beneficial."

    See more detail in our full analysis of which skills are most useful at 80000hours.org/articles/skills-most-employable/.
288. Ericsson, 2006, Macnamara, 2014.
289. Ericsson, et al., 2016.
290. Duckworth, 2016.
291. Grant, 2016.
292. Blackburn, 2003.
293. Parfit, 1986.
294. Harris, 2015.
295. Brooks, 2016. See Bill Gates' summary of the book at www.gatesnotes.com/The-Road-to-Character.
296. Schubert, et al., 2021.
297. Hamming, 1986.
298. For instance, see the following reviews of the literature: Kahneman et al., 1982, Kahneman, 2013 and Ariely, 2009.

    A post on the Replicability-Index blog (Schimmack et al., 2017) contains a detailed critique of Chapter 4 of Kahneman, 2013. In response, Kahneman wrote (McCook, 2017):

    "What the blog gets absolutely right is that I placed too much faith in underpowered studies. As pointed out in the blog, and earlier by Andrew Gelman, there is a special irony in my mistake because the first paper that Amos Tversky and I published was about the belief in the "law of small numbers," which allows researchers to trust the results of underpowered studies with unreasonably small samples. We also cited Overall (1969) for showing "that the prevalence of studies deficient in statistical power is not only wasteful but actually pernicious: it results in a large proportion of invalid rejections of the null hypothesis among published results." Our article was written in 1969 and published in 1971, but I failed to internalize its message."

A later analysis on the same blog (Schimmack, 2020) wrote:

"Daniel Kahneman is a distinguished psychologist who has made valuable contributions to the study of human decision making. His work with Amos Tversky was recognized with a Nobel Memorial Prize in Economics (APA). It is surely interesting to read what he has to say about psychological topics that range from cognition to well-being. However, his thoughts are based on a scientific literature with shaky foundations. Like everybody else in 2011, Kahneman trusted individual studies to be robust and replicable because they presented a statistically significant result. In hindsight it is clear that this is not the case. Narrative literature reviews of individual studies reflect scientists' intuitions (Fast Thinking, System 1) as much or more than empirical findings. Readers of "Thinking: Fast and Slow" should read the book as a subjective account by an eminent psychologists, rather than an objective summary of scientific evidence. Moreover, ten years have passed and if Kahneman wrote a second edition, it would be very different from the first one. Chapters 3 and 4 would probably just be scrubbed from the book. But that is science. It does make progress, even if progress is often painfully slow in the softer sciences."

299. Locke, 2009, pp. 461–480.
300. Arkes et al., 1985.
301. Plus there's evidence that overconfidence, and optimism bias in general, can have its benefits: being overconfident might actually increase our chances of success by causing us to take risks and work harder. How much optimism is optimal? We're unsure, but it's likely to be better to be overconfident rather than underconfident.
302. Read more at 80000hours.org/2012/12/how-to-judge-your-chances-of-success.
303. We go into more detail at 80000hours.org/articles/dont-go-with-your-gut-instinct.
304. See appendix 3.
305. We particularly draw upon Ariely, 2009, Arkes et al., 1985, Heath et al., 2013, Hubbard, 2014, Keeney, 1996, Kahneman, 2013, Locke, 2009, pp. 461–480, Kahneman et al., 1982.
306. See appendix 2.
307. Read more about accidental harm at 80000hours.org/articles/accidental-harm.
308. See appendix 3.
309. See 80000hours.org/2012/12/how-to-judge-your-chances-of-success/.
310. Available at 80000hours.org/career-planning/annual-career-review/.
311. Golwitzer et al., 2006.
312. As of May 2023, from United States Bureau of Labor Statistics, 2023.
313. For more detail, see the distinction between a decision procedure and criterion of rightness. Askell, 2017 provides a short introduction. Or see Ord, 2005 for more detail.
314. Another type of argument concerns uncertainty in your estimates of the positive and negative impact of different options. We're a bit more unsure about these, so they're in a footnote.

    If 'fat-tailed' negatives are more likely than fat-tailed positives (i.e. there are more ways for things to go wrong than to go well), then your estimate of the negative impact is likely to be underestimated relative to positive impact. This could mean that a good rule of thumb for impact is to focus on 'robustly good' paths, and avoid significant negative impacts.

    Relatedly, if the argument is that you can cause a small guaranteed harm in order to have a larger positive impact, this relies on your estimate of the large positive impact being accurate. But your estimate of positive impact is probably too optimistic, which again makes "ends justifies the means" situations less attractive than they first seem.
315. Bourget et al., 2023.
316. MacAskill, 2014. He defended this further in his book *Moral Uncertainty* (MacAskill et al., 2020). Read more about moral uncertainty at 8000hours.org/articles/moral-uncertainty.
317. Read more in an academic paper by an advisor to 80,000 Hours (Ord, 2015), and at 80000hours.org/coordination/.

318. Note, though, that these hypothetical figures assume certainty about the size of the harms and benefits. As covered, in the real world, we likely face huge uncertainty about the benefits, which would suggest taking significantly more caution.

319. Crispin, 2017.

320. 80000hours.org/2013/07/show-me-the-harm/.

321. See 80000hours.org/2017/06/which-jobs-do-economists-say-create-the-largest-spillover-benefits-for-society/ for details.

322. See 80000hours.org/2015/08/what-are-the-10-most-harmful-jobs/ for details.

323. Applebaum, 2015.

324. Noonan, 2015.

325. Shen, 2016.

326. See 80000hours.org/2015/08/what-are-the-10-most-harmful-jobs/ for more.

327. Read how our advice has changed as a result of these events at 80000hours.org/2023/05/how-80000-hours-has-changed-some-of-our-advice-after-the-collapse-of-ftx/.

328. Read more in our article about which skills are most employable at 80000hours.org/articles/skills-most-employable/.

329. See our interview with Brian Caplan for more, at 80000hours.org/podcast/episodes/bryan-caplan-case-for-and-against-education/.

330. See 80000hours.org/2015/02/chronical-on-elite-jobs/.

331. See more discussion of why to take a light course load see Baker, 2021.

332. Newport, 2005.

333. Guillebeau, 2012.

334. We reviewed the evidence at 80000hours.org/2014/01/the-value-of-a-degree/.

335. Read more in Caplan, 2014.

336. Caplan, 2018.

337. See more discussion of the book in our interview with Caplan at 80k.info/bryan-caplan.

338. Dale et al., 2002.

339. Eide et al., 2016.

340. Caplan, 2018.

341. Newport, 2005.

342. Mochary et al., 2021.

343. Horstman et al., 2023.

344. Green et al., 2012.

345. Whitmore, 2009.

346. Covey et al., 2012.

347. Maurya, 2022.

348. Lock, 2009.

349. See Schneider, 2017.

350. Rackham, 1995.

351. Cialdini, 2007.

352. Pink, 2018.

353. Ury, 1993.

354. Ury, 1993.

355. To be published in The Norton Introduction to Ethics, and available at globalprioritiesinstitute.org/william-macaskill-effective-altruism/.

356. MacAskill, 2016.

357. See eaglobal.org for more.

358. Find events at forum.effectivealtruism.org/community/.

359. See our research on this at 80000hours.org/2021/05/how-much-do-people-differ-in-productivity/.
360. Such as The SANS Cyber Security course at sans.org/cyberaces/.
361. At jobs.80000hours.org.
362. See more discussion of these probabilities in the full profile at 80000hours.org/problem-profiles/artificial-intelligence.
363. It's difficult to say exactly how much is being spent to advance AI capabilities. This is partly because of a lack of available data, and partly because of questions like:

    What research in AI is actually advancing the sorts of dangerous capabilities that might be increasing potential existential risk?

    Do advances in AI hardware or advances in data collection count?

    How about broader improvements to research processes in general, or things that might increase investment in the future through producing economic growth?

    The most relevant figure we could find was the expenses of DeepMind from 2020, which were around £1 billion, according to its annual report (Companies House, 2021). We'd expect most of that to be contributing to "advancing AI capabilities" in some sense, since its main goal is building powerful, general AI systems. (Although it's important to note that DeepMind is also contributing to work in AI safety, which may be reducing existential risk.)

    If DeepMind is around about 10% of the spending on advancing AI capabilities, this gives us a figure of around £10 billion. (Given that there are many AI companies in the US, and a large effort to produce advanced AI in China, we think 10% could be a good overall guess.)

    As an upper bound, the total revenues of the AI sector in 2021 were around $340 billion (Shirer, 2021).

    So overall, we think the amount being spent to advance AI capabilities is between $1 billion and $340 billion per year. Even assuming a figure as low as $1 billion, this would still be around 100 times the amount spent on reducing risks from AI.
364. See footnote 3 at 80000hours.org/problem-profiles/artificial-intelligence/ for more details on this number.
365. Snodin, 2022. Snodin defines advanced nanotechnology as "any highly advanced technology involving nanoscale machinery that allows us to finely image and control processes at the nanoscale, with manufacturing capabilities roughly matching, or exceeding, those of consequential APM [atomically precise manufacturing]", i.e. technology that is similar in nature and similarly impactful to atomically precise manufacturing,
366. *Ibid.*
367. We've seen a variety of estimates regarding the chances of an existential biological catastrophe:

    Ord, 2020: 3% by 2120

    Sandberg et al., 2008: 2% by 2100

    Pamlin et al., 2015: 0.0002% by 2115

    Fodor, 2020: 0.0002% by 2120

    Millet et al., 2017: 0.00019% (from biowarfare or bioterrorism) per year (assuming this is constant, this is equivalent to 0.02% by 2120).

    We've looked at the reasoning behind these estimates and are uncertain about which ones we should most believe. Overall, we think the risk is around 0.1%, and very likely to be greater than 0.01%, but we haven't thought about this in detail
368. World Bank, 2023.
369. The population of these countries is around 2 billion. To prevent 100 million DALYs each year each person in these countries would have to be given an average of 1/20th of a DALY each year. Given an existing life expectancy of around 65, this would require extending life expectancy by 3.25 years, or the equivalent in improved quality of health. This seems possible and if anything small relative to health gains achieved by other countries that have eliminated easily prevented

diseases in the past.

370. This number would be higher if we included invertebrates (Rowe, 2020) — many of which may be sentient (Schukraft, 2019) — or counted the number of animals killed or slaughtered in a year, rather than alive at any one point (Šimčikas, 2020).

371. Walker, 2021.

372. See, for example, Ord, 2020 (0.1%), Sandberg et al., 2008 (1%), Pamlin et al., 2015 (0.0005%).

373. The resources dedicated to preventing the risk of a nuclear war globally, including both inside and outside all governments, is probably $10 billion per year or higher. However, we are downgrading that to $1–10 billion per year quality-adjusted, because much of this spending is not focused on lowering the risk of use of nuclear weapons in general, but rather protecting just one country, or giving one country an advantage over another. Much is also spent on anti-proliferation measures unrelated to the most harmful scenarios in which hundreds of warheads are used. It is also notable that spending by non-government actors represents only a tiny fraction of this, so they may have some better opportunities to act.

374. Unintended effects make it hard to say which policies will truly reduce the risks.

375. Including academic research, corporate strategic foresight, and national and international space governance agencies.

376. Caplan, 2008.

377. In chapter 5 of Ord, 2020, Ord considers dystopian scenarios as a form of existential risk. In particular, on enforced dystopian scenarios, Ord writes:

> "We can divide the unrecoverable dystopias we might face into three types, on the basis of whether they are desired by the people who live in them…
>
> The most familiar type is the enforced dystopia. The rise of expansionist totalitarianism in the mid-twentieth century caused intellectuals such as George Orwell to raise the possibility of a totalitarian state achieving global dominance and absolute control, locking the world into a miserable condition. The regimes of Hitler and Stalin serve as a proof of principle, each scaling up to become imperial superpowers while maintaining extreme control over their citizens. However, it is unclear whether Hitler or Stalin had the expansionist aims to control the entire world, or the technical and social means to create truly lasting regimes.
>
> This may change. Technological progress has offered many new tools that could be used to detect and undermine dissent and there is every reason to believe that this will continue over the next century. Advances in AI seem especially relevant, allowing automated, detailed monitoring of everything that happens in public places — both physical and online. Such advances may make it possible to have regimes that are far more stable than those of old.
>
> That said, technology is also providing new tools for rebellion against authority, such as the internet and encrypted messages. Perhaps the forces will remain in balance, or shift in favour of freedom, but there is a credible chance that they will shift towards greater control over the populace, making enforced dystopias a realistic possibility."

378. Ibid. Ord notes, in particular, that:

> "To count as existential catastrophes, these outcomes don't need to be impossible to break out of, nor to last millions of years. Instead, the defining feature is that entering that regime was a crucial negative turning point in the history of human potential, locking off almost all our potential for a worthy future. One way to look at this is that when they end (as they eventually must), we are much more lily that we were before to fall down to extinction or collapse than to rise up to fulfil our potential. For example, a dystopian society that lasted all the way until humanity was destroyed by external forces would be an existential catastrophe. However, if a dystopian outcome does not have this property, if it leaves open all our chances for success once it ends — it is a dark age in our story, but not a true existential catastrophe."

379. Dafoe, 2018 categorises robust totalitarianism as one of four sources of catastrophic risk from AI. Dafoe argues:

    "Robust totalitarianism could be enabled by advanced lie detection, social manipulation, autonomous weapons, and ubiquitous physical sensors and digital footprints. Power and control could radically shift away from publics, towards elites and especially leaders, making democratic regimes vulnerable to totalitarian backsliding, capture, and consolidation."

380. Caplan, 2008.
381. Hecht, 2021.
382. Bar-On et al., 2018 estimate biomass, not number of individuals; as far as we know, only Tomasik, 2019 has estimated numbers of individuals.
383. Tomasik, 2015.
384. Tomasik, 2019.

Bibliography

A+E Networks. "Watch beyond Scared Straight Full Episodes, Video & More." *A+E Networks*, www.aetv.com/shows/beyond-scared-straight. Accessed 23 May 2023.

AI Impacts, "2022 Expert Survey on Progress in AI." *AI Impacts*, 27 Sep. 2022, aiimpacts.org/2022-expert-survey-on-progress-in-ai/.

Aknin, Lara B., et al. "Prosocial Spending and Well-Being: Cross-Cultural Evidence for a Psychological Universal." *Journal of Personality and Social Psychology*, vol. 104, no. 4, 2013, pp. 635–652, doi.org/10.1037/a0031578.

Aksenov, Pavel. "Stanislav Petrov: The Man Who May Have Saved the World." *BBC News*, 26 Sep. 2013, www.bbc.com/news/world-europe-24280831.

Alaybek, Balca, et al. "All's Well That Ends (and Peaks) Well? A Meta-Analysis of the Peak-End Rule and Duration Neglect." *Organizational Behavior and Human Decision Processes*, vol. 170, 2022, p. 104149, doi.org/10.1016/j.obhdp.2022.104149.

Alexander, Scott. "Things That Sometimes Work If You Have Anxiety." *Slate Star Codex*, 13 July 2015, slatestarcodex.com/2015/07/13/things-that-sometimes-work-if-you-have-anxiety/.

Allen, David. *Getting Things Done: The Art of Stress-Free Productivity*. Piatkus, 2019.

Altman, Sam. "How to Hire." *Sam Altman*, 23 Sep. 2013, blog.samaltman.com/how-to-hire.

Altman, Sam. "Productivity." *Sam Altman*, 10 Apr. 2018, blog.samaltman.com/productivity.

Anderson, Christopher J., et al. "Response to Comment on 'Estimating the Reproducibility of Psychological Science.'" *Science*, vol. 351, no. 6277, 2016, pp. 1037–1037, doi.org/10.1126/science.aad9163.

Anderson, David. "Guest Post: Proven Programs Are the Exception, Not the Rule." *The GiveWell Blog*, 18 Dec. 2008, blog.givewell.org/2008/12/18/guest-post-proven-programs-are-the-exception-not-the-rule/.

Andreessen, Marc. "Pmarca Guide to Personal Productivity." *Pmarchive*, 4 June 2007, pmarchive.com/guide_to_personal_productivity.html.

Andreeva, Nellie. "'Beyond Scared Straight' Premiere Sets A&E Ratings Record." *Deadline*, 14 Jan. 2011, deadline.com/2011/01/beyond-scared-straight-premiere-sets-ae-ratings-record-96698/.

ANJ Consultancy Ltd. "Stopp Technique." *ANJ Counselling & Psychotherapy*, www.anjclearview.co.uk/stopp. Accessed 24 May 2023.

Aos, Steve, et al. "Benefits and Costs of Prevention and Early Intervention Programs for Youth." *Washington State Institute for Public Policy*, 2004, www.wsipp.wa.gov/ReportFile/881/Wsipp_Benefits-and-Costs-of-Prevention-and-Early-Intervention-Programs-for-Youth_Summary-Report.pd.

Appelbaum, Binyamin. "How Mortgage Fraud Made the Financial Crisis Worse." *The New York Times*, 12 Feb. 2015, www.nytimes.com/2015/02/13/upshot/how-mortgage-fraud-made-the-financial-crisis-worse.html.

Ariely, Dan. *Predictably Irrational: The Hidden Forces That Shape Our Decisions*. Harper, 2009.

Arkes, Hal R, and Catherine Blumer. "The Psychology of Sunk Cost." *Organizational Behavior and Human Decision Processes*, vol. 35, no. 1, 1985, pp. 124–140, doi.org/10.1016/0749-5978(85)90049-4.

Askell, Amanda. "Act Utilitarianism: Criterion of Rightness vs. Decision Procedure." *EA Forum*, 18 Jan. 2017, forum.effectivealtruism.org/posts/voDm6e6y4KHAPJeJX/act-utilitarianism-criterion-of-rightness-vs-decision.

Baker, Mauricio. "Many Undergrads Should Take Light Courseloads." *EA Forum*, 25 Oct. 2021, forum.effectivealtruism.org/posts/hgiLaE3eL76ovcfdH/many-undergrads-should-take-light-courseloads.

Barker, Eric. "This Is How to Make Friends as an Adult: 5 Secrets Backed by Research." *Barking Up The Wrong Tree*, 22 Feb. 2017, bakadesuyo.com/2017/02/how-to-make-friends-as-an-adult/.

Barkley, Russell A., and Christine M. Benton. *Taking Charge of Adult ADHD*. Guilford Press, 2010.

Bar-On, Yinon M., et al. "The Biomass Distribution on Earth." *Proceedings of the National Academy of Sciences*, vol. 115, no. 25, 21 May 2018, pp. 6506–6511, doi.org/10.1073/pnas.1711842115.

Belcak, Austin. "How to Get a Job without Applying Online." *Cultivated Culture*, 22 July 2021, cultivatedculture.com/how-to-get-a-job-anywhere-no-connections/.

Belluz, Julia, and Steven Hoffman. "Stop Googling Your Health Questions. Use These Sites Instead." *Vox*, 11 Mar. 2015, www.vox.com/2014/9/8/6005999/why-you-should-never-use-dr-google-to-search-for-health-information.

Berg, Justin M., et al. "What Is Job Crafting and Why Does It Matter?" *Center for Positive Organizational Scholarship, Michigan Ross School of Business*, 1 Aug. 2007, https://positiveorgs.bus.umich.edu/wp-content/uploads/What-is-Job-Crafting-and-Why-Does-it-Matter1.pdf.

Berger, Alexander. "Errors in DCP2 Cost-Effectiveness Estimate for Deworming." *The GiveWell Blog*, 3 Feb. 2014, blog.givewell.org/2011/09/29/errors-in-dcp2-cost-effectiveness-estimate-for-deworming/.

Bisset, Victoria. "AI Pioneer Quits Google to Warn Humanity of the Tech's Existential Threat." *The Washington Post*, 3 May 2023, www.washingtonpost.com/technology/2023/05/02/geoffrey-hinton-leaves-google-ai/.

Blackburn, Simon. *Being Good: A Short Introduction to Ethics*. Oxford University Press, 2003.

Boenigk, Silke, and Marcel Lee Mayr. "The Happiness of Giving: Evidence from the German Socioeconomic Panel That Happier People Are More Generous." *Journal of Happiness Studies*, vol. 17, no. 5, 2015, pp. 1825–1846, doi.org/10.1007/s10902-015-9672-2.

Bolles, Richard Nelson. *What Color Is Your Parachute? 2015: A Practical Manual for Job-Hunters and Career-Changers*. Ten Speed Press, 2014.

Bosel, Sarah. "UK Approves Pfizer/BioNTech Covid Vaccine for Rollout Next Week." *The Guardian*, 2 Dec. 2020, www.theguardian.com/society/2020/dec/02/pfizer-biontech-covid-vaccine-wins-licence-for-use-in-the-uk.

Bourget, David, and David J Chalmers. "Philosophers on Philosophy: The PhilPapers 2020 Survey." *Philosophers' Imprint*, vol. 0, no. 0, 2023.

Britton, Scott. "How to Find Email Addresses." *Life-Long Learner*, 2012, life-longlearner.com/find-email-addresses/.

Brooks, David. *The Road to Character*. Penguin, 2016.

Burns, David. *Feeling Good*. William Anderson & Sons Ltd., 2001.

Bye, Lynette. "A Peek behind the Curtain Interview Series." *Lynette Bye Coaching*, 25 May 2022, lynettebye.com/blog/2022/5/25/a-peek-behind-the-curtain-interview-series.

Bye, Lynette. "Five Ways To Prioritize Better." *Lynette Bye Coaching*, 27 June 2020, lynettebye.com/blog/2020/6/26/five-ways-to-prioritize-better.

Bye, Lynette. "How to Improve Your Sleep." *Lynette Bye Coaching*, 27 Oct. 2019, lynettebye.com/blog/2019/10/24/lu1xjfsg8i9rzkatmnqgh2r9ykb0r1.

Cabane, Olivia Fox. *The Charisma Myth: How to Engage, Influence and Motivate People*. Penguin, 2013.

Caplan, Bryan. "How to Win Friends and Influence People? Book Club Round-Up." *Econlib*, 28 Apr. 2020, www.econlib.org/how-to-win-friends-and-influence-people-book-club-round-up/.

Caplan, Bryan. *The Case Against Education — Why the Education System Is a Waste of Time and Money*. Princeton University Press, 2018.

Caplan, Bryan. "The Totalitarian Threat." *Global Catastrophic Risks*, edited by Nick Bostrom and Milan Ćirković, Oxford University Press, 2008, pp. 504–530, doi.org/10.1093/oso/9780198570509.003.0029.

Caplan, Bryan. "What Every High School Junior Should Know About Going to College." *Econlib*, Sept. 2014, www.econlib.org/archives/2014/09/what_every_high.html.

CareerCast. "2015 Jobs Rated Methodology." *CareerCast*, 17 Apr. 2015, www.careercast.com/jobs-rated/2015-jobs-rated-methodology.

CareerCast. "2021 Jobs Rated Methodology." *CareerCast*, 5 Sep. 2021, www.careercast.com/jobs-rated/2021-jobs-rated-methodology.

CareerCast. "The Best Jobs of 2015." *CareerCast*, 14 Apr. 2015 www.careercast.com/jobs-rated/best-jobs-2015.

CareerCast. "The Best Jobs of 2021." *CareerCast*, 5 Sep. 2021 www.careercast.com/jobs-rated/best-jobs-2021.

Carnegie, Dale. *How to Win Friends and Influence People*. Vermillion, 2006.

Carnevale, Anthony P, et al. Georgetown University Center on Education and the Workforce. *The College Payoff More Education Doesn't Always Mean More Earnings*, 2021, cewgeorgetown.wpenginepowered.com/wp-content/uploads/cew-college_payoff_2021-fr.pdf. Accessed May 2023.

Carr, Alan, et al. "Effectiveness of Positive Psychology Interventions: A Systematic Review and Meta-Analysis." *The Journal of Positive Psychology*, vol. 16, no. 6, 2020, pp. 749–769, doi.org/10.1080/17439760.2020.1818807.

Centers for Disease Control and Prevention. "Neglected Tropical Diseases." *Centers for Disease Control and Prevention*, 11 Mar. 2017, www.cdc.gov/globalhealth/ntd/.

Chancel, Lucas, et al. "The World #inequalityreport 2022 Presents the Most Up-to-Date & Complete Data on Inequality Worldwide." *World Inequality Report 2022*, 2023, wir2022.wid.world/.

Charity Navigator. "Charity Navigator 2016 Charity CEO Compensation Study." *Charity Navigator*, 2016, www.charitynavigator.org/index.cfm?bay=studies.ceo.

Chow, Andrew R. "How ChatGPT Managed to Grow Faster Than TikTok or Instagram." *Time*, 8 Feb. 2023, time.com/6253615/chatgpt-fastest-growing/.

Christakis, Nicholas, and James Fowler. *Connected: The Surprising Power of Our Social Networks and How They Shape Our Lives.* Little, Brown Spark, 2011.

Christiano, Paul F. "Integrity for Consequentialists." *The Sideways View*, 14 Nov. 2016, sideways-view.com/2016/11/14/integrity-for-consequentialists/.

Chua, Sacha. "Deliberate Performance." *Living an Awesome Life*, 19 Mar. 2013, sachachua.com/blog/2013/03/deliberate-performance/.

Cialdini, Robert B. *Influence: The Psychology of Persuasion.* Harper Business, 2007.

Clear, James. *Atomic Habits: Tiny Changes, Remarkable Results: An Easy and Proven Way to Build Good Habits and Break Bad Ones.* Cornerstone Press, 2022.

Clear, James. "Core Values List." *James Clear*, Sept. 2015, jamesclear.com/core-values.

Clear, James. "Warren Buffett's '2 List' Strategy: How to Maximize Your Focus and Master Your Priorities." *James Clear*, Jan. 2015, jamesclear.com/buffett-focus.

Companies House. "DEEPMIND Technologies Limited Filing History." *GOV.UK*, 4 Oct. 2021, find-and-update.company-information.service.gov.uk/company/07386350/filing-history.

Copeland, Jack. "Alan Turing: The Codebreaker Who Saved 'Millions of Lives.'" *BBC News*, 19 June 2012, web.archive.org/web/20160404135844/www.bbc.com/news/technology-18419691.

Cotra, Ajeya. "AMF and Population Ethics." *The GiveWell Blog*, 12 Dec. 2016, blog.givewell.org/2016/12/12/amf-population-ethics/.

Coughlan, Sean. "Banking 'Can Be an Ethical Career Choice.'" *BBC News*, 22 Nov. 2011, www.bbc.co.uk/news/education-15820786.

Covey, Sean, et al. *The 4 Disciplines of Execution: Achieving Your Wildly Important Goals.* Simon & Schuster, 2012.

Creamer, John, et al. *Poverty in the United States: 2021 Current Population Reports*, 277th ed., vol. P60, pp. 1–94. U.S. Government Publishing Office, 2022., .

Crispin, Natalie. "Our Updated Top Charities for Giving Season 2016." *The GiveWell Blog*, 7 Aug. 2017, blog.givewell.org/2016/11/28/updated-top-charities-giving-season-2016/.

Curry, Oliver Scott, et al. "Happy to Help? A Systematic Review and Meta-Analysis of the Effects of Performing Acts of Kindness on the Well-Being of the Actor." *Journal of Experimental Social Psychology*, vol. 76, 2018, pp. 320–329, doi.org/10.1016/j.jesp.2018.02.014.

Dafoe, Allan. "AI Governance: A Research Agenda - Future of Humanity Institute." *Future of Humanity Institute*, 27 Aug. 2018, www.fhi.ox.ac.uk/wp-content/uploads/GovAI-Agenda.pdf.

Daily Mail. "The Young Professionals Who Believe Their Best Chance at Trying to Save the World iIs by Joining Wall Street and Making Millions." *Daily Mail Online*, 7 June 2013, www.dailymail.co.uk/news/article-2334682/Young-professionals-joining-Wall-Street-save-world.html.

Dale, S. B., and A. B. Krueger. "Estimating the Payoff to Attending a More Selective College: An Application of Selection on Observables and Unobservables." *The Quarterly Journal of Economics*, vol. 117, no. 4, 2002, pp. 1491–1527, doi.org/10.1162/003355302320935089.

Da Silva, Claudia Cardoso, et al. "Effectiveness of Training Programs Based on Mindfulness in Reducing Psychological Distress and Promoting Well-Being in Medical Students: A Systematic Review and Meta-Analysis." *Systematic Reviews*, vol. 12, no. 1, 2023, doi.org/10.1186/s13643-023-02244-y.

Deming, David. "The Growing Importance of Social Skills in the Labor Market." *Harvard University and NBER*, 5 Apr. 2017, doi.org/10.3386/w21473.

Department of Health and Human Services. "Annual Update of the HHS Poverty Guidelines." *Federal Register*, no. 88 FR 3424, 2023, pp. 3424–3425.

Donaldson, Scott I., et al. "Evaluating Positive Psychology Interventions at Work: A Systematic Review and Meta-Analysis." *International Journal of Applied Positive Psychology*, vol. 4, no. 3, 2019, pp. 113–134, doi.org/10.1007/s41042-019-00021-8.

Donovan, Kate. "The [....]'s Guide to Getting a Therapist: Getting Started." *Freethoughtblogs*, 8 May 2014, freethoughtblogs.com/gruntled/2014/05/08/the-s-guide-to-getting-a-therapist-getting-started/.

Duckworth, Angela. *Grit: The Power of Passion and Perseverance*. Scribner, 2016.

Dyer, Ethan, and Guy Gur-Ari. "Minerva: Solving Quantitative Reasoning Problems with Language Models." *Google AI Blog*, 30 June 2022, ai.googleblog.com/2022/06/minerva-solving-quantitative-reasoning.html.

Easterly, William. *The White Man's Burden: Why the West's Efforts to Aid the Rest Have Done So Much Ill and So Little Good*. Oxford University Press, 2007.

Easton, Mark. "Vicar or Publican - Which Jobs Make You Happy?" *BBC News*, 20 Mar. 2014, www.bbc.co.uk/news/magazine-26671221.

Egger, Dennis, et al. "General Equilibrium Effects of Cash Transfers: Experimental Evidence from Kenya." *Econometrica*, vol. 90, no. 6, 2022, pp. 2603–2643, doi.org/10.3982/ecta17945.

Eide, Erik R, and Michael J Hilmer. "Do Elite Colleges Lead to Higher Salaries? Only for Some Professions." *The Wall Street Journal*, 31 Jan. 2016, www.wsj.com/articles/do-elite-colleges-lead-to-higher-salaries-only-for-some-professions-1454295674.

Epstein, David J. *Range: Why Generalists Triumph in a Specialized World*. Macmillan, 2019.

Ericsson, K. Anders, and Robert Pool. *Peak: Secrets from the New Science of Expertise*. Houghton Mifflin Harcourt, 2016.

Ericsson, K. Anders. *The Cambridge Handbook of Expertise and Expert Performance*. Cambridge University Press, 2018.

Erickson, Kjerstin. "How We Got into This Crunch." *Social Edge*, 21 Oct. 2008, www.socialedge.org/blogs/forging-ahead/archive/2008/10/20/how-we-got-into-this-financial-crunch.

Fadde, Peter J., and Gary A. Klein. "Deliberate Performance: Accelerating Expertise in Natural Settings." *Performance Improvement*, vol. 49, no. 9, Oct. 2010, pp. 5–14, doi.org/10.1002/pfi.20175.

Fennema, M. G., and Jon D. Perkins. "Mental Budgeting Versus Marginal Decision Making: Training, Experience and Justification Effects on Decisions Involving Sunk Costs." Journal of Behavioral Decision Making, vol. 21, no. 3, 2008, pp. 225–239, doi.org/10.1002/bdm.585.

Ferrazzi, Keith, and Tahl Raz. *Never Eat Alone: And Other Secrets to Success, One Relationship at a Tim.* Penguin, 2014.

Fish Welfare Initiative. "Donate." *Fish Welfare Initiative*, Mar. 2023, www.fishwelfareinitiative.org/donate.

Fish Welfare Initiative. "Our Impact." *Fish Welfare Initiative*, Mar. 2023, www.fishwelfareinitiative.org/impact.

Florida, R., et al. "The Rise of the Mega-Region." *Cambridge Journal of Regions, Economy and Society*, vol. 1, no. 3, 2008, pp. 459–476, doi.org/10.1093/cjres/rsn018.

Florida, Richard L. *Who's Your City?: How the Creative Economy Is Making Where to Live the Most Important Decision of Your Life*. Basic Books, 2009.

Fodor, James. "Critical Review of 'the Precipice': A Reassessment of the Risks of AI and Pandemics." *EA Forum*, 11 May 2020, forum.effectivealtruism.org/posts/2sMR7n32FSvLCoJLQ/critical-review-of-the-precipice-a-reassessment-of-the-risks.

Fogg, B. J. *Tiny Habits: Why Starting Small Makes Lasting Change Easy*. Virgin Books, 2020.

Fowler, J. H, and N. A Christakis. "Dynamic Spread of Happiness in a Large Social Network: Longitudinal Analysis over 20 Years in the Framingham Heart Study." BMJ, vol. 337, no. a2338, 2008, doi.org/10.1136/bmj.a2338.

Fralic, Chris. "How to Become Insanely Well-Connected." *First Round Review*, 2021, review.firstround.com/how-to-become-insanely-well-connected.

FRED, "Average Hourly Earnings of All Employees, Total Private [CES0500000003]." *Federal Reserve Bank of St. Louis*, 5 May 2023, fred.stlouisfed.org/series/CES0500000003.

FRED, "Average Weeks Unemployed." *FRED, Federal Reserve Bank of Saint Louis*, 5 May 2023, fred.stlouisfed.org/series/UEMPMEAN.

Frey, Carl Benedikt, and Michael A. Osborne. "The Future of Employment: How Susceptible Are Jobs to Computerisation?" *Technological Forecasting and Social Change*, vol. 114, 2013, pp. 254–280, doi.org/10.1016/j.techfore.2016.08.019.

Future of Life Institute, "Research Priorities for Robust and Beneficial Artificial Intelligence: An Open Letter" *Future of Life Institute*, 2015, futureoflife.org/ai-open-letter.

Galef, Julia. *The Scout Mindset: Why Some People See Things Clearly and Others Don't*. Piatkus, 2021.

Gates, Bill. "The Two Adams." *Gates Notes*, 7 Dec. 2015, www.gatesnotes.com/The-Road-to-Character.

Gelman, Andrew. "Bruised and Battered, I Couldn't Tell What I Felt. I Was Ungeneralizable to Myself." *Statistical Modeling Causal Inference and Social Science*, 9 Mar. 2016, statmodeling.stat.columbia.edu/2016/03/09/bruised-and-battered-i-couldnt-tell-what-i-felt-i-was-ungeneralizable-to-myself/.

Giattino, Charlie, et al. "Excess Mortality during the Coronavirus Pandemic (COVID-19)." *Our World in Data*, Apr. 2023, ourworldindata.org/excess-mortality-covid.

Gilbert, Daniel T., and Timothy D. Wilson. "Why the Brain Talks to Itself: Sources of Error in Emotional Prediction." *Philosophical Transactions of the Royal Society B: Biological Sciences*, vol. 364, no. 1521, 2009, pp. 1335–1341, doi.org/10.1098/rstb.2008.0305.

Gilbert, Daniel T., et al. "Comment on 'Estimating the Reproducibility of Psychological Science.'" *Science*, vol. 351, no. 6277, 2016, pp. 1037–1037, doi.org/10.1126/science.aad7243.

Gilbert, Daniel. *Stumbling on Happiness*. Vintage Books, 2006.

GiveWell. "Cash Transfers." *GiveWell*,
2012, www.givewell.org/international/technical/programs/cash-transfers.

GiveWell. "Condom Promotion and Distribution to Prevent HIV/AIDS." *GiveWell*, Apr. 2019, www.
givewell.org/international/technical/programs/condom-distribution.

GiveWell. "Failure in International Aid." *GiveWell*, www.givewell.org/international/technical/criteria/
impact/failure-stories. Accessed 23 May 2023.

GiveWell. "GiveDirectly – November 2020 Version." *GiveWell*,
2020, www.givewell.org/charities/give-directly/November-2020-version.

GiveWell. "GiveWell's Cost-Effectiveness Analyses." *GiveWell*,
2012, www.givewell.org/how-we-work/our-criteria/cost-effectiveness/cost-effectiveness-models.

GiveWell. "HIV/AIDS Charity." *GiveWell*, Nov. 2010, www.givewell.org/international/health/HIV-
AIDS.

GiveDirectly. "In Their Own Words: Grace, Bonphas, and Joyce." *GiveDirectly*, 22 Sep.
105, www.givedirectly.org/in-their-own-words-grace-bonphas-and-joyce/.

GiveWell. "Your Dollar Goes Further Overseas." *GiveWell*,
2010, www.givewell.org/giving101/Your-dollar-goes-further-overseas.

Giving USA. "Giving USA 2022 Report." *Giving USA*, givingusa.org/wp-content/uploads/2022/06/
GivingUSA2022_Infographic.pdf. Accessed 11 Jan. 2023.

Giving What We Can, "How Rich Am I? - World Income Percentile Calculator: Global Rich List."
Giving What We Can, 2019, howrichami.givingwhatwecan.org/how-rich-am-i?income=14580&count
ryCode=USA&household%5Badults%5D=1&household%5Bchildren%5D=0.

Glaeser, Edward L. *Triumph of the City: How Our Greatest Invention Makes Us Richer, Smarter, Greener,
Healthier, and Happier*. Penguin Books, 2012.

Goleman, Daniel, and Richard J Davidson. *Altered Traits: Science Reveals How Meditation Changes Your
Mind, Brain, and Body*. Penguin, 2017.

Gollwitzer, Peter M., and Paschal Sheeran. "Implementation Intentions and Goal Achievement:
A Meta-analysis of Effects and Processes." *Advances in Experimental Social Psychology*, 2006, pp.
69–119, doi.org/10.1016/s0065-2601(06)38002-1.

Goyal, Madhav, et al. "Meditation Programs for Psychological Stress and Well-Being." *JAMA Internal
Medicine*, vol. 174, no. 3, 2014, p. 357, doi.org/10.1001/jamainternmed.2013.13018.

Grace, Katja, et al. "Viewpoint: When Will AI Exceed Human Performance? Evidence from AI
Experts." *Journal of Artificial Intelligence Research*, vol. 62, 2018, doi.org/10.1613/jair.1.11222.

Graham, Paul. *Cities and Ambition*, May 2008, www.paulgraham.com/cities.html.

Granovetter, Mark S. "The Strength of Weak Ties." *Networks in the Knowledge Economy*, 2003, doi.
org/10.1093/oso/9780195159509.003.0010.

Grant, Adam. *Give and Take: Why Helping Others Drives Our Success*. Penguin, 2014.

Grant, Adam M., et al. "Impact and the Art of Motivation Maintenance: The Effects of Contact with
Beneficiaries on Persistence Behavior." *Organizational Behavior and Human Decision Processes*, vol. 103,
no. 1, 2007, pp. 53–67, doi.org/10.1016/j.obhdp.2006.05.004.

Grant, Adam. *Originals: How Non-Conformists Move the World*. Penguin Publishing Group, 2016.

Green, Alison, and Jerry Hauser. *Managing to Change the World: The Nonprofit Manager's Guide to Getting Results*. Jossey-Bass, 2012.

Guillebeau, Chris. *The $100 Startup: Reinvent the Way You Make a Living, Do What You Love, and Create a New Future*. Crown, 2012.

Guvenen, Fatih, et al. "What Do Data on Millions of U.S. Workers Reveal about Life-Cycle Earnings Risk?" *NBER Working Paper Series*, 2015, doi.org/10.3386/w20913.

Hambrick, David Z., and Alexander P. Burgoyne. "The Difference between Rationality and Intelligence." *The New York Times*, 16 Sept. 2016, www.nytimes.com/2016/09/18/opinion/sunday/the-difference-between-rationality-and-intelligence.html.

Hamming, Richard. "You and Your Research." *University of Virginia*, 7 Mar. 1986, www.cs.virginia.edu/~robins/YouAndYourResearch.html. Accessed 24 May 2023.

Hanson, Melanie. "U.S. Public Education Spending Statistics [2023]: Per Pupil + Total." *EducationData.Org*, 15 June 2022, educationdata.org/public-education-spending-statistics.

Haran, Raghav. "How to Get Virtually Any Job You Want (Even If You Don't Have the 'Right' Experience)." *Medium*, 10 Mar. 2019, medium.com/@RaghavHaran/how-to-get-virtually-any-job-you-want-even-if-you-dont-have-the-right-experience-a622149262d5.

Harari, Yuval N., et al. *Sapiens*. Albin Michel, 2020.

Harris, Russ. "The Complete Set of Client Handouts and Worksheets from ACT Books." *The Happiness Trap*, 2014, thehappinesstrap.com/upimages/The_Complete_Happiness_Trap_Worksheets.pdf.

Harris, Sam. *Waking Up: A Guide to Spirituality Without Religion*. Simon & Schuster, 2015.

Hassenfeld, Elie. "An Update on GiveWell's Funding Projections." *The GiveWell Blog*, 5 July 2022, blog.givewell.org/2022/07/05/update-on-givewells-funding-projections/.

Haushofer, Johannes, and Jeremy Shapiro. "Household Response to Income Changes: Evidence from an Unconditional Cash Transfer Program in Kenya." *GiveWell Interventions Report*, 15 Nov. 2013, pp. 1–57.

Haushofer, Johannes, and Jeremy Shapiro. "The Short-Term Impact of Unconditional Cash Transfers to the Poor: Experimental Evidence from Kenya*." *The Quarterly Journal of Economics*, vol. 131, no. 4, 2016, pp. 1973–2042, doi.org/10.1093/qje/qjw025.

Hazell, Julian, and Michael Plant. "Can Money Buy Happiness? A Review of New Data." *Giving What We Can*, 23 June 2021, www.givingwhatwecan.org/blog/can-money-buy-happiness.

Heath, Chip, and Dan Heath. *Decisive*. Random House, 2013.

Heath, Chip, and Dan Heath. *Made to Stick: Why Some Ideas Survive and Others Die*. Random House, 2010.

Hecht, Luke. "The Importance of Considering Age When Quantifying Wild Animals' Welfare." *Biological Reviews*, vol. 96, no. 6, 21 June 2021, pp. 2602–2616, doi.org/10.1111/brv.12769.

Hendel, Hilary Jacobs. *It's Not Always Depression: A New Theory of Listening to Your Body, Discovering*

Core Emotions and Reconnecting With Your Authentic Self. Penguin Random House, 2018.

Henry, Alan. "How to Clean up Your Online Presence and Make a Great First Impression." *Lifehacker*, 28 Nov. 2012, lifehacker.com/how-to-clean-up-your-online-presence-and-make-a-great-f-5963864.

HIV.gov. "HIV and AIDS Epidemic Global Statistics." *HIV.Gov*, 3 Aug. 2022, www.hiv.gov/hiv-basics/overview/data-and-trends/global-statistics/.

Hoffman, Reid, and Ben Casnocha. *The Startup of You: Adapt, Take Risks, Grow Your Network, and Transform Your Career*. Currency, 2022.

Horstman, Mark, et al. *The Effective Manager*. Wiley, 2023.

Hubbard, Douglas W. *How to Measure Anything: Finding the Value of "Intangibles" in Business*. 3rd ed., Wiley, 2014.

Humphrey, Stephen E., et al. "Integrating Motivational, Social, and Contextual Work Design Features: A Meta-Analytic Summary and Theoretical Extension of the Work Design Literature." *Journal of Applied Psychology*, vol. 92, no. 5, 2007, pp. 1332–1356, doi.org/10.1037/0021-9010.92.5.1332.

Industry - North American Industry Classification System 2002, Occupation - National Occupational Classification for Statistics 2006, vol. 23, *No. 97-559-XCB2006024*. Statistics Canada, 2006.

Ingram, April. "David Nallin." *Science Heros*, 2021, www.scienceheroes.com/nailin.

Institute for Fiscal Studies. "About the Tool." *Institute for Fiscal Studies*, 20 Sep. 2022, ifs.org.uk/about-tool.

Institute for Health Metrics and Evaluation, "Global Burden of Disease Results." *Institute for Health Metrics and Evaluation*, 2019, vizhub.healthdata.org/gbd-results/.

Irlam, Gordon. "In Praise of Viktor Zhdanov." *80,000 Hours*, 23 Feb. 2012, 80000hours.org/2012/02/in-praise-of-viktor-zhdanov/.

Jamison, Dean, et al., editors. *Disease Control Priorities in Developing Countries (2nd Edition)*. The World Bank, 2006.

Jollimore, Troy. "Impartiality." Edited by Edward N Zalta, *Stanford Encyclopedia of Philosophy*, 24 Aug. 2021, plato.stanford.edu/entries/impartiality/.

Jones, Benjamin, et al. "Age and Scientific Genius." *NBER Working Paper Series*, 2014, doi.org/10.3386/w19866.

Judge, Timothy A., et al. "The Relationship between Pay and Job Satisfaction: A Meta-Analysis of the Literature." *Journal of Vocational Behavior*, vol. 77, no. 2, 2010, pp. 157–167, doi.org/10.1016/j.jvb.2010.04.002.

Kahneman, Daniel, and Angus Deaton. "High Income Improves Evaluation of Life but Not Emotional Well-Being." *Proceedings of the National Academy of Sciences*, vol. 107, no. 38, 2010, pp. 16489–16493, doi.org/10.1073/pnas.1011492107.

Kahneman, Daniel, et al., editors. *Judgment under Uncertainty: Heuristics and Biases*. Cambridge University Press, 1982.

Kahneman, Daniel. "Focusing Illusion." *2011 : What Scientific Concept Would Improve Everybody's*

Cognitive Toolkit?, 2011, www.edge.org/response-detail/11984.

Kahneman, Daniel. *Thinking, Fast and Slow.* Farrar, Straus and Giroux, 2013.

Karnofsky, Holden. "Learning by Writing." *Cold Takes,* 22 Feb. 2022, www.cold-takes.com/learning-by-writing/.

Kaufman, Scott Barry. "The Complexity of Greatness: Beyond Talent or Practice." *Scientific American,* 22 May 2013, blogs.scientificamerican.com/beautiful-minds/the-complexity-of-greatness-beyond-talent-or-practice/.

Keeney, Ralph L. *Value-Focused Thinking: A Path to Creative Decisionmaking.* Harvard University Press, 1996.

Kemp, Simon, et al. "A Test of the Peak-End Rule with Extended Autobiographical Events." *Memory & Cognition,* vol. 36, no. 1, 2008, pp. 132–138, doi.org/10.3758/mc.36.1.132.

Killingsworth, Matthew A. "Experienced Well-Being Rises With Income, Even Above $75,000 Per Year." *Proceedings of the National Academy of Sciences,* vol. 118, no. 4, 2021, doi.org/10.1073/pnas.2016976118.

Kinney, Martha. *Landsteiner, Karl,* 9 Sep. 2011, scienceheroes.com/index.php?option=com_content&view=article&id=128&Itemid=137.

Klamer, Arjo, and Hendrik P. Dalen. "Attention and the Art of Scientific Publishing." *Journal of Economic Methodology,* vol. 9, no. 3, 2002, pp. 289–315, doi.org/10.1080/1350178022000015104.

Knowledge at Wharton. "Putting a Face to a Name: The Art of Motivating Employees." *Knowledge at Wharton,* 17 Feb. 2010. knowledge.wharton.upenn.edu/article/putting-a-face-to-a-name-the-art-of-motivating-employees/.

Kollipara, Puneet. "Earth Won't Die as Soon as Thought." *Science,* 22 Jan. 2014, www.sciencemag.org/news/2014/01/earth-wont-die-soon-thought.

Kristof, Nicholas. "Opinion | The Trader Who Donates Half His Pay." *The New York Times,* 4 Apr. 2015, www.nytimes.com/2015/04/05/opinion/sunday/nicholas-kristof-the-trader-who-donates-half-his-pay.html.

Kuhn, Ben. "Giving Away Money: A Guide." *Benkuhn.Net,* June 2014, www.benkuhn.net/giving-101/.

Lead Exposure Elimination Project. "Home - Lead Exposure Elimination Project - Ending Lead Poisoning." *Lead Exposure Elimination Project,* 8 May 2023, leadelimination.org/.

Lee, C.T., et al. "Parachuting for Charity: Is It Worth the Money? A 5-Year Audit of Parachute Injuries in Tayside and the Cost to the NHS." *Injury,* vol. 30, no. 4, 1999, pp. 283–287, doi.org/10.1016/s0020-1383(99)00083-2.

Levitt, Steven. "Heads or Tails: The Impact of a Coin Toss on Major Life Decisions and Subsequent Happiness." *NBER Working Paper Series,* 2016, doi.org/10.3386/w22487.

Levy, Frank, and Richard J. Murnane. *New Division of Labor.* Princeton University Press, 2004.

Lewis, Gregory. "How Many Lives Does a Doctor Save?" *80,000 Hours,* 19 Aug. 2012, 80000hours.org/2012/08/how-many-lives-does-a-doctor-save/.

Liu, Lu, et al. "Hot Streaks in Artistic, Cultural, and Scientific Careers." *Nature,* vol. 559, no. 7714, 2018, pp. 396–399, doi.org/10.1038/s41586-018-0315-8.

Locke, Edwin A., editor. *Handbook of Principles of Organizational Behavior: Indispensable Knowledge for Evidence-Based Management.* John Wiley & Sons, 2009.

Lomas, Tim, et al. "Mindfulness-Based Interventions in the Workplace: An Inclusive Systematic Review and Meta-Analysis of Their Impact Upon Wellbeing." *The Journal of Positive Psychology*, vol. 14, no. 5, 2019, pp. 625–640, doi.org/10.1080/17439760.2018.1519588.

Lopez, Alan D., et al. *The Global Burden of Disease and Risk Factors.* Oxford University Press, 2006.

Lyubomirsky, Sonja. *The How of Happiness: A New Approach to Getting the Life You Want.* Penguin Books, 2008.

MacAskill, William. *Doing Good Better.* Guardian Faber Publishing, 2016.

MacAskill, William, et al. *Moral Uncertainty.* Oxford University Press, 2020.

MacAskill, William. "Normative Uncertainty." *University of Oxford*, 2014, https://80000hours.org/wp-content/uploads/2017/06/MacAskill-Normative-Uncertainty.pdf.

MacAskill, William. "What Do Leaders of Effective Nonprofits Say about Working in Nonprofits?" *80,000 Hours*, 1 Sept. 2015, 80000hours.org/2015/09/what-do-leaders-of-effective-non-profits-say-about-working-in-non-profits-interviews-with-givedirectly-deworm-the-world-initiative-development-media-international-schistosomiasis-control-initiativ/.

MacKay, David. "Phone Chargers - the Truth." *Inference - University of Cambridge, Department of Engineering*, 15 Oct. 2015, www.inference.eng.cam.ac.uk/sustainable/charger/.

MacKay, David. *Sustainable Energy: Without the Hot Air.* UIT, 2009.

Macnamara, Brooke N., et al. "Deliberate Practice and Performance in Music, Games, Sports, Education, and Professions: A Meta-Analysis." *Psychological Science*, vol. 25, no. 8, 2014, pp. 1608–1618, doi.org/10.1177/0956797614535810.

Maddison, Angus. *Contours of the World Economy, 1-2030 AD: Essays in Macro-Economic History.* Oxford University Press, 2013.

Mansilla, R., et al. "On the Behavior of Journal Impact Factor Rank-Order Distribution." *Journal of Informetrics*, vol. 1, no. 2, 2007, pp. 155–160, doi.org/10.1016/j.joi.2007.01.001.

Mathers, Colin, et al. *The Global Burden of Disease: 2004 Update.* World Health Organization, 2008.

Matthews, Dylan. "Join Wall Street. Save the World." *The Washington Post*, 31 May 2013, www.washingtonpost.com/news/wonk/wp/2013/05/31/join-wall-street-save-the-world/.

Maurya, Ash. *Running Lean: Iterate from Plan A to a Plan That Works.* O'Reilly Media, Inc., 2022.

Mayo Clinic. "Office Ergonomics: Your How-to Guide." *Mayo Clinic*, 25 May 2023, www.mayoclinic.org/healthy-lifestyle/adult-health/in-depth/office-ergonomics/art-20046169.

Mayo Clinic. "Simple Ways to Prevent Back Pain at Work." *Mayo Clinic*, 3 June 2021, www.mayoclinic.org/healthy-lifestyle/adult-health/in-depth/back-pain/art-20044526.

McCook, Alison. "'I Placed Too Much Faith in Underpowered Studies:' Nobel Prize Winner Admits Mistakes." *Retraction Watch*, 20 Feb. 2017, retractionwatch.com/2017/02/20/placed-much-faith-underpowered-studies-nobel-prize-winner-admits-mistakes/.

McGuire, Joel, and Michael Plant. "Cash Transfers: Cost-Effectiveness Analysis." *Happier Lives Institute*, Oct. 2021, www.happierlivesinstitute.org/report/cash-transfers-cost-effectiveness-analysis/.

McIntosh, Craig, and Andrew Zeitlin. "Cash versus Kind: Benchmarking a Child Nutrition Program against Unconditional Cash Transfers in Rwanda." *arXiv*, 1 June 2021, arxiv.org/abs/2106.00213.

McIntosh, Craig, and Andrew Zeitlin. "Using Household Grants to Benchmark the Cost Effectiveness of a USAID Workforce Readiness Program." *Journal of Development Economics*, vol. 157, 2022, p. 102875, doi.org/10.1016/j.jdeveco.2022.102875.

McKay, David. "Sustainable Energy - without the Hot Air." *Without the Hot Air*, 9 Feb. 2014, web.archive.org/web/20170414224843/www.withouthotair.com/cI/page_337.shtml.

McKenzie, Patrick. "Salary Negotiation: Make More Money, Be More Valued." *Salary Negotiation: Make More Money, Be More Valued | Kalzumeus Software*, 23 Jan. 2012, www.kalzumeus. com/2012/01/23/salary-negotiation/.

Midjourney. "Midjourney." *Midjourney AI*, 2023, www.midjourney.com/.

Millett, Piers, and Andrew Snyder-Beattie. "Existential Risk and Cost-Effective Biosecurity." *Health Security*, vol. 15, no. 4, 1 Aug. 2017, pp. 373–383, doi.org/10.1089/hs.2017.0028.

Mochary, Matt, et al. *The Great CEO Within: The Tactical Guide to Company Building*. Mochary Films, 2021.

Mongrain, Myriam, and Tracy Anselmo-Matthews. "Do Positive Psychology Exercises Work? A Replication of Seligman et al." *Journal of Clinical Psychology*, vol. 68, no. 4, 2012, doi.org/10.1002/jclp.21839.

Montini, Laura. "The Most Undervalued Employee in Your Business | Inc.Com." *Inc.Com*, 2014, www.inc.com/laura-montini/the-most-undervalued-employee-at-any-organization.html.

Morgensen, Andreas. "Giving without Sacrifice?" *Giving What We Can*, 2014, assets.ctfassets.net/dhpcfh1bs3p6/3jqEdXNDmg8SGAeOeC8KYo/ 63f9caa4de752b15c84455dc9025d537/giving-without-sacrifice.pdf.

National Careers Service. "Finding Job Vacancies." *Find Job Vacancies | National Careers Service*, 2022, nationalcareers.service.gov.uk/careers-advice/advertised-job-vacancies. Accessed 14 October 2022.

National Center for Charitable Statistics. "Charitable Giving in America: Some Facts and Figures." *National Center for Charitable Statistics*, 2015, nccs.urban.org/nccs/statistics/charitable-giving-in-america-some-facts-and-figures.cfm.

National Endowment for the Arts. "How the United States Funds the Arts" *Arts.Gov*, Nov. 2012, www. arts.gov/sites/default/files/how-the-us-funds-the-arts.pdf.

National Institute of Mental Health. "Major Depression." *National Institute of Mental Health*, www. nimh.nih.gov/health/statistics/major-depression. Accessed 24 May 2023.

National Institute of Mental Health., "Mental Illness." *National Institute of Mental Health*, www.nimh. nih.gov/health/statistics/mental-illness. Accessed 24 May 2023.

New, Jake. "College Athletes Greatly Overestimate Their Chances of Playing Professionally." *Inside Higher Ed | Higher Education News, Events and Jobs*, 2015, www.insidehighered.com/news/2015/01/27/ college-athletes-greatly-overestimate-their-chances-playing-professionally.

Newport, Cal. *Deep Work*. Piatkus, 2016.

Newport, Cal. "Do Like Steve Jobs Did: Don't Follow Your Passion." *Fast Company*, 20 Sep. 2012, www.fastcompany.com/3001441/do-steve-jobs-did-dont-follow-your-passion.

Newport, Cal. "Fixed-Schedule Productivity: How I Accomplish a Large Amount of Work in a Small Number of Work Hours." *Cal Newport*, 15 Feb. 2008, calnewport.com/fixed-schedule-productivity-how-i-accomplish-a-large-amount-of-work-in-a-small-number-of-work-hours/.

Newport, Cal. *How to Win at College: Surprising Secrets for Success from the Country's Top Students.* Crown, 2005.

Newport, Cal. "Lesson 2: Four Principles for Decoding Career Success in Your Field." *Scott H Young*, Apr. 2017, www.scotthyoung.com/blog/lesson-2-four-principles/.

Newport, Cal. *So Good They Can't Ignore You: Why Skills Trump Passion in the Quest for Work You Love.* Grand Central Publishing, 2012.

NHS. "Back Pain." *NHS Choices*, 10 June 2022, www.nhs.uk/conditions/back-pain/.

NHS. "Coronary Heart Disease: Causes." *NHS Choices*, 10 Mar. 2020, www.nhs.uk/conditions/coronary-heart-disease/causes/.

NHS. "Physical Activity Guidelines for Adults Aged 19 to 64." *NHS Choices*, 4 Aug. 2021, www.nhs.uk/live-well/exercise/exercise-guidelines/physical-activity-guidelines-for-adults-aged-19-to-64/.

NHS. "Repetitive Strain Injury." *NHS Choices*, 24 May 2022, www.nhs.uk/conditions/repetitive-strain-injury-rsi/.

Nielsen, Michael A. "Augmenting Long-Term Memory." *augmentingcognition.com*, July 2018, augmentingcognition.com/ltm.html.

Noonan, Laura. "Bank Litigation Costs Hit $260BN - with $65bn More to Come." *Financial Times*, 23 Aug. 2015, www.ft.com/content/c6d01d9a-47dc-11e5-af2f-4d6e0e5eda22.

Oakley, Barbara. *A Mind for Numbers: How to Excel at Math and Science (Even If You Flunked Algebra).* Penguin, 2014.

Obama, Barak. "Barack Obama's Berlin Speech – Full Text." *The Guardian*, 19 June 2013, www.theguardian.com/world/2013/jun/19/barack-obama-berlin-speech-full-text.

OECD. *ODA Levels in 2021- Preliminary Data.* OECD Sustainable Development Office, Paris, France, 2022, pp. 1–15.

Oettingen, Gabriele. *Rethinking Positive Thinking: Inside the New Science of Motivation.* Penguin, 2015.

Office of the Assistant Secretary for Planning and Evaluation. *Prior HHS Poverty Guidelines and Federal Register References*, 2023, aspe.hhs.gov/topics/poverty-economic-mobility/poverty-guidelines/prior-hhs-poverty-guidelines-federal-register-references.

Olah, Chris. "Do I Need to Go to University?" *Colah's Blog*, 30 May 2020, colah.github.io/posts/2020-05-University/.

OpenAI. "GPT-4." *OpenAI Research Report*, 2023, openai.com/research/gpt-4.

Oppenheim, Maya. *Sir Elton John Tops List of Sunday Times Most Generous Celebrities Donating £26.8 Million to Charity*, 17 Apr. 2016, www.independent.co.uk/news/people/sir-elton-john-tops-list-of-the-sunday-times-most-generous-celebrities-donating-ps26-8-million-to-charity-in-last-year-a6988096.html.

Ord, Toby. "Aid works (on average)." *Giving What We Can*, 2017, studylib.net/doc/13259236/aid-works—on-average—toby-ord-president—giving-what-we

Ord, Toby. *Consequentialism and Decision Procedure, University of Oxford*, 2005, https://www.amirrorclear.net/files/consequentialism-and-decision-procedures.pdf.

Ord, Toby. "Moral Trade." *Ethics*, vol. 126, no. 1, 2015, pp. 118–138, doi.org/10.1086/682187.

Ord, Toby. "Reflecting on the Last Year — Lessons for EA." EA Global: Bay Area 2023. 2023, Oakland, CA, https://forum.effectivealtruism.org/posts/YrXZ3pRvFuH8SJaay/reflecting-on-the-last-year-lessons-for-ea-opening-keynote.

Ord, Toby. "The Moral Imperative toward Cost-Effectiveness in Global Health." *Center for Global Development*, Mar. 2013, pp. 29–36, doi.org/10.1093/oso/9780198841364.003.0002.

Ord, Toby. *The Precipice: Existential Risk and the Future of Humanity*. Bloomsbury, 2020.

Ord, Toby. "The Timing of Labour Aimed at Reducing Existential Risk." *The Future of Humanity Institute*, 3 July 2014, www.fhi.ox.ac.uk/the-timing-of-labour-aimed-at-reducing-existential-risk/.

Our World in Data. "Primary energy consumption per capita." *Our World in Data*, 2021, ourworldindata.org/explorers/poverty-explorer?time=2023.

Our World in Data. "Share of Population Living in Extreme Poverty, 2021." *Our World in Data*, 2021, ourworldindata.org/explorers/poverty-explorer?time=latest.

Pamlin, Dennis, et al. "Global Challenges – Twelve Risks That Threaten Human Civilisation – The Case for a New Category of Risks." *Global Challenges Foundation*, 2015.

Parfit, Derek. *Reasons and Persons*. Oxford University Press, 1986.

Payscale. "Most and Least Meaningful Jobs Methodology." *PayScale*, 2015, www.payscale.com/data-packages/most-and-least-meaningful-jobs/methodology.

Payscale. "Top Ivy League Schools." *Payscale*, 2021, www.payscale.com/college-salary-report/best-schools-by-type/bachelors/ivy-league-schools.

Petersen, Alexander M., et al. "Methods for Measuring the Citations and Productivity of Scientists across Time and Discipline." *Physical Review E*, vol. 81, no. 3, 2010, doi.org/10.1103/physreve.81.036114.

Peterson, George J., et al. "Nonuniversal Power Law Scaling in the Probability Distribution of Scientific Citations." *Proceedings of the National Academy of Sciences*, vol. 107, no. 37, 2010, pp. 16023–16027, doi.org/10.1073/pnas.1010757107.

Petrosino, Anthony, et al. *Scared Straight and Other Juvenile Awareness Programs for Preventing Juvenile Delinquency*. 2nd ed., vol. 2004, Campbell Corporation, 2004. pp. 1–62.

Pink, Daniel H. *To Sell Is Human: The Surprising Truth About Persuading, Convincing, and Influencing Others*. Canongate, 2018.

Price, Richard. "The Number of Academics and Graduate Students in the World." *Tumblr*, 15 Nov. 2011, www.richardprice.io/post/12855561694/the-number-of-academics-and-graduate-students-in.

R., D. "Our First-Ever College Rankings." *The Economist*, 29 Oct. 2015, www.economist.com/graphic-detail/2015/10/29/our-first-ever-college-rankings.

Rackham, Neil. *SPIN-Selling*. Routledge, 1995.

Radicchi, Filippo, et al. "Universality of Citation Distributions: Toward an Objective Measure of

Scientific Impact." *Proceedings of the National Academy of Sciences*, vol. 105, no. 45, 2008, pp. 17268–17272, doi.org/10.1073/pnas.0806977105.

Randerson, James. "Revealed: The Lax Laws That Could Allow Assembly of Deadly Virus DNA." *The Guardian*, 14 June 2006, www.theguardian.com/world/2006/jun/14/terrorism.topstories3.

Redner, S. "How Popular Is Your Paper? An Empirical Study of the Citation Distribution." *The European Physical Journal B*, vol. 4, no. 2, 1998, pp. 131–134, doi.org/10.1007/s100510050359.

Reed, Scott, et al. "A Generalist Agent." *Transactions on Machine Learning Research*, 2022, www.deepmind.com/publications/a-generalist-agent.

Reynolds, Matt. "Salt, Sugar, Water, Zinc: How Scientists Learned to Treat the 20th Century's Biggest Killer of Children." *Asterisk*, Mar. 2023, asteriskmag.com/issues/2/salt-sugar-water-zinc-how-scientists-learned-to-treat-the-20th-century-s-biggest-killer-of-children.

Rowe, Abraham. "Insects Raised for Food and Feed - Global Scale, Practices, and Policy." *Rethink Priorities*, 29 June 2020, rethinkpriorities.org/publications/insects-raised-for-food-and-feed.

Saeedy, Alexander. "FTX Says $8.9 Billion in Customer Funds Are Missing." *The Wall Street Journal*, 2 Mar. 2023, www.wsj.com/articles/ftx-says-8-9-billion-in-customer-funds-are-missing-c232f684.

Salzgeber, Nils. "'Eat That Frog' by Brian Tracy (Book Summary)." *NJlifehacks*, 16 Feb. 2019, www.njlifehacks.com/eat-that-frog-brian-tracy-summary/.

Sandberg, Anders, and Nick Bostrom. *Global Catastrophic Risks Survey.* Future of Humanity Institute, Technical Report, Oxford University, 2008.

Schimmack, Ulrich. "A Meta-Scientific Perspective on "Thinking: Fast and Slow"." *Replicability-Index*, 30 Dec. 2020, replicationindex.com/2020/12/30/a-meta-scientific-perspective-on-thinking-fast-and-slow/.

Schimmack, Ulrich, et al. "Reconstruction of a Train Wreck: How Priming Research Went off the Rails." *Replicability-Index*, 2 Feb. 2017, replicationindex.com/2017/02/02/reconstruction-of-a-train-wreck-how-priming-research-went-of-the-rails/.

Schmall, Tyler. "Most People Believe Climate Change Will Cause Humanity's Extinction." *New York Post*, 22 Apr. 2019, nypost.com/2019/04/22/most-people-believe-climate-change-will-cause-humanitys-extinction/.

Schmidt, Frank L., and John E. Hunter. "The Validity and Utility of Selection Methods in Personnel Psychology: Practical and Theoretical Implications of 100 Years of Research Findings." *ResearchGate Working Paper Series*, 2016, pp. 262–274, home.ubalt.edu/tmitch/645/session%204/Schmidt%20&%20Oh%20validity%20and%20util%20100%20yrs%20of%20research%20Wk%20PPR%202016.pdf.

Schneider, Michael. "Google Spent 2 Years Studying 180 Teams. The Most Successful Ones Shared These 5 Traits." *Inc.com*, 19 July 2017, www.inc.com/michael-schneider/google-thought-they-knew-how-to-create-the-perfect.html.

Schubert, Stefan, et al. "Considering Considerateness: Why Communities of Do-Gooders Should Be Exceptionally Considerate." *Centre For Effective Altruism*, 2017, www.centreforeffectivealtruism.org/blog/considering-considerateness-why-communities-of-do-gooders-should-be.

Schubert, Stefan, and Lucius Caviola. "Virtues for Real-World Utilitarians." *PsyArXiv Preprints*, 2021, https://doi.org/10.31234/osf.io/w52zm.

Schukraft, Jason. "Opinion: Estimating Invertebrate Sentience." *Rethink Priorities*, 6 Nov. 2019, rethinkpriorities.org/publications/opinion-estimating-invertebrate-sentience.

Schwartz, Nelson D. "In Hiring, a Friend in Need Is a Prospect, Indeed." *The New York Times*, 27 Jan. 2013, www.nytimes.com/2013/01/28/business/employers-increasingly-rely-on-internal-referrals-in-hiring.html.

Seligman, Milton. *Flourish*. Nicholas Brealey Publishing, 2011.

Sethi, Ramit. "How to Sell Yourself Confidently Using the Briefcase Technique." *I Will Teach You To Be Rich*, 20 Jan. 2017, www.iwillteachyoutoberich.com/how-to-sell-yourself/.

Sethi, Ramit. *I Will Teach You To Be Rich*. Workman Publishing, 2009.

Shen, Lucinda. "Goldman Sachs Finally Admits It Defrauded Investors During the Financial Crisis." *Fortune*, 11 Apr. 2016, fortune.com/2016/04/11/goldman-sachs-doj-settlement/.

Shinn, Noah, et al. "Reflexion: Language Agents with Verbal Reinforcement Learning." *arXiv*, 21 May 2023, arxiv.org/abs/2303.11366.

Shirer, Michael. "IDC Forecasts Companies to Spend Almost \$342 Billion on AI Solutions in 2021." International Data Corporation, 4 Aug. 2021, www.idc.com/getdoc.jsp?containerId=prUS48127321.

Shulman, Carl. "What Portion of a Boost to Global GDP Goes to the Poor?" *Reflective Disequilibrium Blog*, 23 Jan. 2014, reflectivedisequilibrium.blogspot.com/2014/01/what-portion-of-boost-to-global-gdp.html.

Šimčikas, Saulius. "Estimates of Global Captive Vertebrate Numbers." *Rethink Priorities*, 18 Feb. 2020, rethinkpriorities.org/publications/estimates-of-global-captive-vertebrate-numbers.

Simonson, Itamar, and Peter Nye. "The Effect of Accountability on Susceptibility to Decision Errors." *Organizational Behavior and Human Decision Processes*, vol. 51, no. 3, 1992, pp. 416–446, doi. org/10.1016/0749-5978(92)90020-8.

Simonton, Dean K. "Age and Outstanding Achievement: What Do We Know after a Century of Research?" *Psychological Bulletin*, vol. 104, no. 2, 1988, pp. 251–267, doi.org/10.1037/0033-2909.104.2.251.

Siskind, Scott. "Depression." *Lorien Psychiatry*, 5 June 2021, lorienpsych.com/2021/06/05/depression/.

Slattery, Peter. "Creating a Newsletter: A Very Quick Guide with Templates." *EA Forum*, 27 May 2022, forum.effectivealtruism.org/posts/QZQHcgXjKxGHtuAEX/.

SmartAsset. "California Paycheck Calculator." *SmartAsset*, 1 Mar. 2023, smartasset.com/taxes/california-paycheck-calculator.

Snodin, Ben. "My Thoughts on Nanotechnology Strategy Research as an EA Cause Area." *EA Forum*, 2 May 2022, forum.effectivealtruism.org/posts/oqBJk2Ae3RBegtFfn/my-thoughts-on-nanotechnology-strategy-research-as-an-ea.

Snow, Shane. "These Are the Ages When We Do Our Best Work." *Fast Company*, 18 Apr. 2016, web.archive.org/web/20160607234708/www.fastcompany.com/3058870/your-most-productive-self/these-are-the-ages-when-we-do-our-best-work.

Solanto, Mary V. *Cognitive-Behavioral Therapy for Adult ADHD: Targeting Executive Dysfunction*. Guilford Press, 2011.

Soma, Jonathan. "The New, Interactive Singles Map." *The New, Interactive Singles Map.*, 2013, jonathansoma.com/singles.

Southern District of New York. "United States Attorney Announces Charges against FTX Founder Samuel Bankman-Fried." *US Attorney's Office, Southern District of New York*, 13 Dec. 2022, www.justice.gov/usao-sdny/pr/ united-states-attorney-announces-charges-against-ftx-founder-samuel-bankman-fried.

Spall, Benjamin, and Michael Xander. *My Morning Routine: How Successful People Start Every Day Inspired*. Portfolio, 2018.

Spicer, Michael. "20 Essential Job Interview Tips." *The Poke*, 26 Jan. 2019, www.thepoke.co.uk/2015/02/03/20-essential-interview-tips-updated/.

Steel, Piers. *The Procrastination Equation: How to Stop Putting Things Off and Start Getting Stuff Done*. Harper, 2012.

Steinhardt, Jacob. "AI Forecasting: One Year In." *Bounded Regret*, 3 July 2022, bounded-regret.ghost. io/ai-forecasting-one-year-in/.

Stein-Perlman, Zach, et al. "2022 Expert Survey on Progress in AI." *AI Impacts*, 3 Aug. 2022, aiimpacts. org/2022-expert-survey-on-progress-in-ai/.

Stevenson, Betsey, and Justin Wolfers. "Subjective Well-Being and Income: Is There Any Evidence of Satiation?" *NBER Working Paper Series*, 2013, pp. 1–24, doi.org/10.3386/w18992.

Tetlock, Philip E., and Dan Gardner. *Superforecasting: The Art and Science of Prediction*. Random House Business, 2019.

Todd, Benjamin. "Expected Value: How Can We Make a Difference When We're Uncertain What's True?" *80,000 Hours*, Sept. 2021, 80000hours.org/articles/expected-value/.

Todd, Benjamin. "How Much Do Solutions to Social Problems Differ in Their Effectiveness? A Collection of All the Studies We Could Find." *80,000 Hours*, Feb. 2023, 80000hours.org/2023/02/how-much-do-solutions-differ-in-effectiveness/ #ways-the-data-might-overstate-the-true-degree-of-spread.

Todd, Benjamin. "Is It Fair to Say That Most Social Programmes Don't Work?" *80,000 Hours*, Aug. 2017, 80000hours.org/articles/effective-social-program/.

Todd, Benjamin. "More Empirical Data on 'Value Drift.'" *EA Forum*, Aug. 2020, forum.effectivealtruism.org/ posts/eRQe4kkkH2pPzqvam/more-empirical-data-on-value-drift.

Todd, Benjamin. "My Updates after FTX." *EA Forum*, 31 Mar. 2023, forum.effectivealtruism.org/posts/jpyMhAPSmZER9ASi6/my-updates-after-ftx.

Todd, Benjamin. "Should You Wait to Make a Difference?" *80,000 Hours*, Apr. 2017, 80000hours.org/ articles/should-you-wait/.

Todd, Benjamin. "Show Me the Harm." *80,000 Hours*, 31 July 2013, 80000hours.org/2013/07/show-me-the-harm/.

Todd, Benjamin. "Stop Assuming 'Declining Returns' in Small Charities." *80,000 Hours*, Nov. 2015, 80000hours.org/2015/11/ stop-talking-about-declining-returns-in-small-organisations/.

Todd, Benjamin. "What Is Effective Altruism?" *What Is Effective Altruism? | Effective*

Altruism, www.effectivealtruism.org/articles/
introduction-to-effective-altruism. Accessed 24 May 2023.

Todd, Benjamin. "What Is Social Impact? A Definition." *80,000 Hours,* Oct. 2021, 80000hours.org/
articles/what-is-social-impact-definition/.

Toli, Agoro, et al. "Does Forming Implementation Intentions Help People with Mental Health
Problems to Achieve Goals?
A Meta-Analysis of Experimental Studies with Clinical and Analogue Samples." *British Journal of
Clinical Psychology,*
vol. 55, no. 1, 2015, pp. 69–90, doi.org/10.1111/bjc.12086.

Tomasik, Brian. "Assorted Tips on Personal Finance." *Essays on Reducing Suffering,* 1 Mar. 2021,
reducing-suffering.org/advanced-tips-on-personal-finance/.

Tomasik, Brian. "How Many Wild Animals Are There?" *Essays on Reducing Suffering,* 7 Aug. 2019,
reducing-suffering.org/how-many-wild-animals-are-there/.

Tomasik, Brian. "The Importance of Wild-Animal Suffering." *Relations. Beyond Anthropocentrism,* vol.
3, no. 2, Nov. 2015, pp. 133–152, doi.org/10.7358/rela-2015-002-toma.

Tomasulo, Dan J. "The Virtual Gratitude Visit (VGV): Psychodrama in Action." *Psychology Today,* 27
Dec. 2011, www.psychologytoday.com/us/blog/the-healing-crowd/201112/the-virtual-gratitude-
visit-vgv-psychodrama-in-action.

Torkington, Simon. "The Jobs of the Future – and Two Skills You Need to Get Them." *World Economic
Forum,* 2 Sept. 2016, www.weforum.org/agenda/2016/09/jobs-of-future-and-skills-you-need/.

Townsend, Michael, and Sjir Hoeijmakers. "2020–2022 Impact Evaluation." *Giving What We Can,* 31
Mar. 2023, www.givingwhatwecan.org/impact.

Tracy, Brian. *Eat That Frog!: Get More Of The Important Things Done Today.* Yellow Kite, 2013.

UK NICE. "NICE Health Technology Evaluations: The Manual." *NICE,*
2022, *www.nice.org.uk/Process/Pmg36/Resources/
Nice-Health-Technology-Evaluations-the-Manual-Pdf-72286779244741.*.

UNESCO Institute for Statistics. "New Estimation Confirms Out-of-School Population Is Growing
in Sub-Saharan Africa." *UNESCO Institute for Statistics,* Sep. 2022, unesdoc.unesco.org/ark:/48223/
pf0000382577.

United States Bureau of Labor Statistics. "Employee Tenure Summary - 2022 A01 Results." *U.S. Bureau
of Labor Statistics,* 22 Sep. 2022, www.bls.gov/news.release/tenure.nr0.htm.

United States Bureau of Labor Statistics. "Industries at a Glance: Finance and Insurance: NAICS 52."
U.S. Bureau of Labor Statistics, 25 May 2023, www.bls.gov/iag/tgs/iag52.htm.

United States Bureau of Labor Statistics. "Table A-1. Employment Status of the Civilian Population
by Sex and Age - 2023 M04 Results." *U.S. Bureau of Labor Statistics,* 5 May 2023, www.bls.gov/news.
release/empsit.t01.htm.

United States Census Bureau. "Post-Secondary Employment Outcomes (PSEO)." *Longitudinal
Employer-Household Dynamics,* United States, Jan. 2023. Accessed 2023.

Urban, Tim. "Life Is a Picture, But You Live in a Pixel." *Wait But Why,* 20 Nov. 2013, waitbutwhy.
com/2013/11/life-is-picture-but-you-live-in-pixel.html.

Ury, William. *Getting Past No: Negotiating in Difficult Situations.* Bantam, 1993.

Vallerand, Robert J., et al. "Les Passions de l'âme: On Obsessive and Harmonious Passion." *Journal of Personality and Social Psychology*, vol. 85, no. 4, 2003, pp. 756–767, doi.org/10.1037/0022-3514.85.4.756.

Van Dalen, Hendrik P., and Arjo Klamer. "Is Science a Case of Wasteful Competition?" *Kyklos*, vol. 58, no. 3, 2005, pp. 395–414, doi.org/10.1111/j.0023-5962.2005.00294.x.

Vermeer, Alex. "8,760 Hours: How to Get the Most out of next Year." *Alex Vermeer*, Dec. 2012, alexvermeer.com/8760hours/.

Vermeer, Alex. "Life Hacking." *Alex Vermeer*, Mar. 2015, alexvermeer.com/life-hacking/.

VIA Institute on Character. "The 24 Character Strengths." *VIA Institute on Character*, 19 June 2019, www.viacharacter.org/character-strengths.

Vos, Theo, et al. "Global Burden of 369 Diseases and Injuries in 204 Countries and Territories, 1990–2019: A Systematic Analysis for the Global Burden of Disease Study 2019." *The Lancet*, vol. 396, no. 10258, 2020, pp. 1204–1222, doi.org/10.1016/s0140-6736(20)30925-9.

Walker, Caitlin, et al. "Global Priority: Mental Health." *Happier Lives Institute*, May 2021, www.happierlivesinstitute.org/report/global-priority-mental-health/.

Walsh, Veronica. "The ABC OF CBT – the Starter Exercise/Handout to Catch Your Negative Automatic Thoughts..." *Veronica Walsh's CBT Blog Dublin, Ireland*, 14 Apr. 2012, iveronicawalsh.wordpress.com/2012/04/15/the-abc-of-cbt-the-starter-exercisehandout-to-catch-your-negative-thoughts/.

Watkins Uiberall, "2012 Nonprofit Compensation Survey." *Watkins Uiberall Accounting*, 2012, assets.speakcdn.com/assets/2800/2012_wu_nfp_survey.pdf.

Webb, Michael. "The Impact of Artificial Intelligence on the Labor Market." *SSRN Electronic Journal*, 2020, doi.org/10.2139/ssrn.3482150.

Whitmore, John. *Coaching for Performance*. Nicholas Brealey, 2009.

Wigert, Ben. "The Top 6 Things Employees Want in Their Next Job." *Gallup.Com*, 21 Apr. 2023, www.gallup.com/workplace/389807/top-things-employees-next-job.aspx.

Wikipedia. "Gorilla." *Wikipedia*, 2 Feb 2017, en.wikipedia.org/wiki/Gorilla.

Wikipedia. "Human Mission to Mars." *Wikipedia*, 26 May 2023, en.wikipedia.org/wiki/Human_mission_to_Mars.

Wildeford, Peter. "Productivity 101 for Beginners." *EA Forum*, 5 Nov. 2014, forum.effectivealtruism.org/posts/TCr8gEfeFyZQcEHFR/productivity-101-for-beginners.

Williams, Mark, and Danny Penman. *Mindfulness: An Eight-Week Plan for Finding Peace in a Frantic World*. Rodale Books, 2012.

Winter, Nick. *The Motivation Hacker*. Nick Winter, 2013.

Wolff, Hans-Georg, and Klaus Moser. "Effects of Networking on Career Success: A Longitudinal Study." *Journal of Applied Psychology*, vol. 94, no. 1, 2009, pp. 196–206, doi.org/10.1037/a0013350.

Wolfram, Stephen. "Seeking the Productive Life: Some Details of My Personal Infrastructure." *Stephen Wolfram Writings*, 21 Feb. 2019, writings.stephenwolfram.com/2019/02/seeking-the-productive-life-some-details-of-my-personal-infrastructure/.

World Bank. "Current Health Expenditure Per Capita, PPP (current international $)." *World Bank Open Data*, data.worldbank.org/indicator/SH.XPD.CHEX.PP.CD. Accessed 31 May 2023.

World Bank. "Current Health Expenditure Per Capita, PPP (current international $) - Low income." *World Bank Open Data*, data.worldbank.org/indicator/SH.XPD.CHEX.PP.CD?locations=XM. Accessed 31 May 2023.

World Bank. "Fact Sheet: An Adjustment to Global Poverty Lines." *World Bank*, 16 Sep. 2022, www.worldbank.org/en/news/factsheet/2022/05/02/fact-sheet-an-adjustment-to-global-poverty-lines.

World Bank. "GDP (Current US$) - United States." *World Bank Open Data*, data.worldbank.org/indicator/NY.GDP.MKTP.CD?locations=US. Accessed 23 May 2023.

World Bank. "Physicians (per 1,000 People) - United States." *World Bank Open Data*, data.worldbank.org/indicator/SH.MED.PHYS.ZS?locations=US. Accessed 19 Feb. 2023.

World Bank. "Population, total." *World Bank Open Data*, data.worldbank.org/indicator/SP.POP.TOTL.

World Bank. "PovcalNet: An Online Analysis Tool for Global Poverty Monitoring." *World Bank*, 1 Oct. 2016, iresearch.worldbank.org/PovcalNet/home.aspx.

World Bank. *Poverty and Shared Prosperity 2022: Correcting Course*, 6 Oct. 2021, doi.org/10.1596/978-1-4648-1893-6.

World Bank. "Poverty Gap at $2.15 a Day (2017 PPP) (%)." *World Bank Open Data*, data.worldbank.org/indicator/SI.POV.GAPS.

World Bank. "Poverty Headcount Ratio at $2.15 a Aay (2017 PPP) (% of population)." *World Bank Open Data*, data.worldbank.org/indicator/SI.POV.DDAY.

World Bank. "Research and development expenditure (% of GDP)." *World Bank Open Data*, data.worldbank.org/indicator/GB.XPD.RSDV.GD.ZS. Accessed 25 May 2023.

Wrzesniewski, Amy, et al. "Managing Yourself: Turn the Job You Have into the Job You Want." *Harvard Business Review*, June 2010, hbr.org/2010/06/managing-yourself-turn-the-job-you-have-into-the-job-you-want.

Young, Scott H. "Lesson 3: How Do You 'Deliberately Practice' Your Job?" *Scott H Young*, Jan. 2017, www.scotthyoung.com/blog/lesson-3-how-do-you-deliberately-practice-your-job/.

Young, Scott H. "Why Most People Get Stuck in Their Careers." *Scott H Young*, Jan. 2017, www.scotthyoung.com/blog/2017/01/16/career-stuck/.

Zhang, Baobao, et al. "Forecasting AI Progress: Evidence from a Survey of Machine Learning Researchers." *arXiv*, 8 June 2022, arxiv.org/abs/2206.04132.

Zhang, Lily. "How to Research a Company Pre-Interview." *The Muse*, 19 June 2020, www.themuse.com/advice/the-ultimate-guide-to-researching-a-company-preinterview.

Index